The Media for Democracy Monitor

A Cross National Study of Leading News Media

The Media for Democracy Monitor

A Cross National Study of Leading News Media

Josef Trappel, Hannu Nieminen
& Lars Nord (eds.)

NORDICOM

The Media for Democracy Monitor
A Cross National Study of Leading News Media

Josef Trappel, Hannu Nieminen & Lars Nord (eds.)

ISBN 978-91-86523-23-7

Published by:
Nordicom
University of Gothenburg
Box 713
SE 405 30 Göteborg
Sweden

Cover by: Daniel Zachrisson
Graphic design: Henny Östlund
Printed by: Litorapid Media AB, Göteborg, Sweden 2011
Environmental certification according to ISO 14001

Contents

Josef Trappel, Hannu Nieminen & Lars Nord
Editorial   7

Chapter 1
Josef Trappel
Why Democracy Needs Media Monitoring   11

Chapter 2
André Donk & Josef Trappel
Indicators and Definitions   29

Chapter 3
Beate Josephi
Australia: Committed to Investigative Journalism   51

Chapter 4
Manuela Grünangerl & Josef Trappel
Austria: Informal Rules and Strong Traditions   79

Chapter 5
Kari Karppinen, Hannu Nieminen & Anna-Laura Markkanen
Finland: High Professional Ethos in a Small, Concentrated Media Market   113

Chapter 6
Frank Marcinkowski & André Donk
Germany: The News Media are Still Able to Play a Supportive
Role for Democracy   143

Chapter 7
Auksė Balčytienė
Lithuania: Mixed Professional Values in a Small and Highly Blurred
Media Environment   175

Chapter 8
Leen d'Haenens & Quint Kik
The Netherlands: Although There is No Need for Dramatization,
Vigilance is Required   203

Chapter 9
Joaquim Fidalgo
Portugal: A Young Democracy Still in Progress   235

Chapter 10
Torbjörn von Krogh & Lars Nord
Sweden: A Mixed Media Model under Market Pressures   265

Chapter 11
Werner A. Meier, Alexandra Gmür & Martina Leonarz
Switzerland: Swiss Quality Media. A Reduced Protection Forest
for Democracy   289

Chapter 12
Peter Humphreys
UK: UK News Media and Democracy. Professional Autonomy
and its Limits   319

Chapter 13
Lars Nord, Hannu Nieminen & Josef Trappel
Democratic Functions under Pressure: Conclusions   347

The Authors   365

Editorial

When the global financial markets lost their balance following the US subprime markets crisis in 2008, when South Africa hosted the Soccer World Championship in the summer of 2010 and when Wikileaks heated up global diplomacy in fall 2010 – the mass media acted as core transmission belts between the events and the global public. But did the mass media do a good job? Why had the US mass media never scrutinized the financial sustainability of Fanny Mae and Freddy Mac before the crash? Does the world audience understand South Africa and its socio-economic framework better now than before the world championship? Did the mass media demonstrate responsibility when they published whistleblowers' material?

Mass media are essential elements of all forms of democratic societies. Their performance may differ from country to country and each democracy may expect different services, but there are common denominators equally applicable to all or at least the vast majority of democracies. In this book, we argue that *freedom, equality*, and *control* are the core fields of media performance in the service of democracy. We therefore ask to what extent the core news media live up to these democratic requirements. Do mass media make the best out of media freedom or do media companies interpret media freedom merely as the freedom to maximize corporate profits? Do leading news media mediate between groups and interests in times of conflict; do they explain social tension and global inequalities? Do the core news media effectively control the possible abuses of those in power?

The examples quoted above show that there is room for improvement. The news media might argue that they lack the resources to follow closely all strands of society for abuses of power; they might claim that readers and viewers are less interested in the socio-economic development of South Africa than in soccer games, and that democracy as an institution is external to them and does not control their business. Despite such claims, the news media do have an impact on the development of contemporary democracies, irrespective of whether they accept their responsibilities.

It is therefore of interest to try to discover to what extent leading mass media in contemporary or mature democracies contribute to freedom, equality and control. The purpose of the *Media for Democracy Monitor,* therefore, is to monitor the structure and performance of the leading news media with regard to these three dimensions. What is taken for granted, notably, is the existence of a stable and reliable legal framework allowing for extensive media freedom with no fundamental shortcomings such as censorship, the state as the major media owner or any other form of legal barriers to professional journalism. This instrument is therefore limited in scope, and would require adaptation if applied to countries with less or little formal media freedom.

Each of the three dimensions is divided into several indicators and for each indicator empirical evidence is provided. Ten countries have participated in this exercise and in each country a team of researchers collected empirical evidence.

The present research project follows up on its initial empirical implementation in 2006. At that time, the pilot exercise was part of the research program "Democracy in the 21st Century", undertaken at the University of Zürich, Switzerland. Encouraged by positive responses from within the scientific community, the authors from each country met again in November 2009. Scholars from five more countries joined the group. The indicators were critically reviewed and collectively adapted. Country reports were prepared during 2010 and went to print in early 2011.

What makes this second empirical implementation unique is the fact that the research was carried out without any central funding or institutionalized sponsor. Each team of authors found the necessary support in their own country. The overall research design, however, was collectively adopted and not subject to change by the authors of the country chapters. The scope was extended from the five initial countries Germany, Lithuania, the Netherlands, Portugal and Switzerland to Australia, Austria, Finland, Sweden, and the United Kingdom. This extension increased the relevance and weight of the instrument *Media for Democracy Monitor*. The selection of countries does not follow any intrinsic logic. It is rather driven by the interest and availability of scholars willing to spend the time and effort needed to participate in this research project.

At the time the research was designed, Hungary was part of the sample, another country from Central and Eastern Europe in addition to Lithuania. Data collection, however, was difficult from the outset. But when the Government of Viktor Orban announced its fundamental revision of the media law in 2010, it became obvious that Hungary would no longer qualify as a research object in this exercise on a par with the other countries. Uncertainty prevailed among Hungarian news media when this book went into print, and it will certainly take time and further fundamental changes in the law before the Hungarian media legislation can be considered equal to that of contemporary democracies.

Chapter 1 of this book argues on theoretical grounds for scholarly media monitoring on a regular basis, not only in countries in transition, but also in the so-called mature democracies. Changes, and indeed media crises, permanently alter the performance of the mass media in democratic societies and require therefore constant observation. The *Media for Democracy Monitor* is one instrument that can be used to follow these changes closely.

In Chapter 2, the instrument is presented and discussed. All 26 indicators are introduced and justified. Each indicator is characterized by a research question, and several criteria for the empirical research are suggested. Moreover, each indicator is graded on a scale from 0 to 3. The more criteria that are met by the leading news media in the respective country, the higher the score becomes. Through this grading exercise, an indicative proposition as to the overall performance of the leading news media in each country under scrutiny is possible. Because the same indicators and empirical methods are used for all countries, the final scores can be compared across countries. However, this scoring only illustrates the research finding, and the scores must not be read without the justifications given for each indicator and each country.

Chapters 3 to 12 are dedicated to the countries participating in the *Media for Democracy Monitor*. With regard to the validity of the instrument, it was important to discuss the dimensions, indicators and criteria and how the team was to apply them nationally. For this purpose, the whole research team (with the exception of one person) met twice during the research process and exchanged their experiences of applying the instrument. During these personal meetings, a common understanding of each indicator was developed.

Chapter 13 finally draws some conclusions regarding the research exercise and presents the findings in a comparative manner. It turned out that the notion of *pressure* appropriately summarizes the situation of journalism in the leading news media: pressure with regard to time, budgets, and investigative resources.

This book addresses, on the one hand, the academic community with the intention to further the debate on the role of leading mass media within contemporary democracies. New developments such as social media and the ongoing media crisis in many countries are likely to require further observation by academic research. On the other hand, the book provides input for the debate going on within media professional circles and their own perception of the role the news media play in democratic societies. The findings expose the leading news media to criticism from different perspectives, but they may also encourage media professionals to study best business practices in other countries – and perhaps to learn from experience abroad. Studying practices in other countries may cause longstanding newsroom habits to be questioned and revised.

As the editors of this book, we would like to express our thanks to all those who participated in this exercise, in particular the authors of the country chapters. Furthermore, we are grateful to SwissGIS, the Swiss Centre for Studies on the Global Information Society, and all other academic institutions for their support in producing the book: Universities of Helsinki, Münster, Salzburg and the Mid Sweden University. Finally, we express our gratitude to the great team at our publisher NORDICOM and in particular to Ulla Carlsson for her flexibility, patience and efficiency.

Salzburg, Helsinki and Sundsvall in August 2011

Josef Trappel, Hannu Nieminen, Lars Nord

Chapter 1

Why Democracy Needs Media Monitoring
Conceptualizing the *Media for Democracy Monitor*

Josef Trappel

The seminal book on normative theories of the media ends on a pessimistic note. The authors summarize their reflections on journalism in democratic societies by concluding:

> "We recognize that the conditions the media operate in are becoming more and more restrictive and oppressive. This is especially true when it comes to the crucial issue of having a financially profitable media system that is both committed to public enlightenment and sufficiently independent and capable of holding agencies of power in society to account – economic, political, and military. Those at the heart of power do not have to answer to the media, and the media are usually reluctant to press the issue for fear of consequences or because they have close ties to the established order." (Christians et al. 2009, p. 240)

In their view, the media find themselves in a delicate position. On the one hand, there is increasing economic pressure following from decreasing revenues from sales and advertising; on the other hand, there is the erosion of their position as outstanding agents of enlightenment, which they inherited from their predecessors and which is rooted in the bourgeois revolution of the 19th century.

Indeed, there are several strands of fundamental critique of the performance of news media in contemporary democracies. One line of critique is articulated among many others by US scholar Robert McChesney. To him, democracy and media power do not match: "I contend that the media have become a significant antidemocratic force in the United States. The wealthier and more powerful the corporate media giants have become, the poorer the prospectus for participatory democracy." (2008, p. 426) In particular, he identifies media concentration as a deadly threat to democracy: "This concentration accentuates the core tendencies of a profit-driven, advertising-supported media system: hyper-commercialism and denigration of journalism and public service. It is a poison pill for democracy." (p. 427) Much along the same line, C. Edwin Baker considers media concentration a multidimensional challenge to democracy (Baker 2007).

Another line of critique, linked to the former, is the claim that the mass media are constantly losing their independence, owing to the fact that most leading news media understand themselves first and foremost as a business, networked into economic and political power structures. "Business connections with other economic branches are strengthened, reducing still further the media's independence. Accountability to shareholders and owners take precedence over professional accountability and public responsibility" (Christians et al. 2009, p. 226). The view, the authors continue, that the media are primarily a business and that the freedom of the media is the freedom to trade, is rarely challenged in the Western world.

Along a similar line of argument, others criticize the media as being "market driven" (McManus 1994; for a detailed outline of media criticism see McManus 2009). The media would follow a commercial and market-oriented imperative, rather than an editorial one. This eventually leads to systematic distortions of the public sphere by, for example, privileging groups with higher purchasing power over groups with less, and by structuring the media supply in accordance with advertising requirements rather than the consumption preferences of the people. In his overview of topical European research findings, Brants acknowledges that the "[a]ppropriation of editorial resources is increasingly taking place more on the basis of market evaluations than on professional of public interest considerations" (2007, p. 109). He concludes, however, that despite the fact that corporate and managerial pressure is increasing and editorial decisions are largely cost/benefit driven, there is no systematic proof that news selection criteria used by European journalists are purely driven by market considerations (ibid., p. 111).

Are the news media putting at stake their civic role for democratic societies? Or are they just adapting to socio-economic and political change following mega-trends such as marketization, commercialization and a general decline of interest in matters of public concern and politics at large?

The answers to these questions are important, because they guide the line of argument. Democratic societies and news media do not just co-exist in parallel. The news media and democratic societies need one another in a complex relation of interdependency. Obviously, news media need society as a market for their products, and they need the state to guarantee press freedom. Moreover, the news media need the state and other institutions as news sources. In turn, society needs the news media for information and the constant observation of itself. Democratic societies grant and guarantee press freedom in exchange for a large variety of media services. It is therefore essential for democratic societies to follow closely the performance of the news media, in particular during times of change. For the media, it is equally important to follow closely the rules defined by the state. There is, however, an element of imbalance in this relation. While the media, represented by their business lobbies, constantly defend their case in the public by using their own platforms of publication, the observation of media performance by civil society is less institutionalized.

Scholars have repeatedly pointed to the fact that media monitoring should become a regular exercise in order to hold the media to account to the people (and not only to shareholders, owners and ultimately advertisers) and to facilitate the public debate on the performance of the media.

> "Monitoring is much more than trend watching: To monitor is to understand in order to act in an informed, well-reasoned way. Monitoring is beyond mirroring what happens in the fourth pillar of society (in addition to State, capital and civil society). To monitor the media is to make them transparent, a basic condition for democracy to function." (Galtung 1999, p. 23)

The most obvious way to monitor media performance is to observe media content. Nordenstreng has repeatedly called for coordinated action to establish content monitoring by pooling together the content analysis carried out at universities (2004, p. 350; Nordenstreng and Griffin 1999: p. xvii). Content analysis, however, must be seen within the context of its production. He admits: "Is not content just a reflection of structures of production and distribution, ultimately ownership? Is not content after all an ahistorical category?" (Nordenstreng 1999, p. 11). In order to understand better and to explain media performance, media monitoring needs to focus on structural features.

This insight corresponds well with the sketch of a future research agenda, presented by Christians et al. "(…) our theorizing should pay more attention to the many extramedia activities of research, monitoring, reflection, and means of accountability that subject the media themselves to scrutiny, both according to diverse perspectives and in a transparent manner." (2009, p. 241)

It follows from these considerations that (1) media monitoring is an important element in maintaining the delicate equilibrium between democratic societies and the news media; and (2) media monitoring should focus on structural features rather than content analysis.

Therefore, our media monitoring research project addresses the following research questions:

> In what way and to what extent do the structures and conduct of leading news media correspond with the fulfillment of their specific role in contemporary democracies and what are the differences between countries?

This research question contains two fundamental notions that need further consideration. First, the notion of contemporary democracy needs to be discussed. The following section presents an outline of different models of democracy and eventually defines in normative terms the notion used for this monitoring exercise. The term 'contemporary' is chosen to distinguish democracies in transition from democracies within a stable political framework. What is of interest in this project are the so-called stable democracies and not countries in the process of democratization, as described by Voltmer (2006). The role of the media in democracies in transition is decidedly different at least during the transition phase (Jakubowicz and Sükösd 2008), and any analysis requires different instruments than an analysis of media performance in a more stable democracy framework. Nonetheless, we expect considerable variations among the group of countries considered to be 'contemporary' democracies.

Second, the role of the media and of journalism in democracy needs further elaboration. It clearly follows from the chosen model of democracy which role journalism and the media are expected to fulfill. Therefore, the subsequent section elaborates on different models and roles of journalism in democracies.

Thereafter, the concept of the implemented research instrument, the *Media for Democracy Monitor (MDM)*, is briefly presented. It refers to the chosen model of democracy and the appropriate role for media and journalism. To date, this instrument has been used twice: In 2008, a pilot project with empirical analysis in five countries was undertaken[1]; in 2010 a modified and improved MDM was empirically implemented in ten countries. The design of the MDM, presented in detail in Chapter 2 of this book, allows for considerable variation from country to country.

The final section of this chapter briefly discusses why the MDM 2010 does not focus more strongly on the potentially democratizing force of new communication technologies. At the time of writing, the overturn of regimes in North Africa and the Arab Spring were going on. Irrespective of the compelling organizing and mobilizing power of Internet- and mobile-phone-based communication, it turned out that these means of communication were easy for the totalitarian regimes to eliminate. There is certainly a great deal of participatory substance in new communication technologies, but their flaws should not be ignored in times of social media euphoria.

In short, the MDM is designed to take a closer look at the structures and the conduct of leading news media in contemporary democracies. The chosen perspective emphasizes the interplay between the news media and democratic requirements. Empirically, the MDM provides a monitoring instrument that focuses on structures and not on content. The ultimate purpose of the *Media for Democracy Monitor* is to help hold leading news media accountable to democratic societies.

Models of contemporary democracies

From the vast arrays of concepts of democracy, several basic aspects are of great relevance to the debate on the interdependency of media, journalism and democracy. Democracy refers to the principle that all power in society is rooted in the people and that government is accountable to the people; it also refers to equality, which is best understood in relation to the principle of 'one man, one vote'; but it also refers to the process of decision-making, where those affected by decisions should participate in decisions. Democracy is a principle of governance and a method of decision-making.

It is based on the fundamental rights of citizens, which correspond with Human Rights, in particular the right to freedom of expression. For our research purpose, it is of prime interest how democratic governing and decision-making processes are incorporated into the conduct of leading news media. Two levels of analysis follow:

At the meso (company) level, we focus on how democratic leading news media make relevant decisions and how democratic processes are enacted within newsrooms and media organizations. At the macro (state) level, democracy can be analyzed against the background of how the Human Right to freedom of expression is enacted and what variations of democratic governance affect the performance of news media.

Media companies (meso level) are not democratic by nature. Nonetheless, democratic values are of importance to them, as they claim to be the main institutional addressees of freedom of speech rules. The beneficiaries would be the public at large. In other words, media companies profit from and their independence is rooted in this fundamental democratic right to free expression. At the same time, democratic procedures of decision-making are not widespread within media organizations. Publicly owned public service media organizations aside, private commercial media companies are in most cases either family businesses or shareholder companies. A small minority of media companies, most of them in the alternative or 'third sector', are organized as cooperatives or similar forms of institutionalization. Very few media companies are owned by the newsroom staff (e.g., *Der Spiegel* in Germany).

"If hardly anyone today disputes democracy as a worthy goal, not everyone expects it to apply to their own decisions and activities. Newspaper editors (…) often champion democratic values on their editorial pages but seldom apply those values in their own newsrooms. And editors usually see no irony in the gap between what they preach and what they practice, because for them democracy denotes a form of government and not a set of requirements aimed at private persons and their private enterprises." (Glasser 2009, p. 92)

Newsroom democracy can take different forms. Consultation, participation, co-decision, or ultimately voting in elections represent different procedures of democratic decision-making, for example when a new editor-in-chief is implemented. In such cases, those affected by the decision (newsroom staff) participate in the decision-making. These kinds of procedures can therefore be considered democratic. But also day-to-day editorial decisions can be made either by consultation and deliberation, or by one person in his/her own capacity and on his/her responsibility. What makes democratic procedures within newsrooms or media companies such a critical matter is the division of power within the organization. The implementation of democratic decisions always means loss of power for some and empowerment of others. Procedures may take more time, and it is uncertain whether the ultimate decisions will be better, but there is an important advantage of democratic newsroom procedures. Journalists whose profession it is to explain the democratic decision-making of others (parliament, government, etc.) to the public should personally experience the strengths and weaknesses of such procedures at their own workplace. Moreover, such democratic procedures might ultimately benefit the media company as well. Journalists who have a say within their own newsrooms can be expected to be intrinsically motivated and to work better.

At the macro (state) level, democracies are usually divided into two models or traditions (Held 2006). Civic republicanism, rooted in the French Revolution and represented in the writings of Jean-Jacques Rousseau, is based on "each citizen's commitment to a civic culture that transcends individual preferences and private interests" (Glasser 2009, p. 94); procedural liberalism, in contrast, is more an Anglo-American concept with John Locke and Thomas Hobbes as its early proponents. Liberal democracy in this tradition can be conceptualized as "essentially procedural mechanism designed to facilitate the expression of individual preferences" (ibid.). Both traditions refer to the same two basic constituents: liberty and equality.

While republican democracy is further subdivided into several categories, liberal democracy is described in political science theory as rather uniform. Starting from Locke and Hobbes, this concept was further developed by Joseph Schumpeter. In his view, democracy means government for the people, but definitely not government by the people (Schumpeter 1976). For good reasons, scholars characterized this model of democracy as "elitist" (Baker 2002, p. 129ff). Decisions are made by informed and competent elites, who are elected by the people. Elections are the time when these elites are held to account. This extensive delegation of power is justified by citizens' lack of interest in governing themselves and their lack of the necessary expertise to do so effectively (Glasser 2009, p. 94). The democratic role of journalism and the media is to identify and make public the wrongdoings of elected representatives.

> "In this vision of democracy, the responsibilities of the press are minimal but crucial. Elections are more likely to deter corruption and reward effective elite response to popular needs if the press effectively exposes transgressions and incompetence that could contribute to the electoral defeat of those currently governing." (Baker 2006, p. 114)

In other words, the essential role of the press in elitist liberal democracies is that of watchdogs who alert people if something is going wrong. Constant information about day-to-day routines is of little importance, as people normally have neither the time nor the interest to follow the routine business of their elected representatives. Consequently, Zaller (2003) coined the term the *Burglar Alarm* standard. Given the assumption that it is beyond the capacity of many people to follow closely political developments, Zaller claims that it would be sufficient to limit political reporting to serious problems requiring attention. Such an alarm-based standard would focus the interest of the people on the really important public issues. Such a model confronts journalism with a considerable burden. "The alarm standard does, however, impose one serious constraint on news: Journalists cannot talk about every potential problem because their audience would ignore them; it is the job of reporters – in cooperation with political and interest groups – to decide what requires attention and bring it to the public" (2003, p. 121). Journalists become not only gate-keepers of political news, they decide for the people what the really important issues are – and what can be left outside public observation. Such decisions require highly skilled and responsible journalists, able to identify in their daily routines those issues that might eventually become important enough to be brought to the attention of the mass audience. In turn, people in their capacity as citizens depend critically on the heavily restricted choices of journalists.

Republican concepts of democracy emphasize the active role of citizens in exercising freedom of expression. These concepts rely on dialogue and debate within a democratic society, rather than on decisions made by elected, though elitist, representatives. In a republican democracy, "the epistemological hope is that those speakers with better arguments will prevail over those without – and this hope presumably requires that these better arguments ultimately gather larger audiences" (Baker 2007, p.11). Therefore, the most characteristic element of republicanism in this sense is "its insistence on the active participation of citizens in democratic self-governance. (...) Republicanism asserts that democracy requires civic virtues from its citizens, (...)" (Dahlgren 2007, p. 59).

Republican democracies come in different shades. Glasser suggests distinguishing *pluralist*, *civic* and *direct* models of republican democracy. While the former model is characterized by the competition of different groups in society, the *civic* model depends on a civic culture that cultivates different voices and different points of views. Journalism is required to accommodate these differences. The latter *direct* model is the most radical proposition and rejects any accumulation or distribution of resources "that would have the effect of creating unequal opportunities for political participation" (Glasser 2009, p. 104). In a *direct* democracy, he continues, "freedom of the press exists to serve the interests of the community, not the interests of journalists and their managers" (ibid.).

In his own classification, Baker suggests the term *complex* for the most sophisticated form of democracy. In such a *complex* democracy, decisions are only made after exhaustive deliberation processes. He argues that

> "(...) the complex democrat recognizes that a group's interests and identity are not preformed and are often in need of internal clarification. Rather, the group's interests are also properly the subject of discursive deliberation. Without adequate opportunities for these internal deliberations, groups, especially weaker or otherwise marginalized groups, will not be able to enter into any broader public sphere equipped for rational participation but rather empirically will be much more likely to be submerged into or dominated by the perspectives of more dominant groups." (Baker 2006, p. 119)

In *complex* democracies the "(…) media should support varying types of discourses – bargaining discourses of the liberal pluralist, discourses aimed at the common good emphasized by republicans, and smaller self-definitional as well as minority cultural discourses especially important to the fairness of the democratic participation of smaller or otherwise marginal groups" (ibid.).

A similar classification is offered by Strömbäck, who argues that democracy is not just an institutional arrangement for elections, but rather a forum for people engaged in public life and different types of political action. *Participatory* democracy thrives when people engage in and work for their causes. "The stronger civil society is, and the more social capital a society has, the more democracy thrives" (Strömbäck 2005, p. 336). Similar to Baker's *complex* model and Glasser's *direct* model, Strömbäck's most challenging democracy model refers to active citizens who make collective decisions based on an exchange of arguments. This *deliberative* model of democracy is based on discussions in the public sphere, values of rationality, impartiality, intellectual honesty and equality, as well as on means of producing agreement or better understanding (ibid.).

In these dialogue- and deliberation-based models of democracy, journalism has not only the obligation to inform about potentially crucial issues (as in the elitist model), but also to act as a forum for the debate; the media should inspire people to participate in the public discourse, and journalism should give voice to groups that need to express themselves in public to make their cause heard.

Such concepts of highly deliberative democracies are criticized for being unrealistic and for underestimating the problems that arise exactly from deliberation. Dahlgren argues that deliberation is not free from social stratification and that (new) hierarchies are established in accordance with the communicative competence and skills of speakers and groups of speakers.

> "Deliberative democracy asserts that meaningful political discussion can only take place if all participants are on an equal footing, that is, if respect, a pluralist outlook, and reciprocity prevail. (…) In fact, one could ask: given that the distribution of communicative skills tends to follow general social hierarchies, and thereby may well serve to reinforce such hierarchies, why should we expect citizens with lower communicative skill to participate, and why should we anticipate that deliberative democracy is a good way for citizens to impact on the decisions that affect them?" (Dahlgren 2006, p. 31)

There is no easy answer to this worrying question. However, in complex or deliberative democracies, journalism is required to take factors that privilege some speakers over others into account when it attempts to enable groups and people to express themselves and make their causes heard.

Whatever model of democracy is taken into account, liberal-procedural or republican – or, more realistically, a mixture of different models – journalism is confronted with normal expectations of various kinds. And journalism itself is subject to internal democratic procedures. The more sophisticated democracy becomes in terms of deliberation, the higher the expectations of journalistic performance become and the more professional – and democratic – excellence is required.

Democratic roles of journalism and media

The existence of different models of democracy implies that we should try to define the roles of journalism and the media according to these models. Liberal-procedural democracies require watchdog journalism on high alert concerning corruption, abuse of power and things going wrong in general. Moreover, journalism in these democracies needs antennas sensitive to developments that may eventually become important enough to be brought to the attention of the people. Within republican democracies, the role of journalism – on top of being watchdogs – is dedicated to offering different groups access to the general public and to facilitating deliberation and discourse.

This distinction looks artificial. While republican democracies require the whole set of journalistic virtues to function, liberal-procedural would only need the watchdog element. Such a reductionist view would be misleading. Both in times of conflict and corruption, as well as in times when such events are (temporarily) absent, legitimate (and even illegitimate) claims of groups, pressure groups and lobbies are articulated. Some of these claims may be urgent and justify the immediate attention of journalism. But others may require public debate and deliberation over some time in order to mature, to explain, or even to develop their justification in public dialogue. These maturing processes require public attention, and journalism is indispensable in evaluating, discussing, dismissing or accepting such claims. Thus far, digital communication technologies have not provided enough alternative opportunities to fully substitute this discursive role of journalism (see last section of this chapter for arguments).

It would seem reasonable, therefore, to develop a set of journalistic roles in democracies, without further distinction along the lines of different models of democracy. Some roles may be more important in certain circumstances than in others, but fundamentally, the roles and virtues of journalism in democracies are inseparable and universal.

One recent and comprehensive attempt to systematize the role of journalism in democracies was undertaken by McQuail. He starts out by describing the basic tasks of journalism as observing and informing, participating in public life by way of comment, advice and advocacy and providing a forum or platform for different voices (2009, p. 116). He then suggests four different roles[2]:

- The *monitorial* role addresses information provision by journalism to the general public. People need and require orientation, and journalistic information should be able to provide points of reference. The *monitorial* role refers to "all aspects of the collection, processing, and dissemination of information of all kinds about current and recent events, plus warnings about future developments" (ibid., p. 125).

- The *facilitative* role covers all aspects of the provision of a deliberative public space. Journalism should promote active citizenship by way of debate and participation. "They [the media] promote inclusiveness, pluralism, and collective purpose. According to the concept of the facilitative role, they help to develop a shared moral framework for community and society, rather than just looking after individual rights and interests" (ibid., p. 126). McQuail points out that the facilitative role is not always in accord with the practices of a press driven by profit and competition. Its focus is rather on minorities, marginalized groups and cultures than on mainstream reporting. Nonetheless, the *facilitative* role is particularly important in deliberative models of democracy.

- The *radical* role "focuses on exposing abuses of power and aims to raise popular consciousness of wrongdoing, inequality, and the potential for change" (ibid., 126). It is not very clear why this role is called radical, as this function is one of classics in the list of journalism's duties. It is radical in the sense that such journalism has the potential not only to raise awareness for any kind of abuse of power, but perhaps also to mobilize resistance or protest.

- The *collaborative* role refers to the collaboration between the media and the state, for example during times of crisis or states of emergency. "Collaboration meets the needs of both parties, recognizing the fact that the media possess an essential societal resource – the public information network – though authorities often control the supply of 'news'. While collaboration of the kind described almost inevitably impinges on the independence of the press and other media, it can usually be legitimated on grounds of immediate necessity" (ibid., 127). This role may at first sight be contradictory to the notion of freedom of the press in democratic societies. Media should certainly not collaborate with the state and other agents of power in society. But it is the irony of such role descriptions that they only rarely correspond with reality. "The collaborative role (…) is often only a more transparent and accentuated case of what goes on much of the time" (ibid. p. 130).

These four normative roles of journalism cover at large the democratic requirements that follow from the descriptions of the different democratic models. While the *collaborative, monitorial*, and *radical* roles fit all forms of democracy, the *facilitative* role with its feature of deliberation is more important in republican models of democracy.

In any case, the role of the media is essential to the sound functioning of democracies. From the perspective of the concerned civil society in whatever democracy, the media's and journalism's responsibility is crucial. Therefore, the conduct of the media as agents of power in democracies should be closely monitored, and media organizations should be called to account. Accountability in this context is understood as a wider concept, not only comprising the output of the media. Accountability "refers to the willingness of the media to answer for what they do by their acts of publication, including what they do to society at large, and refers as well to the feasibility of securing accountability where there is unwillingness" (Glasser 2009, p. 132).

Theory concept of the Media for Democracy Monitor (MDM)

"To monitor is to characterize something according to a criterion. In other words, monitoring means evaluating" (Galtung 1999, p. 18). The MDM intends to provide empirical evidence on the fulfillment of the role of the media for each participating democratic country. Based on the insight that different models of democracy demand similar services from the media and based on a consistent understanding of the role of the media, the following considerations define the analytical framework of the MDM.

There are other instruments of media monitoring with a longer tradition than the MDM. But their purpose is different. When existing media monitoring initiatives are overviewed, two categories can be identified. There are initiatives that watch critically the output of the news media. Such initiatives are typically Internet based and focus on mistakes and misleading information published by their object of study. In Germany, of example, the broadsheet *Bild-Zeitung* is watched by *Bild Blog* (www.bildblog.de). In the United States, three initiatives among many others are *Mediawatch* (www.mediawatch.com), *News Hounds* ("We watch Fox so you don't have to"; www.newshounds.us) and *Grade the News* (www.gradethenews.org). Typically, such watch-blogs are run by individuals or small groups and their sustainability depends on the time and effort these activists are able and willing to invest.

The second category is composed of established institutions with a specific mission statement. Often such monitoring instruments observe the media in democracies in transition and report about violations of journalism rights. Examples of such institutions are *Freedom House* and the *International Research and Exchange Board* (IREX). Such monitoring instruments are typically based on reports from concerned journalists or country experts reporting irregularities during the period of scrutiny. A project that monitors media developments in a highly systematic way is the the US-based *Project for Excellence in Journalism* (PEJ), which publishes a detailed annual report on the content and structure of the leading news media in the United States.[3]

With regard to the purpose of the MDM, these monitoring initiatives are either civil-society-based observation desks with little or no social-science background (watch blogs) or they do not cover mature democracies (IREX) or they scrutinize just one country (PEJ). While the latter can certainly be regarded as a best practice example in its own right, for the purpose of monitoring and thus evaluating media conduct on a comparative level among various countries, these monitoring initiatives are not completely appropriate.

The MDM's ambition, therefore, is to provide a monitoring instrument appropriate to all mature democracies. It starts out from a root concept of democracy with three distinct elements that are firmly anchored in the history of democratic reasoning: *freedom, equality* and *control*.[4]

Figure 1 integrates the four roles of democracy as suggested by McQuail (2009) (left) into the root concept of the MDM (right).

Figure 1.   Roles of media in democracy and the MDM root concept

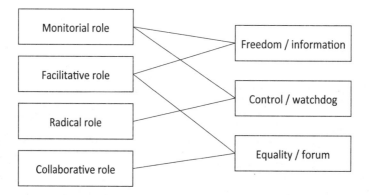

The main line of argument of the MDM's root concept is the following:

Freedom as an elementary notion in democracy has a negative and a positive connotation. Negative freedom refers to the absence of legal and/or political prohibitions and – in the context of media – to the absence of censorship. In a more reductionist view, negative freedom means being free from the interference of the state. Positive freedom, in turn, refers to the freedom to act. In the context of the media, positive freedom is freedom of expression (to receive and, in particular, impart information), freedom of opinion-building, and of the flow of diverse ideas and opinions. In other words, positive freedom is the effective capacity of individuals to have their opinions printed and circulated (Picard 1985, p. 48).

Equality is another elementary principle of democracy and refers, in the first place, to the fundamental notion that all citizens are equal in and before the law. Equality calls for an absence of discrimination or bias in the amount and kind of access available to channels, on equivalent terms, for all alternative voices, as far as is practicable. "Equality (…) requires that no special favour be given to power-holders and that access to media should be given on a fair, if not always an equal, basis to contenders for office and, in general, to oppositional or deviant opinions, perspectives or claims" (McQuail 1992, p. 71). Equality, however, does not include any kind of obligation to provide balanced reporting. Not all claims need to be treated equally by journalists. The media should provide a platform, but not necessarily equal opportunities for all. On the contrary: Conflicts are an intrinsic element of democratic societies. James Curran holds that the media should not pretend that the underlying notion of society is harmony. "Democratic politics is about expressing and managing real conflicts in society." And he continues: "The expression of conflict through the media is positive, and should be encouraged (…)" (Curran 2007, p. 36f).

Control, the third elementary principle of democracy refers to the capacity and obligation of citizens to call power-holders of all sorts to account. While at the institutional political level elections are a powerful instrument for holding political power-holders accountable, there are no set mechanisms to call power-holders in other social realms to account. Curran argues that control should not be limited to the state and institutionalized power, as this could lead to the "neglect of other forms of power – economic, social and cultural – that can also injure or restrict" (2007, p. 35). If we broaden his interpretation, this democratic principle calls for control of all institutions with power over individuals and groups. Media and journalism provide one prominent means to control power-holders by way of public deliberation. In the context of the MDM, however, there is a second meaning of democratic control. As power agents in democratic societies, the media need to be called to account for their own actions as well.

Freedom, *equality* and *control* can be translated into communication functions. The media's communication function, which derives from *freedom*, is the information function; from *equality* follows what might be called public opinion-making or simply the forum function; and from *control* follows the function to act as a watchdog against the abuse of all types of power. The watchdog mandate involves "accuracy, honesty, and investigative zeal" (Baker 2006, p. 114). Curran argues that the watchdog role of the media does not and should not place the burden of investigation on journalism alone. Rather, all of what he calls "investigative resources of a free society – its whistleblowers, dissenting elite members, civil society watchdogs, independent think tanks, and critical researchers" (2007, p. 35) should collaborate. The aim of watchdog journalism in conjunction with all other investigative resources is described by Bennett and Serrin as "documenting, questioning, and investigating those activities, in order to (…) provide publics and officials with timely information on issues of public concern" (2005, p. 169).

Thus, the root concept of democracy translates into a democratic media mandate to serve as (1) a guardian of the flow of information; (2) a forum for public discussion of diverse, often conflicting ideas; and (3) a public watchdog against the abuse of power in all its various forms. This root concept serves as a theoretical fundament for the development of empirical dimensions and indictors. These are presented in the following chapter.

New media, new role in democracy?

The empirical concept of the MDM, structured into dimensions and indicators, focuses on the leading news media in each country under scrutiny. This focus on the traditional news media may seem inappropriate and outdated in times when successful presidential election campaigns rely on the candidate's presence in web-based social media (the United States in 2008), when governments are toppled by Facebook-organized citizens (Tunesia and Egypt in 2011) and when younger generations base their daily information diet primarily or even entirely on Internet sources.

There may be some truth to such an argument. But there are also good reasons to justify the MDM's emphasis on traditional media organizations. Leaving aside the colossal and overwhelming question of whether or not the Internet changes everything, including democracy, we concentrate on the somewhat easier question of whether it is still justified to focus on the conduct and performance of the traditional news media when the role of journalism for democracy is under scrutiny. Indeed, some observers have expressed their optimism that the Internet will develop a democratizing, emancipatory and thus revolutionary force. Cyber-libertarians, as Dahlberg and Siapera call them, believe in the Internet as a non-hierarchical network of free information flow, a space for open debate and opinion formation that enables citizen scrutiny of power (Dahlberg and Siapera 2007: 3). If this were the case, the essential functions of journalism and the media for democracy would be replaced and ultimately rendered obsolete.

In a more critical, sober reflection, Hindman (2009) argues that such euphoria is not justified. His analysis of the Internet and the hyperlink structure in the United States showed that there is a winner-takes-it-all pattern, rather than the often proclaimed digital openness for all voices. Internet links and Internet usage are not evenly distributed, but clustered around a few popular thus powerful sites. These websites are not those of independent bloggers representing diverse views on political matters, but rather those of large media conglomerates. Jenkins and Thorburn argue that "[t]he old intermediaries are still in place, not likely to wither away any time soon, so long as they command national and international audiences and thus retain their power to deliver commercial messages to millions" (2003, p. 12). In a more recent study on the changes taking place in journalism and the news media as a result of new technologies, Fenton confirms this earlier expectation: "It seems ever likely that the voices on the web will be dominated by the larger, more established news providers that will duplicate the same commercial interests according to the same understanding of how news fits those commercial concerns, leading to anything but increased diversity" (2010, p. 13). Given this corporate strength in online news provision, which mirrors power relations in the analogue world, Christians et al. also see no reason for cyber-enthusiasm: "The flow of political communication in cyberspace can be just as biased, manipulative, propagandistic, disinformational, distorted, (…) cynical, and xenophobic as in the conventional channels of present day mass media" (2009, p. 231).

Hindman develops another argument: Websites in cyberspace are not all created equal. Although everyone can express his or her opinion freely in cyberspace, this potentially democratizing force remains weak. "No democratic theorist expects citizens' voices to be considered exactly equally, but all would agree that pluralism fails whenever vast swaths of the public are systematically unheard in civic debates. The mechanisms of exclusion may be different online, but (…) they are no less effective" (2009, p. 12). Ultimately, self-expression only furthers democratic deliberation if there is a fair chance of contributing to the public debate. As for now, contributions in cyberspace need to be repeated and multiplied by traditional news organizations, even if the speaker/blogger enjoys elite status in cyberspace. Hindman concludes and summarizes his research by saying: "It may be easy to speak in cyberspace, but it remains difficult to be heard" (ibid., p. 142).

It follows that the choice of concentrating the current MDM research endeavors on leading news media seems well justified – at least for now and given the current state of development. This choice does not, however, exclude all references to cyberspace from the research design. The empirical design includes indicators referring *inter alia* to the level of (virtual) participation of citizens offered by leading news media, and the research sample certainly includes leading online news media along with newspapers, television and radio. But most of the online news media (with few exceptions) are part of the well-know corporate media world.

Notes

[1] A short version of the MDM 2008 was published in *Communications* 2009; the full version was published in 2011 by Peter Lang. See Trappel and Maniglio (2009), d'Haenens et al. (2009) and Trappel and Meier (2011).

[2] These four roles are described in Chapter 5 of the book by Christians et al. (2009). In the introduction, Denis McQuail is listed as the author of this chapter. The four roles, however, were presented earlier by members of the team of authors, see for example Nordenstreng (2006, p. 38)

[3] For a more detailed description of existing monitoring initiatives, see Trappel and Maniglio (2011).

[4] This root concept is developed in detail in the introductory chapter of the report on the pilot phase of the MDM (Trappel and Maniglio 2011).

References

Baker, C.E. (2002) *Media, Markets, and Democracy.* Cambridge: Cambridge University Press.

Baker, C.E. (2006) 'Journalist Performance, Media Policy, and Democracy', in F. Marcinkowski, W.A. Meier and J. Trappel (eds) *Media and Democracy. Experiences from Europe,* pp. 115-126. Bern: Haupt.

Baker, C.E. (2007) *Media Concentration and Democracy: Why Ownership Matters.* New York: Cambridge University Press.

Bennett, W.L. and W. Serrin (2005) 'The Watchdog Role', in G. Overholser and K. Hall Jamieson (eds) *The Press,* pp. 169-188. Oxford: Oxford University Press.

Brants, K. (2007) 'Changing Media, Changing Journalism', in W.A. Meier and J. Trappel (eds) *Power, Performance and Politics: Media Policy in Europe,* pp. 105-121. Baden-Baden: Nomos.

Christians, C.G., T.L. Glasser, D. McQuail, K. Nordenstreng and R.A. White (2009) *Normative Theories of the Media. Journalism in Democratic Societies.* Urbana, Chicago: University of Illinois Press.

Curran, J. (2007) 'Reinterpreting the Democratic Role of the Media', *Brazilian Journalism Research* 3(1): 31-54.

d'Haenens, L., F. Marcinkowski, A. Donk, J. Trappel, T. Maniglio, J. Fidalgo, et al. (2009) 'The Media for Democracy Monitor applied to five countries: A selection of indicators and their measurement', *Communications* 34(2): 203-220.

Dahlberg, L. and E. Siapera (2007) 'Introduction: Tracing Radical Democracy and the Internet', in L. Dahlberg and E. Siapera (eds) *Radical Democracy and the Internet. Interrogating Theory and Practice,* pp. 1-16. Hampshire, New York: Palgrave MacMillan.

Dahlgren, P. (2006) 'Civic Participation and Practices: Beyond 'Deliberative Democracy'', in N. Carpentier, P. Pruulmann-Vengerfeldt, K. Nordenstreng, M. Hartmann, P. Vihalemm and B. Cammaerts (eds) *Researching Media, Democracy and Participation. The Intellectual Work of the 2006 European Media and Communication Doctoral Summer School,* pp. 23-33. Tartu: Tartu University Press.

Dahlgren, P. (2007) 'Civic Identity and Net Activism: The Frame of Radical Democracy', in L. Dahlberg and E. Siapera (eds) *Radical Democracy and the Internet. Interrogating Theory and Practice,* pp. 55-72. Hampshire, New York: Palgrave MacMillan.

Fenton, N. (2010) 'Drowning or Waving? New Media, Journalism and Democracy', in N. Fenton (ed.) *New Media, Old News. Journalism & Democracy in the Digital Age,* pp. 3-16. Los Angeles: Sage.

Galtung, J. (1999) 'Prospects for Media Monitoring: Much Overdue, But Never Too Late', in K. Nordenstreng and M. Griffin (eds) *International Media Monitoring,* pp. 15-24. Cresskill (NJ): Hampton Press.

Glasser, T.L. (2009) 'The Principles and Practice of Democracy (chapter 4)', in C.G. Christians, T.L. Glasser, D. McQuail, K. Nordenstreng and R.A. White (eds) *Normative Theories of the Media.* Journalism in Democratic Societies, pp. 91-113. Urbana, Chicago: University of Illinois Press.

Held, D. (2006) *Models of Democracy.* 3rd edition. Cambridge: Polity Press.

Hindman, M. (2009) *The Myth of the Digital Democracy.* Princeton and Oxford: Princeton University Press.

Jakubowicz, K. and M. Sükösd (2008) 'Twelve Concepts Regarding Media System Evolution and Democratization in Post-Communist Societies', in K. Jakubowicz and M. Sükösd (eds) *Finding the Right Place on the Map.* Central and Eastern European Media Change in a Global Perspective, pp. 9-40. Bristol, Chicago: Intellect.

Jenkins, H. and D. Thorburn (2003) 'The Digital Revolution, the Informed Citizen, and the Culture of Democracy', in H. Jenkins and D. Thorburn (eds) *Democracy and New Media,* pp. 1-17. Cambridge, MA: MIT Press.

McChesney, R.W. (2008) 'Rich Media, Poor Democracy: Communication Politics in Dubious Times', in R.W. McChesney (ed.) *The Political Economy of Media. Enduring Issues, Emerging Dilemmas,* pp. 425-443. New York: Monthly Review Press.

McManus, J. (1994) *Market-driven Journalism: Let the Citizen Beware?* Thousand Oaks: Sage.

McManus, J. (2009) 'The Commercialization of News', in K. Wahl-Jorgensen and T. Hanitzsch (eds) *Handbook of Journalism Studies,* pp. 218-233. New York, London: Routledge.

McQuail, D. (1992) *Media Performance. Mass Communication and the Public Interest.* London, Newbury Park, New York: Sage.

McQuail, D. (2009) 'Roles of News Media in Democracy (chapter 5)', in C.G. Christians, T.L. Glasser, D. McQuail, K. Nordenstreng and R.A. White (eds) *Normative Theories of the Media. Journalism in Democratic Societies,* pp. 114-135. Urbana, Chicago: University of Illinois Press.

Nordenstreng, K. (1999) 'Toward Global Content Analysis and Media Criticism', in K. Nordenstreng and M. Griffin (eds) *International Media Monitoring,* pp. 3-13. Cresskill (NJ): Hampton Press.

Nordenstreng, K. (2004) 'Media Monitoring: Watching the Watchdogs', in R.D. Berenger (ed.) *Global Media Go to War. Role of News and Entertainment Media During the 2003 Iraq War,* pp. 343-352. Spokane: Marquette Books.

Nordenstreng, K. (2006) "Four Theories of the Press' reconsidered', in N. Carpentier, P. Pruulmann-Vengerfeldt, K. Nordenstreng, M. Hartmann, P. Vihalemm and B. Cammaerts (eds) *Researching Media, Democracy and Participation. The Intellectual Work of the 2006 European Media and Communication Doctoral Summer School,* pp. 35-45. Tartu: Tartu University Press.

Nordenstreng, K. and M. Griffin (1999) 'Preface', in K. Nordenstreng and M. Griffin (eds) *International Media Monitoring,* pp. xiii-xviii. Cresskill (NJ): Hampton Press.

Picard, R. (1985) *The Press and the Decline of Democracy. The Democratic Socialist Response in Public Policy.* Westport/Connecticut: Greenwood Press.

Schumpeter, J. (1976) *Capitalism, Socialism and Democracy*. 5th edition. London: Allen and Unwin.

Strömbäck, J. (2005) 'In Search of a Standard: four models of democracy and their normative implications for journalism', *Journalism Studies* 6(3): 331-345.

Trappel, J. and T. Maniglio (2009) 'On Media Monitoring – the Media for Democracy Monitor (MDM)', *Communications* 34(2): 169-201.

Trappel, J. and T. Maniglio (2011) 'On Media Monitoring – The Media for Democracy Monitor (MDM)', in J. Trappel and W.A. Meier (eds) *On Media Monitoring. The Media and Their Contribution to Democracy*, pp. 65-134. New York: Peter Lang.

Trappel, J. and W.A. Meier (eds) (2011) *On Media Monitoring. The Media and Their Contribution to Democracy*. New York: Peter Lang.

Voltmer, K. (ed) (2006) *Mass Media and Political Communication in New Democracies*. London, New York: Routledge.

Zaller, J. (2003) 'A New Standard of News Quality: Burglar Alarms for the Monitorial Citizen', *Political Communication* 20(2): 109-130.

Chapter 2

Indicators and Definitions

André Donk & Josef Trappel

In the following chapter, we briefly introduce each of the indicators used for the "Media for Democracy Monitor". The choice of indicators is based, on the one hand, on the theoretical concept, outlined in the previous chapter. On the other hand, these indicators were discussed by the members of the research team in various face-to-face sessions. The meaning of each indicator was scrutinized in detail and theoretically applied to the context of the countries concerned. These discussions were based on experiences from the first (pilot) research conducted in 2007/2008 (Trappel & Meier 2011; d'Haenens, Marcinkowski, Donk, et al. 2009) Some of the indicators have been modified; some have been deleted or merged with others. Some new indicators were introduced in order to better balance the whole instrument.

For each indicator, the national research team was requested to grade the performance of their country's media by assigning from 0 to 3 points. This grading scheme was used in the pilot study as well and found suitable for this exercise. In general, 3 points were awarded when all or almost all requirements were fulfilled, 2 points were given if the clear majority of criteria or the most important criteria were met. One point indicates poor fulfilment, but that at least some criteria were met. Zero points were given if the respective indicator did not apply at all or if all major criteria were not met in the country. The grading was done by the academic research team on the basis of research or the evidence available to them. On first glance, this grading might seem to contain arbitrary choices, but in the application of the scheme, the vast majority of grades were easy to apply. In order to create a common understanding of how the grades were awarded, the group of researchers met after data collection again (in October 2010). This grading meeting turned out to be useful for all participants to clear out interpretations and to increase the validity of the instrument.

Indicators

Freedom / Information (F)

This structural feature refers to each specific country and its media landscape. According to this feature, freedom is better guaranteed if the relevant news media are available to all citizens and are widely used by them. The following two indicators deal with the distribution and consumption of news.

The first indicator – *geographic distribution of news media availability* – concerns the geographic distribution of news media. It seeks a media landscape that is characterized by high levels of public access, including marginalized groups, and by the possibility of efficient use of technology to gather and distribute news and information. News media should therefore be widely available and regional divides should not exist. This implies a high degree of technical reach and unrestricted access to news media so that a full supply of all types of news media can be guaranteed. Geographic distribution as an indicator of freedom should not be underrated. It has always been a key principle of media structure, closely connected with social structure: "Differences of geography may also coincide with ethnic, religious or language differences within the national society" (McQuail 1992, p. 115).

(F1) Geographic distribution of news media availability		1
Question	Are the relevant news media available to all citizens? Is there a regional divide?	
Requirement	The higher the level of distribution and availability, the more democratic freedom and the higher the potential that democracy will be promoted.	
Points	3	news media are widely available all over the country
	0	news media are available to the urban population only
Criteria	- coverage of all areas/ nationwide access	
	- strong radio or television signals via cable, satellite, terrestrial networks	
	- access to online media without restrictions	
	- use of multiplatform delivery systems (e.g., making radio and TV available online)	
	- ...	
Data sources	Statistics; Reports	

The next indicator in this field relates to the reach of the primarily used news media. It focuses on the daily share of newspapers, television, radio, and online media use. It shows which news media reach the largest group of citizens and which media therefore have a potentially greater influence on public opinion. What Berelson et al. stated, already in the 1950s, still provides the normative foundation for current political communication research: Democracy needs well-informed citizens (1954, p. 308).

(F2) Patterns of news media use (consumption of news)	2
Question	What does the distribution of media use look like between newspapers, television news, radio news and online-media? What is the reach of the main news broadcasts?
Requirement	The more the news media are used, the more democratic freedom and the higher the potential that democracy will be promoted. Distinguish whole population from younger population (approx. 12-25 years old)
Points	3 entire population young and old watch/read/listen/use news regularly 0 news is of minor importance compared to entertainment, etc.
Criteria	- high reach of main news broadcasts (evening news) - high reach and circulation of quality newspapers - high reach of radio news - high reach of news-oriented online media - high reach among different social segments of the population - ...
Data sources	Statistics; Audience research; Public opinion surveys

The following performance feature refers to selected news media and focuses on the status of editorial and journalistic autonomy within media organizations. In this respect, working free from any interference is a basic principle of media in democracies (Hardy 2008, p. 109; Christians et al. 2009, p. 116). It calls for the preservation of some degree of independence from internal and external influences and pressures. This indicator also assumes that the selection and composition of news needs to be executed according to professional rules and through use of a plurality of sources (Kovach & Rosenstiel 2001, pp. 135-6), and that the news combines results from in-depth interviews with the selected media sample and external research findings to reveal the diversity of news sources used in the news media. The indicator assumes that the use of different news sources better promotes democracy, as it ensures the validation of facts and a plurality of standpoints (Christians et al. 2009, p. 117). First, this implies a large variety of news agencies and no dominance of just one national or international agency in the newsroom. Furthermore, a diversity of news sources implies the use of non-elite sources (e.g., political blogs), the rejection of PR material, and the employment of national as well as foreign correspondents. The selection or omission of relevant news sources for political or ideological reasons reduces the degree of diversity, as it indicates the partisanship of news media. Furthermore, it is asked whether the media cooperate and build up a content syndication and supply each other with certain news sections, such as foreign news.

(F3) Diversity of news sources		3
Question	How diverse are the sources used by the leading news media?	
Requirement	The more diverse the sources used by the leading news media are, the better democracy will be promoted.	
Points	3 large variety of sources, no dominant sources 0 dependency of leading news media on one source (e.g., national news agency)	
Criteria	- dominance of the national news agency; - presence and relevance of other news agencies; - research findings on the use of PR material by the media - number of own national and foreign correspondents - content syndication (do leading news media supply one another with relevant news sections, such as foreign news?) - relation between elite and non-elite sources - selection (or omission) of sources on political grounds - ...	
Data sources	Interviews, external research findings	

Indicator F4 is called *Internal rules for practice of newsroom democracy* and concerns the principle of checks and balances, which is essential to democracy and describes in particular the idea of newsroom democracy and conditions of freedom for the editorial staff (Christians et al. 2009, p. 92; 96). It looks for organizational structures that guarantee the independence of the individual member of the editorial staff and thus the promotion of responsible and responsive journalism (objective reporting). If actual rules aiming at internal democratic practices exist, it is more likely that democratic freedom will be guaranteed and democracy promoted. The indicator seeks to ascertain whether any formal procedures (or strict rules) have been established to ensure journalists' participation in decision-making. There can be different ways to ensure the internal freedom of the press and to involve journalists in the management of information and in important decisions at the heart of a media organization, such as the existence of a newsroom council, internal rules of electing or appointing the editor-in-chief.

(F4) Internal rules for practice of newsroom democracy		4
Question	To what extent do newsroom journalists practice internal democracy?	
Requirement	If effective rules aiming at internal democratic practices exist, it is more likely that democratic freedom will be guaranteed and thus that democracy will be promoted.	
Points	3 democratic practices in the newsrooms are implemented and respected 0 decisions in the newsroom do not involve journalists at all	
Criteria	- newsroom journalists have a formal / equal say in how to portray and frame political issues - newsroom journalists have to arrive at a consensus on how to frame political issues - newsrooms have clear editorial guidelines aiming at impartiality, with sanctions attached - existence of a newsroom council - internal rules for electing/appointing editor-in-chief, other positions, etc. - journalists chose their editor-on-chief - ...	
Data sources	Interviews	

The following performance indicator relates to the degree of interference by the management and other internal supervisors in editorial decisions. It assumes that democratic freedom is greater when more journalists can decide independently on editorial matters: "Owners of media operations may exert influence over content and distribution in a variety of ways […], although this may be rare in large corporations" (McAllister & Proffitt 2009, p. 331). The question certainly does not arise in the same way when government has legitimate control over the media (as in most European public broadcasting systems) and sets legal limits on freedom (McQuail 1992, p. 117). In order to secure the independence of newsrooms and journalists against the management or sales department, however, some internal rules are useful. An important rule, for instance, is that the newsroom and the management must be clearly separated. This prevents internal manipulation and influence as well as involving the newsroom in advertising relationships.

(F5) Company rules against *internal* influence on newsroom/ editorial staff		5
Question	What is the degree of independence of the newsroom against the ownership/ management? Are there rules on the separation of the newsroom from the ownership/ management? Are they implemented?	
Requirement	The more journalists decide independently on editorial matters, the more democratic freedom and the higher the potential that democracy will be promoted.	
Points	3 full independence on editorial decisions by the newsroom journalists 0 no participation in staff decisions;	
Criteria	- formal rules to separate newsrooms from management including the board in both private and public service media - Are such rules actually effective in daily practice? - representation of journalists in management - representation of journalists on the board - presence/absence of advertising department in newsroom meetings - Is editor-in-chief or publisher the formal leader of newsroom work? In case of public service media: - Does the public service remit provide for independence from the state/ government? - Is the selection procedure for the editor(s)-in-chief of public service media independent from the government? - ...	
Data sources	Interviews	

In general, any interference from external parties in the media is regarded as a negative factor for media freedom (Hardy 2008, p. 92). This indicator concerns the degree of interference by external parties in editorial decisions. This refers to such influences that derive from pressures in the operating environment of the media, particularly from advertisers, news sources, and organized pressure groups or public relations bodies. In theory, no commercial conflicts should interfere with the reporting (Foreman 2010, p. 32). In practice, media often rely on several simultaneous sources of income – a condition that conventional wisdom holds to be better for freedom. Particularly in the case of newspapers, we can say that the more financial resources originating from a third party (e.g., government, a single large advertiser or sponsor), the less plausible is the claim of full independence (McQuail 1992, p. 106).

(F6) Company rules against *external* influence on newsroom/ editorial staff		6
Question	What is the degree of interference by external parties (e.g., proprietors, advertisers, etc.)? Do news media receive revenues from a multitude of sources?	
Requirement	The higher the diversity of revenue streams, the more democratic freedom and the higher the potential that democracy will be promoted.	
Points	3 no single large advertiser, no effective political influence	
	0 strong policy interventions, dependence on large advertisers/sponsors	
Criteria	in the case of mixed financed media companies:	
	- multitude of income streams (sales, advertising, license fee, others)	
	- multitude of advertisers, each having only a minor share of the total	
	- sponsoring agreements with influence on content (such as "infomercials", etc.)	
	in case of single revenue financed media companies (e.g., some public service media):	
	- formal rules and practice of distance between revenue source (e.g., State/Government) and news media	
	- Are public service media financed over a short/long period? Can financial provision be changed from one year to the next?	
	- ...	
Data sources	Interviews	

The last feature of this dimension refers to formal rules on how to select and process news. It asks for routines and guidelines for news production: Is a stylebook on news selection available and being used? Do new journalists receive training in news values or selection criteria, what procedures precede publication? Democracy in the newsroom is better established if there is a regular debate on the selection and processing of news, because this may ensure both control and impartiality. Formal rules on the selection guarantee a high degree of professionalism.

(F7) Procedures on news selection and news processing		7
Question	What rules are implemented and practiced in the leading news media regarding the selection and in-house processing of news items?	
Requirement	The more internal debate about news values (selection criteria) and the choice of news that occurs, the more democratic freedom and the higher the potential that democracy will be promoted.	
Points	3 formal rules on how to select and process news exist and are practiced	
	0 news selection and processing are done by the individual journalist based on his/her own preference	
Criteria	- stylebook available on news selection	
	- in-house training for new journalists on the job	
	- defined stages for any news item before it is published/aired/put online	
	- regular newsroom discussions of past and forthcoming decisions regarding news values and news selection	
	- ...	
Data sources	Interviews	

Equality / Interest mediation (E)

This structural feature refers to the country and its entire media system. According to this feature, equality is better guaranteed if there are large numbers of different media outlets (quantitative external diversity). Ownership structure and diversity are accordingly regarded as important elements. Moreover, news should reach the citizen by means of different formats. Finally, there is a greater chance of achieving equality if the mass media are employed by minority groups (alternative media, third sector) and if the dominant mass media report on a regular basis about minority claims.

Claims concerning the threats of ownership concentration for democratic media have been discussed widely among scholars. Arguing from different angles, a high level of media concentration is considered detrimental to media market competition, the diversity of opinions and the representation of different groups in society. According to Doyle (2002), media ownership concentration is highly relevant to democracy, as it may result in the "abuse of political power by media owners or the under-representation of some significant viewpoints. (…) Concentrations of media ownership narrow the range of voices that predominate in the media and consequently pose a threat to the interest of society" (Doyle 2002, p. 6). Furthermore, Doyle argues that media ownership can lead to overrepresentation of certain political opinions that may create power imbalances, entailing risks for democracy and social coherence (ibid. p. 26). More recently, Baker argued that ownership concentration must be seen as contrary to the fundamental ideas of democracy. To him, the egalitarian principle of one man, one vote is not adequately reflected in media ownership concentration. "Dispersal of media power, like dispersal of voting power, is simply an egalitarian attribute of a system claiming to be democratic" (2007, p. 14). Therefore, "(…) concentrated media ownership creates the possibility of an individual decision maker exercising enormous, unequal and hence undemocratic, largely unchecked, potentially irresponsive power" (ibid. p. 16). McChesney concludes that ownership concentration accentuates hyper-commercialism and journalism denigration. He simply calls concentration "a poison pill for democracy" (2008, p. 427). For all these reasons, it is important to examine thoroughly the level of ownership concentration both at the national level (indicator E1) and at the regional (local) level (E2).

The first indicator (E1) refers to the degree of ownership concentration at the national level. The central assumption is that ownership concentration in the media may compromise the plurality of the media landscape. A national market controlled by one operator (monopoly) or by two (oligopoly) can be problematic in this regard. Ideally, more than two competing news media outlets should therefore be available in each news media sector, such as newspapers, news magazines, radio, television, online media.

(E1) Media ownership concentration national level		8
Question	What is the degree of ownership concentration at the national level?	
Requirement	The lower the national ownership concentration, the more democratic equality is guaranteed and the higher the potential that democracy will be promoted.	
Points	3	low concentration ratio (measured by CR3) and more than two competitors for all news media
	0	private monopoly at the national level
Criteria	- plurality of ownership at national level	
	- transparency of ownership	
	- if there is a monopoly: Is it publicly controlled? Is it state-owned?	
	- ...	
Data sources	Statistics (data, calculate the market share CR3 of all media in the country)	

The second indicator (E2) measures the degree of ownership concentration in the market of regional news media. In this context, each country must first define its major communication areas and then show the regional selection of newspapers, broadcasters, and online media. Ideally, more than two competing news media outlets should be available in each news media sector. With lower media concentration, a larger number of players have access to the news markets and more diverse opinions are likely to emerge. Over recent decades, many regional media markets lost on completion between regional or local media owners. Strong media ownership concentration at the local level is particularly difficult for local politics, as politicians have no alternative means to communicate with their electorate other than through the local monopoly media company. The Internet may help to offer additional channels of information and participation, but critics argue that it does not eliminate gate-keepers and does not provide equal access to deliberation. "The Internet has served to level some existing political inequalities, but it has also created new ones" (Hindman 2009, p. 19).

(E2) Media ownership concentration regional (local) level		9
Question	What is the degree of ownership concentration at the regional (local) level?	
Requirement	The lower the regional (local) ownership concentration, the more democratic equality is guaranteed and the higher the potential that democracy will be promoted.	
Points	3	more than two competitors in all regions for all news media types (newspapers, TV, radio, etc.)
	0	full news control of just one private media company in all relevant regions (integrated media companies: newspaper, local TV, radio, online)
Criteria	- plurality of ownership in the regions	
	- transparency of ownership	
	- if there is a monopoly: Is it publicly controlled? Is it state-owned?	
	- ...	
Data sources	Statistics (data, calculate the market share CR3 of main regions in the country)	

The following indicator – *diversity of formats* – measures the diversity of the respective formats and news presentations. It indicates plurality of information through multiple types of newspapers, television, radio, and online media as well as their use to provide news to the public. Each medium has its own specificities in the presentation of news and adds potentially to the diversity of news and information on offer. Accordingly, it is argued that when more options and greater variety of news formats exist, more diversity is provided to the consumer. Moreover, ownership diversity is unlikely to automatically translate into news format diversity (see ownership concentration E1 and E2).

(E3) Diversity of formats	10
Question	Is there a diversity of different formats of news presentation?
Requirement	The higher the diversity of formats, the more plurality of information and democratic equality is guaranteed and the higher the potential that democracy will be promoted.
Points	3 abundance of news formats 0 minimum diversity of news formats
Criteria	- degree of diversity of formats (deliver a list of different format of news, including online-outlets specialized on news, 24-hour news channels, etc.) - multiples types of news media - special forms of news presentation - ...
Data sources	Reports; audience research, format research

Indicator E4 – *minority/alternative media* – refers to the existence of minority/alternative media. It is uncontested that media can contribute to diversity by reflecting differences in society: "Media are expected to represent the prevailing differences of culture, opinion and social conditions of the population as a whole" (McQuail 1992, p.144). Ideally, all major minorities within a given society are served by a variety of special minority/alternative media or are well-represented by other media based on rules or conventions. More democratic equality is likely to be established if minority groups have easy and even privileged access to the media in order to argue their causes. Governance rules within media companies that entail legally binding obligations for the media in favour of positive discrimination of minorities are considered helpful tools in establishing more equality.

(E4) Minority / Alternative media		11
Question	Do minority / alternatives media exist? Are all sorts of minorities served by media? Do they have their own media? As minority qualify: ethnic groups, disabled people, women, minority languages, etc.	
Requirement	The more minority/alternative media exist, the more democratic equality is guaranteed and the higher the potential that democracy will be promoted.	
Points	3 plenitude of minority media exist, largest minorities are served by them 0 no such media exist	
Criteria	- quantity of minority/alternative media - do main / largest minorities have their own media or access to media on a regular basis? - use of languages that reflect the linguistic diversity of the media's target area - use of languages relied upon by marginalized groups - existence and relevance of Weblogs of minorities / ethnic groups, etc. - ...	
Data sources	Research reports; audience research	

According to the next indicator, the news media should be available at a reasonable price to the whole population. In order to provide people with equal opportunities to inform themselves on a regular basis, the price of the available media must be within the financial means of the entire population. Therefore, this indicator measures the cost of access to newspapers (price of subscription and/or copy price), television and radio (license fee, pay TV), and online media (broadband connection). These costs are put in relation to the average household income in order to provide a sound data basis for international comparison.

(E5) Affordable public and private news media		12
Question	What is the price of the media in relation to average household income?	
Requirement	If the price for news media is affordable, it is more likely that democratic equality will be guaranteed and thus that democracy will be promoted.	
Points	3 low price in relation to average household income 0 news media only affordable for elites	
Criteria	All in relation to average household income and to lower income household groups (quantitative): - average price for an annual full subscription for newspapers - annual tax/licence fees for television and radio - price of broadband access - ...	
Data sources	Statistics; prices	

The structural feature *content monitoring instrument* refers to the specific country and its mass media landscape. According to this feature, equality is better guaranteed if there is a large number of politically neutral outlets (internal diversity) or a balance of politically aligned media organizations at the aggregate level (external diversity). For this reason, it is important that there exist bodies or institutions that monitor, for example, the actual political neutrality of the media. This indicator illustrates whether a country's media system has bodies or instruments to monitor news media content. Such instruments should be independent, the results should be publicly available, and operate on a regular basis. Such content monitoring might be institutionalized by the media themselves, by supervising bodies, by university institutes, or other organizations. The existence of a permanent content monitoring institution by itself is considered to have a positive impact on journalists' behaviour and to help foster the idea of media accountability.

(E6) Content monitoring instrument		13
Question	Is there a regular and publicly available issue monitoring instrument for news media?	
Requirement	If an effective monitoring instrument exists, it is more likely that democratic equality will be guaranteed and thus that democracy will be promoted.	
Points	3 continuously and published issue monitoring	
	0 no public monitoring at all	
Criteria	- organized, permanent issue monitoring	
	- published by relevant news media on a regular basis (publicly available)	
	- independence of the monitoring body / private company	
	- ...	
Data sources	Desk research	

The following indicator seeks to determine the existence and the use of an institutionalized and effective self-regulation system for the main news media of a country. It checks whether the internal tools for editorial policies (such as mission statements, codes of ethics, editorial guidelines, etc.) are implemented in line with formal rules. The central assumption here is that the mass media, within a prevailing climate of self-regulation and respect for the journalistic profession, effectively reflect and represent the diversity of views and interests in society. Scholars have pointed to a large variety of possible measures to implement both at the company level and on the national level (Bertrand 2002; Liederke 2004). Relevant for this indicator is the national level and whether codes of ethics exist that are implemented and respected by the leading news media.

(E7) Code of ethics at the national level (structure)		14
Question	Does a code of ethics at national level exist, requiring news media to provide fair, balanced and impartial reporting? Is it known and used?	
Requirement	If an effective code exists, it is more likely that democratic equality will be guaranteed and thus that democracy will be promoted.	
Points	3 code is implemented and frequently used 0 no code, not in use	
Criteria	- Existence of a press complaints commission, etc. - Existence of independent journalist associations, which disseminate good practice, e.g., improving skills and raising ethical standards… - Are there any provisions regarding the accountability of the media to civil society? - …	
Data sources	Interviews	

The structural indicator E7 is combined with the performance feature E8. This indicator is geared towards self-regulation instruments within leading news organizations in each country. Such self-regulation instruments are part of media governance in a broad sense, understood as the collective rules that organize media systems (Boeyink 1994; Freedman 2008; Puppis 2010). It is assumed that instruments such as clear internal rules that apply to all journalists in the newsrooms help to increase quality and provide journalists with guidelines on their day-to-day routines. Such guidelines work on the condition that rules do not only exist, but are used regularly. According to McQuail (2010), such self-regulation instruments can be formal or informal. However, formal self-regulation rules are more transparent and possibly more helpful for journalists than a set of informal rules that are applied by editors-in-chief at their discretion. News organizations with a sophisticated, highly developed, and continuously updated set of internal self-regulation rules are considered to better advance the cause of democratic equality.

(E8) Level of self-regulation (performance)		15
Question	Does a media self-regulation system exist at the main news media, requiring the provision of fair, balanced and impartial reporting? Is it effective?	
Requirement	The better the media's self-regulation system is, the more democratic equality is guaranteed and the higher the potential that democracy will be promoted.	
Points	3 highly sophisticated self-regulation instruments 0 no such instruments at all	
Criteria	- existence of a mission statement/ code of ethics/code of conduct, which refers to democratic values and contains journalistic obligations to report politically balanced - existence of internal rules for the right to reply - existence of formal systems for hearing complaints about alleged violations of ethical standards - Do ombudsmen have their own space in the media? Are they independent? - existence of sanctions against journalists who violate ethical standards - organized process of self-criticism - …	
Data sources	Interviews	

Indicator E9 – *participation* – examines the extent to which news media give citizens the opportunity to voice their own views and reactions to news stories they see, read or hear (Christians et al. 2007, p. 116, McNair 1999, p. 19, Wahl-Jorgensen 2007). In 1947, the Hutchins Commission on social responsibility in journalism proposed that media should provide a forum for exchange of comments and critit-cism (Commission on Freedom of the Press 1947). Moreover, the indicator analyses how well the media encourage citizens to participate in the production of news. Such an approach requires that the news media be open to forms of cooperation with citizens. It can be argued that, generally speaking, the larger the number of citizens who participate, the greater the chance of having a multitude of opinions. Online media are very well situated to organize such a forum by providing web-space for user reactions. Furthermore, other media make use of the Internet to provide a forum for comments and criticisms on their websites. In general, the Internet opens up new modes of citizen participation in the public discourse with fewer gatekeepers and supposedly a re-distribution of communicative power, away from established news outlets like television, radio and newspapers. The public sphere may be broadened and opened up to those with less access to traditional media. However, this form of participation via the Internet has a downside as well. Critics, such as Matthew Hindman, claim that differences remain and that the computer skills necessary to participate are even more stratified than in the analogue world. "These scholars acknowledge the continuing effects of the digital divide, the influence of economic forces and Internet gatekeepers, and the simple fact that all Web sites are not created equal" (Hindman 2009, p. 11).

(E9) Participation		16
Question	Is there an organized way for people to participate in the news process?	
Requirement	The more people that participate in the news process, the more democratic equality is guaran-teed and the higher the potential that democracy will be promoted.	
Points	3 open newsrooms, space in the media for citizens' voice 0 no such possibilities	
Criteria	- Newsrooms open to the public (sometimes, always) - Existence of rules for the right to reply / possibilities to give feedback - Do leading news media offer / organize public debates and discussions? - Do people participate in online fora on news issues offered by the media? - Do leading online media offer public postings? - If leading news media provide space for user generated content: For what reasons? What is the internal justification? - ...	
Data sources	Interviews	

Along with the process of media ownership concentration (see indicators E1 and E2), the importance of internal pluralism increases. Different voices in society are well represented if the leading news media allow for a high degree of internal pluralism in the newsrooms. While in earlier stages of the media development external pluralism was provided by a large number of independent news outlets (newspapers), which showed in their entirety a wide array of opinions, media concentration and in particular the demise of the party press require higher levels of internal pluralism within leading newsrooms. Irrespective of the requirement for each newsroom to follow an editorial line, from the perspective of democratic equality different views and opinions should be represented. But internal pluralism cannot follow from state regulation. It is rather part of the newsroom culture. Empirical evidence can be collected from close observation of the newsroom output (which is not done in this research exercise) or by discussion with members of the newsrooms. Internal pluralism is realized when divergent voices are represented within the same newsroom, when different experts' opinions are being voiced, and when the feedback culture of the newsroom is open to all sides.

(E10) Rules and practices on internal pluralism		17
Question	How do media organizations ensure that different views and perspectives are being reported?	
Requirement	The more different voices are reported by the media, the more democratic equality is guaranteed and the higher the potential that democracy will be promoted.	
Points	3	known and practiced standardized procedures to ensure internal pluralism
	0	no such procedures
Criteria	- How are different positions accommodated within the newsroom? - What rules apply to present divergent opinions of journalists within the same newsroom? - Are there regular internal debates on different positions? - existence (and observance) of internal rules/guidelines specifying that all relevant information and socially significant views must be given their appropriate weight in the coverage - Are journalists free (and expected) to also use information and views favouring the other side when a medium is allied with a particular party or ideology? - Are politicians / experts from all sides given the chance to present their case? - Is the medium's feedback culture (e.g., readers' letters) open to all sides? - ...	
Data sources	Interviews	

Control / Watchdog (C)

This structural feature refers to the specific country and its media system. It focuses on control mechanisms that exercise a watchdog role with regard to the media themselves. Hence, the first indicator examines the existence of instruments monitoring media performance and is based on the assumption that scrutiny from other media leads to overall better performance (Foreman 2010, p. 34). It is important to examine what tools different media have in order to adequately perform as a watchdog as well as to look at to what extent the media actually deal with controversial matters, engage in public criticism, and risk antagonizing either powerful interests or their own audience. Moreover, it is important to analyse the degree to which the media play an active role in their society or community.

(C1) Supervising the watchdog 'control of the controllers'		18
Question	Is there any institutionalized mechanism to control the performance and role of the news media?	
Requirement	If effective institutionalized mechanisms for scrutinizing the performance of the leading news media exist, it is more likely that democratic control will be guaranteed and thus that democracy will be promoted.	
Points	3 permanent debate on the role of the media as watchdogs, which engages a wider public 0 no public debate	
Criteria	- independent observers: news monitor, media blogs, professional journalistic journals, etc. - openness to external evaluation - existence of media bloggers - media journals that report on media coverage - newspaper space / TV and radio programmes on news coverage, the media - ...	
Data sources	Observation, interviews	

The following feature – C2 – refers to the performance of the selected news media as well as to structures of the media system. The focus is on mechanisms that encourage journalistic accountability and promote democratic control of the government and big business (Baker 2006, p. 120). The more the media are independent of power holders such as the owner or the state, and the more this independence is guaranteed by formal rules or even laws, the better the media can fulfil their function as a watchdog, and the better democracy is served (Christians et al. 2009, p. 130; Hardy 2008, pp. 88-9). On the one hand, this structural and performance indicator asks for legal provisions protecting journalists and their sources. On the other hand, it examines the influence of political parties, business interests and other social groups on the news media. For example, are financial investors, representatives of the government or churches present on the board of the leading news media? Do non-media companies own news media? The normative assumption is that media should first feel obliged to the citizens and not to power holders (Kovach & Rosenstiel 2001, pp. 51-2).

(C2) Independence of the news media from power holders		19
Question	How strong is the independence of the news media from various power holders and how is it ensured?	
Requirement	News media's watchdog function requires a high degree of independence. More independence means more control of those in power, thus enhancing democracy.	
Points	3 no formal or ownership-related influence from power holders on leading new media	
	0 strong formal or ownership-related influence of power holders on leading news media	
Criteria	- Are there shield laws in place to protect journalists? - Are sources protected by law or other professional rules? - How important is party affiliation among leading news media? - Are powerful business interests present on the boards of leading news media? - Are non-media companies such as financial investors, political parties, churches, etc. among news media owners? - If yes: Rely on existing data: Ownership share of such non-media companies of total circulation/audience - Is such diagonal ownership concentration transparent? - ...	
Data sources	Legal provisions, public service remit, corporate information (investors' relations), interviews	

Transparency is essential for democracy (Foreman 2010, p. 34). This indicator refers to citizens' possibilities to inform themselves about leading mass media: Is this information published frequently and easily accessible? Thus, this feature directly relates to the media's accountability. Does an imprint exist and is it obligatory to make the ownership of a news medium transparent? Who provides information on leading mass media: journalists' unions, government or regulatory authorities, universities or research institutes? And to what extent is this information available?

(C3) Transparency of data on media system		20
Question	How accessible is detailed information on the media system to the citizens?	
Requirement	Transparency is essential for democracy. The more easily citizens can inform themselves about the leading news media, the better the news media are placed to perform their watchdog function.	
Points	3 information on leading news media is published frequently and easily accessible on Internet or other sources	
	0 information on leading news media is not available or only available to experts	
Criteria	- publication of ownership information in every edition / imprint ("impressum") - information availability on leading news media provided by outside sources such as government, universities, unions, etc. - easily accessible and comprehensive information on leading news media on the Internet - data provided by regulatory authorities - ...	
Data sources	Own research, field tests	

The indicator *journalism professionalism* can be described as a performance feature, which is based on interviews with the news media sample and journalists' unions. Journalistic professionalism encompasses shared norms and standards of journalistic work and ethos (Hardy 2009, pp. 100-1). Professionalism can be regarded as one main form of journalistic accountability (Christians et al. 2009, p. 133). Thus, a high professional ethos helps the media in exercising their watchdog function. On the one hand, this indicator covers questions of journalistic ethics: Do journalists and society discuss media rules and ethics on a frequent basis? Is there any journalistic training on these matters? On the other hand, professionalism requires no pressure in terms of space, time and format (Christians et al. 2009, pp. 115-6). Hence it was asked whether there is an overload of journalistic capacities.

(C4) Journalism professionalism		21
Question	How well developed is journalism professionalism?	
Requirement	Strong professional ethos and sufficient resources are prerequisites for the exercise of the watchdog function. Strong professionalism is therefore good for the watchdog function of the media.	
Points	3 high professional ethos	
	0 no / low professional ethos	
Criteria	- workload of journalists / time for investigative research?	
	- multi-media requirements of journalists? overload of journalistic capacities?	
	- self-organization of journalists, discussing own rules and ethics; frequency of such meetings	
	- public debate provoked by journalists about ethical behaviour	
	- statements of professional rules established by journalists	
	- regular / irregular further education training for journalists on professional ethics	
	- ...	
Data sources	own research, field tests, interviews with journalists' unions	

The next indicator relates to the job security of journalists, assuming that the better they are protected against dismissal due to their reporting, the better they can exercise their watchdog role. On the juridical level, the indicator asks for legal provisions to save journalists from writing against their conviction ("clause de conscience") as well as from getting fired if their conviction is expressed in the commentary, etc. On the level of the labour market, the indicator has to examine the share of freelancers and permanent staff in the newsrooms, as only long-term and secure contracts promote free and autonomous reporting.

(C5) Journalists' job security		22
Question	What provisions are in place to provide a maximum of job security for journalists?	
Requirement	The more securely journalists can do their research and reporting work, the better they can exercise their watchdog function, and the better for democracy.	
Points	3 high degree of legal or professional security 0 no / low job security	
Criteria	- legal provisions to save journalists from writing against their personal conviction ("clause de conscience") - professional rules protecting journalists against dismissal because of personal convictions - labour contracts with long periods of notice (in case of dismissal) - proportion of freelancers and permanent staff - systematic use of short-term contracting - ...	
Data sources	Own research, legislation, interviews with journalists' unions	

Indicator C6 – *practice of access to information* – refers to journalists' possibilities to gain access to public information. As stated earlier, taking the role of a watchdog, journalists need to be free from restrictions when they are researching government or state activities. Otherwise, the media cannot provide efficient and profound control and criticism. The indicator questions whether there is any media law providing free access to public information and how it is implemented.

(C6) Practice of access to information		23
Question	How accessible is public information to journalists?	
Requirement	In order to exercise the watchdog function, journalists need access to public information.	
Points	3 no barriers for journalists 0 high barriers for journalists	
Criteria	- Does the media law allow for access to public information? - Do journalists enjoy privileges in accessing public information? - Are there reports about problems of journalists seeking public information? - Are there relevant restrictions against journalists accessing public information? - Differences between promises and practices - ...	
Data sources	Own research, interviews with journalists and journalists' unions	

The following indicator examines the extent to which the news media perform their mission as watchdogs. The view of the media as a watchdog against the abuse of power and corruption has long been a steady component of the journalistic self-image and of Western democratic political theory (Christians et al. 2009, p. 119; McQuail 1992, p. 120). This indicator intends to reveal the extent to which the watchdog function is perceived as important both in theory and in practice (Foreman 2010; Kovach & Rosenstiel 2001). Furthermore, it seeks to uncover whether a mission statement exists that refers explicitly to active investigative journalism.

(C7) The watchdog and the media's mission statement	24
Question	Does the mission statement of the company or the newsroom contain provisions on playing an active role as watchdogs / on investigative journalism or other forms of power control?
Requirement	If a mission statement concerning watchdog journalism exists, it is more likely that democratic control will be guaranteed and thus that democracy will be promoted.
Points	3 all relevant news media refer to the watchdog role and exercise it 0' no reference
Criteria	- existence of mission statement, which refers to an active investigative journalism and contains duties to act as a trustee on behalf of the public - level of importance of watchdog for the media organization/ - examples for accountable watchdog role - ...
Data sources	Interviews

This indicator provides information on whether journalists are given the chance to take part in professional training courses. The news media can only perform their watchdog duty if they have qualified personnel resources. In order to do so, the news media should provide their staff with training courses in watchdog journalism.

(C8) Professional training	25
Question	What importance is attached to journalism training?
Requirement	If effective professional training on watchdog journalism is provided, it is more likely that democratic control will be guaranteed and thus that democracy will be promoted.
Points	3 continuous "knowledge" training for journalists in news media 0 no such training
Criteria	- continuous training, obligation for continuous training - not skills but knowledge training - enough resources for each journalist (time & money) - ...
Data sources	Interviews

The following performance feature refers to the selected news media. A vital condition for exercising the watchdog role is that sufficient resources be available to journalists in the newsrooms. The more money there is at the disposal of newsrooms, the greater the number of news agencies that can be subscribed to, the more reporters that can be employed, and the more funding there is to be invested in investigative journalism, etc. (Schulz 2000, p. 3). Thus, the indicator refers to the financial resources of newsrooms for performing their watchdog function. To perform their mission as a watchdog in an appropriate way, it is crucial that they have the appropriate means regarding time and budgets. Limited resources have often been cited as a potential cause of constraint on the independence of journalism. Resources for their own investigations reduce the dependency on agency material. Additionally, news media perform better if they can make use of journalists who are specialists on given subjects. In this way, there will be more room for investigative journalism.

(C9) Watchdog function and financial resources		26
Question	Are there specific and sufficient resources for exercising investigative journalism or other forms of power control?	
Requirement	If sufficient resources for the scrutiny of government and business are given, it is more likely that democratic control will be guaranteed and thus that democracy will be promoted.	
Points	3 highest priority given to well-funded investigative journalism 0 relevant news media rely on agency material only	
Criteria	- output composition (agency material, own material) - funds / time / money for investigative journalism - ad hoc provisions by the news medium for in-depth investigation - foreign correspondents - ...	
Data sources	Interviews	

References

Baker, C.E. (2007) *Media Concentration and Democracy: Why Ownership Matters*. New York: Cambridge University Press.

Berelson, B., Lazarsfeld, F., & McPhee, W. (1954) *Voting. A Study of Opinion Formation in a Presidential Campaign*. Chicago: Chicago University Press.

Bertrand, C.-J. (2002) *Media Ethics & Accountability Systems*. New Brunswick, London: Transaction Publishers.

Boyeink, D.E. (1994) 'How Effective are Codes of Ethics', *Journalism Quarterly*, 71, 893-904.

Christians, C.G., Glasser, T., McQuail, D., Nordenstreng, K., & White, R. (2009) *Normative Theories of the Media. Journalism in Democratic Societies*. Urbana: University of Illinois Press.

Commission on the Freedom of the Press (1947) *A Free and Responsible Press: A General Report on Mass Communication: Newspaper, Radio, Motion Pictures, Magazines, and Books*. Chicago: University of Chicago Press.

d'Haenens, L., Marcinkowski, F., Donk, A., Maniglio, T., Trappel, J., Fidalog, J., Balcytiene, A., & Napryte, E. (2009) 'The Media for Democracy Monitor applied to five countries: A selection of indicators and their measurement', *Communications*, 34, 203-220.

Doyle, G. (2002) *Media Ownership. The Economics and Politics of Convergence and Concentration in the UK and European Media*. London, Thousand Oaks, New Delhi: Sage.

Foreman, G. (2010) *The Ethical Journalist. Making Responsible Decisions in the Pursuit of News*. Chichester: Wiley-Blackwell.

Freedman, D. (2008) *The Politics of Media Policy*. Cambridge: Polity Press.

Hardy, J. (2008) *Western Media Systems*. London: Routledge.

Hindman, M. (2009) *The Myth of the Digital Democracy*. Princeton and Oxford: Princeton University Press.

Kovach, B., & Rosenstiel, T. (2001) *The Elements of Journalism. What Newspeople Should Know and the Public Should Expect*. New York: Three Rivers Press.

Liederke, L.V. (2004) 'Media Ethics: From Corporate Governance to Governance, to Corporate Social Responsibility', *Communications*, 29, 27-42.

McAllister, M., & Proffitt, J. (2009) 'Media Ownership in a Corporate Age', in Wilkins, L., & Christians, G. (eds) *The Handbook of Mass Media Ethics* (328-339). New York: Routledge.

McChesney, R.W. (2008) Rich Media, Poor Democracy: Communication Politics in Dubious Times.

McChesney, R.W. (ed.) *The Political Economy of Media. Enduring Issues, Emerging Dilemmas* (425-443). New York: Monthly Review Press.

McNair, B. (1999) *Introduction to Political Communication*. London: Routledge.

McQuail, D. (2010) *McQuail's Mass Communication Theory.* London: Thousand Oaks; New Delhi: Sage.

McQuail, D. (1992) *Media Performance: Mass Communication and the Public Interest*. London: Sage.

Puppis, M. (2010) 'Media Governance: A New Concept for the Analysis of Media Policy and Regulation', *Communication, Culture & Critique*, 3, 134-149.

Schulz, W. (2000, October) *Preconditions of Journalistic Quality in an Open Society*. Paper presented at the International Conference News Media and Politics – Independent Journalism, Budapest.

Trappel, J., & Meier, W. (eds) (2011) *On Media Monitoring. The Media and Their Contribution to Democracy*. New York et al.: Peter Lang.

Wahl-Jorgensen, K. (2007) *Journalists and the Public. Newsroom Culture, Letters to the Editor, and Democracy*. Cresskill: Hampton Press.

Chapter 3

AUSTRALIA
Committed to Investigative Journalism

Beate Josephi

Geography and demographics are important factors affecting Australia's media. As the world's sixth largest country, Australia compares in size to the United States, not including Alaska. This large landmass only has a population of 22.5 million people (Australian Bureau of Statistics 2010), which is concentrated in its state and territory capitals, with close to 90 % of Australians living in urban centres.

History is the other highly influential factor, with Australia having consisted of six British colonies which formed the nation of Australia in 1901. Many British traditions as well as its legal and regulatory framework shape Australia's media to this day. Following the British model, Australia established a public broadcaster, the Australian Broadcasting Commission (later Corporation) in 1932, and the Special Broadcasting Service in 1978. Unlike their British counterpart, the public broadcasters are directly funded by the government. Although the ABC's independence has been guaranteed in the Australian Broadcasting Corporation Act 1983, board appointments have followed the government of the day's political preferences.

Commercial media have also flourished, but given the size of the country and its population distribution, Australia from early on had a high level of concentration of media ownership (Richards 2005). This was accompanied by the phenomenon of media dynasties and media moguls, who were decidedly influential in Australia's first hundred years of history (Griffen-Foley 2002; Griffen-Foley 1999; Chadwick 1989; Wolff 2008; Shawcross 1994). In the latter part of the 20th century, Australia's two wealthiest men were media owners, the late Kerry Packer and Rupert Murdoch. Murdoch's News Corporation, in 2010, is one of the world's largest media companies.

Australia does not have a legal instrument, either a constitutional or statutory bill of rights, guaranteeing freedom of speech for its citizens, nor does it have freedom of the press expressly guaranteed in its constitution (Nash 2003). Its journalists do not constitutionally enjoy any special rights beyond those of an ordinary citizen. However, since the 1990s, the High Court of Australia has recognised an implied right to freedom of political communication in a succession of cases (Nash 2003; Herman 2009). Despite the uncertainties in the legal framework, and the ongoing demand for better shield laws for journalists and an improved Freedom of Information system (Warren 2010), Australia's media are robust and enjoy a relatively free press.

Media policy is legislated by the government of the day. After twenty years of relative constancy in media ownership regulations, with technological changes making the possession of a particular type of media less of an issue, shifts have occurred since 2006. The Australian government's regulatory body dealing with the electronic media is the Australian Communications and Media Authority (ACMA). Its main briefs are to ensure that quality communication services are available and that license conditions, codes and standards are complied with.

Sample

Much of the data provided in this chapter is taken from publicly available websites such as the Australian Communications and Media Authority's site. These figures are supplemented by seven formal face-to-face interviews with editorial level journalists from various media, as well as a number of informal interviews with academics who used to work in the media for many years. In addition, two face-to-face interviews were conducted with spokespeople for the Australian journalists' union, which is part of the Media Entertainment and Arts Alliance (MEAA) and the Australian Press Council (APC).

To obtain a representative sample of the Australian media's performance, interviews were conducted with editorial level journalists from one national paper, The Australian, and several metropolitan papers, The Age, Sydney Morning Herald and West Australian, as well as Fairfax Online. The Australian is Australia's only major national newspaper and, being founded in 1964 by Rupert Murdoch, is News Ltd.'s flagship publication in Australia. Apart from News Ltd., which owns the metropolitan papers in the states of South Australia, Queensland, the Northern Territory and Tasmania, Fairfax is the only other media company of note in the newspaper market. Fairfax publishes the broadsheets Sydney Morning Herald, in Sydney, and The Age, in Melbourne. The West Australian, which is owned by West Australian Newspaper Holdings, in which TV Channel 7 owner Kerry Stokes has a dominant stake, was chosen so as to include representatives of a variety of Australian media companies.

Australia no longer has any weekly papers or news magazines of national significance. With regard to the electronic media, interviews were obtained with the public broadcaster, Australian Broadcasting Corporation, covering both radio and television, and an informal interview with a former journalist of the commercial networks, Channel 9. There was a distinct reluctance to provide formal interviews, which has to be seen in the light of industry uncertainty due to major ownership changes taking place in Australia's commercial television field.

Table 1.   Interviewees

	Other	Media	Public	Private	Reach	Reach
The Australian		newspaper		News Ltd	national	HQ: Sydney
The Age		newspaper		Fairfax	metropolitan	Melbourne
Sydney Morning Herald		newspaper		Fairfax	metropolitan	Sydney
West Australian		newspaper		WAN	metropolitan	Perth
ABC		Radio & TV	X		national	HQ: Sydney
Channel 9 (informal i/v)		TV		Nine Enter-tainment Co	regional	Perth
Fairfax Online		online		Fairfax	national	HQ: Sydney
MEAA (Journalists' union)	X				national	HQ: Sydney
Australian Press Council	X				national	HQ: Sydney

Indicators

Freedom / Information (F)

(F1)   Geographic distribution of news media availability   2 POINTS

Due to Australia's geography and population distribution, regional areas are less well served than the metropolitan centres, where all media are available.

In a country the size of Australia – 21.5 times the size of Germany and 186 times the size of Switzerland – and with a population density of close to 3 persons per square kilometre, it is no surprise that there are regional divides. Large parts of Australia are unpopulated or have so few people living in them that infrastructure, in particular broadband and mobile telephony coverage, has always been a problem for regional areas, and has been hotly fought over politically. Access to the media is no problem in the capital cities and large regional centres.

The media consist of commercial and public broadcaster radio and television stations, daily newspapers, as well as a large array of journals.

Table 2.   Access to telecommunications in Australia

Media type	Household access
Free-to-air TV	99 %
Digital free-to-air TV	77 %
Pay TV	32 %
Internet	78 %
Broadband	62 %

Source: ABS 2009b.

These figures show that analog free-to-air television, provided by the public broadcaster, the Australian Broadcasting Corporation and, in the main, three commercial television networks, is available to 99 % of Australians, while the percentage of digital free-to-air users is increasing. In breaking down these figures, the Australian Communications and Media Authority (ACMA 2008, 7) shows that socio-economic reasons play the large part in determining access to the Internet, whereas country location has the largest impact on broadband access.

Access to radio is put at 99 %, and the availability map for 2007 shows that most of Australia is serviced by one to five stations, and up to twelve in the metropolitan centres (ACMA 2009). There are 274 commercial radio broadcasting licences in Australia, including 150 FM licences and 106 AM licences, with the largest concentrations of commercial radio licences in the major capital cities. Most regional centres are served by two licensees, typically with one AM and one FM service.

Table 3.   Number of commercial radio licences by city

City	Number of commercial licenses
Sydney	11
Melbourne	11
Brisbane	7
Adelaide	6
Perth	6
Canberra	4
Hobart	3
Darwin	2

Source: ACMA licensing information (ACMA 2008, 4).

The public broadcaster, Australian Broadcasting Corporation (ABC), provides 60 local radio stations throughout Australia, and four national broadcast networks: the national talk network, Radio National; the national news network, News Radio; the national youth network, Triple J and the national classic music network, Classic FM. Via shortwave, satellite and online Radio Australia broadcasts in the Asia-Pacific region.

The second public broadcaster, Special Broadcasting Service (SBS), whose brief it is to broadcast to Australia's various migrant ethnic groups (Ang 2008), broadcasts in 68 languages to all capital cities and key regional centres on a mix of FM and AM frequencies. SBS radio provides Australian and international news, homeland news, a mixture of current affairs, interviews, community information, sport and music (ACMA 2008).

In terms of television, the public broadcasters Australian Broadcasting Corporation (ABC) and Special Broadcasting Service (SBS), and three major commercial networks, Seven, Nine and Ten, are the main providers of free-to-air television. The

ABC's analog service is available to more than 98 % of the Australian population. SBS's multilingual and multicultural television services reach 95 % of the Australian population through its analog service and 80 % through its digital service.

Map 1.   Radio availability in Australia by licence area, January 2007

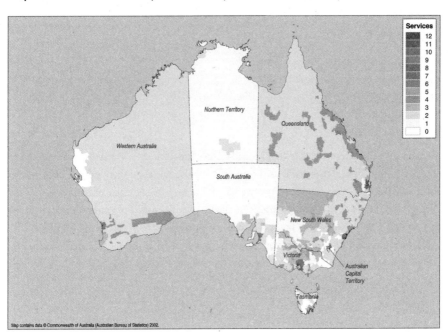

There are 28 distinct commercial television licence areas across Australia. Broadcast planning provides for three commercial television licence operators in Adelaide, Brisbane, Melbourne, Perth and Sydney. The Seven, Nine and Ten networks operate in each of these cities. There are three licensees operating in Canberra and Hobart, and two in Darwin. In regional areas, the majority of broadcasting is provided by the NBN, Prime, Seven Queensland, Southern Cross Broadcasting and WIN networks (ACMA 2008).

Permanent community television services were established in Brisbane, Melbourne, Perth and Sydney in 2004. In January 2007, there were 83 permanent community television licences, 79 of which were remote Indigenous media services (ACMA 2008).

Until 2001 only a limited number of analog free-to-air television channels were available. From 2001 the two public broadcasters and from 2004 the commercial channels have begun to add further digital channels.

In 2006 the reach of the major television companies was given as such:

Table 4.   Reach of television broadcasters

Commercial broadcaster	Channel name	Reach
Seven Media Group	Seven	72 %
Ten Network Holdings	Ten	65 %
Nine Entertainment Co.	Nine	51.5 %
Southern Cross Broadcasting Australia Ltd	Southern Cross Television (Regional)	42 %
Prime Television Ltd	Prime, Golden West Network (GWN) (Regional)	25 %
WIN Corporation Pty Ltd	WIN (Regional)	26 %
Public broadcaster		
Australian Broadcasting Corporation	ABC	98 %
Special Broadcasting Service	SBS	97 %

Source: Jackson 2006.

The reach of the major commercial television broadcasters is calculated according to the number of metropolitan and regional television licences they hold. The Seven Media Group controls five metropolitan and one regional television licences; the Ten Network controls five metropolitan television licences and the Nine Entertainment Co, which also is Australia's largest magazine publisher, controls three metropolitan and one regional television licences. The regionally based Southern Cross Broadcasting has one metropolitan and seven regional television licences. Recent audience share figures show the following:

Channel	Channel 7	Pay TV	Channel 9	Channel 10	ABC	SBS
Audience Share	23.9 %	21.3 %	20.9 %	14.5 %	13.5 %	3.3 %

Source: The Numbers, 1.11. 2010.

Despite an overall decline of metro newspaper circulations (daily and Sunday) in Australia of 7.31 % since 2000, this compares favourably with falls in circulation in other English-speaking countries.

Table 5.   Circulation figures October – December 2009

Newspaper	Oct-Dec 09	Newspaper	Oct-Dec 09
National		Queensland Regionals	
Australian	131,246	NewsMail (Bundaberg)	10,926
Weekend Australian	300,941	Cairns Post	25,626
Aust Financial Review	77,470	Gladstone Observer	6,949
Aust Financial Review (Sat)	84,528	Gold Coast Bulletin	44,232
NSW		Gympie Times	5,630
Daily Telegraph	359,171	Queensland Times (Ipswich)	10,512
Daily Telegraph (Sat)	322,456	Daily Mercury (Mackay)	15,421
Sunday Telegraph	632,009	Sunshine Coast Daily	20,603
Sydney Morning Herald	211,006	Fraser Coast Chronicle	9,406
Sydney Morning Herald (Sat)	353,878	Morning Bulletin (Rockhampton)	18,036
Sun-Herald	442,357	Chronicle (Toowoomba)	22,644
NSW Regionals		Townsville Bulletin	29,147
Border Mail (Albury)	24,734	Daily News (Warwick)	3,344
Barrier Daily Truth (Broken Hill)	5,928	South Australia	
Daily Liberal (Dubbo)	5,299	Advertiser	180,853
Daily Examiner (Grafton)	5,554	Advertiser (Sat)	250,757
Northern Star (Lismore)	14,466	Sunday Mail	300,483
Herald (Newcastle)	48,500	Western Australia	
Northern Daily Leader (Tamworth)	7,454	West Australian	188,211
Daily Advertiser (Wagga Wagga)	11,655	West Australian (Sat)	327,251
Illawarra Mercury (Wollongong)	26,997	Sunday Times	315,024
Victoria		Western Australia Regional	
Herald Sun	514,000+	Kalgoorlie Miner	5,612
Herald Sun (Sat)	503,000+	Tasmania	
Sunday Herald Sun	601,000+	Mercury	45,210
Age	202,100	Mercury (Sat)	61,123
Age (Sat)	291,000	Sunday Tasmanian	58,968
Sunday Age	228,600	Tasmania Regionals	
Victoria Regionals		Advocate (Burnie)	23,545
Courier (Ballarat)	18,631	Examiner (Launceston)	32,245
Advertiser (Bendigo)	13,860	Sunday Examiner	39,307
Geelong Advertiser	29,276	Northern Territory	
Sunraysia Daily (Mildura)	7,268	Northern Territory News	20,553
News (Shepparton)	10,414	NT News (Sat)	31,084
Standard (Warrnambool)	12,801	Sunday Territorian	21,640
Queensland		ACT	
Courier-Mail	211,230	Canberra Times	33,000
Courier-Mail (Sat)	288,924	Canberra Times (Sat)	55,000
Sunday Mail	300,483	Canberra Times (Sun)	33,000

Source: Isaacs 2010b, 9-11.

Australia does not have the diversity of daily print media experienced until recently in the United States or Europe. Its demographic distribution brought about a higher concentration of press ownership much earlier. There are two national papers, The Australian and The Financial Review. Each of Australia's major cities has one local or metropolitan paper, with only Sydney and Melbourne having two papers, one broadsheet and one tabloid.

(F2) Patterns of news media use (consumption of news)   3 POINTS

The Australian citizen is well supplied with news from different sources.

News information is amply available in Australia from a wide variety of sources. With an assumed literacy rate of 99 % and highly ranked in its per capita GDP, media are affordable to most Australians. The broadcast media, newspapers, and to an increasing degree the Internet are the main news providers for the Australian population.

92.6 % of Australians aged 15 years and older reported that they listened to radio, with 91.1 % indicating that they listened regularly (at least once a week). 53.7 of these listened to commercial FM radio while 40.1 % listened to one of the stations provided by the public broadcaster. 25.3 % listened to commercial AM stations, 14.6 % to the ABC's Triple J network, 13.7 to community stations, 5.6 % to other stations and 4.6 % to SBS's ethnic broadcast stations (ACMA 2009, 64).

Table 6.   Use of news and talkback radio 2009

	15-24	25-34	35-44	45-54	55-64	65-74	75+
News	45 %	64 %	65 %	70 %	74 %	83 %	70 %
Talkback	35 %	31 %	48 %	45 %	51 %	57 %	71 %

Source: ACMA (2009, 65).

With regard to radio news, apart from the 15-24 age group, two-thirds of the radio audience or more listened to radio news. Despite these figures, which indicate the popularity of radio, separate research has shown that radio is not considered the main source of news.

Television has long been the major news provider in Australia (Phillips & Tapsell 2007), and recent figures do not change this picture. Between half and two-thirds of the Australian population acknowledges this medium as their source for national news, and even more so for international news. Interestingly, for the younger generation, the Internet is already the second most important provider of international news, whereas the print media occupies this space for older generations.

Table 7.   Media type as sources of national news

National news	14-17	18-24	25-34	35-49	50-64	65+
Newspapers	14 %	17.5 %	17.5 %	15.5 %	24 %	32 %
Radio	17 %	11.5 %	18 %	17 %	16 %	15 %
Television	54 %	57.5 %	48.5 %	56 %	53 %	52 %
Internet	15 %	11 %	16 %	11 %	6.5 %	1 %

Source: Roy Morgan Research 2007.

Table 8.   Media type as sources of international news

International news	14-17	18-24	25-34	35-49	50-64	65+
Newspapers	10 %	9 %	13 %	11 %	16.5 %	19 %
Radio	3.5 %	2 %	6.5 %	9 %	11 %	16.5 %
Television	68.5 %	56 %	59.5 %	64.5 %	64 %	62.5 %
Internet	18 %	23.5 %	19 %	14 %	7.5 %	1 %

Source: Roy Morgan Research 2007.

These figures underpin the fact that television is the major news provider for Australians of all age groups, in particular for international news. While the older generation also takes a large share of information, both national and international, from the newspapers, people up to the age of 34 turn to the Internet, in particular with regard to international news.

In this context it also has to be noted that the major television news providers are not, as in many European countries, the national broadcaster/s, but commercial television stations. Data show the Channel 7 news on weekdays and Sundays and its current affairs program, Today Tonight, among Australia's ten most watched programs. The Channel 7 Sunday news was watched by an estimated audience share of 24 % ("The Numbers" 2010).

With regard to television, the Australian Communications and Media Authority found that Australian television viewers in households with free-to-air sets spent an average of 161 minutes per day watching television in 2008, with commercial channels accounting for the majority of their viewing. Viewers in subscription television households spent 218 minutes per day watching television (ACMA 2009, 61). These figures are likely to shift when considering the increasing use of the Internet. Between 1998 to 2008-09, household access to the Internet at home has more than quadrupled from 16 % to 72 %, while access to computers has increased from 44 % to 78 % (ABS 2009b).

(F3)   Diversity of news sources   2 POINTS

For Australians, as part of the English-speaking community, the Internet offers a wide array of news sources. Also the world-wide media network of News Corporation feeds the Australian market, whereas the public broadcaster has cut its commitment to foreign correspondents.

Australia benefits from being part of the English-speaking community, which permits Australians to easily access, for example, British or American sourced international news. This somewhat restricts the importance of the Australian national news agency, AAP (Australian Associated Press). AAP is owned by the four major Australian newspaper publishers, and mostly concentrates on domestic news but, in the provision of international news, is complemented by alliances with the major international news agencies.

Similarly, the News Corporation's world-wide media network feeds into its Australian papers and its pay television channel, Foxtel. The national newspaper, The Australian, in its business section carries in each edition one page sourced from the Wall Street Journal, and in its world section articles taken from the London Times. But other Australian media have similar alliances, and the ABC (Australian Broadcasting Commission) takes a number of its reports from the BBC. The ABC, until recently, maintained quite an extensive foreign correspondents network. However, due to reallocating resources to its news 24 News Channel, support to the foreign correspondents network, such as translators and fixers, has been cut back.

With regard to the use of PR material, a joint Crickey – ACIJ (Australian Centre for Independent Journalism) investigation, carried out in September 2009, has found that "nearly 55 % of stories analysed were driven by some form of public relations" (Crickey 2009, 3). However, any story based on a media release, a public relations release or other form of promotion was counted in this percentage. A further breakdown of figures into media releases and PR releases or other promotions shows that the highest levels of PR content were found in police (41 %) and arts & entertainment (39 %), and the lowest in energy and environment (11 %) and politics (12 %) (Crickey 2009, 6).

(F4)   Internal rules for practice of newsroom democracy   1 POINT

There are no written rules for newsroom democracy in the Australian media.

All interviewees confirmed that there are no written newsroom rules which would state the rights of the journalist, nor are there newsroom councils in the selected media outlets. However, the Australian journalists union does have 'house committees' of journalists in the various media companies which meet regularly to discuss industrial matters as well as professional and ethical issues. Most interviewees pointed to the news conferences, held twice daily in the print media and once daily in the broadcast media, as a forum of discussion and consultation. While all interviewees agreed that Australian newsrooms follow a hierarchical structure in which the editor is the boss, several mentioned the fact that some editors work in more collegiate ways than others, and that it depends on the seniority of the journalist as to how much direction s/he needs to take.

(F5) Company rules against *internal* influence on newsroom / editorial staff 1 POINT

Media proprietors have long been dominant figures, also in newsroom decisions.

As several interviewees said, this is a complex question. Much depends on the ownership structure of the media company, and several have statements on the independence of the editorial board. All the same, there was agreement on a culture of 'upward referral'. Historically, Australia has been known for its hands-on media owners, notably Rupert Murdoch and the late Kerry Packer. While Murdoch publicly maintains that he does not interfere with the decisions of his editors (Chessell 2010), a high profile court case in 2010, brought by the sacked editor of high circulation Melbourne tabloid Herald Sun, indicates intervention by the Murdoch family (Milovanovic 2010; Guthrie 2010). The allocation of only one point reflects the fact that, while some media companies have statements of editorial independence, with others there is evidence of owners exerting influence on their media companies.

(F6) Company rules against *external* influence on newsroom / editorial staff 3 POINTS

The strong position of Australian media proprietors protects the newsroom from external influence.

Conversely to internal influence on the newsroom, the strong position of media proprietors protects their media companies from external influence. Throughout Australia's history, it is the influence of media owners and editors on politics which has been evidenced rather than any influence in the opposite direction (Griffen-Foley 2003). Interviewees from commercial television spoke of the attempts of advertisers to shape content but rejected the idea that this was successful.

(F7) Procedures of news selection and news processing   1 POINT

Although no formal rules on how to select and process news exist, informal rules are followed in the news selection and processing.

All interviewees mentioned the importance of the daily news conferences – two per day in the print media and one in the broadcast media. Some emphasized that there is a degree of transparency in that visitors can sit in on these conferences. However, the ABC as well as one of the national newspapers has to meet considerable logistics in putting together news bulletins or a paper for a country of the size of Australia, which covers several time-zones. While each state or territory nominates their top stories, the decision as to which of these is of prime importance has to be made centrally, with national, rather than local, news values in mind.

Equality / Interest mediation (E)

(E1) Media ownership concentration national level   1 POINT

Australia has a high media ownership concentration on a national level, which is only slowly broken up by increased availability of media on the Internet.

Newspaper circulation is published quarterly by the Audit Bureau of Circulation. For June 2009, the figures indicate the following market share distribution for daily (weekday) newspapers:

Table 9.   Market share of Australian daily newspaper publishers, June 2009

Company	Total sold	Market share
News Ltd	1,698,124	58 %
Fairfax	811,407	28 %
West Australian Newspapers (WAN)	227,605	8 %
APN News & Media (APN)	154,033	5 %
Other	24,177	1 %

Source: Isaacs 2010c, 6-7.
Note: Figures include capital city and regional newspaper sales in each Australian state.

Table 10.   Market share of Australian Sunday newspapers, June 2009

Company	Total sold	Market reach
News Ltd	2,535,490	77 %
Fairfax	762,094	23 %
APN News & Media (APN)	13,697	0.4 %

Source: Isaacs 2010c, 6-7.
Note: Figures include capital city and regional newspaper sales in each Australian state.

These figures should be viewed in conjunction with the table 'Circulation figures October – December 2009' on page 57. The major papers published by New Ltd are nationally, The Australian (all editions), in NSW, the Daily Telegraph, in Victoria, Herald Sun, in Queensland, Courier Mail, in South Australia, the Advertiser, in Tasmania, Mercury, and in the Northern Territory, the Northern Territory News. Fairfax publishes nationally The Australian Financial Review, the Sydney Morning Herald and The Age (Melbourne). It also publishes papers in major regional centres, such as the Illawarra Mercury (Wollongong), The Newcastle Herald (Newcastle), The Border Mail (Albury-Wodonga) and The Warrnambool Standard (Warrnambool). APN News & Media publishes in regional centres in northern NSW and throughout Queensland.

A comparison with the figures of 2006 (Jackson 2006) shows a decrease in News Ltd's market share which, for almost two decades, was at 68 % of the daily newspaper market, whereas Fairfax, which publishes The Age in Melbourne and Sydney Morning Herald in Sydney, has increased its market share. All the same, these figures clearly indicate the high level of media ownership concentration in Australia, which can be similarly found in the broadcast sector.

(E2) Media ownership concentration regional (local) level   1 POINT

Australia's demographic distribution and resulting economy of scale have led to a high media ownership concentration on a regional level.

In conjunction with the radio availability by licence area map shown above, the map of commercial television services by licence area clearly demonstrates that Australia's demographic distribution and resulting economy of scale are a determining factor on ownership concentration on the regional level.

Differences in media ownership between the western and eastern states of Australia are also noticeable when two Australian regions, Western Australia's South West (population: 163,170; area: 24,000km^2) and Victoria's Gippsland (population: 241,483; area 41,538 km^2) are examined more closely. A total of 15 newspapers serve different towns in the South West's 12 local government areas, but these newspapers are only produced in larger towns, such as Bunbury, Busselton and Margaret River. The market is dominated by West Australian Newspaper Holdings, which owns six of these newspapers plus a regional Western Australian weekly, Countryman, and Fairfax, which owns five. The other four newspapers are locally owned. There are also only three tiers of radio ownership in the South West. Public broadcaster ABC has the widest coverage, holding licenses in nine towns. Southern Cross Media Group holds six licences and West Australian Newspaper Holdings holds four radio licences in addition to its newspaper market share.

Newspaper and radio ownership is more diverse in Gippsland, which has 16 newspapers and 23 radio stations covering towns in six local government areas. Fairfax owns a large share of the newspaper market, with six, and Star News Group with one. But, in contrast with the South West, Gippsland has more locally owned newspapers (nine). Gippsland also has nine community owned radio stations, as well as five ABC and four Southern Cross Media Group stations, and five stations owned by three regional companies.

Free-to-air national and regional television stations owned by ABC, SBS, Prime Television and WIN Corporation are available in analog format throughout most of the South West and Gippsland. Southern Cross Media Group's regional Victorian analog station is available in Gippsland. The content of these stations, however, is mostly sourced from programs shown on these broadcasters' parallel networks in the capital cities (ABC, SBS, Seven, Nine and Ten). News programs offer some localised content. Pay television is provided mostly via satellite to these regions by Foxtel in Western Australia and Austar in Victoria. A wider range of free-to-air channels, including new channels introduced by the main broadcasters, is now available in digital format in larger towns and newer regional developments through analog/digital set top box converters and pay television's satellite and cable services.

Map 2.   Commercial television services in Australia by licence area, January 2007

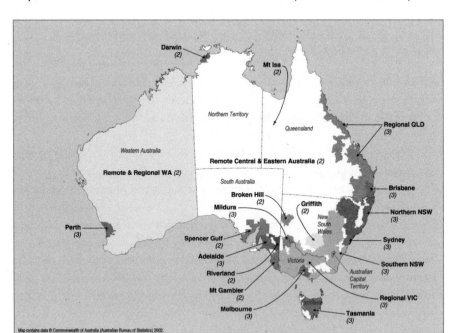

Source: ACMA 2009.

However, there are still many regional towns that cannot receive terrestrial digital signals, which led the government in 2010 to offer subsidies towards households' purchases of satellite dishes and equipment (Brady 2010). The Australian government's Department of Broadband, Communications and the Digital Economy (2010) recently estimated, based on small survey samples, that 80 % of households in Gippsland had already converted to digital television, while only 58 % of households in regional Western Australia were receiving digital signals. For this figure, the Department's survey combined all parts of regional and remote Western Australia. Gippsland will switch permanently from analog to digital television in May 2011, and the South West will be one of the last areas in Australia to switch in December 2013.

(E3) Diversity of formats   2 POINTS

Australia has sufficient news presentation formats of news and current affairs.

One in-depth study on sources of news and current affairs, investigating both the industry and audience aspect, also asked whether there is sufficient diversity of news formats (Pearson & Brand 2001, 191-199). The study was prompted by concerns over Australia's renowned concentration of media ownership. The predecessor of the Australian Communications and Media Authority, the Australian Broadcast Authority as the then regulator, endeavoured to find out the degree of influence that different types of broadcasting services are able to exert in shaping community views in Australia.

According to the study's findings, newspapers and public radio were considered to cover local and regional issues better than other media, with commercial radio and television only doing a somewhat adequate job (Pearson & Brand 2001, 198). With regard to regional news, Internet and Pay TV were ranked even lower. The recent increase in number of digital television and the fourfold increase in Internet use have done little to improve local and regional news. While international news is now available in a wide variety of formats over the Internet, this has not increased the reporting of local and regional news. The same reasons as mentioned by Pearson and Brand are still relevant, in that the provision of local and regional news is affected by newsroom budgets and attempts by larger media groups to affect economies of scale (p. 199).

No such limitations can be said to exist in Australia's large metropolitan centres, where a rich variety of news and current affair formats can be found in the print and broadcast media, and where two 24 Hour News Channels are available – Sky News on pay television and the ABC's 24 Hours news channel on digital HD receivers.

(E4) Minority / Alternative media   3 POINTS

Australia offers an abundance of broadcast and print media in languages other than English.

Australia's second public broadcaster, the Special Broadcasting Service (SBS), is considered unique in that its radio and television services are broadcast in more languages than on any other network in the world. The television program on its first channel in languages other than English – which comprise more than half the SBS Television schedule - are accessible to all viewers through SBS-produced English language subtitles. Its charter is "to provide multilingual and multicultural radio and television services that inform, educate and entertain all Australians and, in doing so, reflect Australia's multicultural society" (SBS 2010).

SBS television broadcasts in 23 languages, including news programs, and SBS radio broadcasts in 68 languages, including news programs. One of SBS's digital channels is almost entirely devoted to news programs taken from stations around the world.

Australia's multiculturalism is equally reflected in the print sector. In New South Wales, papers in 30 different languages are available, which include seven different papers in Arabic, five different Chinese publications, four Korean and Turkish and three Afghan/Iranian papers. The other states do not offer quite the same spread. Victoria offers papers in 17 different languages, with six different papers in Chinese, and four each in Greek and Indian languages. Queensland, Western Australia and South Australia only have four, three and two papers, respectively, in languages other than English. The frequency of publication varies from bi-weekly to weekly, which is the most common form, to fortnightly, and in some cases, monthly (Ethnic Media Organisations 2010).

(E5) Affordable public and private news media   3 POINTS

Media are readily affordable in Australia.

In 2007-08, the average disposable household income was A$811 per week (ABS 2009a), or A$42,172 per year.

The affordability of newspapers is shown in the prices of the national and metropolitan daily newspapers in 2010 in Australian dollars. It should be mentioned that newspapers in Australia, although home delivered, are usually not bought at a special subscription rate.

Table 11.   Newspaper prices in Australia in 2010

Newspaper	Weekday edition	Saturday edition
National daily newspapers		
The Australian	1.50	2.60
Financial Review	3.00	3.00
Capital city daily newspapers		
Adelaide Advertiser	1.10	1.80
The Age	1.50	2.50
Canberra Times	1.40	2.40
Courier Mail	1.10	2.00
Daily Telegraph	1.00	1.60
Herald Sun	1.10	1.50
Hobart Mercury	1.30	1.50
NT News	1.20	1.60
Sydney Morning Herald	1.40	2.40
The West Australian	1.30	2.30

Source: Isaacs 2010a, pp. 4-5.

Because Australia does not charge radio or television fees for the public broadcasters, as these are taken out of the general tax revenue, the only expenses are subscription television or Pay TV.

Table 12.   Monthly pay television costs

Company	Minimum subscription	Maximum subscription	Installation fee
Foxtel	$72	$135	Free-$200
Austar	$42	$124.45	Free
Optus Television	$42	$116.95	$500
Neighbourhood Cable	$19.95	$54.95	$99

All subscription television providers offer news channels, such as BBC, CNN and Sky News, in their minimum subscription packages. The subscription rate for broadband in Australia is between A$50 – A$60 a month. Taking these figures into account, it shows that the supply of a daily paper, plus a subscription to pay television and broadband, lies somewhere between 3 % – 5 % of the average weekly Australian income.

(E6) Content monitoring instrument   2 POINTS

Australia has a number of monitoring instruments, but largely of a self-regulatory nature.

The Australian Communications and Media Authority, which has the task to regulate broadcasting, radio communications and telecommunications and mostly looks after adequate reach, licences and technical industry performance, also steps in when transgressions occur with regard to compliance with licence conditions, codes and standards. This also extends to online content. The government has been severely criticised for using the regulator in this capacity.

A high profile case, commonly referred to as 'cash for comment', prompted ACMA's predecessor, the Australian Broadcast Authority, to inquire into industry standards in commercial radio in 1999. As a result of the inquiry and the finding of systemic failure to ensure the effective operation of the industry's self-regulatory codes of practice, the Australian Broadcasting Authority determined three program standards for commercial radio licensees in 2000 (ACMA 2010).

The public broadcasters, ABC and SBS, have boards which consist of the managing director and five to seven directors, appointed by the government of the day, which has resulted in criticism of the appointees' political affiliation, background, and relative merit. The ABC board is also responsible for ensuring that the gathering and presentation of news and information is accurate and impartial, according to recognised standards of journalism, and that the ABC complies with legislative and legal requirements (ABC 2008).

The Australian Press Council is the self-regulatory body of the print media. It was established in 1976 with two main aims, to help preserve the traditional freedom of the press within Australia and ensure that the free press acts responsibly and ethically, and provides accurate and balanced reporting (Australian Press Council 2010a). While it only deals with complaints received, it does play an active role in promoting freedom of speech and access to information, and in ensuring high journalistic and editorial standards. Its adjudications are available on its website, as are its yearly publications on the state of the press.

(E7) Codes of ethics at the national level (structure) 2 POINTS

The journalists' code of ethics is well-known in the print industry but is becoming less suited to new online environments.

Australia's journalistic code of ethics was first adopted in 1944 (Lloyd 1985, 228), and has been revised twice since. It was drafted by the Australian Journalists' Union and has all the hallmarks of a union-based code (Josephi 1998). For a long time, it was Australia's only journalistic code of ethics. Concise in nature and upheld by the union to which a high proportion of Australian journalists used to belong, it is well-known to journalists and in newsrooms. As confirmed by all interviewees, the Australian journalists' code of ethics has had a deep professional penetration.

Over the past two decades, more and more media companies added their own in-house codes of conduct to the Australian Journalists' Union – now Media, Entertainment and Arts Alliance (MEAA) – code (see, e.g., The Age 2002). As the online presence of print media companies continually extends, several of the interviewees mentioned that they are now confronted with ethical issues that they previously did not have to consider and which their codes do not cover, such as dealing with social media sites. As there are ever occurring transgressions, the debate about media ethics in newsrooms, in the journalists' union and in the media continues loud and clear.

(E8)   Level of self-regulation (performance)   2 POINTS

While the self-regulatory system is far from perfect, a fair attempt is made to implement it.

The main self-regulatory body concerned with the print media is the Australian Press Council. The regulatory body for the broadcast media is the Australian Communications and Media Authority. There are no Ombudsmen, neither in-house in the media companies, nor is there a national Ombudsman for the media.

The Australian Press Council is well aware of the debate about its effectiveness, but reports that it has been more effective in recent times, achieving a mediated settlement in a short space of time in at least half the cases brought to it. This settlement can consist of the publication of an apology, a correction, a clarification or publication of follow-up material. Several papers now have a correction or 'we were wrong' column.

Many of the print media houses have their codes of conduct or editorial ethics policy readily available on their websites, and the public broadcaster has created a special position of director of editorial policies who frequently speaks at public forums.

(E9)   Participation   2 POINTS

Though there is an increasing interaction between journalists and the public, there is no actual participation in the news process.

In the traditional print media, the "Letters to the Editor" is the customary feedback tool. Most Australian papers devote a page to "Letters to the Editor", to which also columns of brief emails from readers are added under the page heading of "Commentary".

The degree of public participation, according to several interviewees, is now as high as it has ever been. One interviewee mentioned that her investigative stories were accompanied by an online forum where the public could send in comments and tips, and that the response was overwhelming and often unmanageable. Yet while there is a far greater interaction between journalists and the public than in the past, this does not amount to an actual participation in the news process.

The public broadcasters ABC and SBS have high profile programs, 'Q & A' and 'Insight', which are built on audience participation, not only of the audience in the studio but also emailed questions and twitter, with a strip of twitter comments running at the bottom of the screen. Almost 36,000 tweets were recorded in an hour in one 'Q & A' during the election 2010 campaign (Scott 2010). The ABC website offers two political blogs under the title of The Drum and Unleashed, which invites the public to "Our rolling gabfest. Drop in, have your say." The major newspapers have similar sites.

(E10) Rules and practices on internal pluralism   1 POINT

There is evidence of internal diversity but little of internal pluralism.

Australian print media have a reasonable degree of internal diversity through their opinion pages, especially in their Saturday editions. These opinion pieces are either written by regular columnists who may or may not be staff on the paper or by invited columnists such as politicians or other public figures.

From the interviews it emerges that some papers permit their journalists to work within a broader framework than others, just as some papers will have not only the journalist's by-line but also his or her photo. As journalism moves to a variety of platforms and the same media company may run a morning news television program or online fora, journalists who participate in these clearly develop more of a profile than those who are merely a name on the page. However, this is only the situation for a small number of journalists. The majority works in newsrooms which, as mentioned earlier, have a clear hierarchical structure.

Control / Watchdog (C)

(C1) Supervising the watchdog 'control of controllers'   3 POINTS

Australia has a number of independent observers of the news media.

The most continual source of 'inside stories' on the media as well as politics, business and environment is the web publication crickey.com.au. Its pages are available to subscribers only, with an annual subscription costing A$160.

Arguably, the best known program is Media Watch on ABC television, which has been shown for over 20 years. Media Watch has a weekly 15-20 minute program slot right after the ABC's major investigative television program, Four Corners, on Monday nights at 21:15 o'clock, and in 2009 averaged 736,000 viewers per program (ABC 2009b). Media Watch picks on factual errors and sloppy journalism, unethical behaviour such as plagiarism, and does not shy away from criticising its own media outlet. Under the motto, 'Stay brave and true', it has had some high profile present-ers, either journalists with years of experience or media lawyers.

The national paper, the Australian, flagship of News Ltd, publishes a weekly six-page media supplement, with articles, commentaries, and "The numbers", which give the audience share of radio or television programs, the top stories of the past week on various platforms and other factual information.

(C2)   Independence of the news media from power holders   2 POINTS

Legal instruments to guarantee greater independence from power holders have only just become law. However, defamation law is used as another pathways by the rich and powerful to silence critics.

The Australian federal parliament's upper house, the Senate, in March 2011 passed the shield law legislation which permits journalists to protect their sources. This is a big step towards journalists being able to guarantee confidentiality to their sources. However, the same law does not yet exist on a state level in some of the Australian states.

The public broadcaster ABC, since 1973, is funded entirely by the Australian government with relatively short funding cycles, and is therefore in a position of dependency. It is a similar scenario for the Special Broadcast Service, though it derives 20 % of its revenue from advertising. With both public broadcasters, the selection procedure for their boards is not independent from government.

Defamation law is seen as another means used by the rich and powerful to deter criticisms. Although the law, which tends to follow English law on defamation issues, is designed to protect people's reputations from unfair attack, it can also be used to protect powerful people from scrutiny. In particular politicians and wealthy individu-als have been known to serve writs quickly when they see unfavourable comment about themselves in the media. Defamation action is very costly and can only be pursued by those with sufficient funds, thus hardly benefitting the ordinary citizen. The 2005 reforms restricted companies from suing for defamation, and established truth as an unqualified defence (Australian Press Council 2010b).

(C3) Transparency of data on media system   1 POINT

Data on media are rarely a topic of debate.

While a vast amount of information is available on the Internet, as for example on the media companies' websites, it takes a dedicated citizen to piece together a picture of the media in the country. Although bodies such as the Australian Communications and Media Authority publish regular reports, these are hardly ever brought to the attention of the general public. The government, universities or the union may offer information on a specialised aspect of the media, but this rarely amounts to a coherent or comprehensive picture of the Australian media. It has to be assumed that the average Australian citizen has little or no knowledge of the political economy of the Australian (news) media.

(C4) Journalism professionalism   2 POINTS

Most journalists receive professional training.

Australia, for the past two decades, has offered journalism degrees at all but two of its 39 tertiary institutions (Koivisto & Thomas 2008, 95). The educational level of Australian journalists has changed significantly over this period. Whereas in 1992 only 35 % of journalists held a degree, the figure was 80 % in 2010. Interestingly, the percentage of those who held an undergraduate degree in journalism had hardly changed, from 33 % to 35 %, which shows that the industry is happy employing people with degrees other than journalism. However, many journalists hold a postgraduate degree in journalism (Josephi & Richards, forthcoming). Cadetships are still being offered by the major media companies, but their numbers have decreased as a casualty of expenditure cuts. Investigative journalism is a subject or topic in most university journalism courses, with one institution – the University of Technology Sydney (UTS) – having established an Australian Centre for Independent Journalism (ACIJ).

(C5) Journalists' job security   1 POINT

It is difficult to provide job security for journalists in this time of change.

While there are redundancy clauses and long periods of notice in the case of dismissal based on the time served, the union acknowledges that this is a difficult climate for the industry in general. According to the MEAA, there is an increasing use of casuals and freelancers, although the more intense period of casualisation occurred in the early 2000s. The union attempts to enforce that, if a journalist has been a casual for more than six months and has worked a regular pattern of shifts, s/he has the right to become a regular member of staff. Yet in a time of credit crunch and structural change, newspaper and other media are reluctant to take on permanent staff. Yet the casualisation can also be seen as an opportunity for all those hundreds of journalists who have been made redundant and now earn their living as freelance journalists.

(C6)   Practice of access to information   1 POINT

The law provides access to public information, but practical problems persist.

The Freedom of Information legislation in Australia was seen as such a hurdle to journalistic work that in 2007 nine major media companies, the two public broadcasters and the MEAA formed the 'Right to Know' coalition to address concerns about free speech in Australia (Right to Know 2010). This coalition set out to work with the Commonwealth and State governments to establish new policy and best practice to improve Australia's relatively poor world ranking for freedom of speech which, in 2010, led to sweeping changes in the Freedom of Information legislation, making it easier for Australians to get information about the federal government. Some of the Australian states also have begun to overhaul their Freedom of Information legislation (Herman 2009, 9-11)

Interviewees pointed to two major problems with regard to Australia's Freedom of Information. One is the time it takes to access the information, and the other is the ongoing secrecy provisions which prevent journalists, and for that matter anyone, having access to the information. As the newly elected minority government has to rely on the vote of one of Australia's best known whistleblowers, it can be assumed that further changes to the Freedom of Information and shield laws will be addressed in this legislature.

(C7)   The watchdog and the media's mission statement   3 POINTS

Australia's media sees itself as a watchdog.

The interviewees saw the watchdog role as their media's most important task. This is substantiated by a recent survey of Australian journalists in which investigating government claims was named as very important by 90 % of the journalists asked (Josephi & Richards, forthcoming). While the Australian media do not pursue politicians or celebrities with the same doggedness as the British media, much of the 'digger' mentality and accompanying distrust of authority can also be found in Australia. For example, it is not surprising that the founder of Wikileaks is Australian.

Those media companies whose editorial policy is available on the Internet, such as The Age and the West Australian, commit themselves expressly to their role as fourth estate (West Australian 2009). The Age (2002) details its commitment: "The public interest includes investigating and exposing crime, serious misdemeanour and seriously anti-social conduct, and investigating and exposing hypocrisy, falsehoods or double standards of behaviour by public figures or institutions."

(C8)   Professional training   1 POINT

Some mid-carrier training is on offer.

Media companies offer training for mid-career journalists, for example to equip print journalists for multi-tasking such as how to add audio and video to their online reporting. They also provide instruction in media law, narrative writing, hostile environment reporting, bushfire training and trauma training. All the same, these courses are more poorly resourced than they have ever been.

The MEAA also provides continuous training, in particular directed towards facilitating the transition to online journalism, or on journalism ethics, which the union sees as the core to journalistic professionalism. One interviewee held the opinion that younger staff is not as committed to, or does not receive the training for, investigative journalism as was the case some years ago.

(C9)   Watchdog function and financial resources   3 POINTS

Commitment to investigative journalism is the Australian media's way to brand themselves.

Most interviewees confirmed that investigative journalism is central to their medium's role. As one interviewee described it, it is the way the paper can 'brand' itself. Many of the media companies, even in lean times, invest resources into investigative journalism by, for example, starting up a special in-depth investigative report section in their Saturday edition. The interviewees agree about the costliness of investigative journalism, pointing out that the expense of investigative journalism lies in the time it takes, rather than travel budgets or special technology, occupying staff time that could otherwise be diverted to filling the pages of the paper.

The ABC always had a strong investigative brief, and it recently revived and somewhat reconfigured its investigative unit. The ABC's Four Corners program, a weekly

45 minute report on television, is Australia's best known investigative program. Its investigations have caused royal commissions and state premiers to step down. But other segments on ABC television, such as its nation-wide 7.30 Report and Lateline, also contain strong investigative elements as do a number of ABC radio programs. SBS frequently shows investigative programs on international topics bought in from other providers. The commercial television stations, too, have current affairs programs, which contain investigative elements, though they are somewhat toned down by the programs' emphasis on the human interest angle.

Conclusion

Australia is an interesting case in that its journalism culture is somewhat at odds with its legal framework. With no constitutional rights enshrining the position of journalism or the media, and shield laws still not uniformly passed throughout the country, Australia's dedication to investigative journalism is ever more amazing. The direction Australian journalism has taken was prepared in colonial times, but Australia has not wavered from this path.

An outstanding feature is the importance of media proprietors in Australian history, and also of journalists in Australian politics – that is journalists turning politicians – especially in the first 50 years of Australia's nationhood (Errington & Miragliotta 2009). By being part of the English-speaking world and being the original home of one of the world's largest media companies, Australia is well provided with international news, however, its geography and demographic distribution favour national and metropolitan over regional news. The power of the big media players ensures that aspects of the external democratic freedoms of the media are observed but make the internal democratic rules in the media harder to implement or enforce.

References

Ang, I. (2008) *The SBS Story: The Challenge of Diversity*. Sydney: University of New South Wales Press.

Australian Broadcasting Corporation (ABC) (2008) The ABC Board. Retrieved 13.09.2010 from http://www.abc.net.au/corp/board/about_board.htm

Australian Broadcasting Corporation (ABC) (2009a) Editorial policies. Retrieved 29.04.2010 from http://www.abc.net.au/corp/pubs/documents/EdPols07_updateFeb09_FIN %20tools.pdf

Australian Broadcasting Corporation (ABC) (2009b) ABC TV ratings hit another new high in 2009. Retrieved 20.10.2010 from http://www.abc-tv-09-ratings-media-release-1.pdf

Australian Bureau of Statistics (ABS) (2009a) Household Income and Income Distribution, Australia 2007-2008. Retrieved 13.09.2010 from http://www.abs.gov.au/ausstats/abs@.nsf/mf/6523.0

Australian Bureau of Statistics (ABS) (2009b) Household Use of Information Technology, Australia 2008-2009. Retrieved 11.09.2010 from http://www.abs.gov.au/ausstats/abs@.nsf/mf/8146.0

Australian Communications and Media Authority (ACMA) (2008) Communications Infrastructure and Services Availability Report 2006-07. Retrieved on 09.09.2010 from http://www.acma.gov.au/WEB/STANDARD/pc=PC_311168

Australian Communications and Media Authority (ACMA) (2009) Communications Infrastructure and Services Availability Report 2007-08. Retrieved on 09.09.2010 from http://www.acma.gov.au/webwr/_assets/main/lib311252/08-09_comms_report.pdf

Australian Communications and Media Authority (ACMA) (2010) Commercial radio inquiry. Retrieved 13.09.2010 from http://www.acma.gov.au/WEB/STANDARD/pc=PC_310821

Australian Communications and Media Authority (ACMA) (2010) All MF/VHF radio served. Retrieved 12.12.2010 from http://www.acma.gov.au/webwr/_assets/main/lib100059/radio_5.pdf

Australian Communications and Media Authority (ACMA) (2010) Television area served. Retrieved 12.12.2010 from http://www.acma.gov.au/webwr/_assets/main/lib100059/tv_9.pdf

Australian Press Council (2010a) About the Press Council. Retrieved 13.09.2010 from http://www.press-council.org.au/

Australian Press Council (2010b) Defamation Law. Retrieved 26.12. 2010 from http://www.presscouncil.org.au/pcsite/fop/auspres.html#defam

Brady, S. (2010) Landmark agreement to deliver Digital TV to Remote, Regional and Blackspot viewers. Retrieved 12.12.2010 from http://www.minister.dbcde.gov.au/media/media_releases/2010/032

Chadwick, P. (1989) *Media Mates: Carving Up Australia's Media.* South Melbourne: Sun Books.

Chessell, J. (2010) Murdoch Passes on Election Call. *The Australian,* august 5.

Crickey (2009) Spinning the media. How much of your daily news is PR? A joint Crickey –ACIJ investigation. Retrieved 29.04.2010 from http://www.crikey.com.au/

Department of Broadband, Communications and the Digital Economy. (2010) Digital Tracker: Measuring Australia's Readiness for Digital Television. Report on quarter 3, July to September 2010. Retrieved 12.12.2010 from http://www.digitalready.gov.au/media/Digital_Tracker_Full_Report_Q3_2010.pdf

Errington, W. & Miragliotta, N. (2009) From the Gallery to the Parliament: Journalists in the House of Representatives and Senate 1901-2007. *Australian Journal of Politics and History*, 55(5), 530-543.

Ethnic Media Organisations (2010) Retrieved 13.09.2010 from www.volunteeringaustralia.org

Griffen-Foley, B. (1999) *The House of Packer: The Making of a Media Empire.* Sydney: Allen & Unwin.

Griffen-Foley, B. (2002) The Fairfax, Murdoch and Packer Dynasties in Twentieth-century Australia. *Media History*, 8(1), 89-102.

Griffen-Foley, B. (2003) *Party Games: Australian Politicians and the Media from War to Dismissal.* South Melbourne: Text Publishing.

Guthrie, B. (2010) *Man Bites Murdoch.* Melbourne: Melbourne University Press.

Herman, J. (2009) *Report on Free Speech Issues.* Australian Press Council Annual Report, 33. Retrieved 29.04.2010 from http://www.presscouncil.org.au/pcsite/pubs/ar33.pdf

Isaacs, V. (2010a) Australian Dailies' Prices at December 2009. *Australian Newspaper History Group*, 56: 4-6.

Isaacs, V. (2010b) Quarterly Circulation Figures. *Australian Newspaper History Group*, 56: 9-11.

Isaacs, V. (2010c) Sales by Company. *Australian Newspaper History Group*, 56: 6-8.

Jackson, K. (2006) Media Ownership Regulation in Australia. Retrieved 11.09.2010 from http://www.aph.gov.au/library/intguide/sp/media_regulations.htm

Josephi, B. (1998) International Comparisons of Journalistic Codes of Ethics. *Australian Journalism Review*, 20(1), 58-71.

Josephi, B. & Richards, I. (2011) Australian Journalists. In L. Willnat & D. Weaver (eds) *The Global Journalist in the 21st Century*. London: Routledge.

Koivisto, J. & Thomas, P. (2008) Mapping Communication and Media Research: Paradigms, Institutions, Challenges. Helsinki: Communications Research Center, University of Helsinki. Retrieved 10.11.2010 from http://www.valt.helsinki.fi/blogs/crc/koivisto-thomas.pdf

Lloyd, C. (1985) *Profession: Journalist.* Sydney: Hale & Iremonger.

Milovanovic, S. (2010) Blunden 'Clashed with Guthrie over Nixon Coverage'. *The Age.* April 29.

Nash, C. (2003) Freedom of the Press in Australia. Retrieved 09.09.2010 from http://democratic.audit.anu.edu.au/Nashpaper.pdf

Pearson, M. & Brand, J. (2001) Sources of News and Current Affairs. Sydney: Australian Broadcasting Authority. Retrieved 29.04.2010 from http://epublications.bond.edu.au/hss_pubs/96/

Phillips, G. & Tapsall, S. (2007) Australian Television News Trends. First Results from a Longitudinal Study. *Australian Journalism Monographs*, 9.

Richards, I. (2005) *Quagmires and Quandaries.* Sydney: University of New South Wales Press.

Right to Know (2010) Media releases and reports. Retrieved 13.09.2010 from http://www.australiasright-toknow.com.au/media

Roy Morgan Research (2007) Television remains main source of news & current affairs. Retrieved 09.09.2010 from http://www.roymorgan.com/news/polls/2007/4182/

Scott, M. (2010) The golden age for Australian journalism. Retrieved 27.12. 2010 from http://www.abc.net.au/news/stories/2010/11/25/3075798.htm

Shawcross, W. (1993) *Murdoch*. London: Pan Macmillan.

Special Broadcasting Service (SBS) (2010) Charter. Retrieved 13.09.2010 from http://www.sbs.com.au/shows/aboutus/tab-listings/page/i/2/h/Corporate/

The Age (2002) Ethics & conduct. Retrieved 13.09.2010 from http://www.theage.com.au/ethicsconduct.html

"The Numbers" (2010, 1 November) Audience Share. *The Australian Media Supplement*, 31.

Warren, C. (2010) Progress under liberty. The State of Press Freedom in Australia. *The Walkley Magazine*. 61, 23-24.

West Australian (2009) Editorial policy of West Australian Newspapers. Retrieved 13.09.2010 from http://au.news.yahoo.com/thewest/shareholders#editorial

Wolff, M. (2008) *The Man Who Owns the News: Inside the Secret World of Rupert Murdoch*. New York: Doubleday.

Chapter 4

AUSTRIA
Informal Rules and Strong Traditions

Manuela Grünangerl & Josef Trappel

The Austrian media system is challenged by several factors: The small national media market is fully exposed to the large language-sharing neighbor Germany. The position of Austria's leading newspaper – *Kronen Zeitung* – is unprecedented in terms of reach and political significance. Television and radio are firmly led by the public service broadcaster *ORF*, and private competitors are still insignificant. Newspaper and news magazine markets are controlled by very few companies, resulting in spectacularly high media concentration ratios. In contrast, however, the formal commitments to press freedom by journalists and the protection of journalists by law are redundantly institutionalized and reflect the high professional ethos of the journalists themselves.

Our media sample consists of seven leading news media representing different types and different ownership: one national quality newspaper (*Die Presse*), one regional newspaper with national distribution (*Salzburger Nachrichten*), the regional subsidiary of the largest tabloid newspaper (*Kronen Zeitung Salzburg*), one political weekly magazine (*Profil*), and a news portal (*derStandard.at*). All editors-in-chief were interviewed. Moreover, public television and public radio are part of our sample. Among our interviewees were the deputy editor-in-chief of *ORF* television and the information chief of *ORF 2*, and the program director and former editor-in-chief of the cultural and information orientated radio program *Ö1*.

Due to the still inferior market position for private media, no private radio and television channel was included in the sample. In addition, the chairman of the journalists' union, who is also president of the recently re-established Austrian Press Council, was interviewed.

Indicators

Freedom / Information (F)

(F1)   Geographic distribution of news media availability   3 POINTS

A wide variety of news media is available to Austrian citizens. The distribution of news media, however, varies by media type.

In total, 16 paid-for-dailies are available to Austrian citizens. All of them are morning dailies, seven of them national and nine regional. Even though all national dailies are Vienna-based, they offer 15 regional editions and are broadly available in all areas (VÖZ/Statistik Austria 2009). Furthermore, 223 non-daily newspapers are available (World Association of Newspapers 2009, p. 214). Free dailies are still rather new in Austria (*Heute, Österreich*). They only play a significant role in urban areas. Because newspaper sales in Austria are mainly based on subscription (62 % compared to 6 % on single copy sales[1]), direct delivery networks have continuously been expanded both by regional and by national newspapers. *Mediaprint* dominates newspaper distribution nationwide.

In Austria, 98 % of all households are equipped with television. There are six terrestrial nationwide channels available to the Austrian population, in addition to 62 regional or local channels and ten regional or local program windows (European Audiovisual Observatory 2009, p. 13). In 2008, more than half of all television households were equipped with digital receivers (cable, satellite or terrestrial). The switchover to digital terrestrial broadcasting was completed in 2010 (RTR 2009a, p. 16). 50 % of television households are equipped with satellite receivers and 42 % with cable receivers. An average of 88 programs, 63 of them in German language, are available to Austrian television viewers (ORF Mediaresearch 2010). In terms of radio broadcasting, 84 channels are available to the Austrian population; 12 of them are part of the *ORF* public service network (either national or regional). Nevertheless, the availability of radio channels in Austrian provinces differs significantly, ranging from two channels in Burgenland to 14 channels in Styria and Tyrol (Statistik Austria/ Arbeitsgemeinschaft Media-Analysen 2009).

Despite the geographical barriers caused by Austria's topography, Internet availability reached 79 % in 2008 (AIM/ORF Mediaresearch 2009). At the same time, 54.5 % of Austrian households were equipped with a broadband connection, either mobile or fixed (European Audiovisual Observatory 2009, p. 13). *ORF* launched its online platform (tvthek.orf.at) in 2010. Mainly in-house productions are offered for free via live-stream and archive (in particular news, magazines, documentaries, sport news, minority content). Furthermore, most radio programs are available as podcasts or web-radio. Private television channels provide similar services for their news programs, magazines and most popular docu-soaps.

(F2) Patterns of news media use (consumption of news)   2 POINTS

Newspapers and public service television are the main sources of information concerning political issues. Among the younger population, the importance of the Internet is increasing. The reach, however, is limited.

Table 1.   Average daily reach of different media types (2008)

Media type	Reach (total)	Daily reach (%)	Availability	Average use (min/day)
Newspapers	5,117,000	72.9 %	100.0 %	30
Television	4,335,000	63.4 %	98.0 %	156
Radio	5,764,000	82.1 %	98.0 %	203
Internet	2,926,000	41.7 %	79.0 %	50

Sources: TV: Teletest 2008; Radio: Radiotest 2008; Internet: ÖWA IV-2008/AIM; Newspapers: ÖAK, all data for population 14+ (Arbeitsgemeinschaft Media-Analysen 2008; RTR 2009a, p. 123)

According to recent studies, a quarter of all Austrians is very interested in political and economic issues (Stark 2009, p. 147). The general interest in political and economic issues varies according to gender and age. Newspapers are still most important; the relevance of television is increasing in the older age brackets, while the Internet as a source of information is of great importance among younger people. Despite the small number of newspaper titles available to the Austrian population, readership remains relatively high, although it is declining (Stark 2009, p. 138). In fact, 72.9 % of all Austrians read newspapers every day for about 30 minutes (Arbeitsgemeinschaft Media-Analysen 2008, p. 67). The main variations in patterns of media use can be seen as a function of age, education and socio-economic status (Stark 2009, p. 140). The daily newspaper with the highest distribution – *Kronen Zeitung* – reaches 41.9 % of the Austrian population. Its position is weaker among the younger population (14-19 years: 34.6 %; 20-29 years: 38.9 %) though it is still unrivaled. An exceptional case is the quality newspaper *Der Standard*, which reaches in total 5.5 % of the population; among the younger population (14-29 years) this percentage is up to 7.0 %.

In Austria, 82.1 % listen to radio programs every day for about 203 minutes (Arbeitsgemeinschaft Media-Analysen 2008, p. 101). However, news content is not the most appealing radio content. The main news format *Mittagsjournal* (Ö1; total reach about 9.2 %) is listened to by 3 % of the population. Nevertheless, short newsflashes every full hour are frequent on all radio channels.

Austrians watch television approximately 156 minutes a day; 63.4 % daily. Television use increases with age; it is lowest among the 12- to 29-year-olds, who only watch approximately 90 minutes a day (RTR 2009a, p. 119). According to a recent study, public service broadcasting is a significant source of information for 76 % of Austrians. Half of the respondents think that newspapers are an important source of information, as well. Other media types (private television, Internet, radio) are seen as a relevant source of information only by 30 % (Stark & Karmasin 2009, p. 368). The main news format broadcasted on *ORF 2 – Zeit im Bild* – reaches more than one million Austrians and has a market share of over 40 %. Nevertheless, this is only a total reach of 14.6 % of the population. Looking at the younger age group (12-29 years), it must be stressed that the percentage of viewers is lower, reaching only 2.2 % of the young population. The late evening news format *Zeit im Bild 2* reaches about half a million Austrians (7.1 % of the total population; 1.2 % among the younger population).

Table 2. Reach of selected news programs (2008)

News program		Total population		Young population (< 29)	
		Reach	%*	reach	%*
Zeit im Bild (ORF)	Main evening news (19:30), daily	1,024,000	14.6	**39,000	2.2
Zeit im Bild 2 (ORF)	Late evening news (22:00), weekdays only	500,000	7.1	**21,000	1.2
Kronen Zeitung	Newspaper with highest reach	2,944,000	41.9	***204,000 ****407,000	34.6 38.9
Der Standard	Quality newspaper	383,000	5.5	***27,000 ****73,000	4.6 7.0
Die Presse	Quality newspaper	241,000	3.4	***15,000 ****32,000	2.5 3.0
Mittagsjournal (Ö1)	Main radio news, 12:00, approx. 1 hour, Monday to Saturday	213,000 212,000 193,000 186,000	3.0 3.0 2.8 2.8	-	-
derstandard.at	Online media with highest reach	740,000	15.0	***64,300 ****156,700	9.6 17.3

*Daily users in percent of population (TV, newspapers, radio), user in fourth quarter 2008 in percent of population (Internet), **Population 12-29, ***Population 14-19, ****Population 20-29.

Source: Television: population 12+ (ORF-Mediaresearch/Teletest), Radio: population 10+, based on quarters/hour (Arbeitsgemeinschaft Media-Analysen 2008, pp. 100-103), Online/Print: population 14+ (Arbeitsgemeinschaft Media-Analysen 2008, p. 86; ÖWA 2008).

Even though 72 % of all Austrians use the Internet on a regular basis, only 41.7 % use it every day for about 50 minutes (Arbeitsgemeinschaft Media-Analysen 2008, p. 137). The Internet's importance as an information source varies by age. Public service television is the main source for gathering information in all age groups, even for 66 % of all respondents between 14 and 29 years. Nevertheless, private television and Internet are important news sources for about 40 % of all respondents in the younger age bracket (Stark & Karmasin 2009, pp. 367-370). This illustrates that cross-media use is common in Austria and that media use patterns are currently changing rapidly. Austrians in the age range 14 to 29 years concentrate on the Internet as their main source of information on political and economic issues (Stark 2009, p. 150). The online newspaper with the highest reach – the quality orientated *derstandard.at* – reached 740,000 readers online from October to December 2008, which means a total reach of 15.0 % of the Austrian population. In the younger age group (20-29 years), it is even 17.3 %.

(F3)   Diversity of news sources   2 POINTS

All editors-in-chief emphasized the predominant role of journalistic research and pointed out that external content could at best serve as a starting point for further investigation.

The national news agency *APA* (*Austria Presse Agentur*) is an important source in the daily business of journalism. It is owned by 15 Austrian newspapers and the *ORF* (APA 2010, p. 2). Most of our respondents stressed the importance of news agencies in the working process and reported using different news agencies (*dpa, Reuters*). Nevertheless, some respondents see the importance of news agencies diminishing due to other directly accessible sources. According to a survey among Austrian journalists, more than two thirds regularly or occasionally use the *APA* archive as a starting point for their research; online research is used by 94.8 % (S. Weber 2006, p. 16). Altogether the respondents stressed the role of news agencies as a backup basis for stories and an archive for research rather than as a dominant or priority source.

Concerning PR material, the position of our respondents was diverse. On a local level, PR material as an information source was acknowledged but not considered as increasing problem. On the contrary, public service media and quality newspapers strictly rejected the use of PR material. Recent studies show that Austrian journalists are at least aware of such external influences: about 60 % noted that advertising or PR interests serve sometimes or even regularly as a reference point for their stories. Approximately 40 % even admitted that their own stories are at least sometimes PR orientated (S. Weber 2006, pp. 39-42). Direct use of external material without further research provoked by time pressure and the increasing potential of an agenda-setting function of such sources were seen as the main problems.

(F4)   Internal rules for practice of newsroom democracy   1 POINT

Newsroom democracy is established by editorial statutes, which are common in most Austrian newsrooms. But journalists have limited influence on hiring decisions regarding the editor-in-chief.

The Austrian Media Act allows media organizations to establish editorial statutes (§ 5, *Mediengesetz* 2009). Stricter rules apply to the public service broadcaster. The law (§ 33, *ORF Gesetz* 2009) requires editorial statutes. 61 % of Austrian journalists work in media organizations that provide statutes (Kaltenbrunner, Karmasin, Kraus, & Zimmermann 2008, p. 64). According to our respondents, democratic practices in the newsroom are less common on a local level, where editors-in-chief are appointed by the owner without participation of the journalistic staff council. Similar situations can be found in the online media sector. At a national level, though, some newspapers have established rules on democratic participation of the newsroom council, especially regarding appointment of the editor-in-chief. The newsroom assemblies of *Die Presse* and *Profil*, for example, can reject the editor's proposal for a new editor-in-chief with a two thirds majority (Kurier 2007; *Redaktionsstatut der Tageszeitung Die Presse*, 1974, § 7). In fact, such rejections have already occurred in both newspapers. Nevertheless, opportunities to make own proposals are few, and participation in other management or staff decisions or in framing future formal rights is also relatively rare.

Concerning the *ORF*, all leading positions have to be publicly announced and staff decisions are rather transparent. Nevertheless, the influence of the newsroom council and its representatives is limited to an advisory function (§ 33, *ORF Gesetz*, 2009; § 5, *ORF-Redakteurstatut*, 2002). Participation rights concerning changes in program schemes and journalistic content exist, however, there is no participation in management or supervisory boards. According to our respondents, journalists are quite aware of their participation rights and practice them seriously.

Regarding the journalistic daily routine and the framing of political issues and opinions, formalized rules and institutionalized decision processes are rare in Austrian newsrooms. Discussions about such issues occur frequently in department and editorial meetings. Nevertheless, the actual decision is up to the journalist himself. For the *ORF*, clear editorial guidelines regarding impartiality and balance are established by the public service remit (*ORF Gesetz* 2009, § 4), the editorial statutes (*ORF-Redakteurstatut* 2002, § 1) and the company's mission statement. Editorial guidelines in a fixed and written form are uncommon in private media companies; only 25 % of Austrian journalists are working in a media organization with a written code of ethics (Kaltenbrunner et al. 2008, p. 64). Nevertheless, moral and ethical rules are informally present and meant to be implicitly understood as a journalistic principle.

(F5) Company rules against *internal* influence on newsroom / editorial staff   2 POINTS

The separation of newsrooms from management is formally practiced by all media organizations in this media sample and can be interpreted as common in the Austrian media system.

Editorial matters are strictly up to the journalists themselves. The effectiveness of the separation depends on the media type and the financing situation. According to a survey among Austrian journalists, about 60 % report occasional conflicts of interest between the editorial department and the newsroom (S. Weber 2006, p. 43).

In public service broadcasting, there is no direct contact between the information section and the advertising department, as common projects (such as infomercials) are prohibited by law. Similarly, all editors-in-chief stressed that the presence of members of the advertising department at editorial meetings was strictly banned. Moreover, they mentioned that meetings with the advertising department are exclusively their responsibility. Nevertheless, concerning special supplements, co-operation between the journalistic staff and the advertising department is inevitable, even though the decision on newsworthy issues is usually incumbent upon the journalists. Some newspapers (*Die Presse*) have so-called "content engines", which are part of the advertising department and in charge of advertorial content. In other newsrooms, freelancers contribute to advertising content. An exception is the online media sector, where members of the permanent staff occasionally produce advertorial content. This is, however, in part contradictory to survey results among journalists; almost half of them pointed out that they had to write advertising content at least sometimes; 11.7 % even do this regularly (S. Weber 2006, pp. 43-45).

In three of the examined media organizations, the editors-in-chief held a double position in that they were also part of the management board. Overall, this was considered as a potential conflict of interest by the editors-in-chief. In particular, situations where journalistic interests collide with financial ones were critically reflected on. Nevertheless, all three editors-in-chief stressed that the inclusion of a newsroom member in management decisions could also have advantages and promote the independence of the newsroom.

(F6) Company rules against *external* influence on newsroom / editorial staff 2 POINTS

All editors-in-chief strictly denied the direct influence of external parties on newsroom work and content, although such attempts were occasionally reported.

Most editors-in-chief mentioned negative impacts on investments due to the tense worldwide economic situation in 2008. While in private media companies two thirds of revenues were obtained from advertising before the crisis, this percentage is decreased to 60 %. In 2008, the *ORF* earned 25.3 % of its revenues from advertising and 48.5 % from license fees[2]. This means a decrease in advertising revenues of 16.7 % (*ORF* 2009, p. 14). Concerning the online medium in our sample, sales revenues are non-existent and 60 % of revenues come from advertising. Nevertheless, the editor-in-chief stressed its exceptional position, generating 35 % from the recruitment and real-estate sections not common in other online media.

Cancellations of advertising contracts due to news coverage do occur in Austria. However, all editors-in-chief stressed their relative independence from such attempts of influence, as single advertising clients never contribute more than 10 % of total revenues. All editors-in-chief regard it as their duty to prevent any advertiser's influence on the newsroom to avoid long-term reputation damage. According to the journalists' union, not all influence can be blocked by the news media and in particular the double function of stakeholders (being politically influential and economically important) is becoming more problematic in times of increasing economic pressures. Attempts to influence the newsrooms of the *ORF* are reportedly made more frequently by political stakeholders than by advertisers. In 2010, for instance, strong interventions by political parties in staff decisions caused journalists from the *ORF* to publicly protest against and reject any further intervention.

(F7) Procedures on news selection and news processing 1 POINT

Institutionalized means of criticizing journalistic working habits only exist in a few newsrooms and are not regularly practiced.

Stylebooks are rare in Austrian newsrooms. The *ORF* has recently developed a code of conduct yet to be accepted by all contributors. So far, the editors-in-chief relied more on the individual professionalism of their journalistic staff than on formalized rules. They emphasized the implicitness of such criteria in the journalistic working process. Discussions on news values and news selection are occasion-driven and part of the journalistic routines. However, all editors-in-chief emphasized that news items should not be published without being checked by at least two people; although they admitted that this may not happen under time pressure. The *ORF* has more institutionalized and complex forms of news selection, as a check and re-check system has been implemented. More general reflections on values and habits are rare in Austrian newsrooms and hardly seen as gainful or commendable experiences.

Equality / Interest mediation (E)

(E1) Media ownership concentration national level   1 POINT

Ownership concentration on a national level is very high as the market is divided among a few big media companies.

The Austrian press market is marked by high press concentration deriving from several waves of concentration up until the mid-1990s (Steinmaurer 2009, p. 505; Trappel 2007, p. 64). The Austrian Cartel Act provides special regulation that requires media mergers to be notified (§ 8) to *Bundeswettbewerbsbehörde* (Competition Authority) if companies exceed revenue limits[3]. But formal rejections of media mergers by the authority are rare.

Table 3.   Audience reach and circulation of Austrian paid-for dailies (2008)

Newspaper	N/R	Associated Media Company	Audience Reach	AR %*	Circulation	Market share %
Kronen Zeitung	national	Mediaprint	2,944,000	41.9	948,615	37.4
Kleine Zeitung	regional	Styria	826,000	11.8	321,957	12.7
Österreich	national	Verlagsgruppe News	702,000	10.0	308,819	12.2
Kurier	national	Mediaprint	625,000	8.9	228,218	9.0
OÖ Nachrichten	regional	Wimmer Verlag	338,000	4.8	140,196	5.5
Der Standard	national	Standard	383,000	5.5	117,131	4.6
Tiroler Tageszeitung	regional	Moser Holding	308,000	4.4	109,716	4.3
Die Presse	national	Styria	241,000	3.4	120,363	4.7
Salzburger Nachrichten	regional	Salzburger Nachrichten	261,000	3.7	94,329	3.7
Vorarlberger Nachrichten	regional	Vorarlberger Medienhaus	208,000	3.0	70,360	2.8
Wirtschaftsblatt	national	Styria	103,000	1.5	39,131	1.5
KTZ Neue Kärntner Tageszeitung	regional	Kärntner DVG	54,000	0.8	32,000	1.3
Neues Volksblatt	regional	OÖ Medien-Data	65,000	0.9	23,000	0.9
Wiener Zeitung	national	Wiener Zeitung	57,000	0.8	20,000	0.8
SVZ Salzburger Volkszeitung	regional	SVZ	-	-	16,300	0.6
Neue Vorarlberger Tageszeitung	regional	Vorarlberger Medienhaus	45,000	0.6	12,328	0.5
Total			5,117,000		2,602,463	
				CR 3 (titles)		62.3
				CR 3 (companies)		77.5

*Readers per edition in percent of population.

Sources: Audience reach: Media-Analyse (2008, p. 67), no data available for SVZ; Circulation: ÖAK (2008, pp. 9-12) except for KTZ, Neues Volksblatt, Wiener Zeitung, SVZ (all data self-declaration).

The Austrian newspaper market is dominated by *Kronen Zeitung*, which reaches 41.9 % of the population and holds a market share of 37.4 % of total newspaper circulation (Arbeitsgemeinschaft Media-Analysen 2008, p. 67). The circulation market share of the three largest newspapers is 62.3 %. All of them are boulevard titles. The nationwide quality newspaper with the highest circulation, *Der Standard*, reaches 5.5 % of the Austrian population with a circulation market share of 4.6 %. In fact, three big private media companies (*Styria Media Group, Mediaprint, Verlagsgruppe News*) dominate the Austrian press market. The circulation market share for those three top media companies (CR3) on the national newspaper market is 77.5 %.

The large national boulevard-style newspapers *Kronen Zeitung* and *Kurier* run *Mediaprint* for shared technical production, distribution and advertising. The second largest Austrian media company (after *ORF*) is *Styria Media Group AG* (Melischek, Seethaler, & Skodascek 2005, pp. 247-251). One regional and two national newspapers (*Kleine Zeitung, Wirtschaftsblatt* and *Die Presse*) as well as several weekly magazines and regional newspapers belong to *Styria*. This company is also active in the radio (*Antenne Kärnten, Antenne Steiermark*) and book market and is the co-owner of *Sat1 Österreich*.

Another large media conglomerate is *Verlagsgruppe News*, which is controlled by majority by the German publisher *Gruner+Jahr* (*Bertelsmann Group*) and which includes among many other titles three major news magazines (*Format, News, Profil*), representing a quasi-monopoly situation on the magazine market. One minority shareholder of these titles is the publisher of Austria's latest boulevard newspaper *Österreich*, with a circulation market share of 12.2 %, reaching 10.0 % of the Austrian population in 2008 (Arbeitsgemeinschaft Media-Analysen 2008, p. 67). Observers criticized several times that strict rules on media mergers and media concentration were established too late to prevent a concentrated media market effectively (Melischek et al. 2005, p. 248; Steinmaurer 2009, p. 508).

In the national television market, private companies were legally admitted in 2001, starting operations in 2003 (*ATV* in Vienna). In 2010, *ATV* and *Puls4* are the main national private television operators, both owned by German companies, and both with insignificant market shares. Competition in the television market is shaped by German television programs available via satellite and cable in Austria, rather than by the two small national broadcasters (see Table 5).

Table 4. Daily reach and market share of TV (national)

Channel	Public/private	Associated Media Company	Daily reach	%*	Market share %
ORF 2	PSB (AUT)	ORF	2,764,000	40.4	25.1
ORF 1	PSB (AUT)	ORF	2,237,000	32.7	16.8
SAT 1	Private (GER)	ProSiebenSat1 Media AG	1,156,000	16.9	7.3
RTL	Private (GER)	RTL Group	1,171,000	17.1	5.6
Pro 7	Private (GER)	ProSiebenSat1 Media AG	1,057,000	15.5	4.8
ZDF	PSB (GER)	ZDF	961,000	14.1	4.3
ARD	PSB (GER)	ARD	959,000	14.0	3.8
ATV	Private (AUT)	Tele München Group, Herbert Kloiber	925,000	13.5	3.0
RTL II	Private (GER)	RTL Group	691,000	10.1	2.5
Kabel 1	Private (GER)	ProSiebenSat1 Media AG	711,000	10.4	2.5
VOX	Private (GER)	RTL Group	-	-	3.9
3sat	PSB (GER)	ARD, ZDF, ORF, SRG	-	-	1.7
Puls4	Private (GER)	ProSiebenSat1 Media AG	-	-	1.2
ARTE	PSB (GER/FR)	ARD, ZDF, France Télévisions	-	-	0.8
Others					16.7
Total			4,335,000	63.4	100.0
				CR 3 (channels)	49.2
				CR 3 (companies)	69.7

* Daily viewers in percent of population.

Sources: All data based on GfK Teletest, population 12+: Market share: AGTT (2009), Steinmaurer (2009, p. 513); Daily reach: Media-Analyse (2008, pp. 114-119).

ORF dominated the television market in 2008, even though its market share is slightly but continuously declining. *ORF 2*, with a market share of 25.1 %, reached about 2,8 million Austrians (40.4 % of the Austrian population) on a daily basis, followed by the entertainment-orientated channel *ORF 1*, with a market share of 16.8 % and reaching 32.7 % of the population. The largest German private television channels (*Sat1, RTL, Pro7*), with market shares between 4.8 and 7.3 %, reach about one million Austrians every day. In 2008, the national Austrian private broadcaster *ATV* had a market share of 3.0 %. The top three television channels unify a market share of 49.2 %. The CR3 for the top three television companies on the national television market, however, is higher: *ORF, ProsiebenSat1 Media AG* and *RTL Group* have a combined market share of 69.7 %.

The radio market is dominated by *ORF* channels, too. Besides the three national radio channels operated by *ORF* (*Ö1, Ö3* and *FM4*), *Kronehit* (owned by *Kronen Zeitung* and *Kurier*) has the only nationwide private license. *Kronehit* reaches 5.9 % of the population and has a market share of 4.0 %. Nevertheless, the Austrian radio landscape is mainly marked by regional and local channels (see also E2). The top three radio channels, all part of the *ORF* network, hold a combined market share of 76.0 %.

Table 5.   Daily reach and market share of leading radio channels (national 2008)

Channel	Public/private	Daily reach	%*	Market share %
Ö2 (regional)	PSB			37.0
Ö3	PSB	2,580,000	36.7	33.0
Ö1	PSB	644,000	9.2	6.0
Kronehit	Private	411,000	5.9	4.0
FM4	PSB	273,000	3.9	2.0
ORF total	PSB	5,013,000	71.4	78.0
Private total	Private	1,623,000	23.1	19.0
Others (foreign)		276,000	3.9	22.0
			CR 3 (channels)	76.0
			CR 2 (companies)	81.0

* Daily listeners in percent of population.

Sources: All data based on Radiotest, population 10+: Market share: ORF Enterprise (2008), Steinmaurer (2009, p. 514) Daily reach: Media-Analyse (2008, p. 100f).

The Austrian online media market is dominated by traditional media companies from other media sectors. The online platform of the *ORF* reaches 1.9 million people with a market share of 21.8 %. Most other online media companies are affiliated with leading companies on the newspaper and magazine market. Only a few of them (like *derstandard.at*) have separate newsrooms with staff working exclusively for the online medium. The top three online media companies, except for *orf.at*, are affiliated with national newspapers (*oe24.at/Österreich, krone.at/Kronen Zeitung*), and unify a market share of 40.0 %.

Table 6.   Reach and market shares of news website (unique users)

Online Newsmedia	Reach	%*	market share %
ORF.at Network	1,902,700	38.5	21.8
oe24-Netzwerk	798,200	16.1	9.2
krone.at	786,000	15.9	9.0
derStandard.at Network	740,000	15.0	8.5
austria.com (network)	681,600	13.8	7.8
NEWS Networld	525,400	10.6	6.0
Kleine Zeitung Online (network)	516,400	10.4	5.9
KURIER	479,600	9.7	5.5
diepresse.at	438,700	8.9	5.0
Vorarlberg Online	290,400	5.9	3.3
ProSieben.at	242,600	4.9	2.8
OÖNachrichten Online Netzwerk	213,500	4.3	2.4
Wirtschaftsblatt.at	209,800	4.2	2.4
Salzburger Nachrichten salzburg.com	183,400	3.7	2.1
tt.com Network	147,800	3.0	1.7
Wiener Zeitung Gruppe (network)	140,400	2.8	1.6
Puls4.com	138,000	2.8	1.6
		CR 3	40.3

*Users in percent of online users (quarter).

Sources: All data based on ÖWA Plus IV (2008); Market share: own calculations.

(E2) Media ownership concentration regional (local) level 1 POINT

On a regional level, ownership concentration is very high. In most Austrian regions one newspaper is dominant; the ORF dominates the local radio market.

With regard to television, local or regional broadcasters play an insignificant role. Non-commercial broadcasting projects are still relatively young and therefore mainly niche programs bound to specific local (mainly urban) areas (e.g., *Radiofabrik Salzburg, Okto TV*). On the contrary, the Austrian radio market is dominated by regional channels. In all nine provinces, the regional public service program (*Ö2*) leads with market shares ranging from 16 % (Vienna) to 45 % (Burgenland). Several small private channels are part of trans-regional chains (*Antenne, Arabella*).

Table 7. Radio: daily reach and market share in Austrian regions (2008)

Channel	Associated media company	Daily reach	%*	Market share %	Channel	Associated media company	Daily reach	%*	Market share %
Vienna					**Salzburg**				
Radio Wien	ORF	237,000	16.7	16.0	Radio Salzburg	ORF	165,000	37.2	39.0
Radio Arabella		138,000	9.7	10.0	Antenne Sbg	Antenne	55,000	12.4	11.0
Ö3	ORF	409,000	28.8		Ö3	ORF	165,000	37.2	
Ö1	ORF	177,000	12.5		Ö1	ORF	40,000	9.0	
Kronehit	Krone/Kurier	85,000	6.0		Kronehit	Krone/Kurier	16,000	3.6	
FM4	ORF	76,000	5.3		FM4	ORF	19,000	4.3	
Total		1,090,000	76.7		Total		369,000	83.3	
Population		1,421,000			Population		443,000		
Lower Austria					**Burgenland**				
Radio NÖ	ORF	430,000	32.0	30.0	Radio BGLD	ORF	109,000	45.0	45.0
Kronehit	Krone/Kurier	127,000	9.4	6.0	Kronehit	Krone/Kurier	21,000	8.7	5.0
Ö3	ORF	532,000	39.6		Ö3	ORF	89,000	36.8	
Ö1	ORF	102,000	7.6		Ö1	ORF	18,000	7.4	
FM4	ORF	41,000	3.0		FM4	ORF	6,000	2.5	
Total		1,137,000	84.5		Total		204,000	84.3	
Population		1,345,000			Population		242,000		
Upper Austria					**Styria**				
Radio OÖ	ORF	369,000	31.5	29.0	Radio STMK	ORF	387,000	37.6	39.0
Life Radio	Moser Holding	163,000	13.9	11.0	Antenne STMK	Styria	174,000	16.9	11.0
Ö3	ORF	462,000	39.4		Ö3	ORF	384,000	37.3	
Ö1	ORF	102,000	8.7		Ö1	ORF	88,000	8.5	
Kronehit	Krone/Kurier	82,000	7.0		Kronehit	Krone/Kurier	46,000	4.5	
FM4	ORF	50,000	4.3		FM4	ORF	29,000	2.8	
Total		967,000	82.5		Total		844,000	81.9	
Population		1,172,000			Population		1,030,000		

Table 7. Cont.

Table 7. Cont.

Channel	Associated media company	Daily reach	%*	Market share %	Channel	Associated media company	Daily reach	%*	Market share %
Carinthia					**Vorarlberg**				
Radio Kärnten	ORF	214,000	44.7	45.0	Radio VBG	ORF	119,000	39.4	41.0
Antenne Ktn	Styria	70,000	14.6	10.0	Antenne VBG	Medienhaus	43,000	14.2	12.0
Ö3	ORF	188,000	39.2		Ö3	ORF	111,000	36.8	
Ö1	ORF	42,000	8.8		Ö1	ORF	21,000	7.0	
Kronehit	Krone/Kurier	16,000	3.3		FM4	ORF	15,000	5.0	
FM4	ORF	14,000	2.9		Kronehit	Krone/Kurier	9,000	3.0	
Total		405,000	84.6		Total		245,000	81.1	
Population		479,000			Population		302,000		
Tirol									
Radio Tirol	ORF	219,000	37.3	34.0					
Life Radio	Moser Holding	43,000	7.3	6.0					
Ö3	ORF	239,000	40.7						
Ö1	ORF	54,000	9.2						
FM4	ORF	24,000	4.1						
Kronehit	Krone/Kurier	23,000	3.9						
Total		503,000	85.7						
Population		587,000							

*Daily listeners in percent of local population.

Sources: All data based on Radiotest, local channels: ORF Enterprise (2008), first and second rank: local public service broadcaster compared to private broadcaster with highest reach in the region, data from first half 2008, all other data: Media-Analyse (2008, pp. 154-194), own calculations.

The leading national newspapers (*Kronen Zeitung, Kurier, Österreich*) provide local editions partly produced by local editorial staff. *Kronen Zeitung* is market leader in four of the nine provinces, being second to regional newspapers in another four and reaching up to 55.5 % of the local population. In Austria's most western province, the *Vorarlberger Medienhaus* occupies a quasi-monopoly on the newspaper market (*Vorarlberger Nachrichten, Neue Vorarlberger Tageszeitung*), reaching 79.9 % of the local population. Moreover, the company is the largest online news provider and runs the only regional private radio station (*Antenne Vorarlberg*) (Melischek et al. 2005, p. 249).

Table 8. Audience share of Austrian paid-for dailies with highest reach on regional level (2008)

Top newspapers	Associated media company	Audience reach	%*	Top newspapers	Associated media company	Audience reach	%*
Vienna				**Upper Austria**			
Kronen Zeitung	Mediaprint	585,000	41.2	Kronen Zeitung	Mediaprint	520,000	44.4
Österreich	Verlagsgruppe News	308,000	21.7	OÖN	Wimmer Verlag	309,000	26.4
Kurier	Mediaprint	262,000	18.4	Österreich	Verlagsgruppe News	115,000	9.8
Population		1,421,000		Population		1,173,000	
Lower Austria				**Salzburg**			
NÖN		647,000	48.1	Kronen Zeitung	Mediaprint	186,000	41.9
Kronen Zeitung	Mediaprint	628,000	46.7	SN	Salzburger Nachrichten	173,000	39.0
Kurier	Mediaprint	240,000	17.9	Population		443,000	
Population		1,346,000					
Burgenland				**Tyrol**			
Kronen Zeitung	Mediaprint	135,000	55.5	TT	Moser Holding	304,000	51.8
Kurier	Mediaprint	43,000	17.6	Kronen Zeitung	Mediaprint	205,000	34.9
Österreich	Verlagsgruppe News	20,000	8.4	Kurier	Mediaprint	19,000	3.3
Population		243,000		Population		587,000	
Styria				**Vorarlberg**			
Kleine Zeitung Graz	Styria	516,000	50.1	VN	Vorarlberger Medienhaus	201,000	66.4
Kronen Zeitung	Mediaprint	445,000	43.2	Neue Vbg. Tageszeitung	Vorarlberger Medienhaus	41,000	13.5
Population		1,030,000		Population		302,000	
Carinthia							
Kleine Zeitung Klagenfurt	Styria	267,000	55.7				
Kronen Zeitung	Mediaprint	224,000	46.7				
KTZ	Kärntner DVG	49,000	10.3				
Population		479,000					

*Readers per edition in % of local population.

Sources: Audience reach: Media-Analyse (2008, pp. 146-193).

(E3) Diversity of formats   3 POINTS

Austrian daily newspapers provide a wide variety of news coverage in different categories, usually including local, national and international news as well as politics, economy, culture and sport sections.

Austria's newspapers provide a larger diversity of formats. Boulevard and quality press titles differ considerably in their news provision. Boulevard newspapers with a stronger focus on entertainment enforced the implementation of social web applications (videos, photos, weblogs) in order to enable users to contribute content; quality newspapers offer more traditional news formats supplemented by postings or chats (Stark & Kraus 2008, p. 313). Some online newspapers also implemented their own community applications.

ORF's main television news formats are broadcasted on *ORF 2*; information formats on *ORF 1* are usually shorter (Woelke 2008, p. 31). Overall, *ORF 2* provides seven different news formats throughout the day, four of them exceeding 15 minutes. A local news format is broadcasted on *ORF 2* before the main evening news, delivered by the regional *ORF* studios. In addition, *ORF 1* delivers shorter news formats five times a day. Besides traditional news formats, there are also special interest magazines on political and economic topics (*Thema, Report*), political discussion formats (*im ZENTRUM*), service magazines (*Konkret*) as well as a weekly discussion format on current affairs inviting journalists from other media to be co-interviewers (*Pressestunde*).

Private television channels have shorter and more sensationalist forms of news presentation. The private channel *ATV* delivers its daily news format (*ATV Aktuell*) twice a day, in addition to news magazines (*ATV Reportage*) and a discussion format (*Am Punkt*) with lower frequency. *Puls 4* produces a news format (*AustriaNews*), which is also broadcasted on *Pro7* and *Sat1* as a local window program, besides a morning and midday news format and a weekly discussion format (*Talk of Town*). There is no Austrian 24-hour news channel, even though some foreign news channels (*ntv, n24, CNN*) are available via cable or satellite.

On most radio programs, short news flashes every full hour are common. *Ö1* offers further news formats: two morning journals including one in English and French, a one-hour news journal at midday (*Mittagsjournal*), and four news formats in the evening. In addition, radio magazines are quite common (Ö1 2010). All public service radio channels and many local private channels provide podcasts or are also available as web radio.

(E4)   Minority / Alternative media   2 POINTS

The availability and institutionalization of minority media depends on whether or not the minority is legally recognized. Overall, a wide range of minority media are available; however their reach is limited.

Austria has six ethnic minority groups recognized by law whose languages have official status: Croatian, Romani, Slovak, Slovene, Czech and Hungarian. Furthermore, Austrian Sign Language is recognized as a minority language. Particularly in the 1960s and again in the 1990s, the number of speakers of Turkish and the languages of the Former Republic of Yugoslavia increased; however their languages do not have official status as minority languages in Austria. For this reason, media initiatives in these languages are either private or non-commercial projects (Bayzitlioglu 2008).

The *ORF* is obliged by law to provide programs in the official minority languages (*ORF Gesetz* 2009, § 5). Some regional studios have special newsrooms that exclusively produce content in minority languages. On television, one nationwide broadcasted format (*Heimat, fremde Heimat*) is dedicated to minority issues such as integration, cultural diversity, etc.; furthermore, regular television and radio news magazines in all official minority languages are available and can also be accessed from the Internet platform *ORF TVthek* (ORF 2010a). The proportion of programs with additional features for people with disabilities is currently about 36 % of the *ORF* output; audio-commentaries for blind people are available for some entertainment and sports formats; extended subtitles are obtainable on *Teletext* for some news and service magazines (ORF 2010b 2010c). Additional offers translated in Austrian Sign Language involve news, parliamentary debates and two formats of children's programs, which are available with digital cable or satellite receivers (ORF 2010d). Nevertheless, critics argue that *ORF*'s minority program is more focused on cultural than on structural differences, and therefore marginalizes political aspects (Böse & Kogoj 2002).

Programs in minority languages that are not officially recognized are frequently broadcasted in so-called free radio and television projects. In 2008, Austria had 14 non-commercial radio projects, all of them limited to specific regions, the largest in Vienna (*Orange 94.0*), Klagenfurt (*Radio Agora*) and Graz (*Radio Helsinki*) (Purkarthofer, Pfisterer, & Busch 2008, p. 19). Furthermore, a non-commercial television initiative with a significant amount of foreign language content is located in Vienna (*OKTO TV*). In addition, a wide variety of alternative and minority magazines and online media are found on the Austrian media market. However, their financial situation is in part critical and highly dependent on limited public subsidies. *RTR* and *KommAustria* are in charge of the public funds established by law (*KommAustria-Gesetz* 2010; § 9i; *Publizistikförderungsgesetz* 2006, § 7). In 2010, subsidies of 1 million EUR were distributed among 16 non-commercial broadcasting initiatives (RTR 2010). In 2008, the first year in which non-German-speaking periodicals could apply for subsidies, € 360,999 in total were given to 93 magazines (RTR 2009a, p. 59).

The number of journalists with an immigrant background in the mainstream media is out of proportion with the number of immigrants in the Austrian society (Gouma 2008, p. 212). Nevertheless, private and non-commercial initiatives for promoting and strengthening the position of minority and alternative news media are becoming more visible through the organization of public discussions, workshops, research, fairs or conferences (*Civilmedia, m-media*). Some programs have recently begun advancing the integration of minorities as contributors to mainstream media newsrooms, like weekly reports written by journalists with an immigrant background in the daily newspaper *Die Presse* (Bayzitlioglu 2008).

(E5) Affordable public and private news media   3 POINTS

All news media are relatively cheap compared to the average income of an Austrian household.

The GDP per capita in Austria is € 33,800, thus exceeding the average GDP per capita of the European Union, which is € 25,100 (Statistik Austria 2010). The average disposable income of an Austrian household in 2008 was about € 33,985 (Statistik Austria 2009). The latest consumer statistics from 2004/05 show that an average household spent about € 2,540 per month; the average costs for radio and television license fees (including cable and satellite fees) were about € 19.4 per month, those for newspapers and news magazines € 18.8 per month; another € 67.0 were spent on communication devices (Statistik Austria 2008). This means that the average costs of mass media (print, radio, television, telecommunication) in Austria range between 0.7 % and 2.6 % of total household expenditures.

The copy price for a newspaper is between 75 cents (with annual subscription) and € 1.02 (direct sale) (World Association of Newspapers 2009, p. 215). Broadcasting reception equipment in Austria must be registered and is subject to a compulsory license fee established by law (*Rundfunkgebührengesetz* 2003, § 2). However, only part of the total amount of the license fee is given to the *ORF*, as some additional regional and national fees are deducted. The monthly fee ranges from € 18.61 (Vorarlberg) to € 23.71 (Styria); the average annual fee is about € 261.12 (GIS 2010). The broadcasting fee is lower if a household is only equipped with radio receivers. In addition, disabled people or low income households can apply for reduction or remission of the license fee.

Broadband connections are an increasing market, despite the already high level. Broadband is technically available in 96 % of all Austrian households, and 56 % of them already used broadband connection in 2008 (RTR 2009a, p. 171). Overall, Austrian households spent on average about € 28.2 on Internet connections in 2008; combined products including telephone, cable television and/or mobile devices with average costs of € 32.7 are becoming more popular (RTR 2009b, p. 15).

Table 9.   Annual costs of different media

Mass media	Average annual price	% of average household income (2008)
Newspaper (subscription)	€ 273.5	0.81 %
Newspaper (direct sale)	€ 372.30	1.10 %
Radio (license fee)	€ 75.75	0.22 %
Television (license fee, including radio)	€ 261.12	0.77 %
Internet (only)	€ 338.40	1.00 %
Internet (in combination with cable, television and/or mobile devices)	€ 384.00	1.13 %

Sources: Newspapers: daily average, own calculations (World Association of Newspapers 2009, p. 215); Radio and Television: monthly, average of all nine regions, own calculations (GIS 2010); Internet: monthly average, own calculations (RTR 2009a, p. 15).

(E6)   Content monitoring instruments   1 POINT

Institutionalized and independent media monitoring instruments are rare in Austria.

The national news agency *APA* in cooperation with *MediaWatch Institut für Medienanalysen* publishes the Prime Politics Index on a weekly basis, monitoring news coverage of the leading politicians of the Austrian parliamentary parties (http://www.apa-mediawatch.at). Furthermore, the *RTR* (*Rundfunk und Telekomregulierungs-GmbH*) publishes several reports about the Austrian media market. A general communication report is published every year summarizing the main developments of the Austrian communication market as well as the work of the regulatory authorities. Still, only a few content-related issues can be found in these reports (RTR 2009a). Since 2007, the *RTR* has financed and published regular reports on the program structure of the Austrian television channels *ORF 1, ORF 2, ATV* and *PULS 4* (Woelke 2007 2008 2010). The main focus of those reports is on a quantitative analysis of the program and issue structures of the Austrian television channels in comparison to other German-speaking countries. The Viewers' Council (*Publikumsrat*) and the Public Value Competence Center of the *ORF* can commission reports concerning content issues. In addition, *ORF* established an annual quality monitoring system in 2008. Besides a representative survey and several statements from experts, this monitoring system includes audience talks (*Publikumsgespräche*) (ORF 2010d).

The Department of Communication at the University of Salzburg has published regular reports (*Bericht zur Lage des Journalismus in Österreich/Journalismus in Öster-*

reich) on working conditions, quality standards, legal and practical developments as well as specific content-related issues since 1996. The purpose of the reports is to present relevant research findings for the journalistic daily business (Abteilung für Journalistik des Fachbereichs Kommunikationswissenschaft der Universität Salzburg 2006, 2009). The Commission for Comparative Media and Communications Studies of the Austrian Academy of Sciences participates in international research projects focusing on the comparative approach of media systems. Based on historical data, the Internet portal *HYPRESS* – with information on the development of the Austrian press market since the beginning of the 19th century – was established. It is still pursued (http://www.oeaw.ac.at/cmc/hypress/); at present, data up until 1934 is available.

Still, there is no systematic independent monitoring instrument supervising media coverage on the Austrian media market on a permanent and continuous basis, comparable to other countries. Attempts at media monitoring are usually not published outside the scientific community and therefore their visibility is rather low.

(E7) Code of ethics at the national level (structure)   1 POINT

A code of ethics exists, but the Austrian Press Council has been re-established in 2010 only.

The Austrian Press Council (*Presserat*) was founded in 1961 as a cooperation between the journalists' union and the publishers' association (*VÖZ: Verband Österreichischer Zeitungen*). The code of ethics established by the Press Council was adopted in 1999 and is formally accepted by most Austrian newspapers. Complaints are examined by one of the Press Council's two senates in case the Ombudsmen cannot mediate between the complainant and the accused newspaper (Österreichischer Presserat 2011, p. 3). Verified complaints must be published by the newspaper concerned. In case that a newspaper continuously or seriously violates the code or refuses to publish the decision of the Press Council, it can withdraw its certification. However, no legal actions or penalties are possible. In fact, after a controversy concerning the news coverage of *Kronen Zeitung* in 2001, the publishers' association withdrew its support from the Press Council (Gottwald, Kaltenbrunner, & Karmasin 2006, p. 9). It therefore was de facto inactive from 2002 to 2010. In 2010, the Press Council was reestablished (Österreichischer Presserat 2011, p. 2), but criticized because its decisions are supposed to be final without the possibility of further legal actions in the same case (I. Weber, 2010) and because the lack of sanctions is likely to limit the effectiveness of the Press Council.

Even though most of our interviewees accepted the guidelines of the code of ethics and affirmed compliance with high ethical standards in their newsrooms, they also asserted the code's irrelevance in the daily journalistic business. None of them uses the code as a reference in internal discussions about ethical standards. Some editors-in-chief even admitted to not knowing the actual content. Moreover, most of our interviewees expressed their skepticism about the effectiveness and significance of the Press Council as a self-governing body.

In addition, there are a few other independent journalists' associations that promote good practice, quality and ethical standards. An association that primarily emphasizes education and further training of journalists is *Kuratorium für Journalistenausbildung* (*Kff*). Another association dedicated to the improvement of journalistic standards is *Initiative für Qualität im Journalismus* (*IQ*), which organizes public discussions about ethical standards and quality in journalistic work.

(E8) Level of self-regulation (performance)   1 POINT

Self-regulation occurs rather informally; institutionalized or codified rules and procedures are rare.

All Austrian news media provide a mission statement declaring their fundamental orientation as required by the Media Act (*Mediengesetz*, 2009, § 25(4)). However, as the law does not contain any further instructions about the length and content of mission statements, those of some news media are rather short and non-specific (e.g., *Kronen Zeitung*, *Profil*). Many of them refer to the independence of the medium and its responsibility for democracy and human rights. In particular, our respondents from quality newspapers emphasized the importance of the medium's mission statement as a reference in internal discussions about news coverage and news production being the medium's fundamental orientation point. However, other interviewees asserted that they rather rely on the internalization of basic rules of journalistic work on an individual and informal basis.

In addition, most Austrian news media have editorial statutes, although only the *ORF* and the national newspaper *Kurier* publish them online. The relevance of those codified orientation papers in the journalistic daily business is quite diverse. The *ORF* hands out its mission statement, the editorial statutes and the *ORF*-Act to every new employee on the first working day, and the rights and duties contained in those documents are regularly discussed. On the contrary, some editors-in-chief (in particular from regional print media and online media) were not even sure about the existence of such guidelines, let alone their actual content.

All of our respondents asserted that a critical review of the journalistic work is part of every editorial conference and takes place at least once a day for 15 to 30 minutes. In weekly news magazines, editorial conferences only take place once a week, but therefore are more extensive. The editor-in-chief of the online medium of our news media sample even mentioned that editorial meetings were held three times a day (mainly via email), including email discussions afterwards. The news department of *ORF* Television has three editorial meetings a day, the radio department two. Most of our respondents were skeptical about the invitation of external critics to their editorial meetings. While some newsrooms practice this regularly by inviting prominent people, journalists from other news media, economic experts, politicians and on rare occasions also academics, some editors-in-chief totally denied the usefulness of such critique. None of the news media in our sample has an ombudsman; the editors-in-chief stated that such a position was rarely ever discussed and generally not considered necessary. Only the quality newspaper *Die Presse* has an external and independent observer who is in part responsible for reader's complaints and publishes his critique about the news coverage of *Die Presse* once a month in the medium itself (*Spiegelschrift*).

Three of our interviewees mentioned that they are currently working on codes of conduct (*Salzburger Nachrichten, Die Presse, ORF*), which however are still subject to acceptance by all contributors. All other editors-in-chief doubted the necessity and usefulness of such written guidelines, as the fundaments of journalistic work were expected to be clear to all journalists. Even though written guidelines for journalistic work are rare, most newsrooms established informal procedures of news production (e.g., that all articles have to be revised by a second person). However, some interviewees admit that in particular in situations of time pressure, such informal rules are neglected. If journalistic standards are violated by an employee, this is usually discussed bilaterally, although consequences are rare. Only the interviewees from the *ORF* refer to the possibility of legal consequences deriving from a complaint before the Federal Communications Board.

The *ORF* established more complex control and feedback structures. First, every news feature must be accepted by the sub-department chief, the department chief and the program responsible. Second, the presenter writes the text on the basis of the news feature. Third, the presenter and the journalist both have to release their versions, which are controlled and accepted once again by the program responsible. This system was established to avoid errors and violations of journalistic standards before going on air. In addition, every journalist has the right to get more general feedback about his/her work from the editor-in-chief during an individual staff appraisal three times a year. Furthermore, the *ORF* regularly consults an external private consulting company.

(E9) Participation   1 POINT

Audience participation is limited to "classical" means of participation, e.g. letters to the editor. Austrian newsrooms are not open to citizens.

In general there are two possibilities for the audience to directly participate in Austrian newsrooms or to get in contact with the newsroom: online postings and letters to the editor. Letters to the editor are in some newsrooms directly read and selected by the editor-in-chief (*Salzburger Nachrichten, Kronen Zeitung Salzburg*), other newsrooms have special staff members for this (*Die Presse, derstandard.at, Profil*). Even though all news media in our sample provide online postings and recognize the increasing importance of online user feedback, some of the editors-in-chief are rather skeptical about the value of postings. All editors-in-chief and the president of the journalists' union conclude that audience members can only fulfill journalistic functions to a very limited extent and do not consider weblogs or online discussion boards a severe competition to their work. Besides classical forms, the possibility for the audience to participate or to get involved is limited.

Access to editorial conferences is generally limited to the newsroom members; public editorial conferences are not practiced in any of the newsrooms in our sample. All interviewees expressed their skepticism about such concepts of transparency. Some editors-in-chief feared that editorial conferences could only have a representative character if they were public. Others mentioned the possible presence of journalists from competing news media as a threat to the exclusivity of their stories. *ORF*, *Salzburger Nachrichten* and *Die Presse* regularly offer guided tours and organize public discussions about journalistic issues from time to time.

(E10)   Rules and practices on internal pluralism   1 POINT

As Austrian newsrooms usually do not have codified guidelines, contradictions and discussions are also subject to informal agreements.

Diverse opinions are generally welcome in Austrian newsrooms and even promoted by the editors-in-chief. It seems that the freedom of the journalist's opinion and its expression is higher in non-daily journalistic work and on a national rather than on a regional level. Most editors-in-chief mentioned quality criteria and the fundamental orientation of the news medium as the limits to the personal convictions of journalists.

Concerning the selection of experts for news coverage, all editors-in-chief concluded that diversity is difficult and therefore sometimes limited, however desirable. Some newsrooms have expert pools or special databases, although most experts are recruited by journalists because of informal contacts. Even though a rotation of experts is preferable for most editors-in-chief, time pressure and limited resources sometimes impede this ideal. More explicit rules on the representation of all socially significant views and inclusion of diverse experts only exist for the *ORF*, as they are required by law to represent this diversity. In print media newsrooms, such principles are expected to be individually internalized and are not regularly discussed or supervised.

Control / Watchdog (C)

(C1)   Supervising the watchdog 'control of controllers'   2 POINTS

Even though weblogs are becoming more popular in Austria, there are only a few media-blogs so far. Media criticism and public debates are centered on the press, but absent from radio and television.

Most media blogs are private initiatives launched by journalists or private people, either critically reviewing the news coverage of one specific medium (e.g. www.krone-blog.at) or the performance of the tabloid media in general (e.g. www.medienschelte.at). Their public presence is limited and public debates on media developments or news issues rather take place in traditional media. Some magazines specialize in media issues, aiming at journalists as readers and discussing the functions and roles of media for society or debates on journalistic ethics and standards (e.g., *Der Österreichische Journalist, Horizont*). Journalists' associations like the journalists' union have their own magazines (e.g., *Kompetenz*).

Furthermore, most newspapers report on media issues and developments, therefore the amount of self-reflection in the Austrian news media is quite high. Compared to other sections, the amount of reports on media developments in Austrian newspapers lies between 2 % (*Die Presse*) and 6 % (*Kronen Zeitung, Der Standard*) and is even higher in online newspapers (Stark & Kraus, 2008, p. 310). An outstanding example is the media section of *Der Standard* (online-version: *derstandard.at/etat*), which features reports on economic and legal media developments, changes in ownership and financial issues, media performance (with a special focus on the *ORF*), national and international media trends and critical reviews on media content. In the television sector such forms of self-criticism are lacking. There is no magazine on media performance or journalistic standards, at all.

(C2)   Independence of the news media from power holders   1 POINT

Overall, a special status is granted to journalists by several laws emphasizing the value of independence for journalistic work. However "promise and practice" often diverge.

The *ORF*-Act grants fundamental independence from power holders to the *ORF* (*ORF Gesetz*, 2009, § 32). Nevertheless, the close relation to political parties and authorities becomes obvious in staff decisions made by the board (*Stiftungsrat*), which is also in charge of appointing the general director (*ORF Gesetz*, 2009, §§ 20 & 22)[4]. To some observers, party affiliation is of importance in staff decisions limiting the political independence of the *ORF* (Kaltenbrunner, 2010, p. 119). However, content analysis of the main *ORF* news formats (*Zeit im Bild*) showed that the news coverage of the *ORF* was well balanced and that the in-depth reporting on democratic values and political issues was comparable to that of quality newspapers (Lengauer 2006, p. 374).

Survey results among journalists show that the importance of *Kronen Zeitung* and *ORF* for the political agenda is unrivaled. In fact, 78 % of journalists think *Kronen Zeitung* has a very great influence on the political agenda; 59 % have the same opinion of the *ORF* (Kaltenbrunner 2010, p. 119f). Even though *Kronen Zeitung* has declared itself as independent and political ambitions have been denied several times, the former longtime editor, Hans Dichand, published his own political preferences regularly in his commentaries. Furthermore, our respondent from *Kronen Zeitung* emphasized the importance of media campaigns initiated by the newspaper and their impact on democratic developments. In 2008 the importance of the newspaper for the political agenda became evident once again when leading politicians of the Social Democratic Party announced a change in the party's position on European issues, in particular the Lisbon Treaty, in an open letter to the editor that was published in *Kronen Zeitung* (Gusenbauer & Faymann 2008, p. 4).

At least two important non-media institutions are present in the Austrian media sectors: the Catholic Church (*Katholischer Medien-Verein, Styria Media Group*) and the financial service provider *Raiffeisen Holding* (*Kurier, Verlagsgruppe News, Profil, Mediaprint, Krone Hit, Sat1 Austria*, etc.). Both are active in all media sectors (book publishing, print, radio and television). Our respondents from news media related to those non-media institutions confirmed regular but informal contact to ownership representatives, however totally denied any direct impact on journalistic daily routines.

Concerning the daily journalistic practice, the president of the journalists' union admitted that attempts to directly influence journalists or newsrooms are made by politicians, and in some cases are also effective. What he considered worse was that political parties were at the same time important advertising clients, which limits the resistance to external influence and can negatively affect the newsrooms' independence.

(C3) Transparency of data on media system   1 POINT

Transparency is given with regard to media legislation and the ORF. Ownership structures of private media companies, however, lack transparency.

Basic data on the Austrian media system, in particular on media legislation, are easily accessible online and provided by the Federal Chancellery. Furthermore, the administrative authority *RTR* provides regular reports on developments in the Austrian media and telecommunications markets (RTR 2009a, 2009c) (see also E6). The *ORF* is obliged by law to annually publish a business report containing information on its financial performance (ORF 2009). Furthermore, the *ORF* publishes a report on the fulfillment of the public service mission since 2008 (ORF 2008, 2010e). Private media companies are not obliged to publish their economic results and refrain from doing so. Therefore data on the advertising revenues of private media companies are not accessible to Austrian citizens.

According to the Media Act (*Mediengesetz* 2009, §§ 24-25), all media companies must provide information on ownership structures and changes as well as on their fundamental orientation in their imprint. Further news coverage on personnel fluctuations or changes in ownership structures occurs occasionally. Due to legal aspects, changes in mission statements rarely take place. Not all media companies provide their mission statements on their websites; those that are members of the publishers' association are published on this website.

Data on the Austrian media system in general and the Austrian news media companies in particular from independent institutions are quite abundant, but usually limited to a specific readership and not widely known. Our interviewee from public service radio criticized the lack of media education in Austria, which led to low awareness of the interrelations of journalistic and democratic values among citizens and little knowledge about the ownership or financial structures of the leading Austrian news media.

(C4)   Journalism professionalism   2 POINTS

The position of journalists concerning professional ethics and standards is quite ambivalent. On the one hand, such principles are highly valued and a crucial status is attributed to them; on the other hand, journalists show little enthusiasm regarding institutionalized forms of self-criticism and reflection.

Public debates on media-related issues often center on the independence of the *ORF* or the (political) weight of *Kronen Zeitung*. In 2006, a popular journalist of the *ORF* publicly criticized the ongoing interventions of politicians; further internal criticism was announced by the platform *SOS-ORF*. It was supported by *ORF* employees worrying about quality standards and independence. Even though the process of self-criticism in the Austrian media sector is quite fluent and all of our respondents at least occasionally take part in public debates on media-related issues, they also admitted that lack of time and a high workload prevent such in-depth discussions. Skepticism about the need for further education and discussion on journalistic basic skills was high among our respondents. About 34 % of Austrian journalists are graduate academics, which can be considered rather low. Concerning further education, journalists are most interested in workshops on writing skills or technical developments (S. Weber 2006, p. 63). According to one of our respondents, education on democratic values is hardly mentioned by the employees. Overall, the self-image of Austrian journalists (in particular those working in political areas) is ambivalent. Austrian journalists consider two roles to be most important: their role as critics and their role as objective mediators of neutral information. Those contrary concepts are very important for over 90 % of journalists working in political sections (Kaltenbrunner, Karmasin, & Kraus 2010, p. 18ff).

Overall, Austrian journalists are pleased with their working conditions: 75 % are very satisfied with working times; 51 % cannot complain about their daily workload and 44 % are very satisfied with the time they have to spend on research (Kaltenbrunner et al. 2008, p. 82). Nevertheless, discontent is present among younger journalists with freelancing contracts concerning remuneration and job security (S. Weber 2006, p. 49). Time pressure is, according to the president of the journalists' union, a problem in the online media sector, but also increasing in other media sectors due to the ongoing rationalization in all areas.

(C5) Journalists' job security   2 POINTS

Journalists are formally well protected by several laws. Nevertheless, pressures occur in the daily journalistic routine.

The Media Act contains a clause of conscience protecting journalists from writing against their convictions (*Mediengesetz* 2009, § 2); furthermore, the Journalist Act includes special privileges and financial compensations for journalists in case of dismissal or termination of contract related to changes in the ownership or political orientation of the medium (*Journalistengesetz* 2002, § 8 & 11). In addition, there are several collective agreements for journalists. The president of the journalists' union defined the legal working conditions for journalists in Austria as "good in theory, bad in practice" and stressed the need for reforms. He also asserted that the situation varies from one media sector to another and is most precarious in the online, private television and radio sector.

According to our respondents, the number of journalists working on freelancing contracts is rather low in Austria. However, the mentioned amount of about 10 % of freelancers lies in strong contrast to the reports of the president of the journalists' union. He estimated that already half of all journalists in Austria worked as freelancers. Presumably this contradiction derives from the unavailability of official statistics and the difference the collective agreement makes between permanent freelancers (with better working conditions and job security) and those employees not covered by the collective agreement. It was reported recently that the economic crisis led to an increasing number of former journalists whose contracts were renewed under collective agreements of non-journalistic businesses to reduce personnel costs for media companies in the long run (Washietl 2009, p. 34). This implies not only financial drawbacks for the employees, but is a loss of special rights and protection of journalists.

(C6) Practice of access to information   2 POINTS

Formally, access to information for journalists in Austria is unlimited even though some restrictions are present.

In Austria the European Convention on Human Rights has constitutional status, therefore freedom of information is granted to all citizens. Nevertheless, the Austrian Constitution (§ 20) also provides for discretion of all official institutions and federal or state-related authorities unless law declares special rights and conditions on access. Therefore some information is subject to official secrecy. However, specific federal and regional laws regulate that requests to official institutions and authorities must be answered to provide transparency in state administration (*Auskunftspflichtgesetze*). Still, the president of the journalists' union was critical, stating that – due to the lack of legislative guarantees obliging public representatives to inform journalists combined with official secrecy status – access to information could be rather difficult.

The Media Act limits the publication of information in case of violation of privacy (§§6-7) or for crimes when children or adolescents are involved (§ 8). Furthermore, any audiovisual recording and broadcasting during legal trials is prohibited. In the past few years, regular discussions on information rights versus the right to privacy have occurred, in particular during important law suits attracting a great deal of news coverage. Recently a tightening of the Penal Code relating to higher penalties for news media in case of violation of privacy or protection of identity has been planned. Some of our respondents therefore expected negative effects on investigative journalistic research and rather preferred forms of self-regulation to tighter legal restrictions.

In particular, interviewees from regional news media reported on the negative effects caused by critical news coverage. Nevertheless, they also stated that this problem could easily be evaded, as a wide variety of alternative information sources were available and therefore it has little effect on their reporting.

(C7) The watchdog and the media's mission statement   2 POINTS

A significant value is attributed to the watchdog function of media in Austria.

The president of the journalists' union mentioned that control of power was one of the most important issues of journalism, even though he argued that awareness of this was higher among older journalists than the younger generation. Our interviewees from the *ORF* considered their control function as crucial for democracy; the respondents from print media also attributed a high value to the watchdog role of journalism. However, some admitted that in small newsrooms the lack of staff interferes with this highly valuable role.

In online media and radio broadcasting, where a large amount of news is produced and published several times a day, the capacities for investigative journalism are limited. On the contrary, our respondent from the weekly news magazine emphasized the importance of watchdog journalism, stating that every piece of journalistic research should be investigative. On a regional level, our respondents expressed skepticism about methods of investigative journalism referring to the negative connotation of "sensational" journalism, which they rejected.

As examples of watchdog journalism, our respondents referred to the discovery of secret foreign accounts of former Austrian politicians, a scandal about financial corruption in the banking sector concerning politicians and bankers, weapons from Austria in war territories or child abuse in organizations of the Catholic Church. It is noticeable that recent examples for watchdog journalism on a local level are rare and that increasing economic pressure, job insecurity among journalists and an increasing workload are the main threats to the watchdog role of journalism.

(C8)   Professional training   2 POINTS

Supply of further education is abundant in Austrian newsrooms; nevertheless workshops on democratic values and ethical standards are rare.

The right for journalists to attend further education does not exist in any of the Austrian newsrooms in our media sample nor is it granted by law. As journalism is a free and unlimited activity, no special education is required and educational measures are voluntary. Nevertheless, some of the newsrooms in our media sample offer internal educational programs for their employees: *Salzburger Nachrichten* is currently planning to set up an internal workshop program, the online medium *derstandard.at* is already organizing courses on journalistic skills and considering an extension of its program. Other editors-in-chief admitted that high costs would prevent them from establishing internal courses, and that they would instead rely on external educational programs (for instance *Kuratorium für Journalistenausbildung*). The editor-in-chief of *Kronen Zeitung Salzburg*, however, doubted the effectiveness of journalistic education at all and considered the profession a vocation which simply requires talent. Thus, in many newsrooms further education depends on the initiative of the journalists themselves. If courses are suggested by journalists, financial support is not guaranteed but quite common in Austrian newsrooms. The final decision usually lies with the editors-in-chief.

The *ORF* has an internal department that organizes education, including courses on democratic, political or legal issues. Nevertheless, the head of information of *ORF* radio stressed that employees must already have basic knowledge about democracy before being hired.

Most educational offers focus on technical aspects or writing skills. Even though most editors-in-chief admitted that courses on democratic values and ethical behavior could be interesting for their employees, internal opportunities are rather modest. Most of our interviewees argued that knowledge about formal and stylistic journalistic skills automatically led to a professionalization of journalists and further measures to raise awareness of democratic rights and duties were dispensable.

(C9) Watchdog function and financial resources 2 POINTS

Austrian newsrooms usually try to provide resources for in-depth research to the extent possible. The decision which issue is most promising is up to the editor-in-chief.

The regional newspaper *Salzburger Nachrichten* has 10 staff members located in Vienna who are in charge of national news coverage in certain areas (economy, national politics, culture, etc.). Other national newspapers, for example *Kronen Zeitung*, have independently organized regional newsrooms providing regional information; their international news coverage is mainly based on international news agencies. Most Austrian newspapers and the *ORF* have a broad range of foreign correspondents. Most of them are neither internal staff members of the medium nor are they exclusively engaged by just one medium; they usually work on freelancing contracts for several German-speaking news media companies. Even though contracts are usually limited, specific rules on rotation are rare and contracts are usually prolonged several times.

The amount of time and money that can be spent on in-depth investigation differs a great deal among the news media in our sample. In fact, so far no Austrian newsroom has journalists who exclusively work on in-depth research of critical stories, even though one editor-in-chief (*Die Presse*) told us about plans to establish an exclusive reporter team, which were delayed due to financial restrictions. Nevertheless, when interesting information is expected, all editors-in-chief mentioned that the exemption of journalists for a couple of days is possible. This is easier in weekly magazines, where stories are investigated over a longer period of time. Nevertheless, there are no established rules and the editors-in-chief decide which journalist will get additional time for research.

Conclusion

The country report draws a rather mixed picture of the democratic implications of the Austrian media system. A small-state media market influenced by reactive media policy in combination with a long tradition of press freedom and strong commitments to democratic values of the journalistic profession led to contradictory situations. The rather modest result of the Austrian grading at all three levels therefore derives from this specific combination of the structural and performative components of the Austrian media system.

Freedom of information is formally secured by Austrian law. Therefore, legal and formal protection of the media and the journalistic profession is abundant and in part even redundant, attributing a democratic role to the media. Distribution and availability of media content is not limited to any great degree by geographic or socio-demographic aspects; nor is media use, which is generally relatively high and diverse. Nevertheless, it is dominated only by a few big players. On a company level formalized rules and guidelines are missing in most Austrian newsrooms. Therefore, democratic practices are rather absent in the journalistic daily working process.

Concerning the Equality indicators, the situation is even worse. High media concentration supported and legitimized by state regulation goes along with the absence of broadly accepted measures of self-regulation. Journalists rather rely on informal agreements and practices, seen as intrinsically known by everyone, showing strong aversion to institutionalized or codified forms of regulation. This leads to a lack of transparency and entails the danger that interest mediation could be negatively affected.

The control function of the media is highly valued by Austrian journalists. The high professional ethos of Austrian journalists concerning independence from and control of power holders is, however, contradictory to the historically developed close relationship between media and economic or political power-holders. The preference for informal practices is also visible concerning the assurance of independence, further education of journalists and other forms of professionalization. Nevertheless, in particular in times of increasing economic pressures on the media, the lack of transparency of working processes due to the absence of mandatory guidelines entails the risk of a gradual neglect of the social responsibility of media professionals for the benefit of economic goals and therefore endangers the democratic role of the media in Austria in the long run.

Notes

[1] Average of 12 national newspapers, own calculations based on circulation, direct sales only (ÖAK 2009, pp. 10-12).

[2] The remaining 26.2 % derive from revenues of the various *ORF* subsidiaries (*ORS, TW1, ORF-Mediaservice GmbH*). Furthermore, the sales on technical equipment (e.g. smart-cards), merchandising and program licenses are part of these further revenues (ORF 2009, pp. 16-21).

[3] The limits are lower than in other economic sectors: Worldwide revenue higher than 300 million Euro, national revenue more than 30 million Euro, or at least two companies with worldwide revenue higher than 5 million Euro (*Kartellgesetz* 2005, p. 6f).

[4] A recent amendment of the ORF Act in 2010 includes the implementation of a new independent media authority, which is not constituted yet.

References

Abteilung für Journalistik des Fachbereichs Kommunikationswissenschaft der Universität Salzburg (*ed.*) (2006) *Journalismus in Österreich. Bericht der Abteilung Journalistik des Fachbereichs Kommunikationswissenschaft der Universität Salzburg 2006.* Salzburg: Universität Salzburg.

Abteilung für Journalistik des Fachbereichs Kommunikationswissenschaft der Universität Salzburg (ed.) (2009) *Journalismus in Österreich. Bericht der Abteilung Journalistik des Fachbereichs Kommunikationswissenschaft der Universität Salzburg 2009.* Salzburg: Universität Salzburg.

AGTT (2009) Marktanteile der TV-Kanäle in allen Fernsehhaushalten 1993 bis 2008. Retrieved August 24, 2010, from www.statistik.at/.../marktanteile_der_tv-kanaele_in_allen_fernsehhaushalten_1993_bis_2008_erwac_021239.pdf

AIM/ORF Mediaresearch (2009) Haushalts-Ausstattung. Retrieved August 26, 2010, from http://mediaresearch. orf.at/c_internet/console/console.htm?y=2&z=1

APA (2010) Offenlegung/Impressum. Retrieved August 30, 2010, from http://www.apa.at/legal/offenlegung_apa.pdf

Arbeitsgemeinschaft Media-Analysen (2008) *Media-Analyse 2008. Jahresbericht 2008.* Wien.

Bayzitlioglu, A. (2008, September 9) Wenn Minderheiten Medien machen. *Die Presse.* Vienna. Retrieved September 14, 2010, from http://diepresse.com/home/panorama/integration/412965/print.do

Böse, M., & Kogoj, C. (2002) Minderheiten und elektronische Medien in Österreich. Von eingeschränkter Vielfalt an Öffentlichkeiten. *SWS Rundschau, 42*(3), 293-307.

European Audiovisual Observatory. (2009) *Yearbook: film, television, video and multimedia in Europe. Vol. 1: Television in 36 European States.* Strasbourg: Observatoire Européen de l'Audiovisuel.

GIS (2010) *Die Rundfunkgebühren im Detail (monatlich)* GIS. Retrieved August 30, 2010, from http://www.orf-gis.at/files/36_gebuehrentabelle_06_2006_brutto.pdf

Gottwald, F., Kaltenbrunner, A., & Karmasin, M. (2006) *Medienselbstregulierung zwischen Ökonomie und Ethik.* Vienna/Berlin: LIT.

Gouma, A. (2008) Fernsehen für MigrantInnen. Ein Grenzfall für den öffentlich-rechtlichen Auftrag? In Steininger, Christian/Woelke, Jens (eds) *Fernsehen in Österreich 2008* Konstanz: UVK, 197-216.

Gusenbauer, A., & Faymann, W. (2008, June 27) Volksabstimmung für neuen EU-Vertrag. *Kronen Zeitung.* Retrieved February 13, 2011, from http://www.krone.at/Nachrichten/Volksabstimmung_fuer_neuen_EU-Vertrag-Brief_im_Wortlaut-Story-105493

Journalistengesetz (2002) Retrieved August 30, 2010, from http://www.medien-recht.com/files/journalistengesetz_0.pdf

Kaltenbrunner, A. (2010) Was bin ich? Leitmotive und Leitmedien im Politikjournalismus. In Kaltenbrunner, Andy/Karmasin, Matthias/Kraus, Daniela (eds) *Der Journalisten-Report III: Politikjournalismus in Österreich.* Vienna: Facultas, 109-134.

Kaltenbrunner, A., Karmasin, M., & Kraus, D. (eds) (2010) *Der Journalisten-Report III: Politikjournalismus in Österreich.* Vienna: Facultas.

Kaltenbrunner, A., Karmasin, M., Kraus, D., & Zimmermann, A. (2008) *Der Journalisten-Report II. Österreichs Medienmacher und ihre Motive. Eine repräsentative Befragung.* Wien: Facultas.

Kartellgesetz (2005) Retrieved August 30, 2010, from http://www.ris.bka.gv.at/Dokumente/BgblAuth/BGBLA_2005_I_61/BGBLA_2005_I_61.pdf

KommAustria-Gesetz (2010) Retrieved August 30, 2010, from http://oesterreich.gv.at/DocView.axd?CobId=24299

Kurier (2007) Das Redaktionsstatut. Retrieved September 1, 2010, from http://kurier.at/service/unternehmen/diezeitung/112215.php

Lengauer, G. (2006) Einfalt oder Vielfalt? Die ORF-Nachrichten im Spannungsfeld zwischen Professionalität, Profit, Publikum und Politik. *Österreichische Zeitschrift für Politikwissenschaft, 35*(4), 361-378.

Mediengesetz (2009) Retrieved August 30, 2010, from http://www.bka.gv.at/DocView.axd?CobId=11995

Melischek, G., Seethaler, J., & Skodascek, K. (2005) Der österreichische Zeitungsmarkt 2004: hoch konzentriert. *Media Perspektiven, 2005*(5), 243-252.

Ö1 (2010) Ö1 Programm. Retrieved September 1, 2010, from http://oe1.orf.at/static/pdf/OE1_Programm_2010.pdf

ÖAK (2008) *Auflagenliste Jahresschnitt 2008*. Retrieved August 30, 2010, from http://www.oeak.at/content/intern/Auflagenlisten/OEAK_2008_JS_KORR.pdf

ÖAK (2009) *Auflagenliste Jahresschnitt 2009*. Retrieved August 30, 2010, from http://www.oeak.at/content/intern/Auflagenlisten/OEAK_2009_JS_KORR_20100824.pdf

ORF (2008) *Wert über Gebühr. Public Value Bericht 2007/2008*. Vienna: ORF. Retrieved August 30, 2010, from http://kundendienst.orf.at/unternehmen/news/public_value.pdf

ORF (2009) *Geschäftsbericht 2008*. Retrieved August 30, 2010 from http://derneue.orf.at/publikationen/gb_2008.pdf

ORF (2010a) Heimat, fremde Heimat. Retrieved September 2, 2010, from http://zukunft.orf.at/modules/orfpublicvalue/upload/09z0099.pdf

ORF (2010b) Audiodeskriptionsservice im ORF. Fernsehen für Blinde und Sehbehinderte. Retrieved September 1, 2010, from http://kundendienst.orf.at/programm/behinderung/hoerfilm.html

ORF (2010c) Gebärdendolmetsch. Retrieved September 2, 2010, from http://zukunft.orf.at/modules/orfpublicvalue/upload/09z0075.pdf

ORF (2010d) *ORF-Qualitätsmonitoring 2009. Repräsentativbefragung, Publikumsgespräche und Experten-/Experinnengespräch*. Vienna: ORF.

ORF (2010e) *Wert über Gebühr. Public Value Bericht 2009/2010*. Vienna: ORF. Retrieved August 30, 2010 from http://kundendienst.orf.at/unternehmen/news/public_value2010.pdf

ORF Enterprise (2008) Factsheet Radiotest 2. Halbjahr 2008. Retrieved August 24, 2010, from http://enterprise.orf.at/typo3conf/ext/up_downloadcluster/pi1/downloadfile.php?filename=FACTSHEET_radiotest-2hj08__2_.pdf

ORF Gesetz (2009) Retrieved August 30, 2010, from http://www.rtr.at/de/rf/ORF-G

ORF Mediaresearch (2010) Fernsehen: Technischer Empfang/Haushaltsausstattung. Retrieved August 26, 2010, from http://mediaresearch.orf.at/index2.htm?fernsehen/fernsehen_heimel.htm

ORF-Redakteurstatut (2002) Retrieved August 30, 2010, from http://kundendienst.orf.at/unternehmen/menschen/redakteurstatut.pdf

Österreichischer Presserat (2011) *Tätigkeitsbericht des Österreichischen Presserats für das Jahr 2010*. Retrieved June 15, 2011, from http://presserat.at/rte/upload/pdfs/taetigkeitsbericht_oepr_2010.pdf

ÖWA (2008) *Datenblatt Ergebnisse ÖWA Plus 2008-IV*. Retrieved August 30, 2010, from http://www.oewa.at/fileadmin/pdf/oewa_plus/oewa_plus_08q4.xls

Publizistikförderungsgesetz (2006) Retrieved August 30, 2010, from http://www.rtr.at/de/ppf/PublFG

Purkarthofer, J., Pfisterer, P., & Busch, B. (2008) *Nichtkommerzieller Rundfunk in Österreich und Europa. Studie 1: 10 Jahre Freies Radio in Österreich*. Vienna: RTR.

Die Presse (1974) Redaktionsstatut der Tageszeitung Die Presse. (unpublished document)

RTR (2009a) *Kommunikationsbericht 2008*. Vienna: RTR. Retrieved August 30, 2010, from http://www.rtr.at/de/komp/KBericht2008/K-Bericht_2008.pdf

RTR (2009b) *Der österreichische Breitbandmarkt aus Sicht der Nachfrager im Jahr 2009*. Vienna: RTR. Retrieved August 30, 2010, from http://www.rtr.at/de/komp/BerichtNASE2009/RTR_Studie_NASE_2009.pdf

RTR (2009c) *RTR Telekom Monitor 2/2009*. Vienna: RTR. Retrieved August 30, 2010, from http://www.rtr.at/de/komp/TKMonitor_2_2009/TM2-2009.pdf

RTR (2010) Förderentscheidungen 2010. Retrieved June 15, 2010, from http://www.rtr.at/de/foe/Entscheidungen2010

Rundfunkgebührengesetz (2003) Retrieved August 30, 2010, from http://www.rtr.at/de/rf/RGG#z2

Stark, B. (2009) Konstanten und Veränderungen der Mediennutzung in Österreich – empirische Befunde aus den Media-Analyse-Daten (1996-2007) *SWS Rundschau, 2009*(2), 130-153.

Stark, B., & Karmasin, M. (2009) Österreich – Land der Zeitungsleser auch im Zeitalter des Internets? Eine empirische Analyse zum Verhältnis von Print und Online. *Medien und Kommunikationswissenschaft, 2009*(3), 353-374.

Stark, B., & Kraus, D. (2008) Crossmediale Strategien überregionaler Tageszeitungen. Empirische Studie am Beispiel des Pressemarkts in Österreich. *Media Perspektiven, 2008*(6), 307-317.

Statistik Austria (2008) *Monatliche Verbrauchsausgaben der privaten Haushalte in kulturbezogenen Ausgabengruppen 2004/05*. Vienna: Statistik Austria. Retrieved August 30, 2010 from http://www.statistik.gv.at/web_de/static/monatliche_verbrauchsausgaben_der_privaten_haushalte_in_kulturbezogenen_au_021508.pdf

Statistik Austria (2009) *Verfügbares Einkommen der privaten Haushalte in Österreich 2008 nach Haushaltstyp*. Vienna: Statistik Austria. Retrieved August 30, 2010, from http://www.statistik.at/web_de/static/verfuegbares_einkommen_der_privaten_haushalte_in_oesterreich_2008_nach_hau_022295.pdf

Statistik Austria (2010) *Wichtigste wirtschaftliche Eckdaten im EU-Vergleich*. Retrieved August 30, 2010, from http://www.statistik.at/web_de/static/wichtige_wirtschaftliche_eckdaten_im_eu-vergleich_021269.pdf

Statistik Austria/Arbeitsgemeinschaft Media-Analysen (2009) Hörfunkveranstalter und Tagesreichweiten des Radios in Österreich 2008. Retrieved August 26, 2010, from http://www.volkszaehlung.at/web_de/statistiken/bildung_und_kultur/kultur/hoerfunk_und_fernsehen/021236.html

Steinmaurer, T. (2009) Das Mediensystem Österreichs. In *Hans-Bredow-Institut (ed.): Internationales Handbuch Medien*. Baden-Baden: Nomos, 504-517.

Trappel, J. (2007) The Austrian Media Landscape. In Terzis, Georgios (ed.) *European Media Governance: National and Regional Dimensions*. Bristol: Intellect Books, 63-72.

VÖZ/Statistik Austria. (2009) Tageszeitungen und Wochenzeitungen 1960 bis 2008 nach Bundesländern. Retrieved August 26, 2010, from http://www.statistik.at/web_de/statistiken/bildung_und_kultur/kultur/buecher_und_presse/021212.html

Washietl, E. (2009) Journalisten ins Gewerbe ausgelagert. *Der Österreichische Journalist*, (04/05), 34-35.

Weber, I. (2010, July 30) Presserat mit Achillesferse. *Wiener Zeitung*. Retrieved August 30, 2020, from http://www.wienerzeitung.at/app_support/print.aspx?TabID=3956&Alias=wzo&cob=509759&mID=12051&ModId=12051

Weber, S. (2006) *So arbeiten Österreichs Journalisten für Zeitungen und Zeitschriften* (Journalistik-Heft Nr.18/2006) Hefte des Kuratoriums für Journalistenausbildung. Salzburg: Kuratorium für Journalistenausbildung. Retrieved August 30, 2010, from http://www.kfj.at/pdf/So_arbeiten_Oesterreichs_Journalisten.pdf

Woelke, J. (2007) Fernsehen in Österreich. Befunde einer TV-Programmanalyse von ORF 1, ORF 2 und ATV. In Steininger, Christian/Woelke, Jens (eds) *Fernsehen in Österreich 2007*. Konstanz: UVK, 49-96.

Woelke, J. (2008) Fernsehen in Österreich. Basisdaten und Programmprofile der Fernsehvollprogramme ORF 1, ORF 2 und ATV. In Steininger, Christian/Woelke, Jens (eds) *Fernsehen in Österreich 2008*. Konstanz: UVK, 13-63.

Woelke, J. (2010) *TV-Programmanalyse. Fernsehvollprogramme in Österreich 2009*. Vienna: RTR. Retrieved November 13, 2010, from http://www.rtr.at/de/komp/Publikationen/Band2-2010.pdf

World Association of Newspapers (2009) *World Press Trends* (20. ed.) London: ZenithOptimedia.

Chapter 5

FINLAND

High Professional Ethos in a Small, Concentrated Media Market

Kari Karppinen, Hannu Nieminen & Anna-Laura Markkanen[1]

Finland is a small country (population 5.4 million), characterized by political and socio-economic structures typical to the Nordic welfare model. The small size of the media market together with a distinct language area contribute to a relatively concentrated media system with well-integrated professional norms and high reach of the main national news media. The Finnish media system is usually considered to represent the "democratic corporatist model" in terms of Hallin and Mancini's (2004) categorization. Characteristics of the model include strong state intervention, reconciled with well-developed media autonomy and professionalization.

In Finland, the media have historically been seen to fulfill an important societal function and until recently the structure of the media market has remained rather stable, reflecting a relative balance of interests. This is supported by governmental policy driven by consensus, rather than major political and economic conflicts (see Nieminen 2010). Recent media policies, however, have been influenced by the general trends of de-regulation and marketization, including the rise of commercial broadcasting, the relative decline of the role of public service broadcasting, and cuts in press subsidies and other forms of state intervention (see Herkman 2009; Nieminen 2010). There are also signs of a shift from consensual to a more antagonistic model, which is reflected, for instance, in the commercial media companies' attacks on public service broadcasting.

The Finnish media system is still characterized by a strong literary culture, and the number of newspapers and readership figures, although declining, are still among the highest worldwide. All print media represent two-thirds of the total media revenue in Finland, while the share of newspapers alone constitutes around one-third (Finnish Mass Media 2010, p. 38). Newspapers alone account for almost half of all media advertising, which is well above the average in the EU countries (ibid., p. 21).

Despite the high number of newspapers and magazines published in Finland, the market is relatively concentrated, with three big companies or chains controlling almost two-thirds (63 %) of the circulation of daily newspapers. Most regional and local markets are dominated by one leading newspaper with little direct competition.

Development of the electronic media also reflects the shift from mutual cohabitation to a more market-driven environment. New commercial radio and television channels have been gradually introduced since the mid-1980s, and even though the status of public service broadcasting remains strong, it no longer dominates the broadcasting market[2]. After the digital switchover in 2007, both free and pay-TV channels have proliferated, but the market has remained fairly concentrated, with the channels owned by *YLE, MTV3,* and *Nelonen* together controlling around 90 % of all viewing. There are very few regional or local television channels in Finland, and they are of little significance. In radio, the public service channels account for 52 % of total radio listening, while all private stations together account for 48 %. National chains own many of the local commercial channels (Finnish Mass Media 2010).

The Internet has challenged the stable position of media institutions in recent years. Nearly 80 percent of the population uses the Internet regularly (Eurostat 2010), and it is increasingly important also as a source of news, especially for younger generations. Since the 1990s, the promotion of the information society has also had a central position in Finnish governmental policies.

The journalistic culture in Finland is characterized by a strong professional ethos and an established self-regulatory system, organized around the *Council for Mass Media*, which represents all main interest groups and oversees the commonly agreed upon ethical codes. In comparison to many other countries, the news media still enjoy a relatively high public esteem and trust (Karppinen et al. 2010). According to recent studies, media professionals are today mostly well educated and share a rather uniform commitment to common professional norms (Jyrkiäinen 2008). The overwhelming majority of journalists are also members of the *Finnish Union of Journalists*.

News media sample

In addition to general observations, six organizations, representing different types of media, were selected for closer analysis and interviews. The sample media include one national, one regional, one local and one tabloid newspaper, as well as the leading public and private broadcasting companies. The online services of the sample media were included in the analysis when applicable. In addition, we have interviewed the president of the Union of Journalists, the Director of editorial issues of the Finnish Newspapers Association, and consulted some independent academic experts.[3]

Table 1.   The news media sample

	Media type	Ownership	Interviewee
Helsingin Sanomat	Daily newspaper	Sanoma Group	Former long-term editor-in-chief
Turun Sanomat	Daily regional newspaper	TS Group	Editor-in-chief
Iltalehti	Tabloid (5 times a week)	Alma Media	Editor-in-chief
Borgåbladet	Local newspaper (Swedish language)	Konstsamfundet (foundation)	Editor-in-chief
YLE	PSB Company	PSB	Director of News
MTV3	Commercial broadcasting	Bonnier	Editor-in-chief (news)
Union of Journalists			President
Finnish Newspapers Association			Director, editorial issues and communication

Indicators

Freedom / Information (F)

(F1)   Geographic distribution of news media availability   3 POINTS

The mainstream news media are accessible throughout the country and there are no major regional divides.

Newspapers, broadcasting and online services are widely available nationwide. The reach of newspapers, in particular, is internationally high. It is estimated that some 90 % of all newspapers sales are based on subscriptions and home delivery. Early morning delivery is available to around 90 % percent of the households (Finnish Newspapers Association 2010). In 2008, a total of 201 newspapers were published in Finland, 53 of those being dailies.

All daily newspapers had an online edition in 2008, while around 75 % of all other newspapers (i.e., mainly local and regional papers) were present online (Finnish Mass Media 2010, p. 175). Thus far, the online editions have had most of their content available for free. Daily free papers are mainly distributed in the larger cities.

The switchover to digital broadcasting initially raised some concerns about equal availability of the services in all areas of the country. In 2008, the technical reach of the digital television network was already at 99.96 % of the population. The digitalization has also increased the supply of free television channels in terrestrial households to 11 channels, compared to just four basic channels carried in the old analogue terrestrial networks. The penetration of digital television equipment in 2008 was 90 %. Around one half (48 %) of the households had cable television and only 6 % had satellite television. One-quarter of all households subscribed to pay channels, a significant growth from some 5 % in the early 2000s (Finnish Mass Media 2010, p. 50-56).

In 2008, there were 54 private radio channels in Finland, one of which had nation-wide coverage and nine of which were near-national. Major cities typically have ten or more local commercial channels available, whereas national and regional public radio channels are available all over the country, in line with the legal obligation of the YLE to provide services for all citizens on equal terms. On average, depending on the area of residence, there are around 15-20 radio channels available to the public in a given location (Kemppainen 2007).

Radio and television contents are also increasingly available online. The most extensive and wide-ranging online television and radio service, *YLE Areena*, makes public service radio and television programs produced by *YLE* available online. The main commercial broadcasters have their own respective online services, which include both free and premium content.

Until recently, broadband connections have not been easily available in some of the more remote areas of the country, but since 2010, the provision of broadband access has been included in the universal service obligations for telecom operators. The penetration of Internet access in 2008 was around 76 % (Finnish Mass Media 2010, p. 50). The operators defined as universal service providers (26 operators) must provide every residence and business with access to a reasonably priced and high-quality connection (at least 1 Mbit/s). The aim of the broadband project is also to provide all households with the permanent fibre-optic or cable network (100 Mbit/s) by the end of 2015, in part with public support (Ministry of Transport and Communications 2010).

(F2) Patterns of news media use (consumption of news) 2 POINTS

The mainstream news media reach a very high proportion of the population in Finland.

According to international comparative studies, the Finnish public seems to be rea-sonably well informed. For instance, one study examining the connections between media systems and citizens' awareness of public affairs cites Finland as an example of a media system characterized by a high level of both news consumption and public knowledge of current affairs (Curran et al. 2009).

Table 2.   The daily reach of different media in 2008

	All	Male	Female	10-24	25-44	45-59	60-
Newspapers	78 %	77 %	78 %	56 %	76 %	86 %	88 %
Television	90 %	91 %	90 %	87 %	88 %	93 %	93 %
Radio	74 %	75 %	72 %	65 %	75 %	78 %	75 %
Internet	60 %	63 %	57 %	76 %	79 %	61 %	25 %

Source: Finnish Mass Media 2010, p. 51.

The main evening news broadcasts of both public service broadcaster *YLE* and its main commercial competitor *MTV3* rank among the most watched programs. At most, the main news broadcasts reach over one million viewers and over a 40 % share of total viewing during the program (Finnpanel 2010a). All leading television channels provide a steady feed of news and current affairs broadcasts during prime-time, which also seems to promote a high level of "inadvertent" news exposure (see Curran et al. 2009, p. 22). In radio, *YLE Radio Suomi,* which broadcasts hourly news bulletins, is the most popular channel with a 38 % national listening share (Finnish Mass Media 2010, p. 88).

High newspaper readership remains one of the main characteristics of the Finnish media system. The leading newspaper *Helsingin Sanomat* has a circulation of 400,000 with around 950,000 daily readers. On average, Finnish people read eight different periodicals and three different newspapers (Levikintarkastus 2009). A sense of concern remains within the industry regarding young readers, among whom newspaper reading is continuing to fall. Of people over 45 years of age, more than 80 percent read newspapers daily, and the average reading time is 35 minutes per day. Of people under 24, only some 56 percent read newspapers daily and their average reading time is less than 15 minutes (Antikainen et al. 2010).

With up to 2 million weekly visitors, the sites of tabloid newspapers and the commercial broadcaster *MTV3* are the most popular websites in Finland, ahead of *Helsingin Sanomat* and *YLE* (TNS Metrix 2010). The Internet in general is increasingly important as a source of information and news, especially among young people: in a survey conducted in 2007, the Internet was the most important source of daily news for 37 % of the people under 25, while television and newspapers clearly remain the dominant news media for older people (Karppinen et al. 2010).

Table 3.   Top 12 Finnish news websites

	Visitors/week	Rank among all websites
IItalehti	1 937 156	1
Ilta-Sanomat	1 823 956	2
MTV3	1 722 725	3
YLE	1 245 148	6
Helsingin Sanomat	1 236 527	7
Kauppalehti	655 093	11
Taloussanomat	643 954	13
Sub.fi	571 855	15
Aamulehti	262 947	23
Kaksplus	245 515	25
Nelonen.fi	206 301	26
Uusi Suomi	204 722	27

Source: Finnish Mass Media 2010, 218.

(F3)   Diversity of news sources   2 POINTS

The diversity of sources is seen to have increased with the Internet, but the influence of PR material and recycling of other media's material are identified as threats in some sectors.

The Finnish News Agency (STT) is a national news provider jointly owned by 41 media companies. With the notable exception of the public broadcaster *YLE*, which quit subscribing to the services of *STT* in 2006 and chose to invest more in its own news service, almost all leading news media subscribe to its services. In addition to *YLE* and *STT*, there is a smaller news service called *UP News Service*, which is historically associated with the *Social Democratic Party* and now provides news for about a dozen newspapers, and a financial news provider *Startel*, owned by the *Sanoma Group*. The leading news media also follow the main international news agencies.

The position of the national news agency in Finland is fairly dominant in defining the news agenda and providing content especially for smaller regional media, which rely heavily on wire services. In our interviews, the editors-in-chief of the leading national news media, which have more resources for their own news gathering, tended to emphasize the role of *STT* as a provider of background information or a baseline for their own news gathering.

It was suggested in the interviews that the influence of the national news agency has slightly diminished recently. Some of the respondents believed that the decision of *YLE* to quit using *STT* services has improved the overall diversity of sources in the Finnish media. At the same time, some representatives of commercial news media were hostile to the decision and saw it as compromising the viability of the commercial news media. Many respondents suggested that their own organizations had sought to invest more in their own news gathering instead of news agency material.

The Internet is widely seen to diversify sources, although it was suggested that the recycling of news items produced by other media has become more common in the Finnish media, as issues, subjects and points of view increasingly circulate from one outlet to another. The increasing influence of the PR material was also acknowledged by the respondents as a potential problem. According to a recent survey among Finnish journalists, 62 percent of journalists agreed that the use of PR material is increasing in the Finnish media because of decreasing resources available for in-house news gathering (Jyrkiäinen 2008, 57).

The leading national news media typically have their own network of national and foreign correspondents and a network of stringers and other freelancers. In 2010, the public service broadcasting company *YLE*, for instance, has a network of some 25 domestic offices, nine foreign news correspondents, and some 20 other freelance contributors abroad. The number of foreign correspondents is comparable to other leading national news media (*HS, MTV3*). Some of these resources are shared between multiple media organizations. The number of correspondents in all media examined has remained more or less stable in recent years. The resources available for foreign news were generally seen as adequate, although it was suggested that foreign news and EU affairs are areas where the dominance of news agency material is most evident and the diversity of sources was seen as the biggest problem.

There is a clear trend towards closer editorial cooperation and syndication within newspaper chains and even between independent newspapers. While this can be seen as decreasing the diversity of news sources, the newspapers involved are mostly regional papers with little overlap in their circulation (Finnish Mass Media 2009, p. 22). Some of the respondents thus denied the notion that the trend would necessarily diminish the diversity of sources, because co-operation can also mean greater diversity in the content of an individual regional newspaper.

A number of editors-in-chief noted that the principle of using multiple sources is mainly followed in their news gathering. Some respondents acknowledged that Finnish journalism generally tends to rely too much on elite sources, such as government officials. A number of interviewees also called for a more critical attitude toward the Finnish economic elite and big corporations. As expected, none of the editors-in-chief considered the selection (or omission) of sources on political grounds to be a problem.

(F4) Internal rules for practice of newsroom democracy   2 POINTS

Individual journalists seem to enjoy a high level of autonomy in daily journalistic decisions, but formal procedures to ensure internal democracy are few.

Assessments of the extent of internal democracy practiced in the newsrooms were somewhat ambivalent. It was argued that individual journalistic autonomy is strongly entrenched in the Finnish journalistic culture. However, the independence and autonomy of individual journalists is generally guaranteed by journalistic culture rather than organizational structures or formal procedures.

The editors-in-chief and experts emphasized the individual autonomy of journalists in choosing and framing news topics. The leading editors generally co-ordinate the work of the newsroom, but they rarely interfere with the individual journalists' decisions concerning how news items are portrayed and framed. While some considered the Finnish journalistic culture markedly individualistic, others emphasized the significance of internal deliberation and discussions within the newsroom.

On the other hand, there are few formal procedures to ensure internal democracy within the newsrooms. While values such as impartiality and autonomy are on a general level documented in codes-of-ethics and editorial guidelines, in practice they are ensured more effectively through journalistic culture and professional norms, rather than written guidelines.

A newsroom council does not have a formal status in any of the selected media outlets, and editors-in-chief and other leading positions are normally appointed by the management without any requirement to incorporate journalists. The newsroom may be consulted informally, and there are some cases in which staff objections have influenced the decisions of management. Aside from rules on the level of individual organizations, the majority of journalists are members of the *Union of Journalists*, whose task is to defend and supervise its members' interests through collective bargaining.

(F5) Company rules against *internal* influence on newsroom / editorial staff 2 POINTS

The autonomy and independence of the newsroom is generally regarded as a central value in the Finnish journalistic culture.

The ethical guidelines for journalists, published by the *Council for Mass Media in Finland* (2005), state that: "Decisions concerning the content of communication must be made in accordance with journalistic principles. The power to make such decisions may not, under any circumstances, be surrendered to any party outside the editorial office." All leading news media are committed to these guidelines, and according to the interviews with the *Union of Journalists* as well as editors-in-chief, the principle of journalistic autonomy enjoys high esteem not only among journalists, but even among the publishers and owners of media companies.

Some problems and causes for concern did surface, however. In some cases, the posts of the editor-in-chief and publisher have recently been combined, which has raised some public concerns about the blurring of journalistic and financial decisions. The new editor-in-chief of *Helsingin Sanomat* also acts as the publisher of the paper. Similar arrangements apply for the tabloid *Iltalehti* and the local newspaper *Borgåbladet*. The dual roles were seen as potentially problematic, for instance, when making financial decisions that affect the work of the newsroom. However, in all cases, the editors-in-chief assured that the management and owners never interfere with individual news items or editorial decisions.

The practical organization of the separation of the newsroom from the ownership largely depends on the type of media organization in question. In some cases, such as the commercial broadcaster *MTV3*, the separation is explicitly mentioned in the company values or other formal documents. In many cases, however, there are no formal rules on the separation of the newsroom from the management, outside of the general professional code-of-ethics.

Most editors-in-chief acknowledged that they have regular discussions with the management, but that both sides have equal respect for the principle of journalistic autonomy. There are still known cases within the profession where the owners have exerted at least indirect influence on the editorial line of a newspaper in individual cases. While influence from the ownership is considered an exception in the Finnish media, it cannot be ruled out.

A study conducted on the corporate correlation between Finnish television and tabloid papers also found some indirect corporate influence. The tabloid newspaper owned by the Sanoma Group produced more positive publicity to its own television channel, while the tabloid paper owned by Alma Media slightly privileged MTV3 in these sections of its tabloid paper (Herkman 2005). The corporate correlation, however, applied only to the entertainment sections of the papers, and not the core journalistic sections.

There is generally no formal representation of journalists in the board of media companies. Of the sample media corporations, none had journalists on the board of the company. Advertising departments are, as a rule, strictly separated from the newsroom and do not interfere with the journalistic work. However, in the case of the local newspaper examined, the small number of personnel made it evident that there is contact and even co-operation between the newsroom and the advertising department.

In the case of public service media, the independence from the state owner is a permanently contested question in terms of both organizational structures and individual news issues. The independence from the government and political parties is emphasized on all levels of the legal definitions, company values, and internal editorial guidelines of *YLE*. In practice, *YLE* continues to enjoy a high level of political independence in its editorial decisions, and there is no evidence of any direct influence by the government.

(F6) Company rules against *external* influence on newsroom / editorial staff   2 POINTS

Direct influence by external parties on newsroom decisions is not seen as a major problem.

All editors-in-chief interviewed insisted that there is no interference by individual advertisers or any other external parties. Many of the editors-in-chief acknowledged that they are regularly contacted by external lobbyists, but that any attempts to influence journalistic decisions are categorically rejected. In line with the previous indicator, most interviewees considered the level of journalistic autonomy and integrity to be fairly high. Strong professionalism was also seen as the most effective safeguard against external influence.

The leading news media all have multiple income streams and a multitude of advertisers, none of which are in a dominant position. Many editors-in-chief also maintained that a strong economic position in part ensures that no single external party can exert influence. It was suggested by some respondents, however, that the degree of external influence may be higher on the local level and in smaller media organizations, which rely more heavily on few major local advertisers. The editor-in-chief of the local newspaper examined acknowledged that tensions occasionally emerge between the editors and local advertisers or authorities, but it was denied that external parties would succeed in directly influencing editorial decisions.

Sponsoring agreements and various forms of product placement have recently become more common in commercial television. Their influence on the contents of current affairs or news programming was strongly denied, although it may be problematic to strictly define current affairs. In case of newspapers, the editors-in-chief insisted that even those sections that contain product reviews are produced entirely on journalistic criteria.

As noted above, the independence of the public service company from any external parties is emphasized on all levels of the public service remit and internal company values (see indicator F5). The government sets the level of the license fee, in line with the criteria set for fulfilling the public service mandate. Thus far, decisions on the level of funding have been made on a long-term basis, but the proposed transition to direct budget funding has raised some concerns that the level of funding will become more susceptible to changes from one year to another.

(F7) Procedures on news selection and news processing 2 POINTS

Stylebooks that include guidelines on the processing of news items are becoming more common, but their significance is still limited.

According to a recent survey among journalists, formal rules and procedures for processing news items have recently become more common in Finnish journalism. Often this development is associated negatively with "industrialized" and standardized forms of news production (Jyrkiäinen 2008, p. 9). Concurrently, it has also been suggested that there has been a gradual shift from a traditional individualistic journalistic culture towards more emphasis on co-operative news processing in Finnish newsrooms.

Defined stages for a news item before it is published are more common in periodicals, whereas daily news and online news, in particular, are usually published as quickly as possible with minimal processing.

Most of the media organizations have some type of stylebook, and these vary from simple instructions on layout and format to comprehensive guidelines that include values, ethical guidelines, and internal practices for news selection. In most cases, the guidelines are only for internal use, although the idea of making such documents publicly available has also gained some support. *The Finnish News Agency*, for instance, has a comprehensive stylebook freely available on its website. The company values and editorial guidelines that include both the ethical guidelines and the practical instructions of public broadcasting company *YLE* are also publicly available. *Turun Sanomat, Iltalehti* and *MTV3* have comprehensive internal stylebooks. Those media that currently do not have a unified stylebook, including *Helsingin Sanomat*, reported that they were currently preparing such documents. Most editors-in-chief considered a stylebook to be necessary, but also noted that questions of news values and selection ultimately hinge on the journalistic culture and professional skills of each journalist.

In-house training for new journalists on the job varies. In newspapers, training typically consists of one-day training, which focuses on practical matters and less on journalistic principles or news criteria, whereas the electronic media houses have training programs of up to one week. Regular in-depth discussions on the past and forthcoming decisions on news values were highly valued by all respondents, but according to a recent survey of journalists, the general sentiment among Finnish journalists still seems to be that there is a need for more deliberation. According to the survey, most journalists also receive surprisingly little feedback from their superiors and colleagues. More feedback and meetings to discuss past decisions and published stories also ranked as the main method to improve journalists' workplaces (Jyrkiäinen 2008, p. 33, 35).

Equality / Interest mediation (E)

(E1) Media ownership concentration national level   2 POINTS

The national media market is relatively concentrated with a handful of companies dividing the market in each sector.

Finland does not have any specific regulation of media ownership concentration, aside from general competition rules. The dominant position of the biggest media company, *Sanoma Group*, in particular, is a distinctive feature of the Finnish media market. The net revenue of the Sanoma corporation in 2008 was 3,030 million, while the total market volume of all mass media in Finland was 4,424 million. Much of the *Sanoma Group's* revenue, however, comes from its operations abroad. In Finland, the *Sanoma Group* controls around one-third of both total newspaper circulation and magazine circulation. The group also owns the broadcasting company *Nelonen Media,* whose channels have around 15 % of the audience share, and the biggest publishing house in Finland (45 % market share). Its other activities include movie theaters, online services, press distribution, and learning solutions.

The position of *Helsingin Sanomat* as the only (de facto) national, quality newspaper is in practice dominant, with no real rivals. As a result of takeovers and mergers, the market share of the biggest newspaper houses has steadily grown since the 1990s (Finnish Mass Media 2010, p. 169). The consolidation of newspaper ownership into chains is also expected to continue at both national and Nordic levels. The most intense competition currently takes place between the two evening tabloids *Ilta-Sanomat* and *Iltalehti.*

The market shares of the top three companies (CR3) have been calculated on the basis of circulation (newspapers) or share of total viewing/listening (television and radio). As indicated in Table 4, the market share of the top three companies is relatively high in almost all sectors of the media, indicating a relatively concentrated market.

Table 4.   Market share of top three companies in different media

	Top three companies	Market share
Television	Yle, MTV3, Nelonen	90 %
Newspapers	Sanoma, Alma Media, Keskisuomalainen	50 %
Radio	Yle, Radio Nova, SBS-Iskelmä	71 %

Source: Finnish Mass Media 2009, The Finnish Audit Bureau of Circulations.

Table 5.   Market share of top three outlets

	Top three channels/papers	Market share
Television	TV1, MTV3, TV2	64 %
Newspapers	Helsingin Sanomat, Aamulehti, Turun Sanomat	41 %
Radio	Radio Suomi, Radio Nova, Yle1	57 %

Source: Finnish Mass Media 2009, The Finnish Audit Bureau of Circulations.

The data on media ownership are transparent for the most part. Most of the large media companies are publicly traded. There is also a website, *Medialinnakkeet*[4], that provides detailed information on changes in ownership, economy and employment issues in the media sector. Major changes in ownership are also reported in the media.

(E2)   Media ownership concentration regional (local) level   1 POINT

Apart from newspapers, the leading news media in Finland are nationally oriented. There are no significant regional or local television channels.

Regionally, there are 28 regional newspapers with practically no competition in their own market areas. Most of the local newspapers, around 150 altogether, also have a relatively stable position in their areas with no major rivals. Many of the regional newspapers also are owned by one of the national chains. Despite the high number of newspapers published per capita, the market for regional media is therefore relatively concentrated.

The only competition these regional newspapers face is against the nationwide newspaper *Helsingin Sanomat* and other national news outlets. Statistics on the circulation of newspapers by regions are not currently available, but based on the total circulation of newspapers published within a given region some CR3 calculations can be made.

Table 6.   Newspaper concentration in some regional marketplaces

Region	Top three newspapers	Regional market share
Finland Proper	Turun Sanomat, Salon Seudun Sanomat, Auranmaan viikkolehti	70 %
Kainuu	Kainuun Sanomat, Ylä-Kainuu, Kuhmolainen	81 %
Uusimaa	Helsingin Sanomat, Ilta-Sanomat, Iltalehti	65 %

Source: The Finnish Audit Bureau of Circulations, Finnish Newspapers Association.

Television channels in Finland are almost exclusively national, so regional concentration does not apply. *YLE* has regional news broadcasts for eight areas on their national channels *TV2*, and news in Sámi on *FST5* [5]. Commercially operated regional or local television channels are few, small-scale, and limited to some cities only (e.g., cable-operated *Turku TV*; local Swedish-language *När-TV* in rural Närpes region).

In radio, *YLE* has 20 Finnish-language, five Swedish-language, and one Sámi-language regional channels with designated windows on the frequencies of *YLE Radio Suomi* and *YLE Radio Vega*. In addition to public service channels, there is one national, nine near-national, and 44 local or regional commercial radio channels (Finnish Mass Media 2010, p. 93). In larger markets, such as the Helsinki region, there is competition between ten or more local commercial radio channels, but more remote areas are served only by *YLE* and a few mainstream commercial channels. A handful of non-profit, public access radio channels (*Lähiradio, Radio Robin Hood*) operate in some cities with limited resources.

The field of local radio stations has also seen considerable centralization in recent years. The ownership of regional and local radio has consolidated into national networks or chains, such as the German *SBS Broadcasting*, which has diminished the proportion of genuinely local programming. The number of Internet radio channels has proliferated, but they do not yet hold a major share of total listening. Regional audience shares are currently available only for the Helsinki region, which also has the broadest supply of radio channels. The audience share of the top three radio stations in the Helsinki region is 47 %, somewhat below the national market share (57 %) of the top three radio channels (Finnpanel 2010b).

(E3)   Diversity of formats   3 POINTS

Formats of news presentation have proliferated especially online, and nearly all major news formats are widely available in Finland.

All leading news media provide a variety of news formats from traditional newspapers and broadcast news to various online and mobile news services. In addition to independent newspapers, there are party affiliated newspapers (although with diminished influence) and financial news outlets. All leading newspapers have online editions and most also offer mobile news services. With online versions, even newspapers now increasingly offer video content on the Internet. Online news services also typically include RSS-feeds, blogs, surveys and other interactive content. Many of the main news media also offer news feeds in various social media platforms.

There are no Finnish 24-hour news channels[6]. Public and main private broadcasters, however, broadcast news bulletins on their main channels throughout the day. Both *YLE* and *MTV3* have around a dozen daily news bulletins, a morning news show and financial news. Both also have a teletext service, comprehensive online news services and mobile news, which are continuously updated. Despite the emergence of online news, the broadcast teletext pages of *YLE* in particular remain very popular, with over 2 million regular viewers.

In addition, *YLE* offers a variety of different types of documentary and current affairs programs on radio and television. All of the current affairs programming on both radio and television are also available online. In addition to the traditional news providers, independent news aggregators have gained popularity recently. The most popular Finnish news aggregator *Ampparit.com* is one of the most frequently visited websites not owned by any of the large media corporations.

(E4)   Minority / Alternative media   2 POINTS

The supply of media in Swedish and Sámi languages is extensive in relation to the size of the population in Finland, but other minority and alternative media are limited.

Compared to most other European countries, Finland remains ethnically homogenous. Although immigration to Finland has increased, the proportion of the foreign-born population (2.5 %) is much below the EU average (Eurostat 2009). In addition to the official languages Finnish (91 %) and Swedish (5 %), the constitution specifically mentions Sámi, Romani and users of Finnish sign language (alongside a vague reference to "other groups") as minorities with a right to "maintain and develop their own language and culture".

With its own established media institutions, it can be stated that the Swedish-language media in Finland constitutes an institutionally complete media system (Moring & Husband 2007). This includes 11 daily regional and local newspapers, one nationwide public service television channel (*FST5*), two public service radio channels (*Radio Vega, X3M*), and a number of periodicals.[7]

The public broadcaster *YLE* is obliged to provide services also in Sámi, Romani and sign language, and when applicable, in other languages used in Finland. The supply of products in the Sámi language include television news broadcasts (*Oddasat*), a regional radio channel (*YLE Sámi Radio*) and an online news portal. *YLE* also has a 24-hour digital radio station *(YLE Mondo),* which broadcasts news in eight different languages. There are also online news portals in English and Russian.

The Ministry of Education allocates some public subsidies to minority and alternative media. Some 500,000 euro is annually allocated to minority language newspapers and magazines. These include Swedish-language newspapers and some periodical publications in Sámi and Romani languages. In Russian, there is a monthly paper (*Spektr*) and a private radio channel *(Radio Sputnik)* that is available in Southern Finland. In addition, there is an English-language weekly newspaper, *Helsinki Times,* and a free monthly magazine, *SixDegrees*, aimed at the immigrant population.

Overall, while media services for recognized "old minorities" in Finland are relatively extensive, few media services are available for immigrants in Finland. The representation of ethnic minorities also remains marginal in the workforce of mainstream media houses. Some new initiatives have been recently launched by immigrant groups to fill the gap (see UJF 2010). *Panorama Television* and *Monivisio* provide news and current affairs programs to immigrants in various languages online and in public access radio with EU and NGO funding.

The Ministry of Education also allocates subsidies to cultural and opinion journals, which "maintain public discussion about culture, science, art or religious life". In 2010, some 1 million euro was allocated to 133 journals (Ministry of Education and Culture 2010). Non-profit actors have a presence in print media and magazines, but in television and radio alternative media outlets are few and they receive little public support. Some public access and community radio stations exist locally (see above), but in television, the increasingly competitive marketplace has left little room for experimental initiatives. Alternative media outlets of civil society organizations and other non-profit actors are thus increasingly confined to the Internet.

(E5)   Affordable public and private news media   3 POINTS

The prices of media services in relation to household income are affordable.

Finland is a comparatively rich country characterized by a general high cost of living. In relation to the average household income (€24,696 per income recipient in 2008), the prices of mass media are generally not exceptionally high. On average, Finnish households spent €1,241 (4.1 % of total consumption expenditure) on mass media (excluding telecommunications) in 2006. The share of mass media of all consumption has slightly declined since 1995 (Finnish Mass Media 2010, p. 51).

The average price for an annual subscription to a daily newspaper is €225, while the annual subscription to the largest newspaper *Helsingin Sanomat* is currently €269.[8] Newspapers also offer various discounts for students, weekend-only subscriptions and combinations of print and online editions. Most newspapers continue to offer at least parts of their content online for free. Free newspapers, distributed in public transportation, are available in larger cities.

The annual television license fee was €231 in 2010. Broadband connection fees have remained more or less stable during the past few years. According to the regulatory authority, the average monthly price for a 1 Mbit/s connection in 2010 was €31 (Ficora 2010), but the prices appear to be cheaper in more densely populated areas, where leading telecom operators currently provide a 8-10 Mbit/s connection for around 25-30 euro. Basic social security (income support) in Finland covers basic media use (telephone, newspaper subscription and TV license), but not broadband connection.

(E6)   Content monitoring instruments   1 POINTS

There are some attempts to develop more systematic instruments for media content monitoring, but they have yet to become fully institutionalized or widely publicized.

The Journalism Research and Development Centre of the University of Tampere has sought to develop an observation system, *Annual Monitoring of News Media (2006 -2012)*, to survey news media output and reveal ongoing trends in the Finnish news media (Suikkanen & Syrjälä 2010). The objects of the analysis include subject matters, people featured by age and gender, the geographical perspective of items, and material on violence and sexuality. In addition, various research projects have developed tools for monitoring reporting on individual issues, such as ethnicity and racism in the media.

   The Ministry of Transport and Communications publishes an annual report on Finnish television programming (Lehtinen 2010). Instead of issue monitoring, however, the report focuses on quantitative analysis of the television output and diversity, based on different program types. A similar type of overview has also been commissioned to produce a description of the programming supply of the license-dependent radio channels in Finland (Ala-Fossi & Haara 2010).

   Outside these systematic monitoring instruments, discussions on the content of journalism take place in academic studies and professional journals, but for the most part these do not constitute continuous monitoring instruments. A number of commercial media monitoring services also keep track of reporting on specific issues for subscribing clients, but their results are not publicly available. Overall, the status of regular content monitoring in Finland seems to be improving, but existing instruments have yet to become fully institutionalized or well-known.

(E7)   Code of ethics at the national level (structure)   3 POINTS

All leading news media have committed to the common code of ethics.

The *Council for Mass Media* is a self-regulating committee established in 1968 by the publishers' and journalists' unions. Its task is to interpret good professional practice and defend freedom of speech and publication. According to the interviews, the status of the guidelines is fairly strong and they are well known within the profession.

   The Council is exclusively a self-governing body, although about one third of its funding comes from public funds. Anyone is free to file a complaint about a breach of good professional practice in the media. If the Council establishes a violation, it issues a notice that all organizations that have signed the charter of the Council are obliged to publish without delay. Practically all Finnish news media have signed the

Charter. The Council can also issue general policy statements. In 2008, the Council received 222 complaints, of which 95 were investigated and 24 led to a notice of violation. All the resolutions are also available on the website of the Council. Occasionally the resolutions have also incited public debate on media ethics.

Despite periodic criticism directed at the effectiveness of the existing self-regulatory practices, the system is strongly established and remains known among journalists. The system has occasionally been criticized for being too reactive and rigid, failing to initiate enough debate on truly fundamental issues, and for leaving out new online actors that compete with traditional professional journalism. In response, the Council has expressed its wish to also initiate debate on important ethical issues in addition to merely reacting to complaints.

In addition to the *Council for Mass Media*, the *Union of Journalists in Finland* also states that it has a special responsibility to defend journalism and its ethical rules. Alongside its 18 member associations, the Union organizes various courses and other activities to disseminate good journalistic practices. It also publishes the biweekly professional journal *Journalisti*, which sustains debate on journalistic practices and ethics. The Guidelines for Journalists include provisions regarding the accountability of the media to civil society, stating that: "A journalist is primarily responsible to the readers, listeners and viewers. They have the right to know what is happening in society" (Council for Mass Media 2005).

(E8)   Level of self-regulation (performance)   2 POINTS

Self-regulation is based on the ethical guidelines whose application varies from media to media.

According to the interviews, the ethical guidelines generally enjoy relatively high esteem and are well known, although some concern was expressed about the younger generation of journalists. Problems of increasing workload and time pressure are typically identified as threats that may compromise ethical standards. In a survey of Finnish journalists, over half of Finnish journalists believed that the ethical standards and autonomy of journalists would decrease in the future (Jyrkiäinen 2008, p. 50).

The right to reply and corrections are guaranteed on the level of both the code of ethics and media law. As noted above, all media organizations are also committed to publishing the notices of the *Council for Mass Media*. Most news media also have their own internal guidelines in one form or another. Mostly, these guidelines are used to complement the *Guidelines of Journalists* and to give more detailed instructions on the practices of the media organization in question.

Most media organizations also have more general mission statements, which almost invariably refer to democratic values, independence, balance, pluralism, and so forth.

Some individual media organizations in Finland have experimented with the use of an independent Ombudsman, but the practice has not become widespread and none of the editors-in-chief interviewed considered it necessary. One respondent claimed that there is no need for an independent Ombudsman to deal with complaints, in part because of the effective national system, but also because editors-in-chief themselves are easily accessible to the public in Finland.

Most media in the sample also claimed to exercise some form of organized process of self-criticism. Resolutions of the *Council for Mass Media* are typically discussed together with the journalists involved and sometimes with the whole newsroom. Some of the respondents also spontaneously acknowledged that recent debates on crisis reporting and political scandals have led to more in-depth discussions on ethics within the newsrooms. Overall, most respondents regarded the current system of self-regulation as serviceable but not perfect. For many, further development of ethical norms and practices is also primarily a matter of professionalism and journalistic culture, rather than written rules, which were largely seen as adequate already.

(E9) Participation   2 POINTS

Audience participation in the news process is increasing, but there was some skepticism about the productiveness of all new forms of participation.

Many of the respondents noted that increasing citizen participation is inevitable, but finding productive and meaningful ways for the people to take part in the news process is still "up in the air" in many organizations. One respondent noted that the aim of participation is not to support citizens' self-expression per se, but to support the media organizations' aims of gaining valuable content that enriches journalism. Many respondents also suggested that they find unmoderated online discussion forums largely unproductive, but that the process of finding more consequential ways for people to participate is still unfinished.

Most Finnish media have also augmented traditional audience surveys with new methods of audience panels and social networks to discover the views and preferences of their audiences (Jyrkiäinen 2008, p. 10). In line with this, respondents invariably noted that media organizations today are generally more receptive to the preferences of the public than before.

The newsroom of the local newspaper *Borgåbladet* is always open to the public, and according to the editor-in-chief, it is fairly common for local citizens to step in with an idea for a news story. In case of larger media, the newsrooms are generally not open to the public. Most of the media, however, organize public debates and other local events that are open to the public. All news media also encourage readers to suggest ideas for news stories.

All newspapers examined also have a section for readers' letters in their print edition, and forums for online discussions and/or possibilities for people to comment and initiate discussion on news stories. The Internet sites of news media typically also contain surveys, feedback features and other interactive content. The discussions forums of all leading national media generally attract a great deal of commentary, especially in relation to more controversial topics.

The leading news media utilize user-generated content mainly in the form of photographs sent in by readers. For many respondents, publishing user-generated content was not a value in itself, but it would need to be justified on journalistic grounds. Overall, the comments and views of the public are quite widely available in a variety of formats. Examples of more robust ways of incorporating citizens in the news process, however, are still lacking.

(E10) Rules and practices on internal pluralism 2 POINTS

Internal pluralism is encouraged and valued, but aside from general professional guidelines and values, there are few formal rules.

None of the media in the sample were officially associated with a particular party or an ideology, but like almost all other leading news media, they subscribe to the ideals of independence, balance and pluralism. Most of the editors-in-chief emphasized that they do not believe in "quota-journalism", stipulated by detailed rules, but that they see balance and pluralism as more general values that guide journalism. These values are also typically enshrined in the general professional guidelines and mission statements. Internal debate between different perspectives is also considered to be a routine part of the journalistic work.

In newspapers, the official line of the newspaper is expressed in the editorials, but according to the editors-in-chief interviewed, the editorials do not in any way guide news selection or otherwise limit the range of perspectives. *Helsingin Sanomat* and *Iltalehti*, for instance, have a policy of encouraging internal pluralism, including opinions that diverge from the main editorial line.

In some of the media, there are more explicit rules for providing equal space for all candidates before the elections or for regulating the opportunities of candidates to act as columnists. *YLE* also claims to constantly monitor the political and regional balance in its reporting. Others noted that balance is monitored through audience feedback and internal discussions.

All respondents insisted that the readers' letters sections are open to all sides, and that it is an intentional aim of the section to initiate debate between different perspectives and bring forward diverging views. The proportion of letters published range from around 20-25 % in *Helsingin Sanomat* to practically all letters submitted in the local newspaper *Borgåbladet*. The respondents did note, however, that some limits to curtail the most contentious material, such as racist views, may be necessary.

Control / Watchdog (C)

(C1) Supervising the watchdog "control of the controllers" 1 POINT

Organized media criticism in general is seen as lacking in Finland.

Public discussion about the role of the media as such is not difficult to find even in the media themselves. Recent events in Finland have also generated public debate on the role and performance of the media. The reporting of violent crimes and crises, for instance, has initiated debate on journalistic ethics and a proper code-of-conduct. The political campaign funding entanglements and frequent sex scandals around notable politicians have also intensified the debate on the increasing power of the media, and strained the relations between the politicians and the media. Occasional media criticism is aired by civil society organizations, individual politicians, and other actors. A number of books have recently been published in Finland about "the power of the media" (e.g., Uimonen 2009; Kunelius et al. 2010). In this sense, media criticism and public debate do exist and they even seem to have become more prominent recently.

More institutionalized arenas for media criticism and the evaluation of media performance include the weekly professional journal *Journalisti*, published by the Union of Journalists, and the annual *Yearbook of Journalism Critique*, which features longer articles on topical issues by both researchers and journalists. Universities have also launched research projects and organized seminars that aim to bring together academic and professional perspectives on the media.

Many of the respondents suggested, however, that academic critiques are often perceived to be too detached from the realities of news journalism and thus have only limited value from the point of view of journalists. Blogs and websites that discuss media performance exist, but none of them have gained wider significance. Most of the respondents failed to name any notable media blogs in Finland. There are also some television and radio programs dedicated to the media criticism, mainly on public service channels. Their focus is more on journalistic self-reflection, and they rarely feature outside observers.

Some respondents noted that specialized forums for "media criticism" can seem somewhat contrived. Instead, it was suggested that good media criticism needs to be spontaneous and issue-driven, rather than institutionalized or too organized. On the other hand, it was also suggested that journalists in general are not very open to external evaluation. This is accentuated by small professional circles, which seems generate a culture in which journalists are reluctant to criticize each other. The flip-side of the strong professional ethos thus seems to be somewhat inward-looking and closed professional circles.

(C2)   Independence of the news media from power holders   2 POINTS

Independence of the Finnish news media from power holders is generally strong.

In general, journalists are not granted a special status in the Finnish law, except for legislation which specifies the responsibilities of editors-in-chief. The confidentiality of sources is guaranteed in the freedom of speech act[9] and in the professional code-of-ethics. Recent government motions to modify the strong protection of sources or privacy regulations, although unsuccessful, were mentioned by many respondents as worrying trends from the perspective of the media.

While the press and public broadcasting in the 1960s and the 1970s had close connections to the political establishment, this political parallelism has declined notably. Many studies have noted that leading news media have become politically more independent (Herkman 2009). The significance of party affiliation has also strongly decreased in the news media. While newspapers affiliated with a specific political party still exist (largely due to state aid to political parties), their significance has been steadily decreasing and almost all leading news media organizations now emphasize political independence.

There are few non-media companies among the owners of the leading news media. Most national media outlets are owned by one of the major media conglomerates, while most local newspapers in Finland are owned by a relatively small company, families or other private individuals with historical roots in publishing.

Rather than ownership or other direct economic ties, respondents suggested that problems of independence in relation to powerful economic actors arise from the strict information management and lack of openness by large corporations who are not bound by the same transparency requirements as public authorities. Many of the respondents also noted that journalists themselves should be more critical and that more resources are needed to fulfil the watchdog role also against private companies and economic power holders. One respondent also suggested that independence is a specific problem in areas such as culture and sports, where journalists in a small country tend to develop close relations to their sources.

(C3) Transparency of data on media system   2 POINTS

Relevant information about the media system is generally available, but not necessarily easily accessible.

Basic information about the media system is provided by the regulatory authorities. The data and publications about market structures and various aspects of content monitoring are generally available to all citizens. According to the law regulating public service broadcasting, *YLE* is required to provide an annual report of public service offered to the regulatory authority, which then gives a statement to the government. These reports or statements are not easily accessible to the citizens.

Various forms of information about the news media are also provided by universities, research institutes, and professional organizations like *The Union of Journalists*. A website co-established by the Union, *Medialinnakkeet,* offers detailed information particularly on changes in ownership, economy and employment issues in the media. Information on media ownership is for the most part openly available, especially as many media companies are now publicly traded. Major changes in the media markets are also reported in the mainstream news media and the financial news. *Helsingin Sanomat,* which is owned by the *Sanoma Group*, has also adopted a policy of publishing a standard acknowledgement of ownership connection whenever it reports on the companies that are owned by the same parent company.

(C4) Journalism professionalism   3 POINTS

The news media are characterized by a strong professional ethos and a high level of unionization.

According to recent studies, journalists and media professionals are mostly well educated and share a basic commitment to common quality standards (Jyrkiäinen 2008). Together with local unions and member associations, *The Union of Journalists* is active in organizing various meetings and further education for journalists. According to the respondents, the professionalism among journalists in Finland is high, and professional and ethical rules are generally well established. The increasing time pressure, however, is seen as a chronic problem that threatens to decrease the time available for in-depth journalism and professional deliberation.

According to a recent survey among Finnish journalists, the increasing workload and time pressures were considered to be by far the biggest problems facing journalism today, while technical skills and multi-media requirements were identified as the most significant area where journalists felt that demands have increased. According to the survey, the number of staff in relation to the amount of content produced has also decreased, which means that there is less time available for writing and planning a single news item. Overall, there is a clear concern among journalists that the increasing demands will ultimately decrease the quality of journalism and hinder the possibilities for in-depth investigations and creativity (Jyrkiäinen 2008).

While the overload of journalistic capacities was widely acknowledged as a real problem in the interviews, many respondents also noted that the resources and tools available for providing quality journalism are still better than ever before. The tension between increasing demands and limited resources thus seems to have become a permanent situation in journalism. One interpretation of the developments is that there is an increasing divide between quality media, which strive to uphold and develop high professional standards, and increasingly routinized bulk journalism that is gaining ground especially online.

(C5)   Journalists' job security   2 POINTS

There are few specific legal provisions that apply only to journalists, but general legal provisions and labor contracts give journalists strong occupational protection.

The Union of Journalists aims to improve the financial and professional position of its members and their work conditions, and to supervise their interests on the level of both collective bargaining and individual organizations. The labor agreements are extensive and terms of employment are generally complied with. The labor agreement also includes ethical counts.

General legal provisions on employment and labor contracts give journalists with permanent contracts, like any other occupational groups, strong protections against dismissal because of personal convictions or any other arbitrary reasons. Collective labor agreements also specify periods of notice. The employer must always be able to demonstrate a financial or production-related reason for termination of employment contracts. The Union has also taken several dismissal cases to courts, which have generally ruled in favor of the journalists by awarding compensations or damages for undue dismissal.

According to the interviews, a professional practice of allowing journalists not to write against their personal convictions is also widely followed in the news media. The proportion of freelancers has increased, and currently around 12 % of the members of the *Union of Journalists* are freelancers. The use of short-term contracting varies between sectors of the media, but in general, short-term contracts, internships or freelance contracts are currently the only way of entering the profession.

As expected, the editors-in-chief interviewed did not consider the increasing proportion of freelancers or the use of short-term contracts to be a major problem in their organization. In *Helsingin Sanomat*, for instance, it was alleged that some 95 % of the content is produced by permanent staff. Some 200-300 jobs were slashed in the media sector because of the economic downturn. According to the Union of Journalists, the unemployment rate among journalists is currently around 4-5 %, although many of those who have lost their jobs become freelancers and do not show up in the statistics.

(C6)   Practice of access to information   2 POINTS

The existing law provides extensive access to public information, but problems remain in practice.

Finland has a long tradition of open access to government files, starting from the world's oldest freedom of information law that was enacted in 1766, when Finland was part of Sweden. The current law, known as *The Act on the Openness of Government Activities* (1999), is considered to provide citizens extensive access to public information. In practice, there are some reports of differences between the principles and practices.

The Act states the principle that all documents are public unless there is a specific reason for withholding them enacted in another law. There are no privileges for journalists in accessing public information. Instead, everyone has the right to access any official document in the public domain held by public authorities and private bodies that exercise public authority. Those asking for information are not required to provide reasons for their request or to verify their identity unless they are requesting personal or otherwise classified information. The law specifies 32 categories of secret documents that are exempt from release according to a variety of potential harm tests depending on the type of information.

The journalistic experiences of the freedom of information legislation and the use of official documents have recently been examined in a research project (Kuutti 2009). In an "accessibility test" designed to assess the behavior of individual officials to information requests, officials were often slow to reply and reluctant to provide the information requested (ibid.). Problems seem to arise from inconsistent legal interpretations of public and non-public issues, from negative attitudes of the authorities providing information requested, and partly from the journalistic practices.

In some cases, journalists are not aware of their rights to access information. In the interviews with editors-in-chief and experts, it was also suggested that rather than the legislation, more critical questions have to do with the skills and resources of journalists to find and access relevant information. The interviews also suggested that journalists often face problems in gaining information about issues in preparation, which hinders public evaluation of the forthcoming plans of the authorities. Overall, most respondents acknowledged that the existing law gives journalists and the general public relatively broad access to public information.

(C7)   The watchdog and the media's mission statements   2 POINTS

The importance of the watchdog role is widely recognized by Finnish media organizations.

The watchdog function seems to enjoy a very high level of importance in the rhetoric of the editors-in-chief. Most of the respondents considered the watchdog role to be among their main functions, if not the most important one. It was also suggested in the interviews that the importance of the watchdog function has recently become increasingly central in the Finnish media.

Most news media have a mission statement of some kind that typically contains references to the freedom of speech, political independence, pluralism, and other democratic values. According to Lehto's (2006) study of the historical development in the written editorial principles of all Finnish daily newspapers, some changes have also taken place in the principles. The notion of "objective journalism", for instance, has disappeared from the documents, while references to the watchdog function and the aim to criticize and evaluate official decision-making have become increasingly prominent (Lehto 2006, p. 413). Overall, it is argued that the development of mission statements indicates that the newspapers have turned their allegiance from political parties and the establishment to the readers.

Most of the editors-in-chief interviewed acknowledged that mission statements have little practical meaning, but it still seems that the watchdog function is strongly entrenched in the dominant professional ideology. As an example of the watchdog role, a number of respondents referred to the ongoing attempts to uncover the campaign funding connections behind leading politicians, which have remained in the headlines of the Finnish media for over two years now and which have also led to a new campaign funding law.

(C8)   Professional training   2 POINTS

The importance of continuous professional training is broadly acknowledged, but not all journalists take full advantage of the opportunities available.

All of the respondents considered journalism training to be increasingly important, but resources and practices seem to vary across media organizations. In principle, most of the respondents considered the resources for training to be adequate. The problem in many newsrooms is that individual journalists don't have the opportunity or time to leave their daily duties and take part in training. According to a recent survey among journalists, a little over half of the journalists thought that possibilities for professional training should be improved. In line with our interviews, many journalists thought that there is enough education available, but not enough opportunities in practice to participate in the training offered (Jyrkiäinen 2008, p. 26, 33).

The Union of Journalists and The Federation of the Finnish Media Industry have agreed on recommendations to advance professional training. The unions agree that education should be diverse, attended regularly, and that part of it should consist of training outside the journalist's own workplace. There is also a chapter on the education programs in the collective labor agreement.

In many instances, journalists can take paid leave for further education. In the selected media organizations, various forms of training are in use. The largest media organizations, like *YLE* and *Helsingin Sanomat*, have their own internal resources for professional training. Most news organizations also use outside consultants or experts for internal training. Much of the regular professional training focuses on technical skills, creative writing, and other professional skills. For more extensive knowledge training, media organizations tend to rely on universities and other places of journalistic higher education. Opinions differ on the recent developments. Some respondents estimated that the total volume of professional training has increased recently, while others noted that there has been a temporary decline owing to the economic downturn.

(C9) Watchdog function and financial resources 2 POINTS

The leading news media give priority to their own material and also seek to undertake investigative journalism.

Most respondents claimed that the resources for investigative journalism are adequate, but that more needs to be done to make investigative journalism part of everyday journalistic culture. Many respondents also noted that journalists themselves should be more daring and active in pursuing their own ideas and investigative stories.

The editors-in-chief interviewed maintained that ad hoc provisions for in-depth investigations are available when necessary.

Public service broadcaster *YLE*, which also has a specific investigative group, has exceptional resources for investigative journalism in the form of documentaries and other current affairs programming. Some newspapers, such as *Helsingin Sanomat*, have also experimented with independent units dedicated to investigative journalism. According to the editors-in-chief interviewed, however, this has not been workable, as it has disconnected the unit too much from the daily process of news gathering. Instead, it was suggested that investigative journalism should be integrated with daily news gathering. The local newspaper *Borgåbladet* had a practice of permanently freeing one journalist from all other duties to pursue investigative journalism and in-depth reporting.

The Finnish Association of Investigative Journalism (*Tutkiva*) was founded in 1992 to promote critical and thorough reporting in the Finnish media. The association tries to facilitate investigative journalism by spreading information and good practices about research methods, principles of transparency, sources and source criticism by organizing discussions and training, and also by awarding an annual prize for investigative journalism.

Summary

On the basis of the above criteria, the overall assessment of the performance and structure of the Finnish mainstream media is fairly positive. In an international comparison, the equal availability and reach of the main news outlets remain on a high level. The challenges, such as increasing market pressures, declining news consumption among young people, and increasing workload and haste in journalistic work, are similar to those of most other countries. Despite these trends, many respondents were surprisingly optimistic, noting that the preconditions for providing quality journalism in Finland have in many respects also improved.

The legal preconditions for freedom of expression and access to public information are generally considered adequate, although some concern about possible changes to the protection of sources and privacy regulations was expressed. Professional ethos among journalists in Finland also remains strong, and it is reflected in established ethical guidelines and professional norms, the position of the Union of Journalists, and relatively good resources for professional training. Issues that were discussed more critically include lack of organized media criticism, the need for a more daring and critical journalism, and somewhat inward looking professional circles. The independence of the news media from political power holders was generally considered strong, but many respondents called for a more critical attitude toward private companies and economic power holders.

The perspectives of the respondents represent the views of experienced leading editors and thus represent rather traditional views of the democratic role of the media. New ways of engaging with public issues that fall outside the scope of institutional journalism, however, are largely beyond the scope of this report, and their influence on the relationship between the media and democracy in Finland remains to be discussed.

Notes

1   In addition to the authors, Pekka Torvinen has contributed to the report by assisting in data collection. The research for the report was funded by the Helsingin Sanomat Foundation.

2   In 2008, the share of public service broadcasting was 45 % of all television viewing. From 1950s until the early 1990s, the public broadcaster YLE rented airtime to the commercial programming of MTV, which left behind a culture of mutual cohabitation that has changed only recently.

3   The following persons were interviewed: Janne Virkkunen, editor-in-chief, *Helsingin Sanomat*; Kari Vainio, editor-in-chief, *Turun Sanomat*; Kari Kivelä, editor-in-chief, *Iltalehti;* Stefan Holmström, editor-in-chief, *Borgåbladet*; Atte Jääskeläinen, director of news, *YLE;* Merja Ylä-Anttila, editor-in-chief, *MTV3*; Arto Nieminen, president of the *Union of Journalists*; Pasi Kivioja, director of the *Finnish Newspapers Association*.

4   http://www.medialinnakkeet.com

5   Co-produced by YLE, Swedish Television SVT, and Norwegian Radio NRK

6   The 24-hour news channel YLE24 was terminated in 2007.

7   As another official language of Finland, Swedish is granted the same position as Finnish in the legislation, and in that sense it is not a minority language per se.

8   All data collected from the respective websites of the newspapers (12 months, automatically renewable subscription).

9   Act on the Exercise of Freedom of Expression in Mass Media, http://www.finlex.fi/en/laki/kaannokset/2003/en20030460.pdf

References

Ala-Fossi, M. & Haara, P. (2009). *Licence-dependent radio supply 2009*. Publication 4/2010. Helsinki: Ministry of Transport and Communications.

Antikainen, H., Kuusisto, O., Bäck, A., Nurmi, O., Viljakainen, A. (2010). Viestintäalan nykytila ja kehitystrendit 2010-2011. *GT-Raportti 1/2010*. Helsinki: VTT.

Council for Mass Media (2005): Guidelines for Journalists. Retrieved from: http://www.jsn.fi/Content.aspx?d=48.

Council for Mass Media in Finland (2010). Self regulation by publishers and journalists. Retrieved from http://www.jsn.fi/Content.aspx?d=50.

Curran, J., Iyengar, S., Lund, A. B. & Salovaara-Moring, I. (2009). Media System, Public Knowledge and Democracy: A Comparative Study. *European Journal of Communication*, 24(1), 5-26.

Eurostat (2009). Population of foreign citizens in the EU27 in 2008. Retrieved from http://epp.eurostat.ec.europa.eu.

Eurostat (2010). Individuals regularly using the Internet. Retrieved from http://epp.eurostat.ec.europa.eu.

Ficora (Finnish Communications Regulatory Authority) (2010). *Laajakaistaliittymien hintakehitys 1/2010*. Retrieved from: http://www.ficora.fi/attachments/suomial/5mlxr9U7V/Laajakaistaliittymien_hintakehitys_1_2010.pdf.

Finnish Mass Media 2009 (2010). Helsinki: Statistics Finland.

Finnish Newspaper Association (2010). *Sanomalehtien jakelu Suomessa 2007*. Retrieved from http://www.sanomalehdet.fi/index.phtml?s=123.

Finnpanel (2010a). Results from the TV Audience Measurement. Retrieved from http://www.finnpanel.fi/en/tulokset/tv.php.

Finnpanel (2010b). Results from the National Radio Survey. Retrieved from http://www.finnpanel.fi/en/tulokset/radio.php

Hallin, D. & Mancini, p. (2004). *Comparing Media Systems: Three Models of Media and Politics*. Cambridge: Cambridge University Press.

Herkman, J. (2005). *Kaupallisen television ja iltapäivälehtien avoliitto. Median markkinoituminen ja televisioituminen*. Tampere: Vastapaino.

Herkman, J. (2009). The Structural Transformation of the Democratic Corporatist Model: The Case of Finland. *Javnost – the Public*, 16(4), 73-90.

Jyrkiäinen, J. (2008). *Journalistit muuttuvassa mediassa* [Journalists in the changing media]. Department of Journalism and Mass Communication Publications Series B50/2008. Tampere: University of Tampere.

Karppinen, K. & Jääsaari, J. & Kivikuru, U. (2010). *Media ja valta kansalaisten silmin.* SSKH Reports and Discussion papers 2/2010. Helsinki: Swedish School of Social Sciences.

Kemppainen, P. (2007): Ääniradion tulevaisuus – onko se radio? [Future development of the sound radio]. Publications 68/2007. Helsinki: Ministry of Transport and Communications.

Kunelius, R., Reunanen, E. & Noppari, E. (2010). *Media vallan verkoissa.* Department of Journalism and Mass Communication Publications Series A112/2009. Tampere: University of Tampere.

Kuutti, H. (2009). The Role of Accessibility Law in Journalists' Work – A Finnish study. Paper for the International Conference *Journalism Research in the Public Interest.* 19-21 November 2009.

Lehtinen, P. (2010). *Finnish Television Programming 2009.* Publication 22/2010. Helsinki: Ministry of Transport and Communications.

Lehto, K. (2006). *Aatteista arkeen. Suomalaisten seitsenpäiväisten sanomalehtien linjapapereiden synty ja muutos 1971–2005.* [From ideologies to everyday life. Editorial principles of Finnish newspapers, 1971–2005]. Studies in humanities 48. Jyväskylä: University of Jyväskylä.

Levikintarkastus (2009). Kansallinen Mediatutkimus: Lukijatiedote 2008 [The Finnish Audit Bureau of Circulations: National Readership Survey 2008]. Retrieved from http://www.levikintarkastus.fi/mediatutkimus/KMT_Lukijatiedote_2008.pdf

Ministry of Education and Culture (2010). Kulttuurilehtien tukemiseen yli miljoona euroa [Over one million Euro to the aid for culture and opinion magazines, press release 24 February 2010]. Retrieved from http://www.minedu.fi/OPM/Tiedotteet/2010/02/kulttuurilehdet.html?lang=fi.

Ministry of Transport and Communications (2010). Laajakaista kaikille [Making broadband available to all]. Retrieved from http://www.lvm.fi/web/fi/243.

Moring, T. & Husband, C. (2007). The contribution of Swedish-language media in Finland to linguistic vitality. *International Journal of the Sociology of Language.* Issue 187-188: 75-101.

Nieminen, H. (2010). Public Interest in Media Policy: The Case of Finland. *Interactions* 1(2), 233-250).

Suikkanen R. & Syrjälä, Hanna (2010). *Suomalaisen uutismedian vuosiseuranta 2010* [Monitoring Finnish news media 2010]. Journalism Research and Development Centre, Publication B 55/2008. Tampere: University of Tampere.

TNS Metrix (2010). Suomen web-sivustojen viikkoluvut [Weekly site rankings]. Retrieved from: http://www.gallupweb.com/tnsmetrix/

Uimonen, R. (2009). *Median mahti.* Juva: WSOY.

UJF (The Union of Journalists in Finland) (2010). New media initiatives to reach out to immigrants. Retrieved from: http://www.journalistiliitto.fi/en/immigrant_journalists/new-media-initiatives/.

Chapter 6

GERMANY

The News Media are Still Able to Play a Supportive Role for Democracy[1]

Frank Marcinkowski & André Donk

The implementation and development of democracy in Germany after World War 2 has been intensively discussed in recent years, as Germany had to face two important anniversaries. 2009 marked the 60-year anniversary of the constitution of the Federal Republic of Germany, which was the founding document for the liberal parliamentarian democracy in the then western part of Germany and remains the constitution of the unified state. And in 2010, the people remembered the unification of Eastern and Western Germany twenty years ago. Thus, on the one hand, we can describe Germany as a solid democracy, which looks back on a 60-year tradition in the western part. On the other, the unification also built up a quite young democracy in the eastern part. We find both old institutions on the federal level and in the western states with a continuous democratic socialization among citizens, and new democratic institutions like the state parliaments as well as a socialist socialization among many older citizens in the eastern states.

As the history of democracy in Western Germany shows, the implementation of new democratic institutions is not directly or automatically followed by the acceptance of these institutions by the citizenry (Gabriel 1999, p. 212). The process of re-education proved that the democratic political system did not change the non-democratic orientations of Germans after World War 2 – neither by its mere existence nor by its own democratic actions. Nevertheless, "[a]bove all, both Western Allies and the Soviets were determined to 're-educate' and thoroughly 'democratise' the Germans" (Humphreys 1990, p. 22-23). But the transfer of a democratic orientation from the level of the institutions and their representatives to the level of the citizens seems to be complex (Kaase 1998, 41). One of the mediating factors in this process is the media system and its performance for democracy. Thus, the post-war West German media policy aimed at creating a media system that ensured "democratic accountability to the 'socially significant groups' in a pluralistic liberal-democratic society" (Humphreys 1990, p. 294-295). In a historical review, we can see which functions the media fulfilled after World War 2 in Germany. First, they had an important democratization function and thus socialized large parts of the citizenry into the social and political norms of democracy. And second, German media contributed to the stabilization of the economic, social and political order (Humphreys 1990, p. 302). Now, sixty years after the foundation of the democratic Germany, and twenty years after its unification, we again pose the question: Can the media play a supportive role for a both transitory and well-established democracy?

Introduction to the German media system

Germany has a large variety of local, regional and national newspapers, even if the diversity of publishers and independent newsrooms has declined over the past years. All in all, there are around about 1,500 titles with a total circulation of more than 20 million (BDZV 2009, p. 4). These impressive numbers cloud the ongoing concentration on the German media market: The number of publishing companies has halved from the 1950s to today, and the number of published units (publizistische Einheiten), which is the number of newspapers whose content is composed by separated newsrooms, decreased from 225 in 1954 to 135 in 2008 (ibid.). The biggest publishing company is Axel Springer-Verlag AG, which owns the most popular national tabloid Bild and the national daily Welt. Furthermore, Springer runs more than a dozen regional newspapers and tabloids. The total circulation of Springer is roughly five million. It is followed by Verlagsgruppe Stuttgarter Zeitung, which owns around about 30 regional newspapers in southern Germany with a total circulation of 1.9 million (Röper 2008). The ten biggest newspaper publishers have a market share of 56.1 % (ibid.).

The German media system – with regard to TV and radio – is divided into a commercially and a publicly run sector. While the press is completely in the hands of commercial publishers or publishing companies, there is a dualism of public and commercial television and radio broadcasting. There are two major public broadcasting corporations at the national level, ARD and ZDF, and two major commercial broadcasting companies, RTL Group and ProSiebenSat1-Media AG, which provide most of the commercial TV channels. In addition, there are nine public broadcasting services in the federal states. The situation is fairly similar for radio: there are public and commercial stations. But the main differences lie in their organizational structures and the diversity of programmes. There are a large number of commercial radio stations in each federal state, and most of the states have regional public broadcasting services with a variety of channels. There are only two national public radio broadcasting services in Germany, Deutschlandfunk and Deutschlandradio Kultur, which both present sophisticated programmes (Altendorfer 2004, pp. 335-336).

While in the early years after World War II licensing by the allied forces was the rule, today print media generally do not need a state licence (Meyn 2004, p. 65). The absence of licensing is formulated in state law. For example, the pertinent law in North Rhine-Westphalia, the biggest federal state, is set down in § 2 Landespressegesetz under the heading of "Freedom of governmental approval". However, the allocation of radio frequencies for commercial broadcasting is regulated by supervising authorities (Landesmedienanstalten), which are funded through licence fees. Because culture falls under the jurisdiction of the individual federal state, broadcasting law is usually enacted by the state parliaments – nevertheless equality is aimed for. Therefore national broadcasting, e.g., the national public broadcasting service, is regulated by treaties between all states and the national government (Medienstaatsverträge) (Fechner 2008, p. 18).

The Sample

We have decided to analyse democratic media performance on the basis of a case study of the main news media. Our choices are based upon the following criteria: first, all the main distributors of news should be represented: TV, radio, the press and online media; and, second, the two dimensions of "leading the elite" (media of the governors) and "leading the citizens" (media of those who are governed) should be applied to the smaple. This selection should represent a comprehensive picture of the German media system. In 2008, our realized sample therefore consisted of the newspapers Süddeutsche Zeitung (quality) and Bild (audience), the TV stations ARD (quality) and RTL (audience), the radio station Deutschlandfunk (quality), the newsmagazine Spiegel (quality) and the Internet news site Spiegel Online (quality). For the 2010 survey, we tried to iterate the selection and vary this sample. Thus, we had to define adequate equivalents, as the sample again had to include a selection of the relevant news media. Additionally, we conducted interviews with journalists' unions to get insights into the working conditions of journalists in Germany.

All sample members were contacted in May 2010 to inform them about the project and to make interview appointments with one of the leading editors (editor-in-chief; deputy editor-in-chief; duty editor etc.). Unfortunately, Focus und Stern, which can be considered as relevant news magazines in Germany, did not take part in our survey. A semi-standardized questionnaire was assembled with regard to the specific indicators. The interviews were conducted either over the telephone or face-to-face. The answers were then analysed – with regard to specific categories derived from each indicator – by using the qualitative content analysis software *Atlas.ti*.

Table 1.   Sample for interviews

	Media Type	Financing		Reach		
FAZ	newspaper		Commercial	Quality (national)		circulation: 368,700
WAZ	newspaper		Commercial		Audience (regional)	circulation: 852,800
WDR	radio	PBS		Quality		daily reach: 7.76 M
ZDF heute	TV	PBS		Quality		market share: 18 %.
N24	TV		Commercial		Audience	market share: 13.1 %
N24.de	online		Commercial		Audience	unique users: 0.86 M
DJU/ Verdi	union	-	-	-	-	-
DJV/ NRW	union	-	-	-	-	-

Indicators

Freedom / Information (F)

(F1)   Geographic distribution of news media availability   3 POINTS

All relevant news media are available to all citizens, there are no regional divides or regional shortages.

Taking a closer look at the accessibility and reach of the single media types, there is no doubt that an almost complete supply of TV, radio and newspapers is guaranteed. The federal political structure of Germany is mirrored in the media system, as there are national as well as regional newspapers and broadcasts. National law stipulates that every citizen shall have access to public television and radio. For this reason, every major communication area has, in addition to private broadcasters, its own publicly run radio and TV stations.

A complete supply of radio programmes is ensured. In the 16 federal states, there are 247 private and 70 public radio stations (ALM-Jahrbuch 2008, p. 173). While there are no numbers for their technical reach, owing to the legal framework one can still assume that there is complete access. In 2008, there were roughly 40 million households in Germany (Statistisches Bundesamt, Mikrozensus 2008) and about 43 million registered radios (Media Perspektiven Basisdaten 2008, p. 6). As the number of radios exceeds the number of households, this figure also indicates a complete supply.

The total number of TV households in Germany, i.e. households that own one or more TV sets, differs because there are two different surveys. The first study counts the number of TV households of German and EU citizens in Germany, which is about 35 million or 87.5 % (AGF/GFK Fernsehpanel). According to these data, the technical reach of the five biggest TV stations (in relation to all TV households) is nearly 100 %: 99 % (ARD) and 99 % (ZDF) for public broadcasting services, and 97.9 % (RTL) and 97.2 % (Sat1) and 97.1 % (Pro7) for commercial stations (Media Perspektiven Basisdaten 2008, pp. 4,5). The other survey focuses on the TV households of all inhabitants in Germany, which includes major populations of Turkish and other non-EU-migrants, and therefore the number is quite a bit higher (Landesmedienanstalten). According to these data, there are 37.7 million TV households, i.e., about 94.3 % of all households (ALM-Jahrbuch 2008, p. 26). How do they get access to TV? More than half of the TV households receive TV via cable (51.7 %), four out of ten (42.4 %) via satellite and only 10.7 % via terrestrial networks. The sum adds to more than 100 %, because some households use different types of access in parallel (ALM-Jahrbuch 2008, p. 27-29). To sum the different figures up, TV is fully accessible all over Germany. Another proof of this fact is the number of TV sets, which is about 43 million (Media Perspektiven Basisdaten, p. 6).

Newspapers are also available in all regions: there are five national dailies (Frankfurter Allgemeine Zeitung, Frankfurter Rundschau, Süddeutsche Zeitung, Tageszeitung, Die Welt) and a large number of regional or local dailies. Besides national dailies, there is at least one regional or local daily for every district; roughly 58 % of German districts are served by just one local or regional daily, about 40 % by two or more (Schütz 2009a, p. 475; 2009b).

With regard to Internet availability, we can state that 99 % of all German households have a telephone connection and a personal computer is owned by 75.4 % of all households (Jahrbuch Fernsehen 2009, p. 297), which is the technical basis for access to the Internet: 54.9 % of all households have broadband access (OECD). Suppliers for broadband Internet connections are available all over West Germany and in large parts of East Germany. A low density is only observed for parts of Mecklenburg-Vorpommern and Sachsen-Anhalt, which also show a low population density (Breitbandatlas).

(F2) Patterns of news media use (consumption of news)   2 POINTS

In Germany, news media use is – with certain reservations regarding the news media use of young people – at quite a high standard.

Together, the five national quality newspapers have a daily circulation of about 1.35 Mio (IVW Auflagenstatistik; own calculation). All German daily newspapers have 46.9 million readers a day, which is more than half of the total population or more than 70 % of all people over 14 years (Media Perspektiven Basisdaten, p. 82; BDZV, p. 27). The reach of daily newspapers differs across age groups: while in the group of older people (60 to 69 years old and older than 70 years) the reach of daily newspapers is more than 80 %, for younger people (14 to 19 years) it is only 47.1 % (Table 2). This figure indicates a decrease in importance of newspapers as a source of information. These results are underpinned by findings from 2004, when only 29 % of the 14- to 29-year-olds agreed with the statement "One should regularly read newspapers" (BDZV, p. 31). In 2008, younger people were asked which media they could not give up: Only 3 % answered newspaper or magazines (ALM-Jahrbuch 2008, p. 183). If we anticipate quite linear cohort effects, this may lead to a decrease in newspaper journalism.

Table 2.   Reach of daily newspapers in 2008 (by age cohorts)

	14-19 y	20-29 y	30-39 y	40-49 y	50-59 y	60-69 y	> 70 y
2008	47.1 %	57.7 %	66.8 %	73.7 %	80.6 %	83.8 %	82.9 %

Source: BDZV, p. 30.

The main news broadcasts in the evening obtain 1.54 to 8.74 million viewers on average; the market share lies between 6.5 and 33 %, which is a slight decrease compared to 2006 (Table 3). Other findings, which confirm our figures, suggest that Germany belongs to a group of countries that are eager for information: these countries pay a great deal of attention to current information and therefore have high rates for the use of newspapers and news broadcasts (Tenscher 2008).

Table 3.   Use of TV News in 2008 (viewers from the age of three)

	Channel	Audience	Market share
Tagesschau	PBS	8.74 Mio	32.0 %
Heute	PBS	3.96 Mio	18.0 %
RTL-Aktuell	Commercial	3.74 Mio	18.2 %
Sat1-News	Commercial	1.54 Mio	6.4 %
Tagesthemen	PBS	2.26 Mio	10.5 %
Heute Journal	PBS	3.33 Mio	12.0 %

Source: Zubayr & Gerhard 2009, p. 107.

There are only two national radio stations that are decidedly news oriented: Deutschlandfunk and Deutschlandradio Kultur. Both have a very low reach of 1.9 % (1.3 million listeners) and 0.5 % (0.4 million listeners), respectively (Media Perspektiven Basisdaten 2008, p. 78; Klingler & Müller 2008, p. 515). Additionally, we can speak of 34.2 million listeners to all regional and national public radio services (Klingler & Müller 2008, p. 515). Because these radio stations broadcast news programmes every hour, this figure suggests a high amount of "inadvertent" usage of news coverage. Looking at TV and radio use among younger people (18/19 years), we see that 86 % of them watch TV and 75 % listen to the radio at least once a week (Klingler 2008, p. 630).

The Internet clearly is not a main source of information. There are only four Internet pages in German language with news orientation in the top-40 list of reach (Table 4). The Internet is "often" and "occasionally" used as a source of information on current news and current regional news by 52 % and 40 %, respectively, of all Internet users (Van Eimeren & Frees 2008, p. 338). If we compare whether the Internet is primarily used for information (instead of entertainment), differences between age groups can be observed. The younger the people are, the less often they use they the Internet to obtain information, as Table 5 shows.

Table 4.   Reach (user / month) of news-oriented online outlets in 2008 (quality news paper / magazines within the top-40 list of reach)

Spiegel Online	5.20 Mio
Welt.de	3.58 Mio
Focus Online	3.26 Mio
sueddeutsche.de	2.41 Mio

Source: AGOF Internet facts I-IV; own calculation.

Table 5.   Use of the Internet for information or entertainment (by age cohorts)

	14-19 y	20-29 y	30-39 y	> 50 y
2008	18 %	42 %	65 %	83 %

Source: Van Eimeren & Frees 2008, p. 338.

(F3)   Diversity of news sources   2 POINTS

Most of the German news media rely on different sources, though there is a tendency towards one dominant news agency

There were five universal news agencies in the German media market in 2008: Two national (dpa, ddp) and three international news agencies (AP, AFP and Reuters). In 2009, ddp and AP merged to DAPD. The biggest German news agency dpa was founded by a consortium of publishers in 1949 and has operated as a registered co-operative since then. Today about 190 associates (publishers, broadcasters, media companies) own dpa. If we compare the size and reach of these five news agencies, we can see that dpa dominates the market, but that the other four can compete to a limited degree:

Table 6.   News agencies in Germany 2008

	dpa	ddp	AP	AFP	Reuters
Journalistic staff (permanent employees)	420	100	70	53	140
Reports per day	800	350	250	200	350
Number of bureaus in Germany	70	22	16	11	4
Number of countries with correspondents	93	-	70	165	97

Source: Grüll 2009, p. 17.

Grüll compared the distribution of these five agencies in the German news media by means of a survey. His sample covers 97 leading editors: 95.9 % of them use dpa, 52.6 % ddp, 48.5 % AP, 38.1 % Reuters, and 45.4 % AFP (Grüll 2009, p. 58.). Another longitudinal analysis confirms Grüll's findings. From the 1990s to today, dpa has dominated the market, the other news agencies having shares between 30 % and 50 %. Significant changes show the shares of AP, which declined from 66.4 % in 1993 to 47.1 % in 2006, and AFP, which increased from 19.3 % to 47.8 % (Wilke 2007, p. 332). Hence, there is competition between news agencies in the German media market; at least half of the news media use more than one agency and the agencies have quite a strong domestic and foreign editorial staff.

Most media subscribe to a news agency, some of them even two or more. Nevertheless, these numbers do not provide any insight into whether the material from news agencies is actually used. Our respondents approved that domestic news is mostly produced by the investigated news media themselves. When asked how much material from news agencies is actually used, the interviewees stated that only 10 % to 30 % of the published and aired domestic news derives from agencies. In the case of foreign news, these numbers differ; especially N24 and N24.de use a great amount of agency reports.

(F4)   Internal rules for practice of newsroom democracy   1 POINT

In Germany, journalists are not in full democratic control of the newsroom. There are some significant barriers to an effective and democratic organization of newsrooms, especially with regard to the engagement of new staff.

On the question of journalists' involvement in staff decisions, the answers differ. Editors-in-chief usually are appointed by the management; in most of the cases, newsroom journalists are not involved in the process. There is, however, a specific characteristic of the public broadcasting service: The editors-in-chief are elected by broadcasting commissions (Rundfunkräte), which are staffed by representatives of the political parties, churches, unions and other social groups. In the case of new employment, it is obligatory to hear from both the staff and the works council. All in all, there are no greater efforts to involve newsroom journalists in staff decisions, although especially WDR claims to have transparency and employee involvement. Nevertheless, there are neither routines for nor obligations to newsroom democracy in electing the editor-in-chief, and there is also no discussion about the filling of other leading positions in the newsroom. Generally, the decision lies with the editor-in-chief or the heads of department. A prevailing hierarchical structure has to be detected.

There are some elements of democratic control of the newsroom, as in most of the cases, there is a newsroom council. Generally, this is referred to as a newsroom statute, established to ensure internal freedom of the press (innere Pressefreiheit). The impartiality of newsrooms is claimed in state laws for public broadcasting service, but there are no sanctions attached. All interview partners agreed that decisions on subjects and framing of the covered issues are debated in the daily editorial meeting, in which all journalists have an equal say. However, it is often the editor-in-chief who makes the final decision. FAZ and WAZ emphasized that controversial opinions on certain political issues among the newsroom journalists are expressed in the commentary.

(F5) Company rules against *internal* influence on newsroom / editorial staff 2 POINTS

The autonomy of newsrooms is generally well-established and implemented in most of the main news media, although sometimes formal rules are still lacking.

All leading editors we interviewed asserted that there is a complete and formal separation of newsroom and management. But are these regulations actually effective in everyday practice? Our interview partners frequently insisted that there has never been any influence at all; most of the editors informed us that they have never experienced any attempt by the management to prohibit or place stories. Generally, the actual implementation of the separation between newsroom and management / advertising department was referred to as "autonomous." Other, more indirect forms of internal influence could be detected in the coverage of programmes and products related to the publishing house or the owning company. But our interview partners claimed that no products from the heading company are to be discussed in articles.

In the case of commercial media, none of our interview partners mentioned direct interventions from management. The editor-in-chief heads the newsroom. In the case of public service media, the selection of the editor-in-chief is formally independent of the government. Although political parties have a say in the broadcasting commissions, they normally do not constitute the majority in these commissions. Nevertheless, in 2010 Hessen's prime minister and his Christian Democratic Union pursued the demission of Nikolaus Brender, editor-in-chief of the ZDF. Thus, one cannot say that the public service media are totally autonomous from political power.

(F6) Company rules against *external* influence on newsroom / editorial staff   2 POINTS

There are no reported cases of external influence, but in the case of the commercial media, there are neither explicit rules nor structural boundaries against such influences.

First of all, it is important to note that, for this indicator in particular, sample effects were to be expected. As the leading German media of our sample are part of bigger and (more or less) well-financed companies, external influence is quite unlikely, because no big advertiser could sustain a boycott for a longer period of time. Also, this indicator involves sensitive data that most of our interview partners were reluctant to share. There is no information about formal rules, but the influence in question seems to be quite insignificant.

With regard to income composition, we find a greater variance that can be explained easily. There are two public broadcasting companies that are almost entirely financed by fees and therefore largely free from advertising.[2] Newspapers and news-magazines have income through sales and advertising; rates are between 40 % up to 50 % for sale and 50 % up to 60 % for advertising. These findings can be under-pinned by current data: The average income composition of German newspapers in 2008 consists of 45.2 % advertising, 46.2 % sales and 8.6 % newspaper supplements (BDZV). Finally, the commercial broadcaster N24 and its online outlet N24.de are nearly completely financed by advertising. If we look at the share of TV advertising revenue, RTL holds 25.9 %, SAT1 18.2 % and ProSieben 17.7 %; the public service media have a very small share of 1.9 % (ZDF) and 2.8 % (ARD) (Television 2008, p. 190). None of our interview partners explicitly recognized a tendency towards a few major advertisers. All sample members that depend (to a varying degree) on advertising asserted that this fact did not interfere with their standards of critical journalism. Most of them emphasized their ability to withstand pressure because their management backs their editorial autonomy. Two editors mentioned that there is critical coverage of big companies even if they are big advertisers as well. While one of them stated that this kind of critical reporting did not have any effect on the advertising activities of these companies, the other one mentioned one case, in which the news media had to waive some millions in income because of their reporting. WDR stated that ads that sound like news are rejected and that there is generally no sponsoring.

As public service media can be described as a single revenue financed media, we have to look at the details of rules and practices of this financing. In Germany, public service media are financed by a fee that is charged by a public authority. This authority is part of the public broadcasting system and not of the government. The amount of the fee is determined by a treaty between the federal states (Rundfunk-gebührenstaatsvertrag) on the basis of a proposal by a financial commission of the public service stations (KEF). Usually, the amount of the fee is fixed for five years.

(F7) Procedures on news selection and news processing   2 POINTS

Rules on how to select and present the news are based on journalists' professional education and regular debates within the newsrooms and therefore widely practised. Stylebooks and other written documents do exist in some media.

In German newsrooms, at least one daily editorial meeting is mandatory. In these meetings, all newsroom journalists have a say in discussing which issues will be covered and how stories will be framed and commented. Most of the interviewed leading editors stated that in these meetings, correspondents are called upon to express their opinions on certain stories or other media are observed. Especially WDR claims that there are regular debates about the programme decisions. And FAZ explicitly understands its editorial meetings as a forum for brainstorming and exchange.

Fixed stylebooks do not exit in most of the cases, only WDR features style guides and logbooks for each of its waves. The lack of stylebooks in German newsrooms can be explained in terms of journalists' education and self-image. Today in Germany, most of the journalists in the main news media have graduated from university and run an editorial traineeship or attended a journalism school. In doing so, they had learned the essential procedures of news selection by the time they started their career. A specific socialization for each medium is not regarded as necessary, as all media agree on the concept of a certain news journalism, which is based on routines and procedures that are obligatory for all news media. The processing of news, as one of the central elements of journalists' self-image in Germany, is a basic competence – all journalists know how to "make the news" after they have been educated and socialized, therefore these procedures do not need to be written down in stylebooks for the newsroom. The rather strong impact of the formal education of journalists in countries such as Germany, which belong to the type of north/ central European media systems, is also described in the current research (Hallin & Mancini 2004, p. 173).

Equality / Interest mediation (E)

(E1) Media ownership concentration national level   2 POINTS

At the national level, there are two or more competitors for all news media, but an increased level of concentration in the TV and print sector can be observed.

The TV market is divided into two big sections: public broadcasting represented by ARD (a consortium of the 9 public broadcasters at the state level) and ZDF, on the one hand, and on the other, commercial broadcasting by RTL-Group and ProSiebenSat1-Media AG with their national programmes RTL, RTLII, Super RTL, VOX, ntv and Pro7, Sat1, Kabel1, n24[3]. There are anti-trust laws and the Bundeskartellamt, an authority that supervises market concentration. The Bundeskartellamt has to approve mergers of companies and can deny such mergers when there is a danger of a monopoly in one sector (Fechner 2008, pp. 91-92; Hans-Bredow-Institut 2006, p. 71; Puppis 2007, pp. 275-283). Boundaries are set for broadcasting companies at a 30 % market share and for the press at 25 million Euros of annual turnover for each company. Taking a closer look at the concentration at the national level, programmes of RTL-Group have a market share of 24.2 %, those of ProSiebenSat1 Media AG 21.7 %. The total market share of the national public broadcasting services is about 43.7 % (KEK 2009, pp. 338; our calculations). As defined by the indicator, we can observe more than two competitors for the national broadcasting market, i.e., there are exactly three.

The five biggest publishing companies (Springer, Stuttgarter Zeitung, WAZ, Du Mont, Ippen Gruppe) share 41.3 % of the daily newspaper circulation (Röper 2008, p. 421). Despite this apparently high degree of concentration, however, there are more than three big competitors in this sector and five national newspapers from different companies. The calculation of CR3 (market share of the three largest companies) shows comparatively high values for the TV and print sectors in relation to the radio sector.

Table 7.   Market share "CR3" in Germany, 2008

	Companies	Market share
TV	RTL-Group, ProSiebenSat1-Media AG, Viacom	46.5 %
Radio (i.e. national stations)	Klassik Radio AG, RTL-Group, sunshine live	2.4 % (daily reach)
Print	Springer, WAZ, Verlagsgruppe Stuttgarter Zeitung	36.6 %
Online	T-Online, WEB.DE, Yahoo! Deutschland	38.4 % (reach unique users)

Source: Own calculations on the basis of: KEK 2009; ALM 2008; AGOF.de, Mediaperspektiven Basisdaten 2008, p. 79.

Finally, some remarks about cross-media ownership. In fact, there are reports on a number of cases of diagonal integration. Just to give a few examples, a big media company like Bertelsmann AG owns radio and TV networks as well as production companies, newspapers and publishing houses, and the big publishing house Springer AG owns a considerable amount of print outlets as well as shares in radio and TV stations. Furthermore, KEK analysed the influence of financial investors in the German media market in 2007: Private equity companies hold a large number of shares in digital TV programmes, which do not have a significant reach. But some financial investors also hold shares (up to 10 % each) in more important media companies, like Axel Springer AG, or Reuters, and the digital pay TV Premiere (KEK 2007, p. 297-301). Furthermore, there are two major cases in the German media market where financial investors hold significant shares in news media: Permira and KKR own ProSiebenSat1-Media AG; Mecom owns Berliner Verlag.

(E2)   Media ownership concentration regional (local) level   2 POINTS

There is some limited competition between regional broadcasters in most of the German states, but monopolization in the field of local press is increasing at the same time.

In order to asses the regional media ownership concentration in Germany, two types of major communication areas need to be defined first. In the case of newspapers, we speak of local and regional news media when they are published in and inform about one of the 439 German districts (Kreise und kreisfreie Städte). Regional news broadcasters operate at the level of the 16 German states. In some cases, these broadcasting stations cooperate, so that instead of 16 there are only 9 public service broadcasters.

A closer look at ownership concentration in the regional newspaper market reveals a tendency towards monopolization. There are different figures, yet all of them yield the same result: in most of the districts, there is no competition between local or regional newspapers. Schütz counts about 239 (53.7 %) district towns with just one newspaper (2009, p. 475); in a secondary analysis on the basis of Schütz' statistics, we counted 217 monopoly districts. Another census counts 250 districts without any competition between local newspapers (Möhring & Stürzebecher 2008, p. 99). We conclude that monopolization in the field of regional or local press is rather high and still increasing.

The situation is much better for radio. There are regional public broadcasting services and at least one commercial provider in all major German regions. Altogether, we find 53 statewide PBS radio programmes, and 54 statewide and 159 regional or local private radio programmes – some of them of course owned by the same broadcasting company (ALM-Jahrbuch 2008, p. 173).

Similar findings were obtained for the TV market: each of the nine regions is served by public broadcasting services. There are no commercial 24/7 services with exclusively regional contents, but some programmes provide regional and local windows (Regionalfenster). Notable, in this context, are the regional programmes produced by the two big commercial broadcasting companies, RTL-Group and ProSiebenSat1-Media AG: their market share varies between 8 and 15 %, depending on the specific region (ALM-Jahrbuch 2008, pp. 117). However, these programmes only get an air time of 30 minutes per day, except Saturdays and Sundays, and are limited to the western part of Germany. Furthermore, in Rheinland-Pfalz and Baden-Württemberg, a new private broadcaster called *RNF Live* aired and reaches roughly 0.5 million households in these states (KEK 2009, p. 319). The only state in eastern Germany with a regional or local window is Brandenburg, where *TV Angermünde* reaches only 40,000 households (ibid.). All in all, there are more than 235 local commercial broadcasters in the 16 states (ALM-Jahrbuch 2008, p. 120), but most of them have no significant reach, as they provide programmes for just one city. Thus there is some competition in regional TV markets between at least two regional competitors, although their output is quite small.

(E3) Diversity of formats   3 POINTS

There is a huge variety of news formats in every media sector in Germany.

For the print sector, we firstly have to refer to five national quality newspapers (Welt, Süddeutsche Zeitung, Frankfurter Allgemeine Zeitung, Tageszeitung, Frankfurter Rundschau), two weekly newsmagazines (Spiegel, Focus) and one major weekly newspaper (Zeit).

For TV, there are two commercial and one public news channels (ntv, n24; Phoenix). The two big public broadcasting services (ARD, ZDF) deliver news throughout the day, starting with a joint morning and a midday magazine, and news shows during the day with longer news programmes at 5, 7 and 8 p.m. Furthermore, both present a late-evening news magazine including reports and commentaries, as well as a news magazine at midnight. Political and investigative magazines, reportages and documentaries constitute an essential part of their programmes. The commercial stations offer a more limited supply of different news formats, as there is generally only one longer evening show and the morning and night programmes that are offered by some stations tend to be of a more sensationalist nature. Even the main private newscasts only present 18 % (RTL) and 27 % (Sat.1) reports on politics, whereas the PBS newscasts have a share of 38 % (ZDF) and 48 % (ARD) political news. The following table shows the proportions of information for the top five stations, and gives an impression of the diversity of formats delivering information:

Table 8.   Proportions of information and formats in TV per day, 2008

	information	news	TV magazines	documentaries
ARD	42.7 %	9.2 %	23.7 %	11.5 %
ZDF	48.2 %	9.5 %	31.7 %	10.4 %
RTL	33.3 %	3.9 %	15.7 %	14.3 %
SAT1	17.6 %	2.4 %	12.8 %	1.9 %
Pro7	23.5 %	0.8 %	13.7 %	8.8 %

Source: Krüger & Schramm 2009, p. 203.

Radio news is delivered every hour by all public broadcasting services and most of the commercial stations. Every regional radio station uses one or two frequencies for special information programmes, e.g., WDR3 and WDR5 in the largest German state North Rhine Westphalia. The two national radio information programmes are: DLF and Deutschlandradio Kultur. Both are clearly news oriented with only small amounts of music.

The online sector is dominated by offerings from the main news stations and newspapers (tageschau.de; Spiegel-Online; sueddeutsche.de).

(E4) Minority / Alternative media   3 POINTS

Minorities' informational needs are respected and served by the German news media.

This indicator has to be differentiated and is related specifically to the situation of a) the largest ethnic minority in Germany, the Turks b) disabled people and c) women – a majority which has been treated as a minority for a long time and still in some parts of the society is. The category "minority languages" is not appropriate for Germany, as there is no second official language.

Unfortunately, there is no updated list of the Turkish newspapers that are published in Germany and report on German issues. So we have to rely on data from 2002, which seems to be consistent with the current situation. Halm lists eleven fairly large daily newspapers (2006). The most current report on the situation of Turkish media in Germany counts eight daily and two weekly newspapers. And there are several local and regional newspapers of limited reach that are displayed, for example, in mosques (Foertsch). Furthermore, there are three fairly important radio stations reporting about and produced in Germany: Radio multikulti, Funkhaus Europa and Radyo Metropol. There are also two bigger TV stations: TRT-Int and Kanal D, of which the latter is owned (as well as the dailies Hürriyet and Milliyet) by the powerful Dogan-Media Group (Schneider & Arnold 2006; Foertsch). Taking a look at reach and patterns of use, the findings indicate a similarity with German media with regard to TV reach (89 % German, 83 % Turkish) and Internet reach (28 % German, 20 % Turkish). A major difference, however, is apparent in radio reach, 84 % for Germans and only 22 % for Turks (Simon 2007, p. 431). Generally, the market share of commercial stations among migrants is quite high, as the programmes mainly watched are ProSieben (13.4 %), RTL (11.7 %) and Sat1 (5.5 %). These stations, however, are not at all news oriented. The media use of migrants does not significantly differ from Germans' media use: 96 % use TV, 76 % the radio, 61 % a daily newspaper and 53 % the Internet more than once a week (Klingler & Kutteroff 2009, p. 305). Investigating whether migrants use media in German or in their mother tongue, Windgasse (2007) showed that the German media dominate migrants' (Windgasse researched Turks, Greeks, Yugoslavs and Italians) media use by far (Table 9):

Table 9.   Media use of migrants in Germany (at least once a week)

	Daily newspaper	TV	Radio	Internet
German-speaking Media	48 %	87.1 %	61.3 %	19.1 %
Native-language Media	27.8 %	48.4 %	21.2 %	5.9 %

Source: Windgasse 2007, p. 157.

With regard to the disabled, we find a notable list of special regular TV programmes including magazines like Stolperstein (BR) and Sehen statt hören (NDR, weekly). In addition, the major public news programme is simultaneously broadcasted in German sign language on the information channel Phoenix. Additionally, the association for handicaps and media (Arbeitsgemeinschaft Behinderung und Medien) produces TV magazines about and for disabled people on a regular basis for the stations Kabel 1, DSF and 3Sat – and local stations in the Munich area.

Finally, the media representation of women's issues is also satisfying. A diversity of formats and magazines exists in both the TV and the print media sectors. We have prominent TV magazines like Mona Lisa or FrauTV (both aired by public broadcasting) and the popular printed magazines Emma and Brigitte. With regard to patterns of media use, significant differences – with the exception of Internet usage – between male and female patterns cannot be detected: TV (207 / 233 minutes per day for men / women), radio (183/ 169 minutes per day), Internet (71.2 % / 57.9 % share of frequent online users) and newspapers (74.4 % / 70.5 % reach) (Gerhards & Klingler 2009, p. 663; Media Perspektiven Basisdaten 2006, pp. 80, 82, 84).

(E5) Affordable public and private news media   3 POINTS

A full media supply is affordable for large sectors of the German society.

In 2008, the average GDP per capita was about 28.800 €[4]. To run a radio or TV set one has to pay general licence fees: 5.52 € for radio alone, and 17.03 € for both TV and radio (GEZ). Cable networks charge, depending on provider and region, between 14.90 € and 19.99 € for a monthly cable TV connection. In addition to this monthly fee, one has to pay a one-time connection fee of between 14.90 € and 49.50 € (Jahrbuch Fernsehen 2009, p. 297). Monthly subscription for newspapers costs about 21.12 € (World Press Trends 2008, p. 392) – this is the most current figure from 2007. And finally, the monthly cost for access to broadband internet starts at 9.99 € – there are a lot of suppliers today who offer access to broadband in combination with cable TV, mobile or stationary telephone services or energy, so that the costs of "pure" access are quite hard to determine. This means full supply with cable TV, radio, newspaper subscription and broadband internet costs at least 63.04 € per month, or 756.48 € per year. This is 2.6 % of the average GDP per capita and seems to be quite affordable.

Also, it needs to be considered that average income does not tell us anything about income allocation. The allocation of income is obviously not homogeneous, and consequently there will be some households with a very high and many households with a very low income. There is a growing section of socially disadvantaged people on welfare receiving state transfers of only 351 € per month / 4212 € per year. Although they are exempt from licence fees, a full media supply with Internet, newspaper and cable TV would still cost them 46.03 € a month or 552.12 € per year, i.e., 13.1 % of their income.

Then again, while the prices for access to broadband in combination with telephone services[5] were cut by 93.4 % (compared to 2000), the prices for newspapers and magazines increased by 108.8 % (compared to 2000).

(E6) Content monitoring instrument   3 POINTS

Content monitoring is delivered on a regular and to some extent free basis.

In Germany, universities and specialized private agencies and companies provide content monitoring. There are some permanent issue monitoring instruments in Germany, which are publicly accessible, although some of them are not free of charge. For the monitoring of TV contents there are two instruments (IFEM - Institut für empirische Medienforschung and GöfaK Medienforschung), which are publicly funded and published in special journals (e.g., Krüger 2009). A third, MediaTenor, sell their results for a fee. The Landesmedienanstalten, which are funded through public licence fees, monitor commercial TV programmes. Their reports are publicly accessible by Internet. Content monitoring for newspapers is often commercial (media clipping services); two major services are available for a fee: MediaTenor and Ausschnitt Pressedienst. Some results of the monitors Landau Media Monitoring and Pressewatch can be obtained free of charge, but generally they are not for free. Totally free monitoring instruments have been established by unions and parts of non-governmental organizations and scientific institutions or by initiatives. All of these monitoring instruments – free or non-free – are normally not published by relevant news media, but only by scientific journals or special interest magazines. Consequently, their public visibility is rather low.

(E7) Code of ethics at the national level (structure)   3 POINTS

A national code of ethics exists, is implemented and widely used.

The German state fosters diligence in research at the level of each federal state through specific press laws (Landespressegesetze). These laws formulate a clearly defined public mission for the press, and derive/infer specific requirements from that public mission. For example, the North Rhine-Westphalian press law determines that the press has to deliver news, to comment on these and thereby contribute to shaping public opinion (LPGNRW §1); moreover, it obliges journalists to check all published information carefully (§6). Lastly, federal states and national government have agreed on a kind of mission statement (Programmauftrag) for public broadcasting services, which is implemented by contract (Medienstaatsvertrag), and which insists on fair, balanced, impartial reporting and underlines the importance of a diversity of opinions. These specific press laws are accompanied by a nationwide – but voluntary – code of ethics. The so-called Pressecodex establishes 16 journalistic standards, such as, §1 "Truthfulness and respect for human dignity," §2 "Diligence," and §7 "Separation of news and advertising." This codex was established by the German Press Council (Deutscher Presserat), whose members are the main newspaper publishers and unions, so it can be assumed that the codex is well-known and put into practice, which is confirmed by out interview partners from the journalists unions. To underpin this assumption, here are some figures (Tab. 10) from the most comprehensive survey of German journalists:

Table 10.   Journalists' self-image / implementation, i.e. approval to the statement "neutral and precise information of the public"

	TV	Radio	Newspaper	Online
Self-image	87 %	94 %	92 %	81 %
Implementation	77 %	80 %	78 %	63 %

Source: Weischenberg, Malik, & Scholl 2006, pp. 280-281.

Two complaints committees are part of the press council: the general complaints committee with two chambers and the complaints committee for editorial data protection. In 2008, the committees received 779 complaints. In the end, they dealt with 294 complaints (Presserat) and decided that 116 of them were baseless. Only in 15 cases did the complaints committee declare a public reprimand. In the view of the journalists' union, DJV, the press council does a good job. Because a legal framework providing ethical and journalistic standards for news coverage does not exist, the German Press Council exerts voluntary self-control of the press. Besides the council there are some initiatives made by journalists. First, there is an initiative for journalistic quality initiated by the biggest journalist's union (DJV), and second, there is the so-called Netzwerk Recherche, a lobbying organization promoting investigative journalism.

(E8)   Level of self-regulation (performance)   2 POINTS

There are parts of a self-regulating system, but these parts are not implemented by formal rules, even though more media seem to establish codes of conduct.

To begin with, mission statements are not the rule in the main German news media. The public broadcasting services do not have a mission statement, but they are legally bound by their public mandate to provide balanced reporting. Only one of the newspapers in our sample has any kind of explicit mission statement: WAZ currently works on a mission statement that defines the newspapers of the company as independent watchdogs defending the principles of democracy and liberty. The remaining news media in our sample do not have such mission statements, but when asked about their self-image, their representatives claimed that they naturally would help to foster democracy.

As we have stated before, a national code of ethics is implemented and widely used, and the journalists' unions believe it is common in most of the media companies. A code of conduct exists in only two cases; in one case it is currently under development. The other investigated news media do not have a set of rules or editorial guidelines in written form. By way of explanation, all of our interview partners argued that a code of ethics / code of conduct was unnecessary, either because it would just reflect the generally accepted and well-established journalistic routines, or because their employment contracts contained special clauses against corruption. Accordingly, a specific ethics guideline was regarded as superfluous. Furthermore, they agreed with the statement that any violation of journalistic standards and suspicion of such violations would be discussed in the editorial conference. None of our interview partners mentioned current violations, though one explained that the code of conduct was developed with harsh sanctions because of grey areas in journalists' behaviour towards local politicians and companies.

In all cases, there is some kind of ombudsman committee or workers council whose authorization is restricted to employment law and that has no say in editorial or ethical matters. The public service media have a special ombudsman for problems with corruption. All the same, many of our interview partners reported that there are daily conferences, which are open to all editors, and which allow for criticism. Furthermore, there exists the possibility of discussions between the editor-in-chief and all journalists. However, it should be noted that these rights are generally not formalized; they are just part of a corporate culture and their acknowledgement depends on the executives rather than on a written code. Journalistic ombudsmen do not exist in many of the main news media. Only WAZ prints a daily column of the ombudswoman.

To sum up, parts of a self-regulating system exist, but these parts are not implemented by formal rules: they could be described as being part of a tradition or of socialization within the news corporation. In comparison with the former report, German media perform better with this indicator, but we actually do not know whether this is a sample effect or a general trend. It has to be monitored.

(E9) Participation   2 POINTS

Audience participation is widely established with classical instruments, but there is a growing amount of new means of audience involvement.

Of course, there are the traditional avenues for participation in the news process, like letters to the editor or audience response by email and telephone. These forms of feedback are widely used and usually answered by special assistants or the journalists themselves. Only very few of these letters, however, will be published in specifically assigned columns or pages of the newspapers and magazines. TV and radio stations do not provide this kind of space for audience feedback. Most of the interviewed editors pointed out that the Internet is generally used as a platform both for the exchange between readers, listeners or viewers and for communication with the news media. Moreover, Internet presence is a place for corrections, especially for TV programmes that do not provide any space for corrections on their programme.

By instituting the so-called eyewitness reporter – which is supposed to represent a representative sample of the German population – one of the news media to offer ample opportunity for participation in the news process is N24. Civic journalism is encouraged by having the readers send in pictures and short videos. This feature cannot be widely used, as there are only two journalists in the newsroom who can supervise those activities. Obviously, the question remains whether these forms of participation meet journalistic standards. WAZ founded reader councils. The local editorial offices consult the readers' advisory board regularly. The influence of the readers' advisory board on the news process must be assessed as high because, according to the editorial office, the board's suggestions are usually implemented. And finally, WDR features a large number of programmes where listeners can call in and interact. In addition to that, WDR regularly provides so-called Listener Days, which give the audience the opportunity to produce radio reports that are aired after being checked by an editor. All in all, there is a lack of opportunities for reader participation in journalism; only a few of the main news media allow editorial space for the public voice. But it seems as if there has been some improvement in this area over the past years: A tendency towards more participation with instruments like reader reporters or reader advisory council can be detected.

(E10) Rules and practices on internal pluralism   2 POINTS

Internal pluralism is widely respected and established, though codified guidelines often do not exist.

In Germany, the media do not feel like partisans or political actors – an assumption that is underpinned by current research (e.g., Weischenberg, Malik, & Scholl 2006).

Even if certain political positions like liberalism or conservatism can be referred to certain news media, the leading editors we have interviewed expressed that they and their media primarily feel a duty to objectivity – the coverage is not coloured by the political standpoint of the media, the publisher or the editor-in-chief. Thus, in all of the investigated news media, daily conferences on the selection and framing of the news take place. These editorial conferences are open to the editorial staff, and all of the newsroom journalists have a chance to articulate their opinions without fear of repression. There are regular debates about the coverage of the news medium that are open to all political standpoints. WAZ and FAZ explained that their newspapers are willing to express different points of view, in the commentary as well as in the letters-to-the-editor section. The public service media, ZDF and WDR, are bound to objectivity and representation of different political opinions by their mission statements (Programmauftrag); WAZ declared itself to be a newspaper of debate. The legal obligations to impartial reporting are written down in the press law, which was described in detail in indicator E7.

The journalists' unions confirm the media's self-image: There are no known cases in media companies of reprisals against journalists because of their political standpoint. Nevertheless, again there are no clear and written rules for respecting internal pluralism – it is more or less a common-sense aspect of journalistic socialization and self-image. Current research on the journalism culture shows that journalists regard their work as influenced by professional standards to a medium degree (Hanitzsch et al. 2010).

Control / Watchdog (C)

(C1) Supervising the watchdog 'control of the controllers' 2 POINTS

There is a quite high degree of media monitoring by media journalism, professional journalistic journals and to a growing extent by blogs, although there is no permanent public debate about the role of media as watchdogs.

Besides extensive monitoring of the media in academic research projects, there are several instruments to control media performance. First, there is the regular coverage of media and journalism in specific sections of every national quality daily newspaper. Second, the regional public television NDR hosts a weekly media magazine called ZAPP. The latest but still well-established development includes media observers in specialised Internet blogs. There are several blogs that comment on just one newspaper, like Bild-Blog and Spiegelkritik.de; others report on media issues in general, such as Watchblog.de or Stefan Niggemeier-Blog. The DJV, the biggest German journalists' union, also maintains a blog with a specific focus on freedom of the press. One can assume that the reach of media blogs is quite low, as well as that of professional journalistic journals like Journalist and Message.

There is also some institutionalized political control of the media. The Landes-medienanstalten, publicly funded supervising authorities, control the content of the commercial programmes in every federal state, making sure that certain standards laid down in their broadcasting licence are met. These standards include, most prominently, a minimum quota of news and cultural programmes, and threshold values for the ratio of advertising and programme content. Public broadcasting service stations are to some extent supervised by special broadcasting councils representing highly influential social groups, such as parliamentarians and church representatives, which consequently indicates a certain amount of political influence on public broadcasting.

In general, the journalists' unions believe in the capacity of these institutionalized mechanisms of control of the controllers. For DJV, it is undoubtedly the case that the Press Council and the Landesmedienanstalten fulfil their controlling functions. However, the unions state that public discussions on media ethics and the media's performance for democracy remain restricted to very specialized media coverage or union congresses, but do not gain much public attention.

(C2) Independence of the news media from power holders 2 POINTS

Independence from power holders is guaranteed by law and widely respected, though there are some minor cases of potential owner influence.

In Germany, freedom of the press is guaranteed by constitutional law (Art. 5 Grundgesetz) and has been fostered by the jurisdiction of the federal constitutional court (Bundesverfassungsgericht) over the past fifty years (Branahl 2006, pp. 15-18; Fechner 2008, p. 33; 268). Article 5 of the constitution guarantees freedom of expression, freedom of access to information and the absence of censorship. In an Interstate Agreement on Broadcast Services (Rundfunkstaatsvertrag), both governmental and state non-intervention in broadcasting are described in detail. The commission for the control of concentration in the media system (KEK) criticized a 2008 renewed passage of this contract. KEK argues that §20 of the contract does not completely ensure that the state or the government cannot exert influence on broadcasters and programmes. Companies that are at least to a certain degree owned by the state, like Deutsche Telekom, are not excluded as broadcasters. Hence, KEK reports for 2008 three minor cases of specialized TV programmes in which the state, by virtue of its shareholding in Deutsche Telekom and Investitionsbank Berlin, may have exerted influence on the media (KEK 2009, pp. 345-347).

With regard to independence of the news media from power holders, only two cases can be reported. First, let us look at Deutsche Druck- und Verlagsgesellschaft

(DDVG), a printing and publishing house owned by the Social Democratic Party (SPD): although DDVG is one of the top ten publishing companies in Germany, their market share (2.4 %) is comparatively small (Röper 2008, p. 421). DDVG mostly owns regional and local newspapers, but in 2008 it also held a 40 % share of *Druck- und Verlagshaus Frankfurt am Main GmbH,* which publishes the national quality newspaper *Frankfurter Rundschau* (DDVG Geschäftsbericht 2008). Second, since 2006, after the sale of ProSiebenSat1-Media AG to the top publishing house (Springer) was prohibited by the German competition authority, this broadcasting company was sold to the financial investors Permira and KKR by the businessman Haim Saban. Thus a non-media company gained control over some news broadcasts like the SAT1-News and the commercial news channel n24. But these broadcasts are small in reach: SAT1-News has a market share of about 6 %, n24 about 1 % (Zubayr & Gerhards 2009; KEK 2009, pp. 339). In 2007, Berliner Verlag, which owns several regional newspapers, was sold to the financial investor David Montgomery and his commercial equity firm Mecom. Montgomery and Mecom finally sold Berlin Verlag in 2009, because the company needed money in the wake of the international financial crisis. Berliner Verlag was sold to the media group DuMont, which today owns quite a high portfolio of regional newspapers.

All leading editors we interviewed rejected any attempts of interference by power holders or politicians. No case was reported. On the contrary, all of our journalistic interview partners were convinced that the management would back them against such attempts. The German media system is widely characterized by distancing itself from the state (Hallin & Mancini 2009, p. 197), and the journalist culture contributes actively to the value of keeping one's distance from power holders (Hanitzsch & Seethaler 2009).

(C3) Transparency of data on media system   3 POINTS

Transparency of the complete media system is given and available for the public.

Print and online media are legally obliged to publicize an imprint – with the name and address of the publisher – in every edition. The clear duty to inform about the publishing person or company is formulated in national law (Telemediengesetz).

The market share of each commercial provider is legally restricted to 30 %. There are legal provisions to ensure plurality: Plurality of ownership is guaranteed by national law and controlled by the Bundeskartellamt, the German antitrust agency. Additionally, there is a special commission that assesses and reports the degree of concentration within the media market with a special focus on the television market (KEK – Kommission zur Ermittlung der Konzentration im Medienbereich). Concentration in the print market is assessed and evaluated by the commercial research institute FormaTT.

Both institutions publish their reports; KEK also provides a free Internet database. Reports on structural data of the German media system are provided by the public service media. Some reports are freely available on the Internet – e.g., the monthly journal Media Perspektiven, which presents the latest results from research on the reach, use and concentration of the media.

The Landesmedienanstalten promote and finance research on the media system, in 2009 with a grant of 20,000 Euros (ALM-Jahrbuch 2008, p. 461). A complete list of all projects is presented in the annual reports.

(C4) Journalism professionalism   2 POINT

There are signs of high professionalism, such as strong unions and frequent ethical debates, but the increasing workload of German journalists is a menace to news quality.

Journalists and journalists' unions agree on the question of workload: Both believe that the daily work load has significantly increased over the past years – and is still increasing. One consequence of this is less time for in-depth investigation. Two of the interviewed news media state that there is not enough staff for investigative research because the newsroom journalists have more than enough work with daily news composition. This work overload might be the result of job cuttings in the media. It cannot be referred to multi-media requirements, as the media companies have employed additional staff for online sites.

In Germany, journalists are organized in the unions DJU and DJV, which of course provide more or less regular training in ethical questions. Furthermore, they offer consultations on law and have national annual congresses where questions of ethics, the future of work or the journalists' self-image are discussed. Congresses and meetings in the federal states' sections of the unions are common as well.

Debates on ethics take place, but media journalists in newspapers as well as in TV, radio, and the Internet do not regularly discuss these matters. Most often these debates are reactions to current issues, like the coverage of the accident at the Loveparade in 2010. In such cases, ethical debates in the media occur, but their effect is limited. Public debates about journalistic behaviour are quite rare.

(C5) Journalists' job security   1 POINT

Journalists only have rudimentary legal protection.

With regard to journalists' job security, the unions provide quite a pessimistic outlook. First of all, the number of permanent staff in the newsrooms is declining, while the number of freelancers increases. One indicator of the increase in freelancers and decrease in permanent staff is the number of persons insured by the companies: This number has continued to fall over the past years (down 180 for the newspapers, down 410 for magazines). DJU also confirmed that round about 2/3 of their 22,000 current members are freelancers. In addition to that, there are cuts in jobs in many media companies, and the wages of permanent staff and freelancers have not increased over the past years. Many of the freelancers have very little money despite having a great deal of work. Especially since the financial crisis in 2008, staff reductions have taken place in every media company, DJV claims.

In Germany, the media are *Tendenzbetriebe*, which means that a company not only has economic but also cultural or political objectives. The government is not allowed to interfere in the political leanings of the news media – neither directly nor immediately through laws that, e.g., might allow a newspaper's workers council to gain influence over the publisher's inclinations. The rulings of the constitutional court and federal law are against any influence on the political leanings of the news media. On the other hand, publishers cannot force their editorial staff to follow their inclinations, i.e. a journalist is not bound to write an article expressing the publisher's viewpoint. In such cases, freedom of expression and the dignity of man (basic principles of the German constitution) legally protect journalists from pressure, which can be interpreted as a clause de conscience. Only the federal state of Brandenburg derived from these constitutional principles a passage in its press law that contains the protection of journalists from the influence of publishers (Fechner 2008, pp. 217-220). Journalists' unions do not report any case of reprisals on journalists based on their political opinions in the newsroom.

(C6)   Practice of access to information   2 points

Formally the access to information and to governmental documents is unlimited, though it does not work in a completely satisfactory manner in daily practice.

Since 2006, the Freedom of Information Act (Informationsfreiheitsgesetz) allows citizens and journalists access to governmental documents. This law obligates all state authorities (national, regional or local) to provide access to requested information for all citizens (Branahl 2006, p. 32; Fechner 2008, pp. 46-49). The journalists' unions claim that state authorities still constrain access to requested documents.

Another problem is the abolishment of journalists' privilege to refuse to give evidence in Germany. Journalists can no longer protect their sources in court, which is particularly problematic when reporting on the government and big companies using information from whistleblowers. Furthermore, journalists have to agree to be checked by state authorities or even the intelligence service in the wake of an increasing number of events. An accreditation more often depends on journalists' permission to save and check their data.

(C7) The watchdog and the media's mission statement   1 POINT

There is no widespread use of mission statements that explicitly foster investigative journalism. However, most interviewees emphasized the importance of investigative journalism.

Our findings corroborate the results of a previous survey showing that no more than 24 % of German journalists see themselves as watchdogs (Weischenberg, Malik, & Scholl 2006, p. 279). The journalists we have asked about how they would define their role in a democracy did not use the term "watchdog" or refer to the corresponding profile of an unflinching watchman over, let alone a critic of, politics and politicians. Only WAZ explicitly used the term watchdog – not only for the newspaper but also for all newspapers in this publishing house. They prefer to define their function as providers of impartial, fair and balanced information. Some editors pointed out that the media are not legally obliged to play the role of controllers of state powers, and that it would consequently be presumptuous to play this role and the part of a fourth branch of government. Others of our interview partners also feel that part of their role is to empower citizens to participate in the political process. In accordance with the fact that most journalists do not identify with the role of a watchdog, there are fewer mission statements that promote this self-image. An international comparison of journalism cultures underlines these assumptions: German journalists do feel obligated to the role of watchdog to a high degree, but consider the role of information provider to be much more important (Hanitzsch 2009; Hanitzsch & Seethaler 2009).

Likewise, there are no mission statements that explicitly advert to active investigative journalism. However, most interviewees emphasized that the importance of investigative journalism was so clearly a part of their self-image and work routines that it did not need to be set out in writing. However, especially the daily news media are often confronted with too many events – investigation and deep research therefore are not always possible. Nevertheless, most of our interview partners stated that critical coverage is obligatory. It is again WAZ that claims to have an extra investigation team of five newsroom journalists.

(C8)   Professional training   2 POINTS

In Germany, there is no serious lack of opportunities for journalism training.

At least three of the sampled news media run their own academy. In most cases, there is also a possibility to attend extra courses at academies and institutes or courses held by experts providing specialized knowledge. Only one editorship does not offer any journalism training. The journalists' unions provide a certain, but small, amount of professional training courses as well.

The next question, of course, is whether there is a great demand for such courses. All editors confirmed that there was a continuous demand and that most of the journalists in their editorial offices regularly took part in training courses. But continuous training is expensive. The newsroom needs to be sufficiently staffed for one or two colleagues to attend a course lasting several days. Also, sufficient funds need to be set aside for on-going professional training. Finally, journalists need to be encouraged by their superiors. Because most of the news media in our sample belong to financially sound publishing or broadcasting corporations, they have sufficient financial and staff resources at their disposal to enable on-going journalism training. ZDF and WDR, for example, emphasized their eagerness to provide training. WAZ claimed to have sufficient financial resources to enable continuous journalistic training and monitoring on the job. Thus, the company is currently working on a programme. In sum, it appears that financial resources, the encouragement of journalists, and a variety of training opportunities in most of the companies provide a solid basis for journalism training. There is, however, no formal obligation to take part in training programmes, and therefore, due to the generally heavy workload in editorial offices, in some cases there simply may be no time for additional courses.

(C9)   Watchdog function and financial resources   2 POINTS

The main German news media are in a quite good financial situation for in-depth investigations.

Given the fact that German journalists do not identify with the role of watchdog, it can be concluded that the priorities for financing journalistic work lie elsewhere. However, our findings indicate that most of the main news media have sufficient financial resources for investigations of their own and do not have to rely solely on agency material. All of the main news media have subscribed to the big national and international agencies. But agencies often function as a starting point for observation and not as a source that will be adopted completely.

Most of the interviewed news media told us that they are in a good financial situation and have enough funding for in-depth investigations. However, a majority added that funding had been cut over the past years. The journalists' unions confirm this finding: They also believe that the financial resources for in-depth research had been reduced. Furthermore, the unions complain that – despite the efforts of some bigger news companies and the public service media – most of the news media in Germany cannot afford their own investigations.

To sum up: the investigated main German news media are in a good financial situation. For all of them investigation is a question of prestige. And apparently this is independent of whether the media are run commercially or publicly or of whether journalists see themselves as watchdogs.

Summary and Conclusion

Altogether, this year's results show no great differences from the last report: The German news media again receive satisfactory scores in all of the analysed dimensions. As the small differences can be explained by sample effects, we conclude that the German news media still perform well and thus contribute to the functioning of democracy. At least two remarkable developments in the German media system, which are obvious in our data, have to named: First, a tendency towards more audience participation can be detected, which might result in positive effects for democracy if it leads to sound criticism of the media and a qualitative discourse about political issues within the audiences. Second, there is also a tendency towards ownership concentration, especially in the local and regional markets. If this development continues, we can anticipate serious problems regarding the plurality of information and opinion especially on the local level. As the local or regional newspaper is also one of the main sources of many citizens' information about national and international politics, less diversity in this sector may affect opinion formation on all relevant nationwide issues at stake.

To give a brief outlook on very current developments that might be relevant for the next report: (1) The German government passed a law to foster freedom of the press. The law contains the following elements: The publication of leaked material is no longer punished as aiding and abetting the betrayal of secrets. Additionally, there are stricter rules to hinder confiscation of journalists' data (epd medien 67, 2010, p. 7). (2) The funding of the public broadcasting system had to face two changes. In 2009, an increase in the annual fees led to increased revenues by 340 million euros (epd medien, 61, 2010, p. 5). Furthermore the states have decided on a new fee system, which charges each household instead of each individual TV or radio-set (epd medien, 83, 2010, p. 8). Though it is unclear whether this system, which is more transparent and easier to control, will provide more or less stabile revenues for PBS (epd medien, 92, 2010, p.10). We hypothesize that the new system will be perceived as more just and therefore gain acceptance among citizens. (3) Two other developments within the PBS are of interest. First, the income of the top management (including the directors) of all PBS stations was first published in 2010, which means more transparency and can be regarded as a positive development (epd medien, 63, 2010, 7; 64, 2010, 11-2). Second, another amendment of the valid Interstate Treaty on Broadcasting (*12. Rundfunkänderungsstaatsvertrag*) regulates whether the public broadcasting programmes are allowed to provide certain services on the Internet. As a consequence of this treaty, a so-called three-step test was introduced. The test checks the Internet offerings of PBS by asking the following three questions: Does the content meet the cultural and social needs of society? Does it contribute to media competition? Are the financial costs justified? This new regime is designed against distortion of the market, to secure the private Internet content providers, but it may affect the quality of news on the Internet as the PBS used to present a great deal of high quality information. However, it is unclear how far the economic crisis will affect journalism in the near future. In recent years, one has been able to observe cost reduction in many media companies, which often resulted in the layoffs of journalists. But we currently do not know whether these are structural changes and whether they will have negative impacts on media's performance for democracy.

Finally we return to our question regarding the supportive role of the media to build up and foster citizens' democratic orientation in a unified Germany. Studies conducted directly after unification showed that some central democratic norms, like the right of demonstration or the need for political opposition, were strongly supported by the East Germans, because they lacked those civil rights (Bauer 1991, p. 443-444). Nevertheless, a remarkable difference could be seen regarding the level of satisfaction with democracy (ibid., p. 448). In 1998, Gabriel found that West and East Germans, older and younger democrats, only marginally differed in their level of satisfaction with democracy (Gabriel 1999, p. 212), which is regarded as surprising as the total collapse of the political and economic system of Eastern Germany had occurred relatively recently. Thus, Gabriel argues that the adaption of patterns of trust in democratic institutions by the East Germans is an indicator of the formation of a unified political community (ibid., p. 230). As German media are thought to have performed well for democracy, it can be argued that this performance was in a way supportive of people's perception of democratic accountability. The very quick unification of people's minds and their acceptance of/ satisfaction with democracy may to some extent have resulted from the media's function of democratic socialization. In 2010, the findings are similar but slightly different: While East and West Germans appreciate the idea of democracy (89 % and 92 %, respectively), satisfaction with the current state of democracy in Germany is modest. Almost 50 % of West Germans are "very" or "rather satisfied" with the functioning of democracy, but the same is true of only 33 % of citizens in the Eastern states (Niedermayer & Stöss 2008). Given that the successful democratic socialization of the German people after World War 2 at least to some extent can be referred to the performance of the media, a similar development for Eastern Germany's citizens after unification can be expected. Long-term monitoring of Germans' media use indicates that no differences between the states can be detected. From 1990 to 2005, people in the East and West German states make use of TV, radio, newspapers and the Internet to largely the same extent. The East Germans actually spend a bit more time on watching TV and reading daily newspapers (Reitze & Ridder 2005, p. 39). Most current data from 2010 confirm these trends. There is neither a great difference in media use nor in the political interest of newspaper readers (Jandura & Meyen 2010, p. 220). The German media system structurally provides the citizenry with political information on an appropriate level, and the media's performance meets people's use of news. These conditions – once, after World War 2, and again after the unification – provided a basis for democratic socialization. Our reports indicate that this foundation continues to exist. Hence, the media are still capable of playing a supportive role for democracy.

Notes

[1] This report is an updated and advanced version of our country report for the *Media Democracy Monitor* 2008 (Marcinkowski & Donk 2011).

[2] Currently, 94 % of public broadcasting is financed by fees and 6 % by advertising and sponsoring (GEZ). PBS-TV is allowed 20 minutes of advertising in their main programmes – and only before 8 pm. PBS-Radio has the right to air 90 minutes of advertising per day. So, WDR is allowed some advertising until the evening in its main programmes Einslive and WDR2, but there are no ads in the news channel WDR5.

[3] As an outlook: In 2010, Pro7Sat1 Media AG sold the news channel N24.

[4] Source: Eurostat

[5] According to the national statistical bureau, there are no longer separate reports on the development of prices for access to broadband and telephone, because suppliers mostly offer combined solutions.

References

Altendorfer, O. (2004) *Das Mediensystem der Bundesrepublik Deutschland. Band 2.* Wiesbaden: VS Verlag.

Bauer, P. (1991) Politische Orientierungen im Übergang. Eine Analyse politischer Einstellungen der Bürger in West- und Ostdeutschland 1990/1991. *Kölner Zeitschrift für Sozialpsychologie und Soziologie, Vol. 43, 3,* 433-453.

Branahl, U. (2006) *Medienrecht. Eine Einführung.* Wiesbaden: VS Verlag.

van Eimeren, B., & Frees, B. (2008) Internetverbreitung: Größter Zuwachs bei Silver-Surfern. Ergebnisse der ARD/ZDF-Onlinestudie 2008. *Media Perspektiven, 7/2008,* 330-344.

Fechner, F. (2008) *Medienrecht.* Tübingen: UTB.

Foertsch, P. (n.d.) Türkische Medien in Deutschland. Retrieved from http://www.kas.de/wf/doc/kas_12799-544-1-30.pdf

Gabriel, O.W. (1999) Integration durch Institutionenvertrauen? Struktur und Entwicklung des Verhältnisses der Bevölkerung zum Parteienstaat und zum Rechtsstaat im vereinigten Deutschland. In Friedrichs, J. & Jagodzinski, W. (eds) Soziale Integration. [*KZfSS, Sonderheft 38*] (pp. 199-235) Opladen: Westdeutscher Verlag.

Gerhards, M., & Klingler, W. (2009) Sparten- und Formattrends im deutschen Fernsehen Das Programmjahr 2008. *Media Perspektiven, 12/2009,* 662-678.

Grüll, P.(2009) *Die Qualität der Nachrichtenagentur aus Sicht ihrer Kunden. Eine Befragung von Nachrichten-redakteuren in leitender Funktion.* Münster: LIT.

Halm, D. (2006) Die Medien der türkischen Bevölkerung in Deutschland. In Geißler, R. & Pöttker, H. (eds) *Integration durch Massenmedien* (pp. 77-92) Bielefeld: transcript.

Hanitzsch, T., Anikina, M., Berganza, R., Cangoz, I., Coman, M., Hamada, B., Hanusch, F., Karadjov, C., Mellado, C., Moreira, S., Mwesige, P., Plaisance, P., Reich, Z., Seethaler, J., Skewes, E., Noor, D., & Yuen, K. (2010) Modeling Perceived Influences on Journalism: Evidence from a Cross-National Survey of Journalists. *Journalism & Mass Communication Quarterly 87(1),* 7-24.

Hanitzsch, T., & Seethaler, J. (2009) Journalismuswelten: Ein Vergleich von Journalismuskulturen in 17 Ländern. *Medien & Kommunikationswissenschaft 57(4),* 464-483.

Hanitzsch, T. (2009) Zur Wahrnehmung von Einflüssen im Journalismus: Komparative Befunde aus 17 Länder. *Medien & Kommunikationswissenschaft 57(2),* 153-173.

Hans-Bredow-Institut (2006) *Medien von A bis Z.* Wiesbaden: VS Verlag.

Humphreys, P. (1990) *Media and Media Policy in West Germany. The Press and Broadcasting since 1945.* New York: Berg.

Jandura, O. & Meyen, M. (2010) Warum sieht der Osten anders fern? *Medien- und Kommunikationswis-senschaft, Vol. 58,* 208-226.

Kaase, M. (1998) Die Bundesrepublil: Prognosen und Diagnosen der Demokratienetwicklung in der Rück-blickenden Bewertung. In Friedrichs, J., Lepsius, R. & Mayer, K.U. (eds) *Die Diagnosefähigkeit der Soziologie [KZfSS, Sonderheft 38]* (pp. 35-55) Opladen: Leske und Buderich.

Klingler, W. (2008) Jugendliche und ihre Mediennutzung 1998-2008. *Media Perspektiven, 12/2008,* 625-346.

Klingler, W., & Kutteroff, A. (2009) Stellenwert und Nutzung der Medien in Migrantenmillieus. *Media Perspektiven, 6/2009,* 297-308.

Klingler, W.& Müller, D.K. (2008) Ma 2009 Radio II: Stabile Nutzungsmuster auch bei erweiterter Grundg-esamtheit. *Media Perspektiven, 10/2008,* 502-515.

Krüger, U.M. (2009) InfoMonitor 2008: Fernsehnachrichten bei ARD, ZDF, RTL und Sat. 1. *Media Pers-pektiven, 2/2009,* 73-94.

Krüger, U.M., & Zapf-Schramm, T. (2009) Politikthematisierung und Alltagskultivierung im Infoangebot. *Media Perspektiven, 4/2009,* 201-222.

Marcinkowski, F., & Donk, A. (2011) Germany. In Trappel, J., & Meier, W. (eds) *On Media Monitoring. The Media and Their Contribution to Democracy.* New York et al.: Peter Lang, 161-184.

Meyn, H. (2004) *Massenmedien in Deutschland.* Konstanz: UVK

Möhring, W., & Stürzebecher, D. (2008) Lokale Tagespresse: Publizistischer Wettbewerb stärkt Tageszeitungen. *Media Perspektiven, 2/2008,* 91-101.

Niedermayer, O. & Stöss, R. (2008) Berlin-Brandenburg-Bus 2008. Einstellungen zur Demokratie in Berlin und Brandenburg 2002-2008 sowie in Gesamtdeutschland 2008. Retrieved from http://www.polsoz. fu-berlin.de/polwiss/forschung/systeme/empsoz/index.html

Puppis, M. (2007) *Einführung in die Medienpolitik.* Konstanz: UVK.

Reitze, H. & Ridder, C. (eds) (2005) *Massenkommunikation VII.* Eine Langezeitstudie zur Mediennutzung und Medienbewertung 1964-2005. Baden-Baden: Nomos.

Röper, H. (2008) Konzentrationssprung im Markt der Tageszeitungen. Daten zur Konzentration der Tages-presse in der Bundesrepublik Deutschland im I. Quartal 2008. *Media Perspektiven, 8/2008,* 420-437.

Schneider, B., & Arnold, A. (2006) Massenmediale Ghettoisierung oder Einheit durch Mainstream. In Geißler, R. & Pöttker, H. (eds) *Integration durch Massenmedien* (pp. 93-120) Bielefeld: transcript.

Schütz, W. (2009) Deutsche Tagespresse 2008. Media Perspektiven, 9/2009, 454-483.

Schütz, W. (2009a) Redaktionell und verlegerische Struktur der deutschen Tagespresse. Media Perspektiven, 9/2009, 484-493.

Simon, E. (2007) Migranten und Medien 2007. *Media Perspektiven, 9/2007,* 426-435.

Tenscher, J. (2008) Massenmedien und politische Kommunikation in den Ländern der Europäischen Union. In: Gabriel, O.W. & Kropp, S. (eds), *Die EU-Staaten im Vergleich. Strukturen, Prozesse, Politikinhalte* (pp. 412-447) Wiesbaden: VS Verlag.

Weischenberg, S., Malik, M., & Scholl, A. (2006) *Die Souffleure der Mediengesellschaft. Report über die Jour-nalisten in Deutschland.* Konstanz: UVK.

Wilke, J. (2007) Das Nachrichtenangebot der Nachrichtenagenturen im Vergleich. *Publizistik, 52,* 329-354.

Windgasse, T. (2007) Die Radionutzung von Migranten im Kontext anderer Medien. *Media Perspektiven,* *3/2007,* 153-161.

Zubayr, C., & Gerhard, H. (2009) Tendenzen im Zuschauerverhalten. Fernsehgewohnheiten und Fernseh-reichweiten im Jahr 2008. *Media Perspektiven,. 3/2009,* 98-112.

Data Sources

AGOF 2009 = Arbeitsgemeinschaft Onlineforschung (eds) Internet facts I-IV. Retrieved from http://ww.agof.de

ALM Jahrbuch 2008 = Arbeitsgemeinschaft der Landesmedienanstalten in Deutschland (eds) ALM Jahrbuch 2008. Berlin: Vistas.

BDZV 2009 = Bundesverband Deutscher Zeitungsverleger e.V. (eds) Die deutschen Zeitungen in Zahlen und Daten. Auszug aus dem Jahrbuch „Zeitungen 2009". Berlin.

DDVG Geschäftsbericht = Deutsche Druck- und Verlagsgesellschaft mbH (Ed.) Geschäftsbericht 2008. Retrieved from http://www.ddvg.de/wirtschaftsdaten/geschaeftsbericht2008.pdf

Destatis: Bundesamt für Statistik. Retrieved from https://www-genesis.destatis.de/genesis/online;jsessionid=CEB 8C5ED1A5C717D9F7996BAE06C20C6.tomcat_GO_1_1?operation=abruftabelleBearbeiten&levelind ex=2&levelid=1283935728329&auswahloperation=abruftabelleAuspraegungAuswaehlen&auswahlverze ichnis=ordnungsstruktur&auswahlziel=werteabruf&selectionname=12211-0102&auswahltext= %23Z-0 1.01.2008&werteabruf=Werteabruf

epd medien = Evangelischer Pressedienst. Fachinformation Medien. Frankfurt a.M.

Eurostat = Statisches Amt der Europäischen Gemeinschaft. Retrieved from http://epp.eurostat.ec.europa.eu/ portal/page/portal/eurostat/home/

GEZ = Gebühreneinzugszentrale. Retrieved from http://www.gez.de

IVW Auflagenstatistik = Informationsgemeinschaft zur Feststellung der Verbreitung von Werbeträgern e.V. (eds) Auflagenstatistik. Retrieved from http://www.ivw.de/

Jahrbuch Fernsehen 2009 = Adolf Grimme Institut, Deutsche Kinemathek, Funkkorrespondenz, & Institut für Medien- und Kommunikationspolitik (eds) Jahrbuch Fernsehen 2009. Köln.

KEK 2008 = Kommission zur Ermittlung der Konzentration in Medienbereich (eds) Elfter Jahresbericht. Berichtszeitraum 1. Juli 2007 bis 30. Juni 2008. Retrieved from http://www.kek-online.de/Inhalte/ jahresbericht_07_08.pdf

KEK 2009 = Kommission zur Ermittlung der Konzentration in Medienbereich (eds) Zwölfter Jahresbericht. Berichtszeitraum 1. Juli 2008 bis 30. Juni 2009. Retrieved from http://www.kek-online.de/Inhalte/ jahresbericht_07_08.pdf

Media Perspektiven Basisdaten 2008 = Media Perspektiven Basisdaten 2008: Daten zur Medien Situation in Deutschland. Frankfurt a.M..

Media Perspektiven Basisdaten 2009 = Media Perspektiven Basisdaten 2009: Daten zur Medien Situation in Deutschland. Frankfurt a.M..

OECD = OECD Broadband Portal. Retrieved from http://www.oecd.org/document/54/0,3343 ,en_2649_34225_38690102_1_1_1,00.html

Presserat = Deutscher Presserat. Retrieved from http://www.presserat.de

Statisches Bundesamt / Destatis = Statistisches Bundesamt Deutschland. Retrieved from http://www.destatis.de

Television 2009 = European Audiovisual Observatory (Ed.) Fernsehen in 36 europäischen Staaten. Strasbourg.

World Press Trends 2008 = World Association of Newspapers (eds) World Press Trends. 2008 Edition. Paris.

Chapter 7

LITHUANIA
Mixed Professional Values in a Small and Highly Blurred Media Environment

Auksė Balčytienė

Lithuania is a small country (population 3.2 million[1]) characterized by political and economic structures as well as media performance characteristics typical of the young democracies of Central and Eastern Europe[2]. Despite the many similarities, media performance in each of these countries is unique to such an extent that its qualitative characteristics can be paralleled with the overall culture in society, and especially the political culture[3]. Modern Lithuanian journalism represents characteristics that have grown out of and endured from press and book publishing histories as well as from the role the press has played in different periods in history (Balčytienė 2009). Moreover, journalism as it is in Lithuania today has evolved from certain historical and situational circumstances. Journalism was and still is affected by such features as the country's geo-political location and marginality, in addition to its cultural and linguistic distinctiveness. For instance, from the Western point of view, for many centuries, Lithuania as well as the other Baltic nations has always represented the East; while from a Russian perspective, these countries have often appeared to be part of the West. Mixed values and norms and duality of interpretation are also currently observed in the behavioral patterns of the political and media spheres, not only in Lithuania but also in the other Baltic countries, namely Latvia and Estonia.

Briefly, media institutions in the Baltic countries represent hybrid structures, and their further evolvement toward one or another media model (or a hybridity of these) is dependent on the challenges of the present day, especially economic and social. The economic recession with its accompanying decline in advertising revenues, tax changes and increasing competition has significantly affected media operations in many countries around Europe. In Lithuania, the advertising market shrunk to dramatic levels (by 39.2 % in 2009), thus all media companies reassessed their business plans, changed programming, recalculated salaries, and postponed investments. In 2009, the advertising revenues were almost 50 % less in newspapers and magazine publishing if compared to 2008; the TV sector had to face 37 % less income from advertising, while the drop in Internet advertising revenues was 32 %. The economic recession has hit the budget of the public service broadcaster (the LRT, the Lithuanian Radio and Television)[4] especially hard, and drastic cuts in programming and changes in content followed: broadcasting time on television and radio was reduced to critical levels, specialized content programs were terminated, and radio programs in the English language were cancelled. Another observation is related to the social pressures on journalistic professionalism associated with increasing media competition and growing media convergence.

At the same time, in spite of these many challenges and drawbacks, a significant number of media companies in Lithuania, especially those operating in alternative and niche markets, have used the moment of crisis for quality improvement, change, diversification and renewal[5].

Selected news media items

In the present overview, the statistics from 2008 and 2009 are used (in a few cases data from 2010 is provided), and the selected media items represent mainstream news media in the country (Table 1). The group is represented by media of different types (TV stations, dailies and news portals) and with distinctive characteristics (quality and popular information providers). In addition to talking to journalists and editors, the president of the Lithuanian Journalists Union was interviewed, and comments were provided by the independent media expert[6]. Altogether, 7 people were interviewed.

Table 1.   Selected news media according to media type and ownership

News media	Media type	Ownership	Interviewee
LTV (Lithuanian Television)	Public service television	Lithuanian Radio and Television (public service broadcaster)	Journalist (regional news reporter)
BNS (Baltic News Service)	News agency	Alma Media (Finland)	Editor in Chief (company director)
Lietuvos rytas	Mid-market daily	Closed Stock Company "Lietuvos rytas"	Editor in Chief
Lrytas.lt	Online news portal of Lietuvos rytas		
15 min	Free daily (regional)	Schibsted (Norway)	Regional news editor
Delfi.lt	Leading news portal	Delfi AS (Estonia)	Editor

Indicators

Freedom / Information (F)

(F1)   Geographic distribution of news media availability   3 POINTS

There are no clear differences noticed in the regional or national distribution of mainstream media; some years ago a few exceptions in use of the Internet were observed among users from different age groups (e.g., young people were more active users of the Internet), but the situation has changed rapidly.

All types of news media are widely available in the country. Although the reach of dailies in Lithuania is not as high as, for example, in the Nordic countries or Germany, it is significantly higher than in the countries of Southern Europe. According to statistics of 2008, the readership of dailies has remained similar to previous years and it was 95 %, which means that almost everyone in the age group between 15 and 74 years in the period of the past six months has read a periodical; moreover, 90 % of those who could be called decision-makers (represented by the age group 20-49) are regular press readers (TNS Gallup 2009). Briefly, Lithuanians consider press reading an important activity.

Television programs in Lithuania are broadcasted via all kinds of electronic networks: terrestrial television stations, cable networks, multichannel microwave television distribution systems, wire and wireless broadband networks, and by satellite. In 2009, there were 1,300,000 households in Lithuania: 372,249 households used cable television, 24,372 households – multichannel microwave television distribution systems. Analogue terrestrial television in 2009 was already not the dominant technology it was in 2008 when it had over 50 % of users (Radio & Television in Lithuania 2009/2010).

Older age citizens are more active users of television than of the press, and children (between 4-14 years of age) on average watch television about two and half hours a day. The average amount of time Lithuanians spent in front of the TV in 2008 was 3 hours and 23 minutes. Statistically, men spend less time with TV than women do. Also, TV viewing time is seasonally affected: in the winter, people spend more time with television than in the summer (a difference of one hour), and television is watched longer on weekends than during the working days.

In 2008, the commercial TV stations were the most popular according to audience share (TV3: 25.8 % and LNK: 20.9 %), while the audience share of the public service broadcaster (the LTV) was 13.3 %. The public service radio program (LR1: 22.6 %) was the most popular in the country, despite the fact that its main audience is older than 50 years. According to statistics for 2008, over 20 % of the people in Lithuania considered the public service broadcaster (LRT) to be the most influential medium, and this indicator has remained unchanged for a number of years (Annual Report of LRT 2010).

Despite this expressed trust in the public service media, comparative data for five Baltic and Nordic countries show that commercial television in Lithuania is the most popular in terms of use (Česnavičius 2010). Lithuania clearly stands out from the rest regarding the overall size of this segment (56.2 %). Scandinavian countries are different in terms of the stronger position of the public broadcaster (30-40 % of the general audience) compared to an average of around 15 % in the Baltic region (Table 2).

Table 2. Total viewing time split by channel segments (5-year average, 2005-2009)

Country	National commercial channels (%)	Public broadcasters (%)	Local & regional TV stations (%)	International cable & satellite channels (%)
Lithuania	56.2	14.4	10.4	19.0
Latvia	36.5	15.8	20.2	27.4
Estonia	39.4	16.7	20.2	27.5
Denmark	32.9	30.2	22.8	14.1
Norway	35.5	40.9	11.0	12.5

Source: Annual Report of LRT 2010.

Despite having a small audience, Lithuania also has a very dispersed audience in terms of which type of media (print, broadcast or Internet) and what kind of programs it uses for information and entertainment. Business leaders, for example, are most fond of news analysis and debate programs on News Radio (Žinių radijas); whereas people over 50 listen to public radio programs (LR1) and younger audiences are more active online.

Internet usage has been growing steadily since 2000. Today, the penetration has started leveling in the age group of young users, while in the group between 30 and 59 years, it is still growing. In 2008, for the first time since a decade of Internet usage measurements, it was noticed that young users no longer dominate the Internet audience.

In comparison to the Internet, media developments in Europe, Lithuania and the Baltic countries (especially Estonia) stand out in terms of Internet access and new media use. Internet penetration in Lithuania is above the European average (60 %), and the three Baltic countries have the highest figures for households connected to the Internet via FTTH (fiber to the home) networks. The top popular media online in these countries are the online-only news portals (Delfi has sister portals in each country) that do not have any connections to mainstream media such as dailies or broadcast stations (see Table 6). The Lithuanian Facebook community has over 700,000 members, which makes it the biggest and fastest growing Facebook community in the Baltic countries. As a response to technological challenges, few media (mainly newspapers owned by Scandinavian investors: *Verslo žinios, 15 min*) have designed their newspaper versions to be applicable for iPad. Another proof of online media's public significance is the fact that over a dozen professional blogs in politics, media, economy, new technologies, and social issues are regularly monitored by different media monitoring companies. The purposes for monitoring vary, but this signals that business and politics already consider social media to be important opinion shapers. In sum, many different things are happening online, where we already can see the emergence of new and exciting links between journalism, civil society and democracy.

(F2)   Patterns of news media use (consumption of news)   2 POINTS

Although the mainstream news media are heavily used in the country, the population in Lithuania is segmented (dispersed into different audience groups) according to its socio-economic status and socio-cultural needs (the type of media and how it is used).

Despite the fact that people consider newspaper reading an important activity, it is television that receives the biggest share of daily media use. The entire population reads and watches news regularly, but clear differences emerge when information use between people living in the cities and peripheral regions of the country is estimated. For instance, people living in bigger cities tend to read more dailies than those living in the outlying regions, whereas people from smaller cities and living in the peripheral regions are more active TV program watchers and magazine readers.

   Among TV news programs, the news program on commercial TV3 television is the most popular (the evening news program on TV3 has a 12 % share of the audience, while the "Panorama" news program on the PSB channel has 6.3 %). Generally, each TV station has two or three news programs – these are thought to be inseparable from the station's image and necessary to produce to uphold the station's reputation.

   Being a small country, Lithuania also has a dispersed audience, which, as television audience studies vividly describe (Česnavičius 2010), is split into a large number of different audience groups, each with a very different relation to such content categories as news/information or talk shows and general entertainment, mainstream or niche programs. In another study (TNS Gallup 2009), a clear difference in value orientations was disclosed between people living in big cities and those living in the outlying regions, although this result is only applicable to the age group between 30 and 49. For instance, people from smaller cities tend to rely more strongly on traditional values (e.g., religion) and are much less interested, for example, in cultural programs, whereas people living in the cities support individualistic values and are more pragmatically oriented (they are more practical, more logical; and they are also more interested in the arts, popular culture and celebrities, but not at all interested in, for example, religion). Interestingly enough, in the two other age groups (15-29 and 50-74) no such clear differences were detected. In sum, all this shows that media use among decision-makers is quite dispersed according to the place where people live (center or periphery) as well as the value orientations and content preferences of those who consume media.

(F3) Diversity of news sources   2 POINTS

News media use diverse sources; however, none of the mainstream news media have a bureau in a foreign country: for international news reporting, news media rely on Internet-based sources or international news agency material. Citizen journalism is popular in news portals.

Leading news organizations subscribe to a variety of news sources. The two national news agencies (BNS and ELTA) are the leaders in the domestic news market, however, only a few news organizations subscribe to both agencies. Normally, only international news and sports news are published directly from news agency material, in all other cases this material is used only as a source (as a guideline to what is important). For some newspapers, originally produced journalistic content amounts to 80 % (in the news portal of the same company the original journalistic content amounts to around 30 %) (*Lietuvos rytas* and Lrytas.lt). Other popular news sources for media are international news agencies (Reuters, Associated Press, Associated Press TV news, AFP), EBU material, international news photo suppliers (Scanpix Baltics) and others. For some news media, an important source of news is press releases. According to our respondents, among the most significant news suppliers for journalists are networks of their own sources delivering political, economic, cultural, or sports news. In addition to relying on news agency material, PR news and other information providers (social media), the readers supplying Internet portals with user-generated content are also considered to be important proof of what is new and interesting to ordinary people. A number of leading news portals (Delfi.lt, 15min.lt) have developed fairly successful citizen journalism projects that have grown into media supported newsrooms with a few dozen amateur citizen reporters and local editors (Pilietis.lt, Ikrauk.lt).

Leading news media organizations employ foreign correspondents, but these correspondents mainly work part time or on a freelance basis. Lithuanian radio (LR1) has the biggest network of foreign correspondents regularly reporting from different countries around the world. "Big" national dailies (*Lietuvos rytas*) also have correspondents regularly reporting from European capitals. However, none of these news media has a foreign news bureau in a foreign country. The main reason for this is economic limitations. Having a foreign bureau is considered to be too expensive (and by some media not really necessary as news is available through Internet sources). The networks of foreign correspondents of those media that have them are organized rather loosely: journalists residing in foreign countries mainly work on honorariums (as freelancers). Public service radio and television (the LRT) used to be the only media group the had a bureau in Brussels with two staff members based in Brussels and regularly reporting from neighboring European capitals (Paris, London, Amsterdam). However, due to severe financial cuts in the LRT budget in the summer of 2009, the Bureau in Brussels was closed[7].

(F4)   Internal rules for newsroom democracy   1 POINT

In most media organizations, there are no formalized procedures for how to involve journalists in decisions on personnel or editor in chief choices.

There is also no formalized or standardized practice for making journalist or editor choices in the Lithuanian mass media. Some of the news media organize open competitions, while other organizations try to promote their own journalists and invest in human resource building by career offers to their own staff members, and especially in such cases negotiations among journalists as to who will become a desk editor do take place. Different news organizations use different promotional means for their staff members. In some news media, journalists are promoted by being assigned greater responsibilities; in others – by additional financial benefits. Again, in all cases, the choice of the candidate for the highest position in the organization (the editor in chief) is the subject of the board decision (e.g., the director general at the public service broadcaster is chosen by the LRT Council).

(F5)   Company rules against *internal* influence on
newsroom / editorial staff   1 POINT

In most cases, the news media do not have written editorial policies (only a few media have these documents available online); some of the news media that do not have written policies acknowledge that having such document is an important strategic policy decision and are planning to develop such documents in the near future.

The main media law prohibits any pressure on journalists to air false or biased information. It requires producers of public information programs to have their own internal codes of ethics, which "must set the journalist's rights, duties, responsibility, employment relations, as well as the journalist's protection against restriction of his rights". It pins down the journalists' duties including the duty "to refuse an assignment by the producer, the disseminator of public information, their representative or a responsible person appointed by them, if this assignment compels [the journalist] to violate the laws or the Code of Ethics of Lithuanian Journalists and Publishers".

According to the interview results, the majority of journalists say they are independent in choosing their topics and feel no pressure from the media owners. Although media organizations do not have formal rules to separate newsroom and advertising departments, these separations are made and, as our respondents claimed, people from advertising departments are never present in editorial meetings. Some other media also have practices of hiring journalists (freelancers) to write commis-´ sioned texts (that include special indications that this journalistic work was commis-sioned by external sources), thus desk journalists are excluded from such practice.

Normally, newsroom management rules are not formalized, and only a few media (business daily *Verslo žinios*) have their editorial policies publicly available (TILS 2008). According to our respondents, all news media organizations have estab-lished traditions of non-interference in journalistic production. The public service broadcaster (the LRT), for example, has a database with job descriptions of its staff members, where all responsibilities of the professions, for instance, of a journalist or an editor, are explained in a standardized form. In other cases, the norms of profes-sional behavior are written in job contracts (this appears to be the most conventional practice in the Lithuanian media).

Institutionally, it seems that media organizations have developed their own profes-sional cultures (for example, with certain rules and norms of professionalism inscribed in job contracts); in reality, however, there are certain drawbacks. A case was reported in the media revealing that in some dailies (Lietuvos žinios[8]), the texts of journalists were edited without their knowledge. Another drawback is that the requirement for an internal code of ethics in most media organizations is implemented only formally, as there is no legally binding commitment to ensure editorial independence.

(F6) Company rules against *external* influence on newsroom / editorial staff   1 POINT

It is difficult to draw a firm conclusion here: some of the news media have clear and transparent rules (reporting policies), but this is not applied as a regular and established practice in all media organizations. One of the failures to meet this criterion is the public service broadcaster, which not only lacks transparent and planned funding procedures, but its funding is negotiated with the government on an annual basis.

News media receive income from a multitude of sources such as advertising and sponsoring, and a few media receive public donations (Bernardinai.lt). In the case of the public service broadcaster, close to 40 % of the funding comes from advertising, while the rest comes through state allocations.

Although program sponsoring is not a new practice in the Lithuanian media (media law has a special chapter on how this type of advertising is regulated, that advertising is forbidden in news programs and restrictions apply in other programs), with the media crisis it has taken a different shape. Normally, sponsorships are indicated clearly in texts and TV programs, but, as reported in different studies (TILS 2007; Jastramskis 2009), hidden advertising is often found in the mass media (in spite of the fact that media companies are fined for such practice and all cases become public in the media)[9]. It is necessary to mention here that some news media have written rules to indicate that journalistic work was funded through external sources. Another group of media companies also announce their policies on the Internet (that they support quality and high standards of professional journalism), mark advertising and audit circulation.

An exceptional case in program sponsoring discussion is linked to reporting about EU-funded projects. The EU parliament members do fund programs on radio, sections on European news are available in different news portals (funded through the European Parliament members or the European Commission Representation in Lithuania), and TV and print media also receive a significant amount of funding by giving visibility to EU-supported projects in science, education, transport or agriculture. This can certainly be treated as a chance to bring new (European) themes into the public agenda by raising public awareness on important issues; yet, in most cases, the news presented as European news lacks the essential professionalism requirements (news value, critical analysis, sufficient background information) and their presentation style resembles PR writing. Hence, the overall practice is considered to be professionally degrading (Nevinskaitė 2008). One respondent in our study said that their company is taking part in EU reporting because they have won a competition from the Ministry of Finance to write about EU-funding and that their journalists will write about these projects, but will uphold journalistic standards and indicate the source of funding (and also make this information free for other news media).

In addition to what has been discussed above about potential external pressures on the media, the situation surrounding funding of the public service broadcaster needs very close consideration. Despite the continual requirements to establish clear and transparent procedures for LRT funding, the government has failed to develop an adequate long-term funding program, thus the broadcaster is still funded on an annual basis. The potential political influence on decision-making regarding budget allocations is the least well-functioning aspect of this practice. With the economic recession, the LRT budget for 2010 has dropped to the levels of 1996, which is a severe drop compared to the budgets of other public institutions, which were not cut so harshly (see Figure 1).

Figure 1.   Budget allocations to LRT, in million Litas

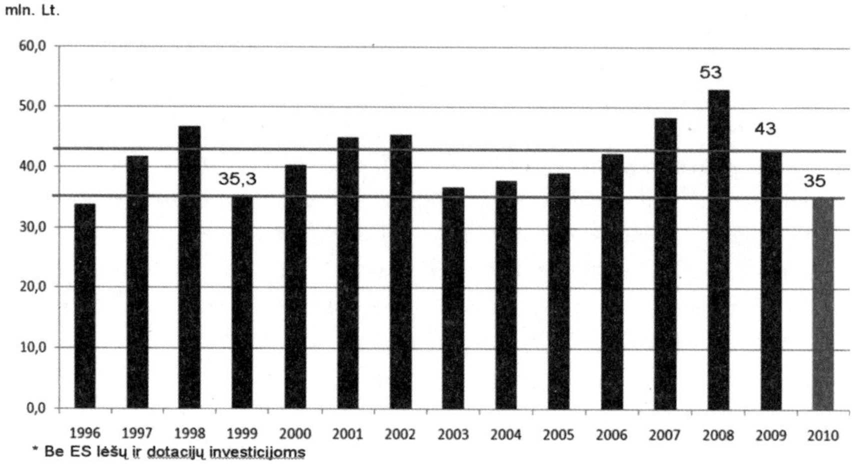

mln. Lt.

* **Be ES lėšų ir dotacijų investicijoms**

Source: Annual Report of LRT 2010.

It needs to be mentioned here that the Lithuanian public service broadcaster is among the least well-funded of the publicly funded broadcasters in Europe.

(F7)   Procedures on news selection and news processing   2 POINTS

Some news media have written documents (stylebooks) for news presentation; these instructions, however, are very general.

The main goal of most media organizations is to inform the audience about what is relevant / important, but also what is interesting. All respondents interviewed stressed that their news organization also seeks to be different from other information providers in their field (or from what is offered on the Internet in general). Thus an important criterion in news selection and presentation is the distinctiveness of news: a different angle, a different source, or a different style of presentation. A number of respondents expressed harsh criticism of their competitors, explaining in what ways their organization is better and how it seeks quality and professionalism (for example, in the journalism that it produces). These journalists have stressed that they see consultations and discussions with colleagues in the newsroom as an important part of their work.

In most cases, news organizations do not have written rules on news selection. Journalists are trained on the job: they are explained the basic principles and policies of the newsroom and learn through their own experience, counseling and consulta-

184

tions. BNS is the only agency in our sample that has a stylebook in which the major principles of professional news reporting are indicated. The instructions put a strong emphasis on the clarity of writing and the reliability of sources. Working at the news agency, journalists know that they must be the first to announce news, but they also must be a reliable source for other news media. Other newsrooms follow their own practices of, for example, sending weekly newsletters to journalists where editorial policies are outlined (*15 min*). In most cases these guidelines are for internal use only.

Generally, all news organizations stressed that there are no preferred and no neglected themes in their newsrooms. In one case it was mentioned that soft news is an important daily news agenda item (*15 min*).

Equality / Interest mediation (E)

(E1) Media ownership concentration national level   1 POINT

Concentration is high in all sectors of media with national coverage (especially in television).

In Lithuania, the legislation contains no special provisions on media concentration. The sector comes under the more general competition law, which forbids dominant positions, meaning over 40 % of a market.

As documented in previous studies (Balčytienė and Juraitė, 2009; Česnavičius 2010), in the TV market, there is hard competition between two commercial television stations, TV3 and LNK, as their popularity among viewers is at similar rates. In the radio market, the situation is different and is in favor of the public service broadcaster, as its station LR1 is the leading one (it controls almost one fifth of the radio market). In general, one could conclude that the highest concentration exists in the television sector (57 %), which is followed by the newspaper market and radio market (see Table 3).

Table 3.   Biggest audience share of the three media companies in different sectors (2008)

Sectors	Media	Media type	Market share	CR3
Television	TV3	Commercial TV	23.5 %	57 %
	LNK	Commercial TV	20.7 %	
	LTV	Public television	12.8 %	
Newspapers	Lietuvos rytas	Mid-market daily	19.3 %	46.8 %
	Vakaro žinios	Tabloid daily	19.1 %	
	Respublika	Mid-market daily	8.4 %	
Radio	LR	Public radio	18.8 %	43.5 %
	Lietus	Commercial radio	13.9 %	
	M-1	Commercial radio	10.8 %	

Even though the online media are rapidly strengthening their positions on the overall media market, competition there is leveling, but Delfi.lt still holds its strongest position among the Top 5 news portals (Table 4).

Table 4.   Top 5 news portals (November 2010)

News portal	Description	Number of users
delfi.lt	Online only	1 107 370
lrytas.lt	Linked to daily Lietuvos rytas	855 507
balsas.lt	Online only	801 619
alfa.lt	Online only	737 291
15min.lt	Linked to daily 15 min	694 843

Source: Gemius Audience (www.audience.lt)

As to ownership type, except for TV3 commercial television which is owned by Modern Times Group (Sweden), all mainstream media in Lithuania are owned by national owners (see Table 7). Being small and economically weak, the three Baltic States do not seem to be very interesting markets for foreign investors.

(E2)   Media ownership concentration regional (local) level   2 POINTS

In general, regional concentration is fairly low in Lithuania; in most cases more than two competing news media outlets are available in each sector.

Regional media are mainly owned by relatively small media companies with different owners. Each of the five biggest cities in the country (Vilnius, Kaunas, Klaipėda, Šiauliai and Panevėžys) has more than two media outlets competing in each sector. Few of the news media (newspapers) belong to the chains of bigger national dailies, but this is not a general trend.

Traditionally, regional newsrooms are small; also journalists working in regional newsrooms are paid less compared to what their colleagues are paid in the capital city. Only a few national media have correspondents outside Vilnius, thus regions are covered by local journalists.

(E3)   Diversity of formats   1 POINT

Different types of content are offered, but entertainment dominates in mainstream media.

The media law contains general guidelines on programming that apply to all broadcasters. They include the requirement to air unbiased information with as many opinions as possible on controversial issues related to politics, economic and social issues. Commercial broadcasters are also obliged by their license contract with the regulator to air a certain proportion of generic programming every week.

The generic diversity is fairly large across the four national coverage channels (1 PSB and 3 commercial stations), ranging from hard news to softer programming and entertainment, but the generic composition among different types of broadcasters (public service and commercial stations) looks very much the same (Table 5). Offering more hours in some sectors of softer programming (music and entertainment), commercial stations aim to keep balance in their output by providing news and information programs as well as niche programs in religion, culture and education in comparable amounts with the public service broadcaster. As the data show, all four stations with national coverage are dependent on advertising revenues and devote a substantial number of hours to advertising in their programming (4-8 % of all output hours).

Table 5.   Output of broadcasting by genre in Lithuania, 2008

Genres	PSB output, LTV		Commercial stations output (hours)	
	Hours	%	Hours	%
Information programs	1,258	11.11	7,082	7.96
News (including sports)	458	4.04	4,096	4.6
Other information programs	800	7.06	2,986	3.35
Education	20	0.18	1,121	1.26
Culture	412	3.64	2,877	3.23
Religion	35	0.31	340	0.38
Entertainment	3,463	30.58	26,232	29.48
Movies, soap	1,991	17.58	6,082	6.83
Music	464	4.1	9,191	10.32
Sports, excluding sports news	491	4.34	735	0.83
Other entertainment	517	4.57	10,170	11.43
Other unclassified programs	931	8.22	10,728	12.05
Advertising	484	4.27	7,355	8.26
Total	11,324	100 %	88,995	100 %

Source: Culture, the Press and Sport 2009.

LRT gives special attention to national production – documentaries, films and drama (Table 6). In 2009, a total number of 2008 hours of European production was broadcasted, which is 63 % of the total international production. The share of foreign programs on both PSB channels was around 30 % of total programming time and amounted to 3200 hours (animation – 124 hours, documentaries – 480 hours, series – 1400 hours and films – 1200 hours).

Table 6.   Weekly program output on LTV

TV programs output	Min.	Share
News and information programs	1,675	15 %
Social and education programs	1,274	11 %
Publicistics and TV magazines	1,104	9.4 %
Children and youth programs	860	7.4 %
Culture	1,095	8 %
Entertainment	30	0.3 %
Music	3,455	29.8 %
Minority programs	90	1 %
Religion	60	0.5 %
Sports	420	3.6 %
Films and TV series	1,630	14 %
Total	11,693	100 %

Source: Annual Report of LRT 2010.

Indeed, it would make economic sense for smaller or less wealthy countries to buy all their television programs cheaply from larger, richer countries that can afford to invest in higher quality productions and sell below the cost of production. As studies in other European countries also show, this does not happen in practice. The external benefits of television (its role of informing, entertaining and educating about local issues) militate against complete reliance on imports, thus the need to support the domestic market and national culture is recognized by national governments as well as by supra-national institutions through the use of subsidies and quotas aimed at enhancing European works and independent domestic production.

(E4)   Minority / Alternative media   2 POINTS

Media for national minorities exist only as niche media.

Generally, Lithuania is an ethnically homogenous country. Lithuanians in 2009 accounted for 84 % of the country's entire population, with none of the national minorities topping the threshold of 10 %. The largest minority in Lithuania is Polish (6.1 %), followed by Russians (4.9 %) and Belarusians (1.1 %). Other minorities (Ukrainians, Germans, Jews, Latvians, Tatars and Roma) account for less than 1 % of the population.

Lithuanian legislation does not include any special quotas for language and minority groups. Business daily (*Verslo žinios*) and several news portals (Alfa.lt), as well as the portal of the public service broadcaster (Lrt.lt), publish news in the English language, while public television and radio have programs for minorities in Polish, Russian and Yiddish, and Delfi.lt (the biggest news portal in the Baltic States) also has its edition in Russian.

LRT has 12 full-time staff members who produce programs in minority languages (Russian, Polish, Belorussian, Ukrainian and Yiddish); however, its daily news program in English, broadcasted on LR1 for 44 years, was terminated due to financial cuts[10].

The Law on LRT does not set specific quotas, but includes some specific requirements for LTV. For instance, it obliges LTV to allot time to Lithuania's traditional and State-recognized religious communities to broadcast religious services in accordance with the conditions and procedure stipulated in bilateral agreements between the public broadcaster and various religious communities. LTV also airs three weekly programs for religious communities (Catholics, the Evangelical community and for the Christian Orthodox community). It also airs masses during the most important Catholic religious events. Roman Catholics in Lithuania comprise a majority. According to the last census in 2001, 79 % of the population consider themselves Catholic, 4.1 % Orthodox, and none of the other religious persuasions account for more than one per cent of the population. In 2009, programming for national minorities accounted for 1 % of LTV's broadcasting time.

The Fund for the Support of the Press, Radio and Television annually allocates some public subsidies to minority and alternative media. The annual budget of the Fund is around 5 million Litas (1.5 million Euro), and the sources of funding are state subsidies, license tax on commercial broadcasters, and other funds.

(E5) Affordable public and private news media 3 POINTS

All media are inexpensive and available at a low cost.

According to Statistics Lithuania, the average gross monthly earnings is 2081.8 Litas (603 EUR), which is slightly higher in the public sector and lower in private business. Generally, all mainstream media are inexpensive and easily accessible. There are no license fees for radio and TV in Lithuania. Moreover, one free newspaper (*15 min*) is available in the three biggest cities of Lithuania (Vilnius, Kaunas, Klaipėda) – with the media crisis, however, its number of weekly issues was reduced from five to three. The mainstream print media are available at a low cost, too. For instance, one issue of the most expensive daily *Lietuvos rytas* (mid-market daily) costs around 1 Euro if bought from a kiosk and 30 cents through a subscription. Tabloids are significantly cheaper. Quality political news monthlies are more expensive (a sold issue costs 1.5 Euro). In the Internet media field, only one business daily requires payment for access to its print editions and all other dailies offer free content.

Briefly, all mainstream news portals offer free content, there are no taxes to pay for the public service media (TV and radio) and newspapers are facing serious competition and dropping numbers of readers, thus they are competing with different subscription offers. As different media are available (and at a low cost), generally, the amount of media consumed is increasing in all sectors. Internet subscription is also inexpensive as different types of offers are promoted.

(E6) Content monitoring instrument 2 POINTS

Organized and regular media monitoring is performed by diverse organizations such as NGOs, media regulatory bodies, and higher education institutions; large-scale and regular media monitoring practices, however, are lacking.

In Lithuania, media content is monitored by the institution of the Inspector of Journalist Ethics and the Radio and Television Commission (the RTC). Both institutions perform these functions according to the law. The Lithuanian Journalism Centre (an NGO) has different projects, some of which are related to media content and performance monitoring as well as policy drafting.

In principle, media-performance-related discussions are fairly often found in the public discourse. Debates also take place in the Internet media (all leading news portals have special sections on media), and these activities are coordinated by media scholars, public intellectuals and media professionals. However, an organized process of self-criticism in the mass media is quite rare, except for a few projects (one radio program and several Internet projects) that offer programs resembling the logic of "media reviewing the media". These are fairly small projects and are treated as a niche media. Academic media studies are also accessible to the public, but their results are often based on small-scale studies, thus there is a need to supplement these studies with long-range media monitoring. Generally, the absence of thorough, regular, independent and publicly accessible media monitoring data is considered to be a serious shortcoming in the media.

(E7) Code of ethics at the national level (structure) 2 POINTS

Lithuania has an institutionalized system of media self-regulation with two institutions established according to media law; in 2009, the Lithuanian Journalists Union established their own self-regulation institution.

According to media law, Lithuania has a "regulated self-regulation" system. Two institutions are involved in handling complaints on media performance, namely the Ethics Commission of Journalists and Publishers and the office of the Inspector of Journalist Ethics (both institutions are written in media law and were established in 1996).

The Ethics Commission functions according to the principles of media self-regulation and the office of the Inspector of Journalist Ethics is a regulatory institution. The
Ethics Commission mainly deals with journalist ethics, and the major document on
which it bases its decisions is the Ethics Code. The Office of the Inspector observes
how the Law on the Provision of Information to the Public (media law) functions as
well as adherence to the regulation according to the Law on the Protection of Minors
against Detrimental Effect of Public Information and others laws.

The Lithuanian system was inspired by the Swedish model of media self-regulation,
but in practice its function is limited due to certain drawbacks. One among many
drawbacks is financial – the Commission is funded by the state (through the Press
Fund) and its budget is limited only to administrative purposes (honorariums to
members paid for each meeting). The Commission does not perform media monitoring and limits its functions only to decision-making. The Office of the Inspector
is funded by the state, and the Inspector is a public servant (he is employed by the
state); his office employs experts for media monitoring, especially for cases that
might deal with violation of the rights of minors. The Inspector also has the power
to penalize an information provider (by administrative order) if he/she detects that
the media firm has offended the law.

One aspect that becomes crucially important in the analysis of media performance
is the question of whether the mass media adhere to the demands of the designated
institutions to publish negations (corrections). As research studies reveal, the media
only seldom publish negations in a form that is clearly identifiable. Both institutions
have the power to announce their decisions on public radio, however in a ten-year
period representatives of these two bodies have only used this possibility on a few
occasions. The Commission follows a practice of writing letters and warnings to the
chief editors of media that violate the Code. Another way to make this issue public
is to assign a special label of "a medium that does not comply with the rules of the
Code", and inform the mass media of this. In 2010, two dailies were assigned this
label (*Lietuvos žinios* ir *Respublika*).

As a response to different limitations in the working practices of these institutions, in 2009 the Lithuanian Journalists Union established their own institution of
self-regulation. Its main mission is to give an account of media performance and to
clarify different clauses of the Ethics Code (for example, on the conflicts of interest
of media professionals and so forth).

(E8) Level of self-regulation (performance) 2 POINTS

Sophisticated means of media self-regulation do exist in some newsrooms; there are also examples of organized self-criticism in some media.

The main self-regulatory tool for editorial policies in the media is the Code of Ethics for Journalists and Publishers, approved by the Lithuanian Journalists Union in 1996. The Code sets basic requirements for news reporting, ethical standards and protection of individual privacy. It also speaks about the relations between journalists and owners, and among journalists themselves. The Codex was updated in 2005.

Many of the leading news media organizations have requirements for journalists to follow the Ethics code in their job agreements. One exception is the *Lietuvos rytas* company, which follows its own codex (based on a foreign prototype that outlines 10 core principles of ethical professional conduct). Overall, most of the respondents see the ethical rules as important principles for their professional conduct.

Independent journalist associations also play an important role in improving skills and raising ethical standards. In Lithuania, two such organizations exist: Lithuanian Journalists' Union and Journalists' Association. The figure for their membership is 800 and 100 journalists, respectively. Keeping in mind that there are generally between 3000 and 4000 journalists in Lithuania, members of these organizations form approximately one third (or one fourth) of all journalists. The Union also has different associations of sports journalists, photojournalists and others who discuss professional issues on a more specialized level. Respondents, however, had ambivalent opinions about the Journalists' Union.

(E9) Participation 3 POINTS

Media in Lithuania offer a variety of ways for their audiences to take part in the public sphere.

Different forms and channels are used to involve the audience in news production. Indeed, readers have many ways of participating in the media, and among the most popular forms of participation are phone calls or emails to live radio and TV programs, email communication, readers commenting on online news and so forth. Journalists have confirmed that they keep regular contacts with their readers (especially those working in online media); they also read reader comments online and respond to constructive criticism. As already discussed, two of the news portals have developed citizen journalism projects. This practice shows that newsrooms are investing in finding new and innovative ways to communicate with their readers. In other media (television), traditional audience surveys (TV meters) are used as a primarily source of information on who is watching what, and programming is often shaped by these data.

(E10)   Rules and practices on internal pluralism   1 POINT

No written rules exist and most of the newsrooms have their own non-interference norms and practices; research studies, however, show that the mainstream media are susceptible to external pressures, and with the media crisis this has worsened.

Representatives of all news media confirm that rules of internal news management do not exist in a written form; according to most respondents, this field (newsroom management) is characterized by spontaneity. In most newsrooms, journalists and editors work in a consultancy regime and often discuss issues that are unclear or require difficult decisions. The manner in which these discussions are organized varies in different news organizations: some of the news media organize regular editorial meetings (*Lietuvos rytas*), in other cases new technologies are applied such as email, telephone or Skype conferences (*15 min, LTV*).

Officially, none of the media in Lithuania is associated with a particular party. One of the reasons for this is that media law enacted in 1996, which even then had a chapter restricting party ownership of media. The absence of clearly defined ideological lines in the mass media – absence of "party-press parallelism"[11] – is therefore a direct outcome of media regulation. But the absence of stable ideological alignments does not imply that the media have no connections with political and economic interests. Although both editors in chief interviewed in the study claimed that their newsrooms (*Lietuvos rytas* and BNS) do not support political or business interests, or pay attention to who advertises in the media, research studies still reveal that most mainstream media do not comply with the principles of objectivity and neutrality (Jastramskis 2009). As discussed earlier, today's politics in Lithuania is shaped by power fights between different interest groups, where clientelistic (or particularistic) interests guide choices, rather than ideological conceptions of the public interest. Mainstream media play an active role in these power games, and with the media crisis this situation has even worsened.

Control / Watchdog (C)

(C1) Supervising the watchdog 'control of the controllers'   2 POINTS

Public criticism and regular public debates on media performance are found in the media; this, however, happens only on an irregular basis.

Structural changes in the media and related matters are regularly reported in some news portals. Mainstream news portals have special sections dedicated to changes in the media field. These sections are often read and the content is monitored by media professionals: journalists, PR and marketing specialists. The issues covered in these sections center around the facts and figures (changes in media ownership or advertising revenues) and do not lift discussions to a more conceptual level, for example, the news does not provide analysis on what these changes mean for democracy or the quality of public discourse in general.

A unique project in the field of raising media awareness is the media literacy project that was launched at the Lithuanian schools with the aim to promote an understanding of media-related matters among very young audiences. In some cases, subjects related to the media business, such as media functions for democracy, media representations, media ethics as well as others, are taught as single subjects; also, these issues are discussed as complementary issues and serve as examples used in teaching other subjects in the class. As far as we know, this is the only project of its kind among the European countries.

(C2) Independence of the news media from power holders   0 POINT

Mainstream media do not have established rules and procedures to cope with pressures from power holders.

In Lithuania, most of the main news media are owned by strong business groups with interests outside the field of media (see Table 7). Media in the regions (local and regional newspapers as well as television and radio stations), in contrast, are still owned by relatively small companies with different owners.

Table 7.   Media groups formed by national owners (2010)

Owner	Main business/activities outside the media field	Owned media outlets
MG Baltic, closed stock company	Business ranging from consumer goods and services to real estate investments and media business	LNK (commercial television), Alfa. lt (news portal), publishing houses Neo-press and UPG Baltic
Achema Group, closed stock company	Various types of business activities in production and trade, cargo handling and logistics, construction and maintenance, financial institutions, hotels/health care and entertainment	BTV (commercial television); Radio stations: Radiocentras, RC2, Zip FM, Russkoje Radio Baltija; *Lietuvos žinios* (national daily); regional newspapers, printing houses, advertising agency
Hermis Capital, private equity group	Business activities in consumer goods and services, heavy industry, electronics and oil	Regional dailies: Vilniaus diena, Kauno diena, Klaipėda, Magazine: TV diena
Snoro Media Investicijos, closed stock company	Various types of business activities in finance management, real estate and other businesses	*Lietuvos rytas* (national daily), Lrytas TV (national television), *Ekstra* (magazine)
SC Baltic Media, closed stock company	The scope of investments in finance, publishing, real estate, energetics and trade	Magazines: L'Officiel, IQ:The Economist, IQ.lt, Intelligent Life, Miesto IQ
Augustinas Rakauskas (president of association of enterprises "Senukai")	Trade in building and household goods	Radio station Žinių radijas

Source: Ministry of Culture, www.lrkm.lt, company web sites.

All respondents in the present study stressed in their answers that their media organization does not have any preferred issues or political or business interests that they would seek to give exceptional positive attention. The editors in chief were especially critical to other media groups. One of the chief editors interviewed is also a director of the company, and he acknowledges this as a case where conflicts of interest might arise. In such situations, clarity in decision-making and established rules of news processing are employed.

In addition to potential owner interests, another serious problem in a small market is related to journalists' relationships with their sources. As indicated elsewhere, the question of proximity in small markets poses problems that are not obvious in larger markets. Indeed, in a small market, journalists' relationships with sources are structured differently than in a large market (often in a small country only a limited number of sources are available for journalists to comment on a particular political or economic issue). Respondents in the study also mentioned attempts to put external pressures on journalists, such as professionalized political PR.

(C3)   Transparency of data on media system   2 POINTS

Media ownership data are available to the citizens.

According to media law, all media organizations have to present annually their financial data to the designated institution, which is the Ministry of Culture. These data (company names and ownership data) are publicly available on the Internet; hence anyone interested can check and get information on who owns what and how much in the media field. Despite this, lack of public accountability and absence of transparency are among the most serious drawbacks of the Lithuanian media. As mentioned, most of the news media do not have written editorial policies, and if they have – these are not publicly accessible (for example, on the Internet). Among those media that are least transparent are *Respublika* and *Vakaro žinios,* which also do not have open editorial policies and an Internet website. As mentioned, another observation is that the mainstream media in Lithuania do not adhere to demands to publish corrections, and if they do publish corrections, they are not in clearly identifiable places. Newspapers do not publish their circulation numbers (only magazines audit their circulation).

(C4)   Journalism professionalism   1 POINT

Professionalism values vary across different media, and this is associated with trans-
formations taking place in the media field, such as economic (media crisis and budget
cuts) and technological (media convergence and new demands on journalists) changes.

Generally, in most of the media, journalists are well educated and, assessed from a
theoretical point of view, their professionalism is relatively high (journalists often
confirm that the value of objectivity is among the most important requirements for
quality journalism). In the present study, respondents have also mentioned a number
of particular drawbacks that have emerged in the media field in recent years and have
affected professionalism standards. These are due to the emergence of new forms
and formats in the media field, such as blurring boundaries between journalism and
non-journalism, between previously distinct operations of media as business, professional journalism, public relations and media ownership. Today the media field is a
mixture of hybrid discourses, when journalism often also takes over strategies and
techniques and mimics practices previously applied in other fields. Signaling changes
in the media, this practice also confirms the growing power and professionalization
of public relations, especially in the political field.

   According to respondents, general journalism professionalism and quality standards do not differ a great deal across different media types, however it is evident that
technological convergence has affected how the news is reported in newspapers and
television. In general, all media professionals are talking about fundamental shifts in
profession, and these are associated with time pressures, as well as changes in working
conditions (job cuts in mass media, increasing competition, demands to be multi-
skilled and professionalized in multi-modal communication formats). If journalists
were previously required to produce news items that are important as well as interesting, today they are required to also think about new forms and formats of reporting.

(C5)   Journalists' job security   2 POINTS

In most media organizations journalists are working on job contracts.

The most common form of employment for journalists is a job contract. Very often
media professionals also receive additional payment in the form of honorariums
(which is fixed and written in job contract). The manner in which journalists get
promoted differs in different organizations: some of these organize open competitions
(Delfi.lt, other online news media), others follow rules and traditions in promoting their own media staff members (*Lietuvos rytas*). Lithuanian labor laws protect
employees from being fired, and the Lithuanian Journalists Union employs lawyers

to protect their members against unfair working conditions. Still, despite these different measures, a significant number of journalists were laid off as a response to budgetary savings in different media organizations.

(C6) Practice of access to information   1 POINT

Additional demands are formulated for journalists.

Generally, information is accessible to journalists. Respondents also stressed the importance of having established networks of primary sources. With growing demands to produce important and interesting news, the requirement to find a new angle, a different aspect in news presentation, is becoming crucial. Having good sources is not only required by journalists who report on domestic politics; with growing media competition it has gradually become a general requirement that is applied in all fields (politics, economy and sports). Other studies also have shown that informal channels of communication (personalized connections) are considered to be very important among Lithuanian journalists.

(C7) The watchdog and the media's mission statement   2 POINTS

The watchdog mission is understood (and sometimes also implemented) as an important, but not a primary function of the contemporary news media.

Although, generally, the watchdog function is mentioned as one of the most important functions of the news media, it is the aim to inform the public that dominates in the answers of all respondents in the study. As the interviewees noticed, investigations have gradually almost disappeared from TV news. These reports have found their place in political news analysis or analytic programs. Newspapers are in a better situation than television: in spite of budget cuts, investigative journalism has survived in some major dailies, although the resources were significantly reduced. Indeed, in most cases, the media function is also dependent on the news media type (whether it is a newspaper, news portal, TV news program or news agency), which again shapes the professionalism criteria that are assigned to journalism. In addition to being important, news needs to be interesting – all representatives also stress the importance of finding a new frame, a new aspect, a new angle, and a new source in news presentation. In short, being different in news presentation seems to be among the most recent demands on Lithuanian journalism. In addition to reporting news that has tangible consequences for ordinary citizens (bringing news to the audience), respondents also discuss the function of the media to explain and comment on complex issues, as well as to educate.

(C8)   Professional training   2 POINTS

There is a well-established practice of continuous training of media professionals.

There is a tradition of training in the newsrooms, however with the media crisis this practice was terminated in almost all news media organizations. The Lithuanian Journalists Union regularly organizes training courses on the basis of the needs expressed by the profession. Over recent years, the greatest attention has been paid to the media in the outlying regions, and training courses were offered in online reporting and editing, newsroom management, journalism ethics, elections reporting, European news reporting and so forth. However, in the media industry, professional training courses are carried out on a less regular basis. Regular training courses were organized at the public service broadcaster, but many of these were terminated for financial reasons.

(C9)   Watchdog function and financial resources   1 POINT

No pre-planned budgets are allocated to perform investigative journalism and fulfill the watchdog function.

Even though investigative journalism is a significant tool for controlling the powers that be, the selected news media do not engage in these activities on a regular basis. Lack of financial resources, adequate time planning as well as lack of professionals qualified to do investigative journalism are among most frequently mentioned reasons for this. The representatives of the selected news media describe investigative journalism as one of the most important functions of the media, yet the highest priority is given to the mission of informing society and presenting the biggest scope on various events. At the same time, some of the news media allocate their journalists the time needed for investigation – sometimes it can be 3-4 days, other times 2-3 weeks (depending on the news media type and the issue that is being researched). It is important to mention that none of the news media organizations in our sample has a unit that performs investigative journalism as its main function; basically, decisions to allocate financial and human resources and invest in investigative journalism are made depending on the needs of the moment (for example, to disclose wrongdoings in politics, business, or sports).

Discussion

Without a doubt, the above discussion shows that the mainstream media's performance in Lithuania in meeting demands for democratic performance is questionable according to all three dimensions. In certain cases, however, different requirements and professional procedures seem to be in place. For instance, a few of the mainstream media either already have or acknowledge that having publicly accessible editorial policies is an important part of newsroom management. Also, all media organizations studied here are sufficiently open to the public – media ownership data are accessible from the designated institution's website; media are also inexpensive and offers different means of public participation and input.

As the monitoring data show, in many respects, news and information are available and easily accessible to citizens. But because the audience in Lithuania is segmented, media use across different audience groups is diverging along socio-economic and socio-cultural lines. Thus the goals and functions of different mainstream media are also susceptible to these two important indicators (economic status and cultural needs).

However, the "Freedom" dimension also shows that internal freedom is very weak in Lithuanian newsrooms, and traditions of democratic newsroom management are missing, as most of the media studied here represent hierarchically organized structures where major decisions are taken by editors in chief or staff with middle management positions. Journalists practically have no or very little voice in the mainstream media.

The media also do not have established routines for how to cope with external pressures – although newsrooms and commercial departments are separated in all media companies, other means to assist journalists to cope with external or internal influences are applied on an irregular basis (such as consultations) or are generally missing.

Also, there is no tradition in the media to have written and publicly accessible editorial policies, and for new journalists, all learning takes place on a spontaneous basis and happens through learning on the job.

Media performance in terms of meeting demands for "Equality" is somewhat better. The media are open to the public – they are affordable and open to public inputs.

Media concentration on a national level has reached critical levels. With increasing competition, generic diversity is decreasing rapidly and entertaining content becomes dominant (especially on commercial television). Seeking to maintain their share of the market, the mass media become an active player by searching for additional funding possibilities and by looking for new ways to meet the demands posed by fierce competition. With the media crisis this situation has even worsened. Regularly performed and independently funded media monitoring is absolutely necessary to reveal the scale and scope of hidden advertising in the mainstream media.

The watchdog function is also problematic. Although acknowledging the necessity of this function, the mass media do not consider it primarily important. In addition, with budget cuts, the mainstream media do not have the financial or human resources needed to support investigative journalism.

To conclude, the present media performance monitoring study has disclosed that, generally, the media field in Lithuania is very polarized, and each media sector operates under its own logic: the mainstream media operate under the logic of commercialism, whereas alternative and niche media aim at fulfilling the needs and expectations of underrepresented (niche) audience groups. Therefore, including niche media items is considered to be a necessary and integral part of future research studies.

Notes

[1] In addition to being described as small, Lithuania may also be characterized as a "Diasporic Nation". According to Statistics Lithuania (www.stat.gov.lt), the yearly average emigration is 30,000 people.

[2] These countries represent blurred societies with ideological cleavages resembling high ideological diversity, which is found in party programs and political rhetoric, yet in reality these declarations mean little beyond popular words, and political decision-making is guided by personalized politics rather than strategic decision-making (Golubeva & Gould, 2010). Political conflicts are also frequent there, and political parallelism is confusing and unclear in most of these countries. Civil society structures in these countries are also weak and public participation is exceptionally low. And what is more important, the free media and independent journalism development tradition in these countries is also very young.

[3] A thought outlined by James Carey seems to be very useful here. According to Carey (1989), the function of news media is not just the transmission of news and information, but rather the confirmation of a certain social order in which journalistic activity is carried out. In other words, this approach implies that media performance as well as media products can be analyzed in the light of the broader culture of society in which media production occurs and where media products take shape. This particular approach does not isolate media production (with its traditions, routines, norms, values and considerations) from the widest social and political context, namely the behaviors and norms that are characteristic of society in general and that are not only part of any particular professional culture.

[4] In 2009, the budget allocations for LRT were 43 million Litas (19 % less than in 2008, 53 million), and advertising revenue was 14 million Litas (51 % less than in 2008, 29 million).

[5] A number of niche magazines were established, which indeed diversified the market of magazines ranging from popular and celebrity magazines, to specialized interest and political and economic news analysis monthlies (*The National Geographic, GEO, IQ: The Economist*); also, a number of alternatives emerged online – all of them signaling the arrival of standards of quality journalism.

[6] One of the independent media experts is a lecturer at the School of Journalism in Vilnius University and he is also a professional blogger.

[7] In Soviet times, the English program was used as a propaganda instrument, but with independence its character transformed and the audience has turned into English-speakers based in Lithuania and in foreign countries. The closure of this program is considered to be among the most severe losses on the Lithuanian Radio.

[8] The concept of party-press parallelism (or political parallelism) is used to identify ideological alignments and identifiable values represented in the party structures and media systems of a particular country (Hallin & Mancini, 2004).

References

Annual Report of LRT (2010) (www.lrt.lt, accessed in January 2011).

Balčytienė, A. (2009) The Baltic Media and Journalism in Context: Sketching the Regional Picture. In Donskis, L. (ed.). *A Litmus Test Case of Modernity: Examining Modern Sensibilities and the Public Domain in the Baltic States at the Turn of the Century.* Peter Lang, pp. 147-167.

Balčytienė, A. & Juraitė, K. (2009) Impact of Economic and Cultural Factors on Television Production in Small Nations. Medijska istraživanja, Vol. 15, No. 2, pp. 33-47.

Carey, J. (1989) *Communication as Culture: Essays on Media and Society.* Winchester.

Česnavičius, A. (2010) *Television in a Changing World of Media.* Ph.D. Theses. Vilnius University Press.

Culture, the Press and Sport 2008 (2009) Vilnius: Statistics Lithuania.

Golubeva, M. & Gould, R. (2010) *Shrinking Citizenship: Discursive Practices that Limit Democratic Participation in Latvian Politics.* Rodopi: Amsterdam – New York.

Hallin, D. & Mancini, P. (2004) *Comparing Media Systems: Three Models of Media and Politics.* Cambridge: Cambridge University Press.

Jastramskis, D. (2009) *Žiniasklaidos organizacijos nuosavybės struktūros ir žiniasklaidos priemonės šališkumo raiškos santykis* (Relationship between Media Organizational Structure and its Partiality). Ph.D. Theses. Vilnius University Press.

Nevinskaitė, L. (2009) EU structural Funds' Publicity and the Practice of Journalism and Public Relations in Lithuania. *Central European Journal of Communication,* Vol. 2, No 1(2), pp. 149-167.

TILS (2007) *Skaidresnės žiniasklaidos link* (Towards Media Transparency); (www.transparency.lt, accessed in January 2011).

TILS (2008) *Lyginamoji Lietuvos, Latvijos ir Švedijos žiniasklaidos atskaitingumo studija* (Comparative study of media accountability systems in Lithuania, Latvia and Sweden); (www.transparency.lt, accessed in January 2011).

TNS Gallup (2009) *Metinė žiniasklaidos tyrimų apžvalga* (Annual Report of Media Research); (www.tns-gallup.lt, accessed in January 2011).

Chapter 8

The Netherlands
Although There is No Need for Dramatization, Vigilance is Required

Leen d'Haenens & Quint Kik

The worldwide economic recession of 2008 and 2009 has entailed the loss of a large number of jobs in the Netherlands as well (Statistics Netherlands 2010), and this trend was also noticeable in the media sector. Newspapers in particular are witnessing hard times as the economic crisis coincides with structural problems such as digitization, a slump in revenues from advertising, the advent of free news channels and a falling interest on the part of readers in news they have to pay for. Many readers are discontinuing their subscriptions and turning to digital versions. Newspapers now have to come up with alternative models in order to induce readers to again accept the papers' core business, i.e. presenting news that the public is willing to pay for. Apart from the newspapers, the broadcasters too have been heavily hit, especially the commercial operators, dependent as they are on advertising revenues. The downturn goes hand in hand with an upturn in the number of studies analyzing the situation and forecasting future scenarios. For the time being, however, things should not be overly dramatized: the position of the media such as it can be deduced from data from 2008 is not fundamentally different from the analysis made for 2006 (d'Haenens 2010).

As far as broadcasting is concerned, the public broadcasting system is considered a lasting player with an important cohesive social task, operating in a competitive environment consisting, generally speaking, of ten broadcasters, among which three are public networks. In our present-day multicultural society, it is especially important that all individuals be reached and feel addressed. While Dutch society used to be split up into social and cultural segments ('pillars': Christian-protestant, catholic and socialist), today it is characterized by diversity in terms of age, geographic and cultural origin and life-style. For the Dutch public broadcasting system, openness is a prime feature, so that a broadcasting organization representing a given tendency alive in Dutch society can become a member of the public broadcasting system. Since September 2010, two organizations have thus joined the public broadcasting system. The first is WNL (*Wakker Nederland* or 'Vigilant Netherlands'), which is positioned on the right hand side of the political spectrum and claims to counterbalance the views put forward by the public broadcaster, views that in WNL's perception are one-sidedly leftist. The second is PowNed (*Publieke Omroep Weldenkend Nederland en dergelijke*, 'Public Broadcasting Right-Minded Netherlands and the like'), which originates from the provocative populist weblog *geenstijl.nl* ('no style.nl'), set up in 2003 and since 2008 fully owned by *Telegraaf Media Groep* or TMG. The rank and file of these two organizations are groups in Dutch society consisting of at least 50,000 contributing members each. An organization that left the public system at the end of August 2010 is *Llink*, a group with a green ideology that was given a negative assessment by the Visitation Commission in April 2009: prospective members of the public system must be shown to constitute an extra value for the system, which in the case of Llink was not sufficiently clear; moreover, the ratings of Llink were poor and its financial policy was inadequate.

In the written media, it is mainly the publishers of dailies and weeklies that in recent years have had to face a decline in circulation coming on top of the increased costs of production and distribution. In June 2009, the so-called Brinkman Commission (*Tijdelijke Commissie Innovatie en Toekomst Pers*, 'Interim Commission Innovation and Press'), proceeding on the assumption that from 2014 on the first newspapers in the Netherlands will become structurally loss-making, recommended that the press urgently seek to innovate its management methods. Acting on this advice, the government provided subsidies to the tune of €8 million in 2010 for innovative projects and another €4 million for hiring young members to the editorial staffs (viz. one new staff member per sixty journalists, without older and more experienced journalists being made redundant).

In order to create opportunities for cross-medial co-operation while still avoiding the concentration of too much power in the hands of one news provider, the government had already eased the provisions of cross-ownership legislation in 2007: a maximum of 25 % of the circulation of paid newspapers that could be owned by one operator had been raised to 35 % of all (i.e., including free) newspapers (temporary law on media concentrations). The Royal Decree of 21 December 2009 stipulated that where two or three markets are combined (radio, television and/or newspapers), the limit of 90 % (of 300 %) must not be exceeded. Meanwhile, this temporary measure (which was meant to last until 1 January, 2012) was withdrawn in November 2010 so as to create, as of 2011, a stimulating cross-media environment. The NMa (*Nederlandse Mededingingsautoriteit*, 'Competition Authority'), overseeing all industries of the Dutch economy, continues to monitor undesired concentration levels.

The remarks above outline the economic crisis, the structural predicament of the press and the supportive and regulatory government measures that form the context in which the media selected for the present study have to operate. These media are presented in the following section.

Method

This follow-up study is based on desk research and fifteen in-depth interviews with professionals in Dutch print, audio-visual and ICT media and with representatives of the academic world[1]. The secondary analysis of relevant documents, including quantitative data, bears on the year 2008, unless stated otherwise. Information collected from the interviews reflects the most up-to-date situation.

From the print media, five national newspapers, one regional paper and one weekly were examined. They are briefly characterized as follows:

- *De Telegraaf*: popular daily with the largest nation-wide circulation and with a Sunday edition;

- *De Volkskrant*: quality paper, the third largest national daily;

- *NRC Handelsblad/nrc.next*: quality papers sharing one editor-in-chief, though each steers a course of its own, nrc.next addressing a younger readership;

- *Het Financieele Dagblad*: specialist paper with financial and economic news;

- *De Gelderlander*: the largest regional newspaper;

- *Sp!ts*: of the three free papers distributed nationally, *Sp!ts* has the largest but one circulation and the largest reach among the target group of 18- to 35-year-olds;

- *Elsevier*: largest weekly.

For radio and television the following were selected:

- *NOS*: within the Dutch public broadcasting system (NPO, *Nederlandse Publieke Omroep*), NOS is the broadcaster with clearly outlined tasks as it is legally bound to provide daily newscasts for three television channels, NOS Teletekst, the digital thematic channel *Journaal 24* and eight radio stations. The most important news bulletin on television is the NOS *Acht uur journaal*. Radio 1 is NPO's 24-hour news and sports station;

- The RTL news bulletin of *RTL4*, the largest commercial television channel and, as far as the format is concerned, the only counterpart to the NOS *Acht uur journaal*;

- *BNR Nieuwsradio*: a commercial radio station that used to focus on financial and economic items (BNR standing for *Business Nieuws Radio*), but has become a wide-ranging newscaster since it changed its format in 2007, focusing on economic affairs, mobility, housing and living styles and sports. As far as format is concerned, the only counterpart to the public broadcaster's Radio 1.

Finally, the following online news media were selected:

- *nos.nl*, the news website of the public broadcaster;

- *nu.nl*, the largest commercial website, focusing on news from the Netherlands. Owned by Sanoma, the largest Dutch publisher of magazines;

- *geenstijl.nl*, a provocative weblog, a 'shockblog' alternating news with scandalous gossip, and part of Telegraaf Media Groep.

Dimension

Freedom / Information (F)

(F1) Geographic distribution of news media availability   3 POINTS

A wide variety of news and information media is available to all Dutch citizens, although regional news coverage varies from province to province.

Print media

In 2008, the situation with regard to the print media is as follows. There are 11 national and 26 regional newspapers (CvM 2009). There are, moreover, 4 free papers and 4 weekly news magazines. The average circulation of newspapers stands at 5.3 million copies. Among the national papers there are 4 quality papers (among which are *De Volkskrant* and *NRC Handelsblad/nrc.next,* with an average daily circulation in 2008 of 216,126 and 83,363, respectively), 2 popular papers (including the largest newspaper of the Netherlands, *De Telegraaf,* with a circulation of 666,555), 2 papers with a Christian-protestant profile and 4 specialist papers, among which is *Het Financieele Dagblad* (circulation 64,449). Each of the twelve Dutch provinces has at least one regional newspaper. *De Gelderlander* is the largest regional paper (circulation 157,263); its readership is to be found in the province of Gelderland. Free newspapers such as *Sp!ts* (430,331) are distributed nation-wide, mainly in the Dutch railway stations. The largest of the 4 weekly news magazines is *Elsevier* (142,581 copies). Most national dailies and weeklies are available in the whole of the country, either in single issues or by subscription. Single copies of regional papers are available in the region on which they focus, and by mail subscription.

Television and radio

In 2008, we find 20 television channels specifically focusing on the Netherlands (CvM 2009). Half of them are generalist channels with wide-ranging programs and divergent genres. The others are niche channels, special-interest channels for music, children's television, documentaries or sports. Six of the 10 generalist channels carry newscasts in one form or another. The average viewing time per day amounts to 184 minutes; some 70 % of this time is divided between the general-interest channels of the public broadcaster and its two major commercial rivals. The three channels of the public broadcaster NPO carry several news bulletins per day, the chief one being the *NOS Acht uur journaal* of *Nederland 1*. For the public broadcaster, the first-line newscast is an obligation imposed by legislation. The commercial counterpart is *RTL Nieuws*, a daily newscast at 19.30h on *RTL4*. *RTL7* for its part provides daily financial-economic news items labeled *RTLZ* (the Z standing for the Dutch *Zaken* or 'business'). *SBS6* has a program *Hart van Nederland* ('Heart of the Netherlands'), a news bulletin focusing on regional news. Apart from news bulletins, the three public channels also present current affairs and opinion programs as well as a few investigative programs. In addition to the national public channels, each Dutch province also has its own regional public television channel; moreover, there are 122 local television channels addressing one or more towns and villages. They provide, among other things, regional and local news bulletins. Finally, Dutch audiences can also tune in to a large number of foreign channels, including the public channels of Flemish Belgium, Germany and Britain and various commercial channels, among which is the American CNN.

There are twenty-odd radio stations catering to the Dutch audience, nearly all presenting a music format. Yet virtually all stations interrupt their programs every hour and sometimes even every half hour to air short news bulletins, which are provided to the public stations by NOS and to their commercial rivals by the press agency ANP. Only the public *Radio 1* station and the commercial *BNR Nieuwsradio* carry news bulletins around the clock. Average daily listening time amounts to 195 minutes, about 60 % of this being divided between the public broadcaster and its two major commercial counterparts. Just as for television, there are regional radios in every province and there are a further 265 local stations carrying news bulletins. Finally, Dutch listeners can also receive public as well as commercial radio stations from neighboring countries.

Both television and radio broadcasts are mainly received via the cable network. Cable-network operators have to offer a basic package as defined in the 1997 Media Law: it includes at least 15 television channels and 25 radio stations. The three Dutch public broadcasters are governed by the must-carry principle, as are the regional and local public broadcasters and the two Flemish public broadcasters. The remaining channels in the package are selected by the cable operators, with local programming boards having an advisory role. A standard package consists of about 35 television and 40 radio channels. In less densely populated areas and in areas with a relatively large population of ethnic minorities, dish antennas are also often used. At the end of 2008, 98 % of all Dutch households owned one or more television sets, and more than half of the households had digital television (de Vries 2008). A standard digital package offers a multitude of television and radio channels, among which are the thematic channels of the public broadcaster. Of special significance as far as newscasts are concerned is *Journaal 24* (looped repetitions of the latest bulletins) and *Uitzending gemist* ('Missed Broadcasts', catch-up programs among which is the *NOS Acht uur journaal*).

Online platforms

Eurostat statistics (2010) reveal that, in 2009, 90 % of Dutch households had access to the Internet. A large majority of the population can therefore surf to (news) sites and blogs and get information about news and current affairs all over the world. All Dutch newspapers have an online version, as do the news magazine *Elsevier* and the television news bulletins of NOS and RTL. The major web-only news media are *nu.nl*, *kranten.com* and *geenstijl.nl*. *NRC Handelsblad* was the first daily in the Netherlands that could be sent over wifi and a special feed to an e-reader (Bright 2008). The websites of news media can also be consulted on mobile (3G) phones and wireless wifi connections. Moreover, since April 2010 trains of the Dutch railways are equipped with free wireless Internet connections. In other words, the free newspapers that used to lure younger readers away from paid newspapers are now in turn faced with competitors in the field of free news.

(F2) Patterns of news media use (consumption of news)   3 POINTS

Seven out of ten Dutchmen read a newspaper every day. Of all television channels, it is the first public channel that has the largest market share, with one out of four Dutchmen tuning in everyday. The reach of most online media is on the rise.

Print media

All Dutch newspapers together reach an average of 70 % of the population on a daily basis; in other words, seven out of ten Dutchmen read a newspaper every day (NOM Printmonitor). As far as its readership is concerned, *De Telegraaf* is the largest paper, followed by the two free papers *Metro* and *Sp!ts*. From July 2008 up to and including June 2009, *De Telegraaf* reached a daily average of nearly 2.1 million readers of 13 years and older (NOM 2009). In the same period, *Sp!ts* had a daily average of 1.6 million readers, *De Volkskrant* had 825,000 and *nrc.next* over 320,000. The largest regional paper is *De Gelderlander* (over 500,000). The largest opinion magazine is *Elsevier* with a monthly average of 834,000 readers.

Television and radio

The 2008 average market share of television channels carrying newscasts varies from 10.6 % (*RTL7/RTLZ*) to 37.4 % (*Nederland 1*) of the Dutch population. Of all television channels, it is *Nederland 1* that has the greatest market share: it is the channel that nearly one out of four Dutchmen tunes in to every day. Trailing far behind is *RTL4*, with 25.9 %. The RTL news bulletin is the only newscast that is, as far as format is concerned, comparable to the NOS *Acht uur journaal*. On any given evening, these two bulletins are watched by 1.7 million and 1.3 million people, respectively (Nieman 2007).

The 2008 average daily market share of the news radio *Radio 1* stands at 10.2 % of the Dutch population, that of *BNR Nieuwsradio* at 1.5 %. After the regional public broadcasters taken together (13.2 %) and after music station *Radio 538* (12.9 %), *Radio 1* thus ranks third as to market share, with one out of ten Dutchmen listening to it every day.

Online platforms

Of all news sites focusing on the Netherlands, the web-only *nu.nl* had the highest monthly reach (30 %), followed by *telegraaf.nl* (27.4 %) and *nos.nl* (20.9 %). This means that three out of ten Dutchmen surf to *nu.nl* every month. Others in the top ten of Dutch news sites and weblogs with the greatest reach are the newspaper sites *volkskrant.nl* (12.8 %) and *nrc.nl* (11.4 %). The 'shockblog' *geenstijl.nl* ranks seventh with 12.6 %. The reach of most of the online news media mentioned here has been on the rise since 2004. Recent data for 2009 show that *telegraaf.nl* now reaches three out of ten Dutchmen.

(F3) Diversity of news sources   3 POINTS

For quite a long time the Dutch press agency ANP used to enjoy a dominant position in providing news and scoops. Recent developments on the Internet have put an end to that hegemony. Other sources mentioned are the national and regional newspapers and the regional broadcasters, which often function as pointers to given issues.

For quite a long time in the past, press agencies used to enjoy a dominant position in providing news and scoops. Recent developments on the Internet have put an end to that hegemony. Journalists as well as ordinary citizens can now keep abreast of events thanks to e-mails, Internet forums and weblogs. The archetypal task of press agencies is to collect (inter)national news and pass it on as newsfeeds to their subscribers, viz. newspapers, broadcasters and websites. In addition they function as alarm systems and put items on the editors' agendas. In this connection, it is worth pointing out that the *Algemeen Nederlands Persbureau (*the Dutch press agency ANP*)* is trying out an sms-service that reports news items even before they have been checked. Many believe that this approach sacrifices reliability and independence to speed. Press agencies would thus lose quality and therefore also their extra value, and their continued existence would become uncertain (Vermaas & Janssen 2009).

The journalists interviewed in the context of the present study list a large variety of news sources. Even though nearly all of them mention the Dutch press agency

ANP, it is striking that several journalists emphatically refer to the network of sources built up by domestic and foreign correspondents. Other sources mentioned are the national and regional papers and the regional broadcasters, which often function as pointers to given issues. Eighteen regional newspapers for their part use the *Geassocieerde Pers Diensten* (GPD or 'Associated Press Services') for their national and international reports. The papers of the Wegener group, among which is *De Gelderlander*, increasingly turn to their own central news service, which delivers regional news items to the seven papers making up the group. *Nu.nl* participates in a number of co-operation agreements with magazines belonging to the publisher, which also operates the news site. Apart from resorting to ANP, the large national media also subscribe to the services of foreign press agencies; financial-economic media turn to specialized press agencies and to their own colleagues from abroad. Most newsrooms receive newsfeeds on an ongoing basis from press agencies and/or always have *NOS Teletekst* or *RTLZ Teletekst* on their screens. One further source mentioned by a few journalists is the expertise of their own readers or viewers, who may even act as regular informants (*De Telegraaf*), and the expertise of police reports. It goes without saying that the editorial staff has also become dependent on the Internet. The use that they make of the Internet is not solely confined to the websites of divergent news media: news logs and social network media too are rapidly becoming interesting sources of information. One member of the editorial staff of *De Volkskrant* is in charge of browsing through social network sites such as *hyves.nl* and filtering them for useful news items. The Twitter website has become quite popular since the controversial elections in Iraq, even though it primarily serves as a mere signal that needs further checking. *Sp!ts* was among the first to resort to Twitter on the occasion of the visit that Geert Wilders, the right-wing politician, made to Britain to show his anti-Islam film Fitna. Finally, a few journalists explicitly state that they do not use press releases or other PR messages issued by the authorities or by companies.

(F4) Internal rules for practice of newsroom democracy 2 POINTS

Nearly all news media have internal rules or by-laws outlining a procedure for appointing an editor-in-chief. The management will not easily disregard the viewpoint of the editorial board.

Nearly all the news media under study have internal rules or by-laws outlining a procedure for appointing an editor-in-chief. The editorial board has some influence in the matter, as it has a say in the appointment of members of the commission that scrutinizes applications, a commission on which the board is actually represented. In addition, the board has the right to veto or accept a candidate put forward by the management, a provision of some consequence as a chief editor without support of the rank-and-file cannot function adequately. In practice, therefore, the management will not easily disregard the viewpoint of the editorial board.

In this context, it is worth citing the procedure adopted by *NRC Handelsblad/ nrc.next*, not only because it is exceptional but also because it could be observed in practice in 2010, after the editor-in-chief resigned quite unexpectedly. The quest for a successor is initiated by the editorial board and not by the commission for applications. The board suggests a candidate to the manager-publisher, who in turn introduces the candidate to the chairman of the board of directors of the investment company controlling NRC Media. The manager-publisher's role is a marginal one, though he or she is given extensive information during the course of the process. If the candidate nominated by the board does not meet with the manager-publisher's approval, the editorial board nominates a second candidate. A candidate is only nominated if at least two thirds of the editorial board agree. This procedure is in sharp contrast with the other end of the spectrum, where we find the editorial staff of *Nu.nl*, who are not numerous enough to have a board, let alone editorial rules, and who have no formal or informal say in appointments at all.

Actually, these editorial by-laws, so typical of Dutch news media, do not go undisputed among foreign publishers and owners. The Belgian publishing group *De Persgroep*, for example, accepts no interference in the appointment of an editor-in-chief for its Belgian media. As Piet Bakker (chief lecturer of communication science at the University of Amsterdam) says, *De Persgroep* (owner of, among others, *De Volkskrant*) considers the editorial by-laws an impediment to the sound management of a publishing company. In their opinion, strict adherence to these rules is one of the factors that led to the decline of *PCM*, the former owner of *De Volkskrant*. They contend that an elected candidate should not hold the post of editor-in-chief, but quite simply the most suitable candidate, an outstanding and talented journalist, himself or herself active among the other journalists, who can motivate and inspire the staff and who understands the readers and their preferences.

The degree of the editorial staff's participation in deciding on the content of the newspaper is defined by the hierarchy within the organization. As far as decisions regarding content go, it is the chiefs who are formally responsible: the chief of the news desk makes a preselection from among the available news items and the final editor decides what goes into the newspaper, the website or the news bulletin and what does not. If these two people cannot reach a decision, it is the editor-in-chief who has the final say. In radio and television, the various desk editors and final editors will check, for each program, the choices they have made with the editor-in-chief, who – and this goes for all news media examined – is responsible for the policy adopted (in the widest sense). In a number of cases, the editorial by-laws explicitly settle the influence of the editorial board on the course steered by a particular news medium. In the 1960s, these rules or by-laws were won after a hard fight by journalists versus owners, but today their significance is slowly being eroded, at least according to Huub Evers, lecturer at the Fontys College for Journalism in Tilburg. The reasons, he says, are many: the new owners do not take the slightest notice of editorial by-laws, editors-in-chief now bear a great commercial responsibility, and the workload of journalists has increased so that they have less time for the editorial board or for a journalists' union.

(F5) Company rules against *internal* influence on newsroom / editorial staff   2 POINTS

Editorial by-laws endorse the chief editor's final responsibility and protect the strict separation between editorial staff, on the one hand, and management and shareholders, on the other. However, present-day practice shows that the editor-in-chief's role is shifting away from editorial responsibilities to general management. The litmus test for whether editorial by-laws really function well is not taken until things begin to go badly for the news medium concerned.

The editorial by-laws or internal rules discussed in the section on indicator 5 are a formal guarantee of the influence that journalists can exercise over the content of the news medium they work for and of their say in important appointments. Also, they endorse the chief editor's final responsibility and they protect the strict separation between editorial staff, on the one hand, and management and shareholders, on the other. However, in the view of media historian Huub Wijfjes, present-day practice shows that the editor-in-chief's role is shifting away from editorial responsibilities to general management. At the request of the manager-publisher, the editor-in-chief now takes a seat on the management board and is held responsible, together with a commercial manager, for the overall policy of the company or the broadcaster of which the news medium in question is a part. His or her traditional role as guardian of the newsroom's independence may thus come into conflict with the requirements of the new role he or she has to play, a role in which the editor-in-chief, together with his or her new management colleagues, is supposed to evaluate and reflect on policies of innovation, such as solutions to the problem of changing media uses on the part of news consumers.

Strikingly, under these changing circumstances, some journalists too have begun to treat the strict separation between editorial staff and management in a more relaxed fashion. For example: by way of the editorial board and the by-laws of *De Volkskrant,* the independence of the staff is given a formal guarantee, but at the same time a more constructive stance toward the owner-publisher is sought. The owner's interference with content and organization is acknowledged on the logical basis that *De Persgroep* has invested in the newspaper and wishes to have a return on its investment. Should the editorial staff always refuse to budge for reasons of principle, the owner might invoke budgetary rights and thus create a deadlock that benefits neither party. The position of *De Persgroep* is that everything proceeds from a journalistic mission or ambition, but needs to go hand in hand with an efficiently managed organization; interesting and financially sound newspapers are a prerequisite for a media company to survive in the future.

The former editor-in-chief of *NRC Handelsblad/nrc.next* took a different view. After the ownership of the NRC newspapers and websites changed in 2009, she became co-responsible for the commercial policy of the group. In 2010 she came into conflict with the new publisher (and indirectly with the chairman of the new owner's board of directors) because he wished to have a say in the journalistic content of any future commercial publications related to NRC Media. The editor-in-chief insisted on her editorial independence and eventually stood down. In the opinion of the NRC journalist interviewed within this context, her resignation shows the need for future strengthening or safeguarding of the editor-in-chief's position in the management set-up.

It is to be noted that nearly half of the journalists interviewed rely less on the internal rules or by-laws than on their own assessment of the situation. Piet Bakker too has his doubts about the value of the editorial by-laws: the litmus test of whether they really function well is not taken until things begin to go badly for the news medium concerned. In any case, according to Piet Bakker, guarantees of effective editorial independence can hardly be put to the test.

(F6) Company rules against *external* influences on newsroom / editorial staff   2 POINTS

Rules or by-laws provide for the formal separation between editorial and commercial considerations. The majority of the journalists interviewed are in principle opposed to any outside influence. Some news media tend to accept more non-spot advertising and advertorials or commercial specials for the job, real estate and travel markets. Such practice will make it more difficult to insist on respecting the editorial rules.

Rules or by-laws provide for the formal separation between editorial and commercial considerations. The majority of the journalists interviewed are on principle opposed to any outside influences. This is also clear from the practical positions taken by several editorial teams: "any interference from advertisers is bound to fail" (*De Telegraaf*), "we feel very strongly about editorial responsibility" (*RTL*), "if any doubts arise, ties with the sponsors will immediately be ruptured" (*BNR Nieuwsradio*), "any commercial interference would do damage to the sound and reliable image of the newspaper" (*Het Financieele Dagblad*); and see F5 for the position of *NRC Handelsblad/nrc.next*. Apart from editorial rules and the Media Law, NOS also has an indirect way of separating editorial and commercial interests. The *Stichting Ether Reclame* (STER, 'Foundation Advertising on Radio and Television') distributes advertising air-time to the various media platforms of NPO and collects the revenue. The revenue is then transferred to the government, which puts it in a fund for newspapers in distress, a fund managed by the *Stimuleringsfonds voor de Pers* ('Press Fund'). At the same time, STER secures the independence of NOS with regard to advertisers and media agencies.

Because the editor-in-chief and the commercial manager are both on the management team, the practice has developed in some news media to accept more non-spot advertising and advertorials or commercial specials for the job, real estate and travel markets. In most cases, it is understood that formal design must differ from that in editorial articles in the paper, for example as to column width and/or letter size. Still, the reliability of the advertisement will be perceived to be greater as the text is placed in the context of a specific newspaper. This is what we find in free papers or on news sites, but also, for example, in the regional paper *De Gelderlander*. Media historian Huub Wijfjes is of the opinion that it will become more and more difficult to insist on respecting the editorial rules on this particular point. In his view, the only concession that one may realistically hope for is an explicit note that the article in question is an advertorial written in co-operation with commercial parties.

(F7)   Procedures on news selection and news processing   2 POINTS

In the absence of formal rules underlying the selection of news or documents outlining a definition of what news is and what it is not, the meetings and discussions held by the editorial staff can be considered informal procedures for making the selection.

None of the news media under investigation can resort to formal documents outlining a definition of what news is and what it is not, nor do they have any rules stating how this is to be determined. A number of the journalists interviewed state that, in selecting news items, they mainly go by their own judgment of what has news value, while others admit that their choice strongly depends on the items available on any given day. Whether an event is newsworthy is influenced by its impact and its vicinity to the newspaper's readers, the number of people involved and the degree to which the event departs from the ordinary. Furthermore, the choice of what goes into the bulletin or the newspaper is also a matter of trends: a large number of journalists feel that the extent to which an item may appeal to the public determines its news value. The readers, listeners or viewers need to appreciate the importance of a given event, for example because the users of the news medium can identify with it. Clearly, even though the selection of newsworthy items is usually made on an ad hoc basis instead of guided by formal rules, it is always made from a coherent and rational journalistic viewpoint and helped by an ongoing discussion among colleagues. In the absence of formal rules underlying the selection of news, the meetings and discussions held by the editorial staff can be considered informal procedures for making the selection.

Equality / Interest mediation (E)

(E1) Media ownership concentration national level   2 POINTS

The overall market of national, regional, free and specialist newspapers is dominated by three large groups, as is the overall television market. Although less concentrated, the overall radio market too is dominated by just a handful of players. No figures on market shares are available for the Internet.

Print media
In 2008, the overall market of national, regional, free and specialist newspapers was dominated by three large groups: *Telegraaf Media Groep* or TMG (*De Telegraaf, Sp!ts* and a few regional papers), *Koninklijke Wegener* (mainly regional papers, among which *De Gelderlander*) and PCM *Uitgevers* (*De Volkskrant, NRC Handelsblad/nrc. next, Trouw,* the free paper *DAG,* and a few regional dailies). TMG is the largest of the three, with a market share of 27.5 % on the basis of circulation (CR1), followed by Wegener with 20.3 % (CR2 = 47.8 %) and in the third place PCM with 17.7 % (CvM 2009). In 2008, Wegener and PCM still had a joint venture in *AD Nieuwsmedia* (publisher of *Algemeen Dagblad* and 8 regional newspapers) with a market share of 9.1 %, which also has to be taken into account. The joint total of the three groups (CR3) thus stands at 74.6 %, three quarters of the overall market for newspapers in the Netherlands (CvM 2009). The 2008 situation as described here had practically remained unchanged since 2005. More recent figures for 2009 reveal a slight decline of CR3, which takes the Herfindahl Hirschman Index (HI II) to 0.19, so that the line between a concentrated market (between 0.10 and 0.18) and a strongly concentrated one (>.18) is just exceeded (CvM 2010). The changes from 2008 to 2009 are explained by the take-over of PCM and AD Nieuwsmedia by the Belgian group *De Persgroep* in March 2009 and the subsequent sale of *NRC Handelsblad/nrc.next* (March 2010) as ordered by the Dutch Competition Authority.

Radio and television
The overall television market too was dominated in 2008 by three large players: the public broadcaster NPO (*Nederlandse Publieke Omroep*) (Nederland 1, Nederland 2 and Nederland 3), RTL Nederland (RTL4, RTL5, RTL7/RTLZ and RTL8) and SBS Nederland (SBS6, Net 5, Veronica) (CvM 2009). NPO's share of viewing time stood at 34.9 % (CR1), *RTL* had 23.6 % (CR2 = 58.5 %) and SBS had 19.3 % (CR3 = 77.8 %). Jointly, therefore, these three broadcasters controlled ten general-interest

channels and over three quarters of the television market. When compared with 2007, both the CR3 figure and the HHI (0.28) had risen slightly because of the take-over of the channel *Tien* (owned by Talpa) by RTL (the channel was renamed RTL8). Since the advent of the first commercial television channels in 1989, the degree of concentration has considerably diminished, but recent figures for 2009 still reveal an HHI of 0.26, in other words a strongly concentrated market.

The overall radio market is slightly less characterized by concentration, though it too is dominated by just a handful of players: the *Nederlandse Publieke Omroep* or NPO (with eight stations, among which the news station Radio 1), *Telegraaf Media Groep* or TMG (four stations, among which Sky Radio), *RTL Nederland* (i.e. Radio 538) and *De Persgroep* (Q Music). In 2008, NPO had a share of listening time of 30.2 % (CR1), TMG had 17.6 % (CR2 = 47.8 %), RTL had 11.1 % (CR3 = 58.9 %) and De Persgroep 7 %. These four groups together therefore control about two thirds of the radio market. The HHI has for the past ten years hovered on the borderline between a concentrated and a strongly concentrated market (0.18).

Online platforms

No figures about market shares are available for the Internet. On the basis of the average monthly reach achieved by publishers and broadcasters on the Internet (calculated by adding up all the websites they control), we find that *Sanoma* (*nu. nl*), *Telegraaf Media Groep* and the *Nederlandse Publieke Omroep* all rank among the top 10 (CvM 2009). Sanoma (ranking second) stands for a reach of 68 %, TMG (ranking fourth) has 54.7 % and NPO (ranking seventh) 50.7 %. Since 2003 the monthly reach of these three providers has doubled. Though *PCM Uitgevers* (i.e. *De Persgroep Nederland* since the take-over of 2009) ranks only fifteenth with a 37.9 % share, its sites volkskrant.nl and nrc.nl are among the top 10.

(E2) Media ownership concentration regional (local) level   1 POINT

Three major players dominate the regional newspaper market. By contrast, concentration in the regional radio and television market is considerably lower.

Print media

The major regional publishers in 2008 are *Koninklijke Wegener, NDC/VBK de uitgevers,* and *Telegraaf Media Groep* (CvM 2009). Wegener has a dominant position in six provinces: Overijssel (99.5 %), Gelderland (95.0 %), Zeeland (99.9 %), Noord-Brabant (99.9 %), Limburg (99.9 %) and Flevoland (62.4 %). NDC is dominant in the provinces of Groningen (99.2 %), Friesland (86.3 %) and Drenthe (99.0 %). *AD Nieuwsmedia*, a joint venture of Wegener and PCM uitgevers, dominates the market in the provinces of Utrecht (88.8 %) and Zuid-Holland (88.1 %). *Telegraaf*

Media Groep, finally, dominates in the province of Noord-Holland (72.8 %). When *De Persgroep* took over PCM, it also took over the joint venture *AD Nieuwsmedia*. In nine of the twelve provinces, more regional than national newspapers are distributed. The three exceptions are Noord-Holland, where the share of regional papers is 43.3 %, Utrecht (35.9 %) and Flevoland (18.2 %). The dominant share of regional papers in the province of Zuid-Holland is very tight (51.9 %), and we should therefore conclude that in the rim city (or 'Randstad', the large conurbation comprising the cities of Amsterdam, Rotterdam, The Hague and Utrecht) generally speaking more national papers than regional ones are read.

Radio and television

By contrast with the market of regional papers, concentration in the regional radio market in 2008 is considerably lower. This is partly explained by looking at the number of players (there is at the most only one player of any significance in each province – the regional public broadcaster), but mainly by the dominant position of national broadcasters. Commercial non-national broadcasters play only a marginal role. Shares of listening time in the regional radio market are conspicuously higher than shares of viewing time in the regional television market. Exceptions to this rule are the provinces of Groningen and Friesland, where the regional public radio stations account for about one quarter of all listeners. In those provinces that partly overlap with the large conurbation of the 'Randstad', they achieve much lower shares of listening time (4-12 %). For television, the shares of viewing time of regional public broadcasters do not amount to more than 1 to 3 %. The greatest competitors of regional broadcasters are the national commercial channels taken together, and this is even more true of radio than of television.

(E3)   Diversity of formats   2 POINTS

Although the chief business of print media remains the production of a paper version, the Internet is increasingly used to offer complementary functions and services. All news bulletins of the public and private broadcasters are available online, offering the latest news.

Print media

The print media studied all have an online version freely accessible to the public, though given sections of the site, for example the online archives, are available at a charge only (free for subscribers). One newspaper, *De Telegraaf*, allows non-subscribers to read the paper online via the function 'day access via sms'. As many modern mobile phones make it possible to surf on the Internet, this is another way of reading a newspaper provided it is presented in a user-friendly format. Newspapers and their editors nowadays have great expectations of the iPad and are looking into ways of dividing the news up, presenting the paper by sections, by sets of topics, by articles as is done in iTunes, or by monthly subscription. Yet another option is the use of RSS feeds, a function that compiles information or news from different websites and sends it to the consumer. All of the print media analyzed here offer this facility. It should be clear, however, that the chief business of print media continues to be the production of a paper version, although the Internet is increasingly used to offer complementary functions and services. The big question is how long the production of a paper version of a newspaper or a news magazine will remain profitable.

Television and radio
All of the public broadcaster's news bulletins of any given day, both on radio and television, are available online on *nos.nl*. NOS has an application for mobile carriers, one via SMS and one that can be downloaded. RTL4 has a page of its own on the RTL website where the latest news can be read. Those who surf to the *BNR Nieuwsradio* website can listen to the newscasts live. One more way to follow the news is a traditional one, viz. on teletext. The NOS website offers this application online, as does *Twitter*. Finally, the RTL and SBS channels also use teletext.

(E4)   Minority / Alternative media   3 POINTS

The public broadcaster aims at inclusive broadcasting through which the largest possible number of groups in society, among them (ethnic) minorities, can make their voice heard. In spite of quite a number of subsidized actions undertaken to support newspapers for minorities, their future is far from rosy.

It is the public broadcaster that provides the most important way for the largest possible number of groups in society, among them (ethnic) minorities, to make their voices heard. Within the public broadcasting system of NPO 20 large and smaller broadcasting organizations divide air time on radio and television among themselves. Of these 20 there are 9 large membership-based broadcasters, 2 task-based ones (i.e., responsible under the law for providing programs about news, art and culture and education), 7 smaller broadcasters with air time for religious denominations or other communities based on spiritual persuasions. The last-mentioned group provides limited space on radio and television channels to programs with a Hindu, Buddhist, Jewish or Islamist content. In addition, every five years prospective membership-based broadcasters can try to join the public broadcasting system; to this end they have to draw up a business plan and prove that they represent a given ideological trend, as shown by at least 50,000 paid-up members. Two 'newcomers', representing a more right-wing populist stance, joined the public broadcasting system in September 2010.

One organization that aims to promote equal participation of ethnic minorities in the media is *Mira Media*, which sets up various activities that help to reflect the multicultural character of Dutch society. *Mira Media* regularly organizes workshops in which minorities can participate to increase their chances of playing a role as media professionals. An online initiative of the same kind is *wereldjournalisten.nl*, which comments on news from an alternative angle, for example by presenting journalists who have come to the Netherlands as refugees and report on news from their native country. The website was set up with the support of the *Stimuleringsfonds voor de Pers* ('Press Fund') and collaborates with *ex Ponto*, a magazine focusing on refugees and migrants. In spite of quite a number of subsidized actions undertaken to support newspapers for minorities, their future is far from rosy. The three main reasons for their scant success are the limited paid-for circulation, the extreme segmentation of the target group, and the unrealistic unbridled ambition of the publishers. For the time being, alternative media can continue to resort to temporary subsidies of the Press Promotion Fund; the scheme introduced in 2002 was extended for two years at the end of 2009, with a yearly overall maximum of €300,000. The condition for obtaining a grant is that the plurality of the press stands to be enhanced. It is not inconceivable that the temporary subsidization measures will be discontinued and that the grants will be transferred to a general subsidization facility.

(E5) Affordable public and private news media   3 POINTS

Pricing is highly flexible: news consumers can choose the subscription that best fits their budget.

Print media

The E5 indicator checks the extent to which the Dutch news media are within the financial means of an average household. To this end, the same comparison is made as in the 2006 monitor: the price for an annual subscription to three newspapers (*De Telegraaf*, *de Volkskrant* and *De Gelderlander*) is compared with that of similar papers in three neighboring countries with similar disposable incomes. We can thus determine whether the affordability of Dutch newspapers has changed since 2006.

Table 1.   Price comparison newspapers

	Quality paper		Popular paper		Regional paper	
NL	Volkskrant	€ 279.90	De Telegraaf	€ 202.50	De Gelderlander	€ 275.00
B	De Standaard	€ 336.00	Het Laatste Nieuws	€ 264.00	Belang van Limburg	€ 267.00
F	Le Monde	€ 324.00	Le Parisien	€ 318.80	Nouvelles de l'Alsace	€ 342.66
D	Die Welt	€ 442.80	Bild	NA	Berliner Zeitung	€ 252.30

NA = not available.

Sources: Newspaper websites.

The prices above (Table 1) are those for an annual subscription in 2010; a subscription to an online newspaper does not usually exceed half of the price for a home-delivered paper version (about €150). One conclusion is that the Dutch quality paper *de Volkskrant*, or at least a subscription to it, is cheaper than the three quality papers in the neighboring countries. The same applies to the popular paper *De Telegraaf*. Only the regional paper, *De Gelderlander*, is relatively expensive. On the whole, quality papers tend to be higher priced than popular ones, probably because publishers assume that the readers of quality papers are willing to pay a higher price. All the papers listed in Table 2 offer different kinds of subscriptions. A common characteristic of them all is the degree of flexibility: today, subscriptions to the week-end edition tend to be the rule rather than the exception. Clearly, news consumers can choose the subscription that best fits their budget.

Television, radio and online platforms?
In 2009 a digital basic package on the cable cost, on average, €0.28 per channel; with an average of 61 channels in a package this amounts to a monthly sum of over €17 (nlkabel.nl 2010). The Netherlands also has several (wireless) Internet providers: the price of an Internet connection varies from €15 to €60 per month, dependent on the period one wishes to be connected and various extra options (among which is speed of the connection). There is, furthermore, the ability to combine an Internet subscription with a television and a telephone connection (triple pay). Prices for such a combination fluctuate between €20 and €80 per month (internetabonnement, 2010). In other words, determining the yearly overall media cost for a Dutch household, given the variation in subscription offers and the TV license fee being paid through taxes, is not a simple task: about 1,500 euros may be a good estimate (leaving out costs for mobile platforms, depending on use and household size). For the sake of comparison: the average disposable income of the over 7 million Dutch households in 2008 was €33,500 per year (CBS 2009).

(E6)   Content monitoring instrument   3 POINTS

The Dutch Media Authority publishes the Media Monitor, an annual report analyzing the ownership relations and markets pertaining to newspapers, television, radio and opinion magazines. In addition, the News Monitor is published periodically.

One of the tasks entrusted to the Dutch Media Authority (*Commissariaat voor de Media*) is to watch over the separation between the editorial and the commercial element on television and radio (cvdm.nl). It does so through the Media Law, which lays down rules for public and commercial broadcasters and applies them to the national, regional and local levels. The Media Authority is also in charge of grant-ing broadcasting licenses for radio and television and audits the annual accounts of public broadcasting organizations. In addition, the Authority publishes the Media Monitor (see E8), an annual report analyzing the ownership relations and markets pertaining to newspapers, television, radio and opinion magazines. The Monitor is usually available in May, and the data bear on the previous year. Since 2005, separate studies have been carried out each year on the news market in the Netherlands. The latest thematic study was published in the autumn of 2009 and dealt with a content analysis of the news on a day chosen at random and a study of the role of reports made by the Dutch news agency ANP in news articles and background information in the newspapers. The News Monitor is published periodically (see E8).

(E7) Code of ethics at the national level (structure) 2 POINTS

Most media conform to the Guidelines of the Press Council and the Code of the Association of Editors-in-chief and/or observe a behavioral code of their own. Ethical decisions are usually made ad hoc in discussions among journalists and editorial staff. The advent of Internet journalism is seen as one of the most important causes of the weakening of journalistic standards and values.

The Guidelines (*Leidraad*) of the *Raad voor de Journalistiek* ('Press Council') list general rules to further objectivity in journalistic usage. The Press Council resorts to these guidelines when dealing with complaints. A second code is that written by the *Genootschap van Hoofdredacteuren* ('Association of Editors-in-chief'). The code is a more specific manual than the Guidelines; it lists a number of concepts that constitute the basis of an open and democratic society. The members of the Association are bound to honor these rules. Our university interviewees all find that the importance of the Code has diminished in recent years and point to the lack of determination on the part of the Press Council as the main cause of this decline. Moreover, com-plaints lodged with the Press Council do not result in any direct redress in the form of fines or other penalties; for those complainants must take legal action. One more problem is that *De Telegraaf* and the opinion magazine *Elsevier* no longer recognize the authority of the Council. Piet Bakker quite rightly points to the danger that news media thus call down upon themselves: in the absence of self-regulation, politicians may feel called upon to intervene.

In brief, most media observe a behavioral code of their own. Generally speaking, they stick to the Guidelines of the Press Council and the Code of the Association of Editors-in-chief, but it is also true that some of the news media interviewed here never signed these documents. Although news media such as NOS and RTL have specific rules for what they will and will not put on the screen, and although *NRC*

Handelsblad/nrc.next and *de Volkskrant* have a detailed style manual, decisions of an ethical nature are usually made ad hoc in discussions among journalists and editorial staff. Besides, most journalists interviewed are convinced that they have an implicit understanding of and feeling for standards and values and that there is therefore no need for a stringent and explicit code. Among the rules that news media do impose upon themselves, we find subjects such as the approach the journalist takes (showing reticence in naming family names and nationality, explicitly introducing oneself as a journalist, letting both sides be heard) and his/his integrity. Some media have taken initiatives to render their own code more up-to-date, for instance *De Gelderlander* by adapting the standards of the paper to practices on the Internet. In this context, it is worth citing a remark made by a journalist of *nu.nl*, who claims that as an Internet journalist he does not necessarily feel freer in applying journalistic standards and values. Just like the staff of the traditional news media, the editors of *nu.nl* are anxious that the visitor of the website might turn away if ethical standards are lowered. That is actually what happened when *De Telegraaf* reported on the air crash in Tripoli (May 2010) and made contact by phone with the only survivor, the nine-year-old Ruben: an action was launched on Twitter by outraged readers and one thousand readers canceled their subscriptions. Piet Bakker is therefore convinced that, as far as ethical standards are concerned, news media are best restrained, not by a code, but rather by news consumers expressing themselves on Internet forums and in readers' panels.

Huub Wijfjes and several of the interviewed journalists draw attention to what might well be the most important cause of the weakening of journalistic standards and values: the advent of Internet journalism. In this context, a journalist working for *Sp!ts* refers to the unequal ways in which news consumers judge responsibility for content and accuracy in comparing traditional media with indiscriminate news blogs written by citizens acting as journalists. If they wish to offer their readers something unique, news sites and free newspapers need to trifle a bit with ethical principles, for example by publishing privacy-sensitive material that is often already available on the Internet. If these news sites and free newspapers obstinately hold on to codes, they do lasting damage to their commercial position vis-à-vis the Internet.

(E8) Level of self-regulation (performance)   3 POINTS

The Press Council, examining complaints about media coverage, is an organization for self-regulation. The News Monitor, funded by grants from the Press Promotion Fund, provides empirical material for the evaluation of news coverage.

The Press Council (*Raad voor de Journalistiek*) is an organization for self-regulation in the media. The Council examines complaints lodged by citizens about reports and articles in the media. The primary aim is to find a compromise between the two parties so that a lawsuit can be avoided. To this end, the Council has written down a code of conduct or guidelines in a Guidebook, which serves as the basis for high-quality and objective journalistic practice that will not prejudice anyone's rights. A second instrument to promote journalistic quality is the *Nederlandse Nieuwsmonitor* ('Dutch News Monitor'). It is a research tool set up by the *Stichting het Persinstituut* ('Foundation The Press Institute') to check on and guarantee the quality of Dutch journalism, and results from the co-operation between *Nederlandse Dagblad Pers* (NDP, Dutch Newspaper Press), the *Nederlandse Vereniging van Journalisten* (NVJ, the Dutch Association of Journalists), the Radboud University of Nijmegen and the University of Amsterdam. The News Monitor is funded by grants from the Press Promotion Fund. The Press Institute Foundation, in its endeavor to guarantee journalistic quality, provides empirical material to the News Monitor,which can thus assess the quality of journalistic practice in the Netherlands. The Monitor analyzes and evaluates news articles and examines ways to improve quality of reporting and journalistic practice. The primary aim is not to make assessments on the basis of good/bad criteria, but rather to focus on the news process as a whole, for which an ongoing follow-up is of course essential. The reports of the News Monitor are published periodically. There are three types of reports: the *Continue Monitor,* the *Event Monitor* and the *Issue Monitor.* The *Continue Monitor* looks into general characteristics of content such as topic, news genre and sources. These characteristics are then checked in the national papers, a number of regional papers and a few news programs on television. The *Event Monitor* deals with controversial issues, scandals and sensational events that are highlighted in the media during a relatively short period of time. The Event Monitor therefore focuses on cool, objective and reliable reporting; the media it examines are the same as in the Continue Monitor. Finally, the *Issue Monitor* studies major social issues that remain in the media limelight for a longer time (Nederlandse Nieuwsmonitor 2010).

(E9) Participation   3 POINTS

Every newspaper has an online version with a facility to post a response. Various social media have intensified the trend of reacting to and participating in news distribution.

Today it is inconceivable that readers should not be able to react to news articles in their newspaper. Every newspaper therefore has an online version with a facility to post a response. The website of *De Telegraaf,* for example, has a 'your opinion' tab, which sends the surfer to a separate website where he or she can post a reaction to any article in the paper. *De Volkskrant* has a separate section for posting readers' replies, and on the website of *NRC Handelsblad/nrc.next,* the reader can write a reaction without even being referred to a different page. Various social media, such as Twitter, Facebook and Hyves have intensified the trend of reacting to and participating in news distribution. The availability and the popularity of smart phones makes it easy to be online at all times and in all places, so that a reaction can be posted any time. The resulting trend of 'civic journalism' makes it possible for diverging points of view to be noticed and for new angles to be explored in the news media.

(E10)   Rules and practices on internal pluralism   2 POINTS

Most news media enjoy a culture of openness: their editors-in-chief are accessible and willing to listen to young journalists with a fresh view of things who make their views known, solicited or not.

At all the news media studied, we find at least one large editorial meeting per day and several meetings of sections of the staff. These meetings are on principle open to all journalists. Two news media go further and explicitly require the presence of their journalists at editorial meetings; attendance is encouraged by those in charge and discussed during the performance interview. Though in most cases hierarchic structures are decisive and the editor-in-chief, the final editor and the head of the newsroom have a great say in any editorial choices, most news media enjoy a culture of openness; their editors-in-chief are accessible and willing to listen to young journalists with a fresh view of things who make their views known, solicited or not.

Control / Watchdog (C)

(C1)   Supervising the watchdog 'control of the controllers'   2 POINTS

One leading example is the 'Foundation Media Debate Bureau', the website denieuwereporter.nl is another. Both invite media professionals as well as citizens to think about quality, reliability and diversity in the media.

Two major examples of the watchdog function are the *Stichting Mediadebatbureau* ('Foundation Media Debate Bureau') and the website *denieuwereporter.nl.*
    The independent *Stichting Mediadebatbureau* was set up in 2005 by NVJ (the Dutch Association of Journalists), the public broadcaster and NDP (the association of newspaper publishers). The objective of the Foundation is to initiate discussions of methods, content and ethics in the Dutch press and journalistic practice, setting

media professionals as well as citizens thinking about quality, reliability and diversity in the media. This kind of debate may create better understanding and new insights, which may in turn trigger an appropriate response. The reports written by Media Debate can be consulted on their website so that all those interested can read the recommendations and perhaps implement them (Mediadebat.nl 2010). The website *denieuwereporter.nl* is an equally refreshing source of ideas for debate and self-reflection in journalistic circles. It is an independent weblog about journalistic practice offering a forum for debate and comments about developments in the media (De Nieuwe Reporter 2010).

Finally, several newspapers and broadcasters also have ombudsmen to whom citizens can address questions, remarks or criticism. It is their task to be approachable for the public at large and to act as watchdogs with regard to the good practice of journalists and editors (Evers, Groenhart & Van Groesen 2010).

(C2) Independence of news media from power holders   1 POINT

The Dutch news media enjoy relative independence from power holders. There are examples of diagonal concentration involving a publisher and a broadcaster in the same group as well as an investment company as the largest shareholder.

The *Telegraaf Media Groep* (TMG) and *RTL Nederland* are partly owned (20 % and 26 %, respectively) by the investment company Talpa Media/Cyrte of John de Mol, ex-chairman of Endemol. Another investment company, Mecom, owns 87 % of the shares in *Koninklijke Wegener*. *SBS Nederland* is partly owned (57 %) by the investment companies Permira and KKR.

In the Netherlands, there are no examples of broadcasting companies that are also active in the newspaper market. The reverse, however, does occur: *TMG* controls 87.5 % of the Sky Radio Group (four radio stations) and *De Persgroep* was already the owner of radio Q Music even before it took over *PCM Uitgevers*. In fact *De Persgroep* was compelled to sell the papers it had acquired through *PCM* (*NRC Handelsblad/nrc.next*) when the Dutch Competition Authority judged that *De Persgroep*, as a result of the take-over, stood to have too large a market share (>33 %) in Amsterdam and the region around it.

There are two more examples of diagonal concentration involving a publisher and a broadcaster in the same group as well as an investment company as the largest shareholder. FD Mediagroep comprises both *Het Financieele Dagblad* and *BNR Nieuwsradio*, controlled (98 %) by HAL Holding. And *NRC Handelsblad/nrc.next* were taken over (2010) by Egeria and the shareholders of the television channel *Het Gesprek*. The bankruptcy of the channel in the summer of 2010 had no impact on the newspapers.

(C3)   Transparency of data on media system — 3 POINTS

On its website mediamonitor.nl, the Media Authority describes the most recent situation as to media ownership relations.

The websites of the parent concerns of the commercial media studied here and their annual accounts generally provide all the data needed about the (major) shareholders of the news media. However, the information given in indicators E1, E2 and C3 is not mentioned in the colophons of papers or magazines nor on the websites of television or radio channels. On the website *mediamonitor.nl*, which is of course open to the general public, the Media Authority (*Commissariaat voor de Media*) describes the most recent situation of ownership relations in the media.

(C4)   Journalism professionalism — 3 POINTS

The Dutch newsrooms engage in various forms of self-reflection on and appraisal of the work they do and the way in which they do it. However, most self-reflection occurs on an ad hoc basis and usually after the fact.

The newsrooms of the Dutch media engage in various forms of self-reflection on and appraisal of the work they do and the way in which they do it. The journalists and editors of the news bulletins on *NOS* and *RTL* hold a daily meeting in which the editor-in-chief and his staff members cast a critical look at the previous day's main newscast. However, as far as self-reflection as such is concerned, the majority of journalists interviewed say that this is done on an ad hoc basis and usually after the fact, whenever current events may make it useful or necessary. At the other end of the spectrum, we find the newsroom of *De Telegraaf,* where no extensive or formal sessions of self-reflection are organized. Instead the paper tries to discover through research what its readers feel is important; on regular occasions, the readers can phone in to the newsroom and ask questions about content and journalistic choices.

At *De Gelderlander,* the editor-in-chief has a monthly talk with the editorial staff about, among other things, ethical issues, and at a annual plenary meeting with readers, the editorial staff explain their methods and the course steered by the paper. At various other media, the editors-in-chief write a blog for their readership and at times engage in self-reflection. *NRC,* for its part, organizes a self-reflection session once a week, at fixed times, and invites outsiders to discuss the previous week's papers with staff. In the weekend edition, the editor-in-chief lets readers have a glimpse behind the scenes of the paper in his column *Lezer schrijft/krant antwoordt* ('the reader writes/the paper answers'). Several media have a special editor for their readers, the most radical form of self-reflection being found at *de Volkskrant* and *NOS,* viz. an ombudsman who comments on the methods used by the newsroom, doing so independently of the editorial staff as a whole. The publisher of *de Volkskrant* (since 2009 *De Persgroep*) regards the ombudsman (who has fulfilled this role for eight years) as an unequivocal sign that the paper takes its readers seriously. Huub Wijfjes believes that the news ombudsman and the blogs written by editors-in-chief are a buffer against the clamor on the part of readers for more accountability. The journalist from *NRC* whom we interviewed observes that a truly independent news ombudsman should, of course, not be on the paper's wage-list. As of 2010, the Press Promotion Fund finances a *Stichting Media Ombudsman*, a foundation set up based on dissatisfaction with the way in which the Press Council has functioned thus far; the aim is to create a platform for studying the use of, for example, a news ombudsman and to create a separate ethical code for Internet journalism.

(C5)   Journalists' job security   2 POINTS

In general, the Association of Journalists controls the basic working conditions for professional journalists in the Netherlands.

In general, the NVJ (Nederlandse Vereniging van Journalisten, 'Association of Journalists') controls the basic working conditions for professional journalists in the Netherlands: negotiating collective employment agreements and author's right contributions, providing legal advice to its members, discussing insurance issues, etc. More specifically, none of the journalists we interviewed had heard of conscientious objectors among their colleagues. As far as they can see, there are no legal provisions to protect them when they have qualms about the way they have to do their job. Two of them are aware that, should such a situation arise, they can turn to the editorial board. Journalists are not compelled to write articles they object to, and the medium concerned would certainly not be helped. However, generally speaking, a journalist does what he or she is asked to do. Still, *De Telegraaf,* for example, will make allowances for a journalist's private circumstances: if he or she has had to suffer a family tragedy, the paper will not ask him or her to report on a similar event. Furthermore, objections stemming from religious convictions – for example refusal to work on Sundays – will usually have been dealt with during an intake interview. In Piet Bakker's view, the editorial room of any Dutch news medium is an environment without very formal rules. Journalists do not tend to seek out borderline cases, they are 'socialized' by their colleagues in the newsroom.

(C6) Practice of access to information   1 POINT

One important source is government information, for which Dutch legislation on the public nature of government records is the primary tool, as it gives citizens (and journalists) the right to access government data. The way in which the law functions and the lengthy procedures involved have recently come under attack.

For citizens to be well informed, it is important that journalists have easy access to information. One important source is government information, for which Dutch legislation (*Wet op de Openbaarheid van Bestuur, WOB*) on the public nature of government records is the primary tool, as it gives citizens (and journalists) the right to access government data. It is of great importance that this kind of information be easily accessible and comprehensible; it would be unacceptable if things were otherwise. Democracy stands to benefit if the government's activities, at whatever level, can be followed and scrutinized. The way in which the WOB law functions has recently come under attack, especially from journalists. It takes lengthy procedures to gain access to this kind of information and the results of one's patience often turn out to be unsatisfactory, a state of affairs that has caused resentment in VVOJ (the *Vereniging van Onderzoeksjournalisten)*, an association of investigative journalists. They demand that important information be made available to all those working in this particular field, without laborious procedures. They have appealed to the Press Promotion Fund to launch an investigation into the functioning of the WOB law in order to gain easier access to government information.

When looking at the views of the journalists we interviewed, it is worth making a distinction between those who claim they do not find it difficult to get access to government information (at least not more than to other sources) and those who have to put up with 'the terror of spokesmen'. Several interviewees in fact feel that the growing army of government spokespeople and the slick strategies adopted by information services result in the increasing dependence of journalists on leaks and whistleblowers. In the past five years or so, government officials have worried more and more about hypes and the possible impact of a damaged reputation or image, and this trend, in the view of *NRC Handelsblad/nrc.next*, is a great danger to the independence of journalistic work. Huub Wijfjes, too, blames the growing power of information services, especially the quasi-journalistic reports produced by them at great expense. These documents rarely mention any sources, so much so that the origin is to all appearances a journalistic medium, whereas it is in fact a government agency or a commercial organization. The business of image building has grown enormously, and the balance between independent journalism and public relations is lost. Today it seems as if political, economic and sports journalism have gradually degenerated into a form of embedded journalism, with a number of journalists going along with the trend in the interest of given politicians and parties, company chairmen and companies, or coaches and sports federations.

(C7)   The watchdog and the media's mission statement   3 POINTS

The media themselves decide on the basis of their distinctive characteristics to what extent they play their role as watchdog seriously.

It goes without saying that it is the media themselves that decide to what extent they will play their role as watchdog. In the view of *De Telegraaf*, for example, its task is to report the news and also provide the reader with a measure of entertainment: as the paper no longer looks upon the Guidelines of the Press Council as its framework of reference, it can be assumed that they take their watchdog role less seriously. *De Volkskrant*, for its part, sets as its aim to provide open, honest and serious reporting, and looks upon the continuous innovation of its approach as a major value. *NRC Handelsblad/nrc.next* has a statement of principle in which it is stated that the paper has no links with any "political or religious groups or with interest groups", that the paper "seeks to provide objective news reporting" and that "it has a critical role within the Dutch parliamentary system". Finally, the regional *De Gelderlander* gears its selection of news, analyses and comments to a very high degree to what it takes to be the fields of interest of its readers and the concerns of the region it considers to be its market.

The chief task of the audio-visual media is to provide information via different platforms and thus address the widest audience possible. Both *NOS* and *RTL* consider this task to be of great importance, but obviously the two channels interpret it on the basis of their distinctive characteristics as a public broadcaster, on the one hand, and a commercial one, on the other. For *NOS* it is essential to mainly emphasize its public functions and to take its role as watchdog seriously. The commercial *BNR radio* addresses the entrepreneurial groups in society, and it follows that its news, background analyses and comments are in close keeping with the outlook of the target group.

(C8)   Professional training   1 POINT

Practically all news media offer their employees a chance to follow courses or complete their education. Due to economies and falling revenues from the advertising market, the possibilities are limited.

Practically all news media offer their employees a chance to follow courses or complete their education. There are, however, several pronounced differences, as is clear from the answers of the journalists interviewed. In more than half of the cases under review, the focus is on internal training sessions in which the editorial staff as a whole participates. The interviewed journalists from *De Gelderlander*, *NOS* and *nu.nl* explicitly point out that, in addition to the internal training sessions, they can also take external courses.

Journalists working for NOS also mention ongoing training programs, which can be internal as well as external, the latter bought from the Media Academy. Most of the courses focus on management and various training courses deal with design, online search strategies, final editing, writing, style, image processing and conducting interviews. Three journalists emphatically mention three technical courses, viz. finance for non-financials (*De Gelderlander*), sessions with lawyers including WOB procedures (on access to government records) (*De Telegraaf*) and training in legal issues and in accountancy (*Het Financieele Dagblad*).

At *De Gelderlander*, every journalist can resort to a budget of €500, which he or she can use discretionally; most editorial staffs, however, have a kitty reserved for training of their members. However, at half of the news media studied, the journalists concerned paint a gloomy picture of the time and the budget available. This may be due to economies and falling revenues from the advertising market.

(C9) Watchdog function and financial resources

1 POINT

The worldwide financial crisis did not affect the time or the budget made available for investigative journalism. Even before the crisis economies had been imposed, mainly as a result of shrinking revenues from advertising and recent take-overs of broadcasters and publishers.

Four of the journalists we interviewed say that the paper they work for allows them adequate time and financial resources to engage in investigative journalism. Four more admit that they can do so only occasionally, while two others claim that their newspaper leaves no room at all for investigative work. All our interviewees agree that the worldwide financial crisis, which hit the Netherlands too in the autumn of 2008, did not affect the time or the budget made available for investigative journalism. Even before the crisis economies had been imposed, mainly as a result of shrinking revenues from advertising and recent take-overs of broadcasters and publishers.

Although *de Volkskrant* emphasizes general news reporting, the paper still continues to employ a substantial number of investigative journalists. The *Volkskrant* journalist whom we interviewed insists that investigative work at *de Volkskrant* is not funded from some insignificant item on the budget, but that the paper considers it an essential part of its task. *NOS* goes even further, claiming that it has more people doing investigative work than ever before, in an attempt to compensate for the decline in investigative journalism on the part of the newspapers by means of investigative programs produced by individual broadcasting organizations within NPO.

By its own account, *RTL* has little scope for investigative journalism, yet it has for some six years had a special staff of four journalists who specifically try to get the latest scoops in the field of domestic news. Even *nu.nl*, which is after all an Internet news medium with a proportionately small newsroom, is very well aware of the importance of investigative journalism and has recently recruited a free-lance journalist for this particular purpose. By contrast, regional papers do have to cope with shrinking budgets for investigative work. Time pressure at *De Gelderlander* has increased so much that journalists barely have time to do their normal work of news reporting, as they are expected to make extra efforts to generate general regional news and to write pieces for their paper's website. Occasionally one journalist may be given time to conduct an investigation, but that is a matter of days rather than of months. The journalists working for *BNR Nieuwsradio, Het Financieele Dagblad* and *NRC Handelsblad/nrc.next* also say that in their newsrooms as well investigative work is only done on an ad hoc basis. Journalists of the *FD Mediagroep* are supposed to be polyvalent and to be able to assume many different roles: they have to write for *Het Financieele Dagblad,* work for the newscasts of *BNR* radio, and provide news content for the newspaper's website and for the channel. Huub Wijfjes confirms this picture: in the past ten years, he has seen investments decline and records grow poorer in the areas of economic affairs and regional and local politics. He adds that, as far as investigative journalism is concerned, the emphasis has shifted away from solid, in-depth research to cursory, superficial revelations without any social relevance.

Among the reasons for the relative decline in investigative journalism in many newsrooms, *NRC* journalists cite not only the current focus on the quest for cursory news, but also the uniform nature of the various journalistic training curricula. The (Flemish) editor-in-chief of *NRC,* who was appointed in September 2010, has promised that one of the spearheads of his policy will be the structural integration of investigative journalism in the paper. Actually, Piet Bakker and Huub Evers believe that investigative journalism will not disappear entirely. The former argues that there appears to be a market for investigative journalism, as testified by the success of a number of investigative books; the latter points to the American trend of rich philanthropists supporting investigative journalists with grants. In this context, the *Vereniging van Wetenschapsjournalisten in Nederland* (the 'Association of Scientific Journalists') needs to be mentioned. The Association seeks to make and maintain contacts with institutions and agencies that play a role in journalistic work as far as science and technology go. More precisely, it promotes the information flow from research and scientific institutions in order to safeguard and guarantee the quality of journalistic reporting. Furthermore, there is the *Fonds voor Bijzondere Journalistieke Projecten* ('Fund for Special Journalistic Projects'), which enables journalists and writers in general to set up projects of a special nature or quality. The Fund seeks to find new angles from which special projects can be carried out.

Conclusion and comparison with MDM 2009 results

Most news and information media have maintained their position in 2008 when compared with 2006 (the reference year for the MDM 2009; d'Haenens et al. 2009), although a few media channels have changed owners. The most noticeable changes occurred in 2009, more particularly in regard to national newspapers. In July 2009, the Belgian publisher *De Persgroep Nederland* acquired *PCM Uitgevers* BV. In April 2010, *NRC Media* (with *NRC Handelsblad* and *nrc.next*) was purchased by the investment company Egeria, an operation that resulted in the resignation of two of the three directors. The values and the mission of the media examined have remained the same, but news gathering and news distribution via online media platforms have seen their importance increase. There can be no doubt that online social media have added a new dimension to the Dutch media landscape with all its core and peripheral activities.

Looking at the scores of the monitor (for an overview see table in chapter 13), we find that the Dutch media score 17 out of a maximum of 21 for the freedom dimension. The loss of points is greatest in the area of the procedure of news selection, in which we chiefly examined press agencies. There appear to be no strict rules for the selection of news, which is usually done on the basis of hunches and professional experience. Neither are there any strict and specific rules on how to deal with internal and external pressure, though the principle is that there is no giving in to external pressures. The danger, however, resides not in external influence, but rather in internal power-play. The director-manager wishes to have a greater say (e.g., the relations between *De Persgroep* and *NRC*), the editor-in-chief is the equal of the commercial manager and co-responsible for the policy adopted by the publisher as a whole. The question can rightly be raised of what the use and merit of editorial rules or by-laws are when the publisher-owner decides on budgetary matters, the journalists go along with these decisions without taking a principled stand, and editorial independence has shrunk to such a degree that it can hardly be measured. On the count of the remaining three indicators (geographic coverage, patterns of news consumption and diversity of news sources), the Dutch media score very well.

For the equality dimension, the score of the Dutch media (24 out of 30) is comparable to that for the freedom dimension (17 out of 21). The availability of alternative media continues to be a point of concern: the chances of survival of alternative media focusing on specific target groups are relatively slim. New media initiatives are eligible for temporary subsidies, but their prospects of profitability remain very uncertain. Self-regulation does not prove to be firmly anchored in news-rooms, and a 'code' is virtually unheard of as ad hoc choices abound. Citizens acting as journalists do not bother with codes and guidelines, and free news media and news sites are forced to cross certain thresholds if they want to hold on to their readers. However, joint actions undertaken by watchful news consumers (whether masterminded by social network media or not) can very well put a stop to daring journalistic choices that could be considered too extreme.

The score for the third dimension, control mechanisms and watchdog function, is no more than moderate (17 out of 27). It is mainly further professional improvement and training that are lacking as a result of financial hardship. And of course time pressure does not benefit professionalism either. Add to this the phenomenon of diagonal concentration, with commercial news media having in recent years been acquired by investment companies rather than by newspaper publishers.

A new criterion measured in the 2011 monitor, absent from the 2009 monitor, is access to government information. There is much dissatisfaction on this point, criticism being leveled against the procedures needed; also, it is felt that costly PR products disguised as journalistic articles threaten independent journalistic efforts. Finally, investigative journalism risks becoming the victim of the financial crisis and the crisis in the news sector (in the public broadcasting system, for example, funding is provided by the various broadcasting organizations and not by NPO).

Overall, in comparing the 2006 (reference year for the MDM 2009) situation of the Dutch news and information media with that of 2008 (reference year for the MDM 2011), the conclusion is that things have remained fairly stable. We find that various initiatives continue to be taken to keep the citizenry adequately informed. Yet, in view of the rapidly changing media environment, the future is not entirely secure. Monitoring therefore remains indispensable.

Note

[1] Fifteen in-depth interviews were held: 3 academics (Piet Bakker, Huub Evers, Huub Wijfjes) and 12 media professionals (2 editors; 1 radio director; 2 news chiefs; 4 (vice) editors-in-chief; 1 editorial director; 1 newsreader/editor; 1 editor/president editorial council).

References

BNR Nieuwsradio (2010) *Mediazaken.* [03-05-2010: http://www.bnr.nl/radio/programmas/mediazaken/14772226].

Bright (2008) *NRC vanaf vandaag uit op e-reader iLiad.* [01-02-2010: http://www.bright.nl/nrc-vanaf-vandaag-uit-op-e-reader-iliad].

Broadcastmagazine.nl (2010) *Marktaandeel publieke omroep in februari op 41,8 %.* [10-05-2010: http://www.broadcastmagazine.nl/Kijkcijfers/marktaandeel-publieke-omroep-in-februari-op-418.html].

Commissariaat voor de Media (2009) *Mediamonitor: Mediabedrijven en mediamarkten 2008.* Hilversum: Commissariaat voor de Media.

Commissariaat voor de Media (2010) *Over het Commissariaat voor de Media.* [19-04-2010: http://www.cvdm.nl/content.jsp?objectid=7011].

d'Haenens, L. (2011) The Netherlands. In J. Trappel, W. A. Meier (eds) *On Media Monitoring The Media and Their Contribution to Democracy.* New York: Peter Lang. pp. 135-160

d'Haenens, L., F. Marcinkowski, A. Donk, J. Trappel, T. Maniglio, J. Fidalgo, et al. (2009) 'The Media for Democracy Monitor applied to five countries: A selection of indicators and their measurement', Communications 34(2): 203-220.

De Journalist (2009) *Dossiers. Code van Bordeaux.* [26-04-2010: http://www.dejournalist.nl/dossiers/journalistieke-codes/code-van-bordeaux/)

De Nieuwe Reporter (2010) *Over DNR.* [03-04-2010: http://www.denieuwereporter.nl/colofon/].

De Persgroep (2010) *Nieuws.* [08-05-2010, de Persgroep: http://www.persgroep.be/].

De Volkskrant (2007) *Bronbescherming journalisten in wet.* [07-05-2010: http://www.volkskrant.nl].

De Vries, W. (2008) *Meer dan de helft Nederlandse huishoudens beschikt over digitale televisie.* [03-05-2010:http://tweakers.net/nieuws/57424/meer-dan-de-helft-nederlandse-huishoudens-beschikt-over-digitale-televisie.html].

Eurostat (2010) *Households having access to the Internet at home.* [01-03-2010: http://nui.epp.eurostat.ec.europa.eu/nui/show.do?dataset=isoc_pibi_hiac&lang=en].

Evers, H., Groenhart, H. & Van Groesen, J. (2010) *De nieuwsombudsman, waakhond of schaamlap?* Diemen: AMB.

Internetabonnement (2010) *Internet abonnement vergelijken.* [25-03-2010, http://www.internetabonnement.nl/].

Kijkwijzer (2010) *Wat is kijkwijzer?* [03-05-2010: http://www.kijkwijzer.nl/pagina.php?id=2].

Leugens.nl (2010) *Waarom.* [03-05-2010: http://www.leugens.nl/over/].

Luistercijfers.nl (2010) *Helft Nederlanders luistert naar Sky Radio 101 FM.* [04-03-2010: http://www.luistercijfers.nl/nieuws-radio-nederland/363-helft-alle-nederlanders-luistert-naar-sky-radio-101-fm].

Maniglio, T., Trappel, J. (2008) *The Media for Democracy Monitor (MDM)* Zurich: University of Zurich.

Mediadebat.nl (2010) *Home.* [03-04-2010: http://www.mediadebat.nl].

Nederlands Genootschap van Hoofdredacteuren (2010) *Code voor de Journalistiek.* [26-04-2010:http://www.genootschapvanhoofdredacteuren.nl/het_genootschap/code-voor-de-journalistiek.html].

Nederlandse Nieuwsmonitor (2010) *Index.* [19-04-2010: http://www.nieuwsmonitor.net/index_nl.html].

Nederlandse Vereniging van Journalisten (NVJ) (2010) *Over de NVJ.* [19-04-2010: http://www.nvj.nl/over/].

Nieman, R. (2007) *Is er nog nieuws?* Amsterdam: Nieuw Amsterdam.

Nom (2009) *Nom Print Monitor 2008-II/2009-1: gemiddeld bereik 13+.* [15-02-2010: http://www.nommedia.nl/docs/Persbericht %20NPM %202008-II %202009-I_bijlage.pdf].

Raad voor de Journalistiek (rvdj) (2010) *Wat is de Raad voor de Journalistiek?* [15-04-2010: http://www.rvdj.nl/katern/43].

Sanomadigital.nl (2010) *Corporate.* [03-05-2010: http://www.sanomadigital.nl/en-web-Over_Sanoma_Digital-Corporate.php].

Sanomadigital.nl (2010a) *Nu.nl, omschrijving.* [03-05-2010: http://www.sanomadigital.nl/en-web-Adverteren-Productinformatie-NU.nl.php].

Statistics Netherlands/Centraal Bureau voor de Statistiek (2010). *Arbeidsmarkt in vogelvlucht.* [03-05-2010:http://www.cbs.nl/nl-NL/menu/themas/arbeid-sociale-zekerheid/publicaties/arbeidsmarkt-vogelvlucht/default.htm].

Stichting KijkOnderzoek (2009). *Jaarrapport 2009.* [04-03-2010: http://www.kijkonderzoek.nl/images/stories/rapporten/sko_jaarrapport_2009_def.pdf].

Stichting Media Ombudsman Nederland. *Media – Ombudsman Nederland. Mission Statement.* [26-04-2010: http://www.media-ombudsman.nl/mission-statement].

Stimuleringsfonds voor de Pers (2010) *GPD en ANP – Gemeentewerken.nl.* [10-05-2010: http://www.bedrijfsfondspers.nl/uno_kredietenEnSubsidies/detail.asp?pageId=335&mode=&besluitId=473].

Stimuleringsfonds voor de Pers (2010a) *Organisatie.* [26-04-2010: http://www.bedrijfsfondspers.nl/emc.asp?pageId=267].

Tijdelijke Commissie Innovatie en Toekomst Pers (2009) *De volgende editie.* http://www.nrc.nl/multimedia/archive/00232/TCITP_rapport_23-06_232451a.pdf

Trappel, J. & Maniglio, T. (2008) *The Media for Democracy Monitor (MDM)* University of Zurich: Institute of Mass Communication and Media Research.

Van der Haak, K. & Van Snippenburg, L. (2007) The national level: The Netherlands. In L. d'Haenens & F. Saeys (eds) Western Broadcast Models. Structure, conduct and performance (pp. 285-286) Berlin/New York: Mouton De Gruyter.

Vara (2010) *De Leugen Regeert.* [03-05-2010, Vara: http://omroep.vara.nl/De-Leugen-Regeert.961.0.html].

Vergelijking (2010) *Breedband-abonnementen.* [25-03-2010, http://www.vergelijking.be/internet/breedband.php].

Vermaas, K. & Janssen, F. (2009) *Het persbureau in perspectief. Het verleden, het heden en de toekomst van de Nederlandse persbureaus.* The Hague: Stimuleringsfonds voor de Pers.

Villamedia (2007) *Onderzoek naar belang redactiestatuut.* [26-04-2010: http://www.villamedia.nl/nieuws/bericht/onderzoek-naar-belang-redactiestatuut/19142/].

Visitatiecommissie Landelijke Publieke Omroep 2004-2008 (2009) *De publieke omroep: het spel, de spelers, het doel.* The Hague: Oranje Van Loon BV.

Chapter 9

PORTUGAL
A Young Democracy Still in Progress

Joaquim Fidalgo

The Portuguese media landscape has been strongly influenced by its specific political, economic, cultural and social evolution during most of the 20th century. Five main factors should be considered:

1. The small size of the country (population of 10.6 million), associated with a very low rate of news media consumption, which makes it difficult for media outlets to achieve sufficient scale to be viable;

2. The economic weakness of the country (an annual GDP of €15.800 *per capita*, when the average for EU/27 countries is € 23.500 – see Eurostat 2010), which means low purchasing power for media consumers and little advertising for the media industry;

3. The rather brief experience of life in democracy, after almost half a century (from 1926 to 1974) of political dictatorship, when basic rights – freedom of expression, freedom of the press, freedom of association – were either forbidden or strictly controlled;

4. The long-standing tradition of a centralized society, very dependent on the State and with low levels of autonomous social dynamism – which tends to 'solve' problems at the macro-level of the law, but not necessarily at the micro-level of actual practices;

5. The faster development of the country (in economic, cultural and technological terms) in more recent years, particularly after joining the European Union in 1986.

The legal and regulatory framework for the media still has marks of the revolutionary period lived in the country between 1974 and 1975, when democracy was recovered and important changes occurred: for some years, the State was the owner of virtually all the media, as a result of nationalization of the main industries. When the democratic regime stabilized and began to follow Western European patterns, in the 1980s, all print media were privatized again and new commercial projects emerged.

Nowadays, the presence of the State as a shareholder in the media is reduced to public television and public radio, as well as to the national news agency.

As a result of this political evolution, the legal framework for the media is different from that of other countries with a liberal tradition. There are many laws: a Press Law, a Radio Law, a Television Law, a PBS Law, a Journalist Statute, an Electronic Communications Law, an Advertising Law, a Law for the Media Regulatory Entity. The State has been very 'present' in terms of media regulation, although the effective respect for the laws raises frequent doubts.

The importance granted to this sector is evident when we look at the Constitution of the Portuguese Republic itself. Freedom of expression and freedom of information have constitutional dignity (art. 37), as do freedom of the press and of the mass media (art. 38), the obligation of media regulation through an administrative entity (art. 39) and the rights to reply, to rectify, to respond politically and to have access to broadcast time (art. 40). The obligation of the State to offer a national public service of radio and television is also inscribed there. Some rights of the journalists – the right to participate in the "editorial orientation" of the news media they work for, the right of access to official information sources, the right to elect newsroom councils – have constitutional dignity as well.

Regarding the media landscape, television consumption is very high in Portugal, but more for entertainment than for information. Since 1992, public television has coexisted with two private channels, one of them leading in terms of audience. There is also an increasing number of channels distributed by cable and paid by subscription.

Radio has both a national and a regional/local presence. The liberalization of the sector occurred in the late 1980s and hundreds of stations were then launched. Many of them did not survive and, at the local level, only a few have their own information service. The public service is present in radio through three different channels, but the leading station is owned by the Catholic Church.

Newspapers have modernized only recently. According to the general world trend, their circulation rates have been falling. Apart from the five daily national newspapers, Portugal also has three daily sports newspapers and two economy dailies. The biggest newspaper sells 120,000 copies a day.

The Internet is developing very fast, in terms of both use of computers and broadband access. Most media companies have been investing in their websites, usually associated with a specific title (a newspaper, a radio or TV channel), but with information content that goes beyond that.

The sample

The general, quantitative data underlying this report refer to the whole country and to all news media. Other data, more qualitative, were gathered among a sample of media companies intended to be somehow representative of the Portuguese situation (in terms of mass-media primarily devoted to news and information). In these cases, the data and opinions were gathered both through access to internal documents and through personal interviews with the editor-in-chief or, in some cases, with a deputy editor-in-chief. Informal interviews with members of different newsrooms were also conducted in order to obtain data from the "rank-and-file" journalists and their practical experience. The interviews were originally made for the 2006 edition of this report, and now were updated and completed, with data from 2009 or 2010. Besides representatives of the media chosen for our sample, we conducted two more formal interviews: one with the deputy editor-in-chief of the news agency *Lusa* (the only Portuguese news agency), and another with the president of the journalists' union (*Sindicato dos Jornalistas*), the only national-wide professional association of this kind.

The four main criteria for our choice were: to have a balanced presence of public and commercial media (which applies to television), to guarantee the presence of different types of media (newspaper, radio, television, on-line), to focus on the most relevant media in terms of news and information, to have a balanced presence of 'popular' (audience-driven) and 'quality' (elite-driven) media.

Table 1.   The sample

	Media type	Financing	Reach	Obs. (2009 data)
Correio da Manhã	Daily newspaper	Commercial (*Cofina* group)	National, popular	Circulation: 122,000
Expresso	Weekly newspaper	Commercial (*Impresa* group)	National, quality	Circulation: 111,000
Público	Daily newspaper	Commercial (*Sonae* industry group)	National, quality	Circulation: 37,000
Destak	Daily newspaper – free	Commercial (*Cofina* group)	National, popular	Printed copies: 99,000
RTP 1	Main public service TV channel	Public – PBS (*State*)	National	Share: 24 % (third position in the ranking)
TVI	Main private TV channel	Commercial (*MediaCapital* group / Spain)	National, popular	Share: 28.7 % (first position in the ranking)
Rádio Renascença (RR)	Main radio station (group)	Commercial (*Catholic church*)	National	Share: 41 % (group) Share of its first channel: 13.5 %

Sources: Marktest (2009) and APCT (2009).

Regarding *on-line media*, the leading positions in Portugal belong consistently to the on-line versions of traditional print media. There are two on-line national 'newspapers' (*Diário Digital* and *Portugal Diário*), but their presence is not relevant in the country's media landscape. Because of that, we did not include any of them in our sample. Instead, we looked both at print and on-line editions of the media indicated above, thus taking into consideration the on-line flow of information that is increasingly important also for traditional media.

Indicators

Freedom / Information (F)

(F1)   Geographic distribution of news media availability   3 POINTS

Relevant news media are generally available to all citizens.

Newspapers – Newspapers are generally accessible all over the country, except for most of the free dailies, which are distributed only in the larger cities. The online editions have most of their content freely accessible. There are a total of 725 newspapers in the country (INE 2008), but the vast majority of them are very small: their total annual circulation is 8,350,733, which means an average of 11,500 copies per year. There are 31 daily newspapers, but only 10 have a rather national distribution. All the regional ones print less than 10,000 copies a day.

Open television – The main open-access, free-to-air TV channels (two public – *RTP1, RTP2* – and two private – *SIC, TVI*) can be watched all over the country. Actually, 99.4 % of Portuguese households have a television set (INE 2008). The commercial channels are free; the public ones are subject to an annual tax of about 21 Euros per household, compulsorily collected with the energy invoice (ca. 2 Euros per month).

Cable television – In 2006, 73 % of households were served by cable; three years later, this figure increased to 78 % (ERC 2009). But no more than 66 % of households (ca. 2.5 million people) actually subscribe to cable TV and, therefore, to several dozens of chains, most of them broadcasting from abroad. There are three major pay-TV operators, with the following market shares: *ZON/TV Cabo* – 64.4 %; *MEO / PT* – 23.0 %; *Cabovisão* – 10.2 % (Anacom 2009).

Radio – The national radio stations are generally accessible all over the country, either because they cover all the territory or because they broadcast in chains of regional or local stations. And their current investment in online distribution is strong as well.

Internet – More than 55 % of the population use a computer regularly, and 51 % use the Internet (see Tables 2, 3 and 4). These figures vary significantly according to age: in the younger group (16-24 years), the percentage of regular users of a computer increases to 94 %. The broadband penetration rate rose from 24 % of households in 2006 to 46.2 % in 2009 (Anacom 2009).

Table 2.   Households with computer and Internet access

	2006	2009	2010
Households with access to a computer	45.4 %	56.0 %	59.5 %
Households with connection to Internet	35.2 %	47.9 %	53.7 %
Households using broadband	24.0 %	46.2 %	50.3 %

Table 3.   Population (16-74 years) using computer and Internet

	2006	2009	2010
% who regularly use a computer	42.5 %	51.4 %	55.4 %
% who regularly access the Internet	35.6 %	46.5 %	51.1 %

Table 4.   Young population (16-24 years) using computer and Internet

	2006	2009	2010
% who regularly use a computer	82.7 %	92.2 %	94.0 %
% who regularly access the Internet	75.2 %	88.1 %	89.3 %

Sources: Pordata and INE (2010) – Inquérito à Utilização de Tecnologias da Informação e da Comunicação pelas Famílias.

(F2)   Patterns of news media use (consumption of news)   2 POINTS

Consumption of news is less important than entertainment or fiction, especially given the overwhelming presence of television.

The growth of Internet access and use, the increasing audience of cable TV, and the changes in free-to-air TV leadership (in favour of a strongly market-driven channel) are the three main elements to consider in the evolution of recent years (Santos 2010).

Television has an overwhelming presence: its total reach is 81.2 % of the population more than 4 years of age (about 8 million people) – see Table 5.

Table 5.   Reach, rate and share of television

	Reach*			Rate*			Share*		
	2006	2009	Dif.	2006	2009	Dif.	2006	2009	Dif.
TVI (private)	66.8 %	64.7 %	-2.1 %	4.4 %	4.2 %	-0.2 %	30.0 %	28.7 %	-1.3 %
SIC (private)	65.6 %	63.4 %	-2.2 %	3.8 %	3.4 %	-0.4 %	26.3 %	23.4 %	-2.9 %
RTP1 (public)	64.6 %	63.1 %	-1.5 %	3.6 %	3.5 %	-0.1 %	24.5 %	24.0 %	-0.5 %
RTP2 (public)	50.7 %	49.8 %	-0.9 %	0.8 %	0.8 %	0.0 %	5.4 %	5.8 %	0.4 %
Cable/Satellite	31.4 %	34.4 %	3.0 %	2.0 %	2.6 %	0.6 %	14.0 %	18.2 %	4.2 %
Total TV	81.4 %	81.2 %	-0.2 %	14.6 %	14.5 %	-0.1 %	100 %	100 %	0 %

Sources: MARKTEST, "Anuário de Media & Publicidade 2006", and MARKTEST, "Anuário de Media & Publicidade 2009".
* Reach – Total audience: the percentage of people who contacted the channel at least for one second.
Rate – Average audience: total number of seconds spent by the population contacting the channel vs. the year under analysis.
Share – Percentage of the watching-TV population contacting each channel (average for the year).

In 2009, every citizen spent an average of 3 hours and 29 minutes a day watching TV. In spite of this, news and information do not have a very strong presence in the programming of the main channels, when compared with entertainment and fiction (particularly the popular Portuguese and Brazilian soap-operas – *telenovelas*). Still, the evening news bulletins of the three main chains (*TVI*, *SIC* and *RTP1*), all broadcasted at the same time (20h00), are usually present among the top-ten programmes every week, with audience rates around 12-14 % (meaning ca. one million people). But these news bulletins are very often a mix of (few) hard and (many) soft news items, entertainment and *fait-divers*, causing them to last for about one and a half hours. Since the information programmes (debates, interviews, news magazines, etc.) virtually disappeared from the free-to-air channels, the evening news bulletins got longer and longer, including those genres that usually would be part of specific information programmes (Lopes 2009).

In cable TV, there are three chains devoted to news and information: *SIC Notícias* (*SIC* group), *TVI 24* (*TVI* group) and *RTPN* (*RTP* group – PBS). This means that the three main players in free-to-air television also have a smaller news channel in cable TV, although with comparatively low audience rates.

Compared with television, newspapers have a much lower reach (see Table 6). In terms of readership, Portugal consistently scores among the European countries with lower rates: only 59.5 copies per 1,000 inhabitants (adult population) are sold daily, compared with 99.2 daily copies per 1,000 inhabitants in Spain, 146 in France, or 538.3 in Norway, just to mention a few examples (WAN 2009). The figures for the main newspapers show important losses between 2006 and 2009, in terms of circulation. The same apparently does not occur in terms of audience, because more people read the online versions.

Table 6.   Newspapers' circulation and audience

	Circulation (number of copies sold per edition)			Audience (% of the population over 15)		
	2006	2009	Dif.	2006	2009	Dif.
Expresso (quality weekly)	133,000	111,000	-16.5 %	7.3 %	7.7 %	0.4 %
Sol ('quality' weekly)	***	45,000	***	***	3.0 %	***
Correio da Manhã (popular daily)	115,000	122,000	6.1 %	9.3 %	12.4 %	3.1 %
Jornal de Notícias (popular daily)	97,000	91,000	-6.2 %	11.4 %	12.1 %	0.7 %
Público (quality daily)	46,000	37,000	-19.6 %	4.5 %	4.5 %	0.0 %
Diário de Notícias (quality/popular daily)	38,000	34,000	-10.5 %	3.2 %	4.1 %	0.9 %
I Informação** (quality daily)	***	10,000	***	***	***	***
24 Horas *** (popular, sensationalist)	43,000	29,000	-32.6 %	3.0 %	2.9 %	-0.1 %
A Bola (sports daily)	n.a.	n.a.	***	8.0 %	9.4 %	1.4 %
Record (sports daily)	80,000	73,000	-8.8 %	7.9 %	10.1 %	2.2 %
O Jogo (sports daily)	41,000	30,000	-26.8 %	5.9 %	6.3 %	0.4 %
Destak (free daily)	168,000*	99,000*	-41.1 %	5.4 %	5.5 %	0.1 %
Metro (free daily)	158,000*	105,000*	-33.5 %	5.6 %	6.0 %	0.4 %
Diário Económico (economy daily)	13,000	15,000	15.4 %	1.9 %	2.6 %	0.7 %
Jornal de Negócios (economy daily)	8,000	11,000	37.5 %	1.9 %	2.0 %	0.1 %

* For free dailies, it is not possible to give circulation figures, but only figures for 'print copies'.

** The daily I Informação was launched in May 2009.

*** The daily 24 Horas closed in June 2010.

Sources: APCT (Associação Portuguesa para o Controlo de Tiragem e Circulação), and MARKTEST, "Anuários de Media & Publicidade" 2006 e 2009.

As for the online diffusion, the sites of traditional newspapers count among the most visited in the country, in terms of news. There is a clear leadership of two sports dailies, fairly distant from general information dailies such as *Público* or *Correio da Manhã*. But the relevant element here is the impressive growth of visits to online sites, as exemplified in Table 7.

Table 7. Access to online sites of some daily newspapers

		Dec. 2007 (millions)	Dec. 2009 (millions)	Dif. (%)
A Bola (sports daily)	Visits	8.8	15.8	+ 79.5 %
	Page-views	34.5	84.4	+ 144.6 %
Record (sports daily)	Visits	6.4	13.3	+ 107.8 %
	Page-views	24.4	64.0	+ 162.3 %
Público (quality daily)	Visits	3.4	5.7	+ 67.6 %
	Page-views	18.3	25.0	+ 36.6 %
Correio da Manhã (popular daily)	Visits	2.9	5.1	+ 75.9 %
	Page-views	15.0	33.7	+ 124.7 %

Sources: MARKTEST – Netscope (Ranking de tráfego de entidades Web).

The total reach of radio is 57 % of the population over 15 (Marktest 2009). But the radio station almost exclusively devoted to news (*TSF*) has an average audience of 4.2 %, which means less than 400,000 people. Still, the time spent listening to the radio seems to be stable over time, although there are changes concerning the places where people listen to radio – less at home, more in the car and over the Internet (Cardoso *et al.* 2009).

The overwhelming presence of television has relevant consequences for the business too: its share of advertising is much higher than the share for newspapers (see Table 8).

Table 8. Distribution of advertisement among media

	2004	2005	2006	2007	2008	2009
Share of advertisement in TV	63.2 %	68.3 %	70.2 %	70.3 %	71.3 %	73.4 %
Share of advertisement in Press	22.5 %	19.3 %	18.2 %	18.6 %	17.9 %	15.5 %
Share of advertisement in Radio	n.a.	5.2 %	4.0 %	4.2 %	3.8 %	4.1 %
Others (outdoors...)	14.3 %	7.2 %	7.6 %	6.9 %	7.0 %	7.0 %

Source: MARKTEST, "Anuário 2009 – Anuário de Media & Publicidade".

(F3)   Diversity of news sources   1 POINT

There is little diversity of news sources, with a high dependency on a single national agency.

There is only one news agency (which has the State as its major shareholder), and its presence as a news source for the media is enormous. *Lusa* has newsrooms in

Lisbon and Oporto, apart from regional delegations in all the districts. Besides the provision of news and photos, in the past two years the agency started providing its clients with sounds and videos as well, thus increasing its presence in all the media.

It is not uncommon for journalists, following orders from above, to hide the fact that this or that piece of news has *Lusa* as its source, either not quoting the source or rewriting the original material in order to make it look 'original'. This trend increased in the on-line sections of media companies, where most of the newsrooms are composed of very few, and very young professionals, which causes most of the journalistic work to be no more than "desk work". And because the speed of publication is the first rule in many information sites, the presence of the agency in the area of breaking news is huge, turning it into "the biggest agenda-setter in the country", to quote the deputy editors we interviewed.

Two other trends are widespread: the high dependence on institutional, official sources, and the increasing ability of Public Relations (PR) organizations to place their material in the pages of the news. A recent study on the origin of the political news in the four main Portuguese dailies (Ribeiro 2009) showed that about 60 % of news items had been originated by PR material, or by communication agencies, rather than by the initiative of the media themselves. As one leading PR manager recently said, "For better and for worse, news sources are installed in the newsrooms" (as cited in Souza 2008).

(F4)   Internal rules for practice of newsroom democracy   2 POINTS

Several laws and mechanisms for journalists' democratic participation exist, but they are not always followed in practice.

The formal involvement of journalists in newsroom decisions has been granted by law since the '25 April 1974' (the revolution that brought democracy to the country). The Constitution states the right of journalists to elect newsroom councils, as well as their right to have a word in the editorial orientation of the news media. The underlying concept is that media activity is not just a business like any other (Kovach & Rosenstiel 2001), only regulated by the supply-and-demand market laws; on the contrary, it deals with a 'public good' of great importance for social and political life, nourishing democracy and stimulating citizenship. For this reason, journalists are expected to actively work to guarantee that media meet their social responsibilities. Furthermore, because the media deal with sensitive issues concerning the fundamental rights of citizens, they are supposed to adopt serious principles and standards of ethical behaviour, to which journalists must be specially committed, even when they conflict with management priorities (Fidalgo 2008). The permanent tension of the journalistic field between the "cultural pole" and the "commercial pole" (Bourdieu

2006) – with a clear over-valuation of the commercial dimension in recent times (Garcia 2009) – makes this participation more sensitive.

All news media with a minimum of five journalists must have a newsroom council. And most of them have it (one known exception is the leading radio station *Rádio Renascença*, another is the free daily *Destak*), even if their function is sometimes confined to just formal consultations.

The weekly *Expresso* has a detailed Code of Conduct and the daily *Público* has a Style Book that goes far beyond the technical standards of news-making. It is an important instrument of accountability, because it is often quoted when readers present their complaints to the newspaper's ombudsman. There is also a draft of a Style Book with these characteristics in the public television (*RTP*).

Some democratic control by journalists in the newsrooms still exists. However, the economic and financial problems of the media industry put a great deal of pressure on the newsrooms, which somehow threatens journalists' jobs and contributes to their demobilization.

(F5) Company rules against *internal* influence on newsroom / editorial staff · 2 POINTS

The degree of independence of the newsroom against ownership is high in the leading media, but weak in others.

Portuguese laws formally guarantee the independence of journalists from the owner (and the exclusive responsibility of the editor-in-chief over the content of the publication). Some media reinforce them through internal rules. The question is what happens at a more informal level, in the daily routines of journalistic choices.

All of the editors interviewed for this report insisted that there is complete independence of the newsroom from the ownership and management. In its first issue (in 1990), the quality daily *Público* even published a text, endorsed both by the editorial board and by the owner, in which a formal commitment to independence was made.

Rádio Renascença is in a special situation, as it is owned by the Catholic Church and makes it clear that it is a radio station "with a Christian inspiration". But the editor-in-chief does not think it puts editorial independence at stake, because the station clearly distinguishes between what is "pluralism of information" and what is "a doctrinal inspiration".

The issue of independence of the Public Broadcasting Service (PBS) in relation to the Government is a permanent matter of debate in Portugal, especially in what concerns television. Their editors-in-chief pledge that the information area is completely independent from the Government, but opposition parties now and then raise their doubts and concerns about it.

Independence from the marketing and advertisement departments of media companies is also a generally underlined rule, although no one denies some more or less timid attempts to break it. Stories of 'promiscuities' between editorial and commercial areas are increasingly told. But they are usually denied by those directly involved, because it would harm their credibility.

The 'golden rule' of separation between the editorial area and the commercial / management area is a strong rule. But there seems to be a problem of self-censorship. As one of our respondents confessed (requesting not to be identified), "when we work in a company owned by an important group, of course we don't forget that situation and, even in a non-explicit way, that tends to influence our choices". And this "can be felt at different levels of the newsroom", beginning at the top and going down to the "individual work of some journalists".

(F6) Company rules against *external* influence on newsroom / editorial staff   1 POINT

Although news media generally receive revenues from a multitude of advertisers, they are increasingly permeable to advertising formats that allow some confusion between the editorial and the commercial areas.

Portuguese news media, in general, face a serious problem of economic survival: because the audience rates and circulation figures are generally very low, their major (or unique) source of income is advertising. But the advertising market itself is small for all the existing competitors, which puts them all under an enormous pressure, as they must accept either some unpleasant advertising formats or important price reductions. In recent years, it is more and more common to find 'intrusions' of advertising in the editorial area. In spite of this, all the editors interviewed in our sample strongly deny any abusive interference from external parties. Independence from advertisers is rather common in the biggest or more important news media, but the same does not apply to smaller companies (regional or local newspapers and radio stations).

Regarding sponsorship, some newspapers now have the good habit of informing readers whenever their reporters travel by invitation of some company or institution.

The big problem seems to be the economic weakness of Portuguese media companies. There is strong competition and, in such a scenario, it becomes easier for advertisers to get what they want; if they don't, the likelihood is great that another competitor will.

(F7) Procedures on news selection and news processing 2 POINTS

Rules and standards for news processing exist, but they are not always present in the day-by-day routines.

Again, this indicator must be balanced between what is formally prescribed in some newsrooms and what the day-by-day routines actually show. Furthermore, it must be balanced between what the editors say about the allegedly existing procedures and what the rank-and-file journalists comment on the subject, with the first guaranteeing that clear procedures are generally followed, and the latter complaining that team-work and collective dynamics in the newsroom are disappearing. The economic crisis, the decreasing circulation figures, the downsizing of most newsrooms – all of these things seem to favour a climate of uncertainty, of demobilization, and of fear of losing one's job, which reinforces an individualistic approach to work and a disinterest in more collective initiatives.

The leading reference newspapers, such as *Público* and *Expresso*, have defined extensive internal rules for selecting and processing news. They are commonly followed and seem to be very useful, for example, in the process of integration of new journalists. But this should be regarded more as an exception than as a rule.

In the past decade, the role of press ombudsman in recalling the principles for news processing, and in adding a reflective voice to the speed of journalistic routines, has been important. Three of the major dailies (*Jornal de Notícias*, *Público* and *Diário de Notícias*) used to have an ombudsman, but presently only *Público* keeps its "readers' advocate", apparently because it is not easy to pay for such a job when the number of journalists is being severely reduced.

Equality / Interest mediation (E)

(E1) Media ownership concentration national level 2 POINTS

There are three or more competitors for every area, but the level of ownership concentration is rather high.

Four big groups (*Impresa*, *Controlinvest*, *Cofina* and *MediaCapital*) control most of the TV and radio stations, newspapers, magazines and online news sites – see Table 9. The State has an important position too, as does the Catholic Church (leading radio station, regional newspapers). Among the most important news media, only the quality daily *Público*, the newcomer daily "*i*" and the sports daily *A Bola* do not belong to any of these media groups. The fact that the market is small and news-consuming habits are not very high makes it difficult for single companies to invest in a news medium and survive.

There are three competitors in open access Television (the State – owning *RTP1* and *RTP2*, one Portuguese media group – owning *SIC*, and a foreigner media group – the Spanish *PRISA* – presently owning *TVI*). All these companies also have paid-for channels, distributed through cable. There are also three major cable TV suppliers (the first one, *Zon/TV Cabo*, with a market share of 64.4 %).

There are four competitors in the national generalist daily press. One media group owns two (*Jornal de Notícias* and *Diário de Notícias*) of the five existing newspapers[1] – plus one of the three sports dailies. There is now only one competitor in the market of generalist free dailies: they were three, but one closed and two others merged.

In the radio, there are more than three competitors at the national level, and particularly at the regional and local levels. As for Internet, there are also more than three competitors in the market (2008), although a company with the State as the shareholder with a "golden share" (PT-Portugal Telecom) has a prominent position.

Table 9.   The main media groups in Portugal (2010)

Groups \ Media	CONTROLINVESTE	IMPRESA	COFINA	MEDIA CAPITAL
Daily newspapers	- *Jornal de Notícias* - *Diário de Notícias* - *O Jogo* (sports) - *Açoriano Or.* (reg.) - *DN Madeira* (reg.)		- *Correio da Manhã* - *Record* (sports) - *Jornal de Negócios* (economy) - *Destak* (free) - *Metro* (free)	
Weekly newspapers and news magazines	- *J. Fundão* (reg.) - *Ocasião* (advert.)	- *Expresso* (weekly) - *Visão* (newsmag.)	- *Sol* (weekly) - *Sábado* (newsmag.)	
Online news	(All newspapers, newsmagazines, tv and radio stations also have online editions)	(All newspapers, newsmagazines, tv and radio stations also have online editions)	(All newspapers, newsmagazines, tv and radio stations also have online editions)	(All newspapers, newsmagazines, tv and radio stations also have online editions) - *PortugalDiario* - *MaisFutebol* (sport) - *Agência Financeira* (economy)
TV (open access)		- SIC		- TVI
TV (cable)	- *SportsTV*	- *SIC Notícias* - *SIC Radical* - *SIC Mulher* - *SIC Internacional*		- *TVI 24*
Radio	- TSF			- Rádio Comercial - Cidade FM - Rádio Clube Português
Others	- Advertising in sports events - Television transmission rights (football)	- News agency (part) - Printing - Newspaper distribution	- Newspaper distribution	- TV producing company *(NBP)*

Source: Elaboration by the author, with data from ERC (2006) and ERC (2009).

A more strict law on media concentration was presented by the socialist government in 2008 and approved by the Parliament in 2009, but was not promulgated by the President of the Republic, with the argument that it was not urgent and that "a broader political consensus" on that matter should be reached.

(E2) Media ownership concentration regional (local) level   3 POINTS

Ownership concentration at the regional level is very low.

"Regions" are not a political entity in Portugal. In spite of that, considering the geographical scope of the publications, there are many regional and local newspapers, but generally very small: for the dozen of dailies, circulation rates are usually between 5,000 and 10,000 copies; for the weeklies (more common at the regional level), there are hundreds, but usually small, rather traditional and not very professionalized. The largest ones (*O Mirante* – 28,000 copies, and *Jornal do Fundão* – 13,000 copies) are exceptions in terms of size.

There are also many local radio stations, but all very small too: most of them do not even have a newsroom or information services. There are no regional TV stations, because they are not allowed by law, which some consider "a serious democratic shortcoming" (Cádima 2009). The exceptions are some local web TV stations, diffused by the Internet, and the two regional channels of the public television for Madeira and Azores.

One of the biggest national media groups (*Controlinvest*) owns three regional newspapers. There are two regional groups of some importance at this geographical level, both in the centre of the country – *Adriano Lucas* and *Sojormedia*. The first one owns four small dailies (one only on-line) and one weekly. The second owns one small daily and six weeklies (plus two regional radio stations and a regional web TV). But they do not mean much concentration in a landscape where regional and local titles can be counted in the hundreds.

(E3) Diversity of formats   1 POINT

There is an increasing homogenization of formats, meaning less diversity.

Television – Although time devoted to news and information has been increasing in free-to-air TV programming, the presence of entertainment and of the fiction area (which mostly means *"telenovelas"*) is still much stronger, particular in commercial channels. This trend is clear when we look at the comparative shares – measured in terms of time devoted to each item – offered by the main channels (see Table 10).

Table 10.   Diversity of thematic areas in television

	TVI (commercial)		SIC (commercial)		RTP1 (public)	
	2006	2009	2006	2009	2006	2009
News and information	14.6 %	15.4 %	10.8 %	14.8 %	21.6 %	26.1 %
Fiction	36.9 %	30.1 %	34.7 %	30.3 %	21.1 %	19.2 %
Entertainment	13.9 %	16.2 %	14.4 %	14.7 %	25.0 %	29.7 %
Sport	2.1 %	2.5 %	0.9 %	1.3 %	4.8 %	5 %
General culture / knowledge	2.6 %	1.9 %	2.5 %	3.1 %	4.9 %	4.2 %
Children and youth	2.5 %	2.3 %	8.7 %	6.1 %	3.0 %	1.5 %
Others	3.4 %	8.8 %	4.0 %	11.4 %	3.8 %	3.3 %
Advertising	24.0 %	22.9 %	23.9 %	18.3 %	16.6 %	11.2 %

Source: MARKTEST, *Anuário 2006* and *Anuário 2009.*

News and information programmes, in the main TV channels, are almost reduced to the evening news bulletins (20h00). But other news formats (interviews, debates, in-depth reporting, etc.) are very much absent, except for some specific situations in public television (*RTP1* and *RTP2*). Besides this, the evening news bulletins, as said before, include a great deal of soft news, *fait-divers*, shocking reporting, and trivial subjects.

Each of the three main TV stations also has a channel exclusively devoted to news and information: *SIC-Notícias* (a subsidiary of *SIC*), *RTPN* (a subsidiary of *RTP*) and *TVI-24* (a subsidiary of *TVI*). But all of them are distributed through cable and are paid for, which means they do not reach more than half of Portuguese families, with low audience rates. This limitation notwithstanding, those channels have a more diverse set of news formats, including debates, extensive interviews, and special features.

More innovative news formats are being developed online, especially by the online editions of traditional media, and multimedia approaches (infographs, podcasts, videos) are expanding.

As for newspapers, the trend goes more towards popularization, soft-news and 'light' products, even among quality papers. The differences between newspapers are not as evident as they used to be. As for the free dailies, they are very similar too. They grew very fast in the years 2006-2008, but they have been quickly decreasing in circulation (see Table 11), because they did not invest in their newsrooms and they failed to get enough advertising.

Table 11. Rise and fall of the Portuguese free (not paid-for) newspapers

	Jun-06	Dec-06	Jun-07	Dec-07	Jun-08	Dec-08	Jun-09	Dec-09	Oct-10
Destak	174,016	177,403	177,416	172,576	168,758	138,807	93,775	117,696	93,400
Metro	159,825	160,409	182,207	162,604	181,515	157,167	102,548	112,916	102,500
GlobalNoticias	X	X	X	150,483	196,787	195,088	99,567	100,574	XX
Meia Hora	X	X	X	88,551	71,589	34,009	25,871	XX	XX
OJE (eco)	15,420	18,150	24,473	25,847	27,778	27,993	27,690	26,644	25,783
Diário Desportivo (sport)	X	X	87,704	XX	XX	XX	XX	XX	XX
TOTAL DAILIES	349,261	355,962	471,800	600,061	646,427	553,064	349,451	357,830	221,683
Sexta (weekly)	X	X	X	312,131	319,516	212,162	XX	XX	XX
TOTAL DAILIES + WEEKLY	349,261	355,962	471,800	912,192	965,943	765,226	349,451	357,830	221,683

Note: The 'X' mark means that the newspaper in question had not been launched yet; the 'XX' mark means that the newspaper in question ceased publication.
Source: APCT

(E4) Minority / Alternative media 1 POINT

Relatively little attention is paid to minorities in the mainstream media, and they have few media of their own.

There are 455,000 foreigners living in the country. The largest group (116.000) comes from Brazil, which means they have no linguistic barriers to accessing the national media. The same is true of other communities coming from former Portuguese colonies (Cape Verde, Angola, and Guinea). But, in recent years, the percentage of immigrants from Eastern European countries has grown rapidly (there are presently 52,000 Ukrainians, 32,000 Rumanians and 21,000 Moldavians, for example).

There are a few newspapers written in foreign languages (in some cases, bi-lingual). But they are not relevant in the media landscape (circulation figures can be counted at most in the hundreds). They usually have been created by the foreigner communities' associations – and there are more than 100 of these associations in Portugal, according to the "High Commissioner for Immigration and Intercultural Dialogue".

There are sometimes some complaints made by those communities regarding the way immigrants are mistreated by the mainstream media. A study funded by ERC and conducted by a group of scholars concluded that the visibility of immigrants in the main media was, in the period 2003-2008, usually associated with "crime" and "social transgression" (Férin 2009, p. 124). And the news reporting on those issues tends to give a voice to security forces (police) and institutional sources, rather than to immigrants' associations or common people from these communities of foreigners (*ibidem*).

As regards television, a very small percentage of programmes are specifically devoted to ethnic or cultural minorities: during 2009, less than 1 % of the general content of *SIC* and *TVI* was devoted to them, while this percentage grew up to 3.4 % in the public channels (*RTP 1* and *RTP2*), although most of it concentrated in *RTP2* (ERC 2009).

As for the disabled, public television usually broadcasts some of its leading programmes with sign language or with subtitles in Portuguese. Presently, some TV popular contests, series and soap-operas are regularly subtitled. A technically advanced system (Tecnovoz) has been in use since 2007, allowing *RTP1* to automatically deliver – with a delay of some seconds – subtitles in Portuguese for programmes being broadcasted live. As for sign language, four daily news programmes and three weekly programmes are presented simultaneously in this way.

The Regulatory Entity for the Media (ERC), following a prescription inscribed in the Television Law in 2007, finally established (in October 2009) a set of obligations for the main TV operators – both public and private – regarding more attention to people with disabilities: a three-year plan, to be fulfilled until 31 December 2012, will greatly increase the number of programmes with subtitles and with gesture language.

The enormous increase of the Internet, and particularly the strong development of weblogs, brought new possibilities for various minorities (political, religious, sexual, cultural…) to have their own information flows.

(E5) Affordable public and private news media   2 POINTS

Prices are decreasing and much free content is offered, but the cost of news media is still relatively high for an average household.

Annual subscription to a quality daily newspaper (Público)	320 Euros
Annual subscription to a weekly newsmagazine (Visão)	130 Euros
Annual subscription to broadband access 12 MB (average: 20x12)	240 Euros
Annual subscription to general Cable TV (average 100 channels)	348 Euros
Annual tax for Public Service of TV and Radio (compulsory)	22 Euros
TOTAL	1,060 Euros

Considering that the average income *per capita* in Portugal is around 15,000 Euros, the amount spent on basic news media, in a scenario like the one shown above, amounts to about 7 % of the annual income. It seems to be a fairly high price: spending about 90 Euros/month for access to the main media and Internet means an important effort in a country where the minimum salary, legally prescribed, is now 450 Euros a month.

Nonetheless, prices for Internet access and cable TV decreased very quickly, especially with "triple-play" packages (Internet + fixed telephone + cable TV). The offers of the two main players in this field vary presently between ca. 40 and 150 Euros a month, according to the number of TV channels received and to the speed of the Internet connection.

Most of the content of the main newspapers is freely available on-line.

(E6) Content monitoring instrument   3 POINTS

There are different monitoring instruments and they are publicly available.

There are four main entities that regularly deal with media monitoring issues:

- **ERC (*Entidade Reguladora para a Comunicação Social*)** This is the official regulatory body for the media, with its members elected by the Parliament by a minimum majority of 2/3 of the votes. Apart from other activities (licensing, regulating, sanctioning), ERC also has a monitoring function to check whether the general rules and obligations (for example, in the Public Broadcasting Service) are fulfilled. Besides its annual report, including a great deal of data on the media field, it regularly publishes a newsletter and conducts – in partnership with universities – studies on specific issues about media activity and performance.

- **OBERCOM (*Observatório da Comunicação*)** Although private, this observatory has great involvement in public institutions connected with the media and uses State facilities to carry out its work. The most important associations and media companies are partners. It regularly publishes a "Yearbook" with a detailed description of the media business in Portugal, and leads (or funds) studies and research projects aimed to achieve "better knowledge of the communication area". It also publishes an online scientific refereed journal.

- **MARKTEST** This private company is responsible for monitoring activities regarding media audiences and audiometric, either in television or radio, the press or the Internet. The results of its monitoring work are regularly used when anyone wants to describe the state of the media, from the point of view of its reception and audience. Some major figures from its findings go public regularly, but the detailed information must be paid for.

- **APCT (*Associação Portuguesa para o Controlo de Tiragem e de Circulação*)** This is also a private entity, created by the voluntary association of the press companies, and was designed to permanently monitor the number of copies printed, diffused and actually sold. Membership is voluntary, but all the relevant print media (with one single exception) joined it.

Besides the regular activity of these institutions, some media monitoring work is also done by research groups at universities[2] and by individual or collective blogs concerned with the media business. Not to mention the increasing debate over these issues in the social networks, particularly *Facebook* (with its three million users).

(E7) Code of ethics at the national level (structure) 2 POINTS

There is a national Code of Ethics but is not always widely implemented.

There is a Code of Ethics for journalists, prepared under the responsibility of the national Journalists' Union – the only national association of journalists in the country. Within the Journalists' Union, there is also an Ethics Council.

The Code is well known, but the fact that it was created in the context of the Journalists' Union, added to the fact that Portuguese journalists are not obliged to join the Union (and more than 50 % actually don't), raises frequent questions about its reach and jurisdiction. In 2007, this situation changed by the initiative of the Government. Apart from the Union, there is a national commission (presided over by a judge) that has the responsibility to grant the journalists' professional credential – no one can work as a journalist in Portugal if he/she does not have the professional card (*Carteira Profissional de Jornalista*), which must be renewed every two years and which depends on some legal conditions. Since 2007, this Commission also has disciplinary powers regarding the journalists' ethical duties. This means that, under the new law, a journalist, regardless of whether he/she belongs to the Union, can suffer sanctions if it is proved that he/she disrespected the Code of Ethics.

Although this Commission is composed entirely of journalists, half of them elected by the professional group and the other half appointed by the media companies, the new system raised strong debates among the Portuguese journalists, who would prefer ethical questions to be treated by the journalists themselves, on an autonomous (self-regulatory) basis, and not by a Commission 'imposed by law' (a model of 'regulated self-regulation'). On its behalf, the Government argued that this measure was taken simply because the journalists' professional group had not proved to be capable of dealing with this problem autonomously.

There is no Press Council. Whoever wants to complain about media ethical abuses must address either the Media Regulatory Entity (ERC) or the Commission of the Journalists' Professional Chart (CCPJ).

(E8) Level of self-regulation (performance) 2 POINTS

Some self-regulation mechanisms exist on the level of the main news media.

As explained above, there is not a national self-regulatory entity (like a Press Council), although there are several self-regulation instruments in the leading news media.

Everyone has an Editorial Statute, with a mission statement emphasizing their independence from political and economic powers, their respect for the people's fundamental rights, their commitment to democratic values, and their attachment to the journalistic ethical principles. But these are, in most cases, just formal statements with very general intentions. Some of these media have more detailed internal accountability mechanisms, which is the case for, e.g., *Expresso* (with a Code of Conduct dealing with such issues as objectivity, accuracy, plagiarism, identification of information sources, error correction, limits to gifts offered to journalists, etc.), *Público* (with a Style Book that has a first part entirely devoted to ethical questions, to journalism social responsibility, to conflict of interests, etc.), or *RTP* (with an Editorial Statute that underlines the particular responsibilities of a public service television, the obligation to promote pluralism and diversity).

A news ombudsman has existed since 1997 in one of the five national dailies (*Público*). Two other dailies had an ombudsman for several years (*Diário de Notícias* and *Jornal de Notícias*), but the position is vacant now – according to our sources, financial constraints have obliged media outlets to invest less in these instruments of 'quality control'. Since 2006, there has also been a news ombudsman in public television and another one in public radio[3]. They, too, have a broadcasting time every week, prepared under their exclusive responsibility.

As for the right of reply, it is a constitutional obligation.

(E9) Participation. 1 POINT

People are not particularly encouraged to participate in the news process, in spite of some improvements in the online context.

The traditional section of "Letters to the Editor" is the most common way for people to participate in the news process. It exists in every newspaper, sometimes enlarged to other small sections where the readers' opinion (or the readers' active participation, either with texts or with photos or videos) is requested.

The Internet and the development of these newspapers' online editions have strongly expanded opportunities for public participation, with comments on the news, voting in day-by-day opinion pools, etc. The newspapers are open to these forms of participation and encourage them, but in a rather disorganized way: they usually do not promote real public discussions or debates, and they do not have regular contacts with the readers.

Some national radio stations (*TSF, Antena Um*) have daily forums open to the public, to discuss a given subject, according to the news of the day. But not all of them agree with this: the leading *Radio Renascença* is against forums in which "anyone can say anything".

In public television and radio, there is an Opinion Council representing different areas and social groups.

(E10)   Rules and practices on internal pluralism   3 POINTS

Internal pluralism is fairly well promoted in the main news media.

In Portugal, there is no tradition for news media to publicly endorse a political party or a candidate. All main media insist on 'independence' as their supreme value, promising to offer their audience all the relevant perspectives on any issue under debate. The lack of any kind of institutionalized 'external pluralism' is, thus, allegedly fulfilled by 'internal pluralism', both in the newsroom and in the set of outsiders invited to regularly write opinion columns. Notwithstanding this general position, the fact is that we often listen to complaints by the public against bias in the media, up to the point of some suggesting that everything would be more transparent if those media assumed a clear political position instead of a false independence.

News media tend to be critical of government and of the ruling party, following a tradition of counter-power that is usually associated with journalism and with its watchdog function. The opposite occurs when it comes to the PBS, or even to the news agency: there is a consistent suspicion that government tends to get better coverage by these media, because they depend directly on public funding. The Regulatory Entity for the Media (ERC) now systematically monitors the existence or absence of political pluralism in the PBS news bulletins, and has concluded that, during the past three years, there has tended to be some over-representation of the Government and of its supporting party (the Socialist Party) in the news, apparently at the cost of the main opposition party (the Social-Democrat Party), which is often under-represented (ERC 2009). The results of this monitoring activity are somehow 'present' in the minds of the editors of public television, as we were told by different sources from the newsroom: there is nowadays more concern in PBS when it comes to deciding what to cover in the political agenda, with an effort to balance the journalistic relevance of the issues with the need to respect the 'quotas' of broadcasting time defined by ERC (in terms of "reference values") to each political party.

Control / Watchdog (C)

(C1) Supervising the watchdog 'control of the controllers' 2 POINTS

There are institutionalized mechanisms to control media performance as a watchdog, but these issues are not very present in the public debates.

The Regulatory Media Entity (ERC) must guarantee that the news media respect everyone's rights, act with independence, fairness and accuracy, allow the exercise of the right to reply, respect pluralism and promote diversity, etc. In this context, it acts as a clear control mechanism of media performance, either on its own initiative or in the sequence of complaints received from the public. It started working in 2006 (although there was, in its place, another institution with some similar purposes). Apart from the political controversies about its statute (its members are appointed by the Parliament, according to nominations supported by the biggest political parties), and about the need for media regulation (contested by some media owners and editors according to an increasingly disseminated 'neo-liberal' ideology), the fact is that some more attention is being paid to media performance and to the media's complex roles in contemporary societies.

Besides this, the general landscape concerning news monitoring and debating within the journalistic community is not very stimulating. The Journalists' Club publishes a monthly magazine ("*Jornalismo e Jornalistas*") and regularly updates an online site devoted to media and journalism issues, where some stimulating debates arise from time to time. Some interesting blogs by journalists (individual or collective) should also be mentioned: a dozen of them are, today, the most consistent, attentive and stimulating instruments for media analysis and media criticism.

The role played by universities that offer journalism courses (and journalism / media research centres) is relevant as well. Some of them have been responsible, during recent years, for the publication of dozens of books dealing with media issues. This means that the discussion of these questions is now more open to the general public than it used to be, when these books circulated only within the academy.

(C2) Independence of the news media from power holders 2 POINTS

Some independence is guaranteed by different laws, but the actual practice shows increasing difficulties.

The Journalist Statute grants journalists a set of important rights and guarantees in order to protect their activity: the right to independence and to "free creation and expression" (containing the so-called 'consciousness clause'), the right "to participate in the editorial orientation" of the media, the right of access to "official sources of information" and to "public places", the right to "professional secrecy" (meaning that he/she is allowed not to disclose the identity of his/her sources[4]).

This does not mean, however, that problems do not arise now and then. For example, the separation of the editorial area and management is not respected in all situations: in 2009, a weekly news bulletin of the leading television channel TVI (which had gained its reputation for being very strongly against the Portuguese prime minister) was terminated by a direct order coming from the board of managers, and not by the editor-in-chief. This was considered illegal by ERC, but the fact is that the news bulletin did not show up again.

There seems to be a feeling among most journalists that, due to the precarious situation of many of them, it is not easy to defend those rights. Keeping silent and trying not to raise too many questions is, apparently, an option more and more followed by journalists, particularly when media companies are economically weak or when journalists are young interns trying to get a more stable job.

In terms of diagonal concentration or cross-media ownership, there are also a number of situations to be considered:

- the owner of the reference daily *Público* is one of the biggest businessmen in the country (SONAE group), whose major assets are supermarkets and shopping centres;

- *Controlinvest*, the owner of the dailies *Jornal de Notícias, Diário de Notícias,* and *O Jogo* (sports), as well as of *SporTV* (cable), has important interests in the advertising industry, in the football industry and in transmission rights for football games;

- *Cofina,* the owner of the dailies *Correio da Manhã, Record* (sports), *Jornal de Negócios* (economy), *Destak* and *Metro* (free), has various interests in industrial areas;

- the owner of the leading radio station, *Rádio Renascença*, is the Catholic Church, which also owns a number of small regional newspapers.

(C3) Transparency of data on media system   3 POINTS

Information on news media exists and is easily accessible.

Every news medium is legally obliged to publish regularly the list of its main shareholders, but this is not always a guarantee of full transparency, either because of cross-ownership situations or because of financial investors who are difficult to identify. Nowadays, however, as the main news media of the country are concentrated in the hands of four or five well-known groups, the question of ownership is not really a disputed issue. And most of the Internet sites of those news media usually provide some information about all the other media belonging to the same group.

A new step in this field was very recently (2010) made by the Regulatory Entity for the Media (ERC), through the creation, on its site, of a "Database for the Transparency of Media Ownership", where information is available for most of the media companies in the country. The database provides information not only on the main shareholders of each company, but also on the other companies that are part of them.

(C4) Journalism professionalism   2 POINTS

The professional ethos is not too high in global terms, considering the heterogeneity of the professional group.

Following the classification of media systems by Hallin and Mancini (2004), Portugal belongs to the so-called "polarized pluralist model", which has as one of its main characteristics a relatively low level of professionalization of journalists. This means a low degree of professional autonomy, some weakness in the definition and implementation of distinct professional and ethical norms, and a relative lack of public service orientation. These traits somehow apply to the Portuguese situation, although with nuances.

During most of the 20th century, because there was no freedom of expression or of association, journalists' professional organizations had no autonomy at all. In such conditions, it was particularly difficult for them to implement their specific ethical values and professional norms, and this contributed to a "weak professional culture" (Correia & Baptista 2007). Things changed fast after 1974, when democracy prevailed. One of the first laws to be put into practice was a new press law. Journalists organized themselves in a (now free and autonomous) strong national union, and were able to convince the political powers to make laws on a large set of items considered to be very important to journalistic work. If the instruments of journalistic professionalization had been absent, now they were 'conquered' by the professional group, although more as a result of pressure over the State rather than as a result of a dynamic autonomous process. But dependence on a very centralized state, which is typical of the 'pluralist polarized systems', somehow continued in the country.

Portuguese journalists have important laws to protect their activity, they have their code of ethics, but they were never able to put into practice an efficient and consensual mechanism of self-regulation. The existing 'Ethics Council' works in the context of the union, but many of the ca. 7,000 professional journalists[5] do not belong to it (in 2009, the union had 2,978 members, which means about 40 % of the existing journalists – see SJ 2009) and, therefore, tend not to acknowledge its jurisdiction.

The teaching of journalism is very recent as well: it only appeared at a Portuguese university in 1979.

Journalists are a rather heterogeneous professional group and still have not succeeded in putting forward a strong collective dynamic. Some progress in recent years is partly counterbalanced by the negative economic situation in the media industry, which pushes journalists more towards 'proletarianization' than professionalization.

(C5) Journalists' job security   2 POINTS

There is a relatively high level of job security in the legal framework.

Portuguese journalists do not have many reasons to complain about job security, when it comes to legal dispositions. But, in practical terms, the economic structural weakness of most media industries and the actual crisis play a major role when it comes to assessing their effective security. Apart from the legal guarantees, the day-by-day routine in concrete media companies shows that, according to multiple sources, things are becoming increasingly difficult for journalists, and this leads to silence and resignation rather than to confrontation and a struggle for one's rights. "It's better to try to avoid problems than to be involved in a long process in a court of law", as was said by a seasoned journalist at a major newspaper.

In the past three years, all of the most important Portuguese news media downsized their newsrooms, dismissing dozens of journalists – some of them, but not all, through friendly negotiations. Between 2007 and 2009, more than 400 journalists lost their jobs. The fear of being the next to be chosen somehow spreads and invites more passive behaviour. With this scenario, it is increasingly difficult for young people to find a new job in the media. Because hundreds of them leave the universities every year, the competition is very strong. Therefore, it is not difficult to find someone who will accept precarious labour conditions (Graça 2007), usually in the form of short-term contracts (or no contracts at all).

(C6) Practice of access to information   2 POINTS

No legal barriers exist to accessing public information, but access is often difficult in practice.

According to the Journalist Statute, the right of journalists to access information sources must be guaranteed by the organisms of public administration, and whoever refuses that access may be legally prosecuted "with urgency" (art. 8). This applies not only to journalists: in the name of "transparency of public affairs", everyone has the right of access to administrative documents from the public sector, with "no need to invoke any particular interest" (law nr. 46/2007).

Because the law is sometimes disrespected, or because the interpretations of what falls under the category of restricted information may be divergent, a special commission works next to the Parliament (since 1995) as an instance of appeal. Every year, about 400 hundred complaints are brought to this "Commission of Access to Administrative Documents" (http://www.cada.pt/), several of them presented by journalists.

Traditionally, the Portuguese public administration tended to be very closed and to keep most of its documents secret, but this behaviour is slowly changing. Sometimes, journalists complain that public administration, although not forbidding access to this or that information (because of the law), raises practical problems of consultation, obliging them to seek what they are looking for among hundreds and hundreds of files. This is why the work of the aforementioned Commission is important.

(C7)   The watchdog and the media's mission statement   1 POINT

News media only indirectly refer to the watchdog function in their mission statements.

An analysis of the Editorial Statute of the different news media points to the main idea of independence:

Radio Renascença: Emphasizes the catholic affiliation of the station and, therefore, insists mostly on Human Rights and on the defence of the dignity of all human beings. It also insists on the need for pluralistic, comprehensive, objective and honest information, with respect for journalistic professional standards and journalism ethics.

RTP: The particular social responsibility of a public television station is stressed in the company's mission statement, together with the need for "accurate and independent" information. Independence from any kind of power is stressed, because the station must be committed only "with its duty to inform citizens".

Público: The newspaper insists it is totally independent from any kind of political or economic powers, considering itself responsible to its readers, and nobody else. It stresses that "the existence of a well-informed and active public opinion is a fundamental condition for democracy and for the existence of an open, dynamic society".

Destak: In its very short Statute, this free newspaper says it will be "independent from any political or economic power", also refusing any ideological influence.

Expresso: The issue of independence from any powers (including "its advertisers") is referred to as well. It insists that news media should not serve any particular interests; they should always be "autonomous institutions through which the citizens (...) can look for all the information they need to make their choices".

Correio da Manhã: "Total independence" from all "powers and interests", whether economic, political, religious or professionals, is underlined by this newspaper. Furthermore, it states it will be "firm" in condemning any "abuse of power".

Only indirectly do the news media refer to their watchdog mission or to their commitment to investigate and control the different powers present in society.

(C8)   Professional training   1 POINT

Very little importance is given to journalists' training, except for technical skills attached to the new 'convergence' efforts.

All the editors interviewed for this report assign "a great importance" to journalism training – which does not necessarily mean that activities devoted to journalism training are part of the companies' routines. Most of the training offered to journalists has to do more with 'skills' than with 'knowledge'. Because these media use more and more new technologies, and several of them are involved in multimedia projects, they need to update their staff to meet the new industrial requirements. Sometimes they organize internal sessions for this training; sometimes they hire specialized training companies or universities provide a course.

Continuous training sessions for journalists sometimes are organized by entities outside the media companies, as happens with the Centre for Training of Journalists (*Cenjor*) or the Journalists' Union. Courses on legal matters, on war coverage, on education subjects, for example, have already taken place in recent years. But they do not occur on a regular basis or depend on the direct commitment of the news media themselves. In this field, the situation is rather poor – with the single exception of training of the new skills required to use new technologies or by the 'convergence' trend occurring in most media outlets.

(C9)   Watchdog function and financial resources   1 POINT

Investing in investigative journalism is more an exception than a rule in the main news media.

The financial situation of the Portuguese news media is generally rather weak, and seems to be worse in 2009 when compared with 2006. Economic survival is their first priority, because most of them actually lose money every year, and the situation is evolving negatively. A small market, not much advertising, low rates of news media consumption, an increasing presence of free Internet sites… All these factors help to explain the crisis. And, when it comes to budget cuts and to downsizing measures, the first area to suffer is usually human resources. With smaller newsrooms, news media have increasing problems to invest in investigative reporting, because such reporting takes more time and more money.

Several editors interviewed for this report complained more or less about this situation: "Of course we haven't enough resources to develop our own agenda, although nobody expects that a free daily like ours will publish very long investigative stories" (*Destak*); "We have limitations as far as material resources are concerned, but we try not to depend too much on news agencies" (*Rádio Renascença*); "The ambition and mission of a newspaper like ours would require many more resources, both human and material" (*Público*).

More optimistic are the views in *Expresso* and *Correio da Manhã* (both with a better economic situation): "We have enough resources for our work, including our own investigative reporting" (*Expresso*); "We have all the necessary resources to produce our model of newspaper. Never has an investigative story been abandoned due to lack of material resources" (*Correio da Manhã*).

In general terms, and looking further than this sample of news media, the fact is that Portuguese newspapers, television and radio stations still depend a great deal on news agencies. Investigative reporting is more an exception than a rule, and tends to concentrate in two or three news media. Coverage of international affairs (with the exception of football games and very big disasters) is most often accomplished through news agencies as well.

Conclusions

Trying to summarize:

1. In economic terms, the structural weakness of the Portuguese media industry, worsened by the present crisis, makes it difficult to run a profitable business and to guarantee good conditions for journalists to do their work.

2. In political terms, the relatively recent conquest of democracy, after a long period of dictatorship and of isolation from the outside world, helps to explain the strong presence of a centralized State and the absence (or fragility) of autonomous social dynamics. In accordance, the existence of important progressive laws is not always strong enough to counterbalance the weight of practices in the day-by-day routines.

3. In cultural terms, a long history of low literacy and of low reading habits is somehow responsible for very low rates of media consumption – with the exception of television, although the fast development of the Internet may help to change things.

Media in Portugal have made an important contribution to democracy, and gave a precious help to consolidate democracy itself. But there still seems to be a great deal to do in order to guarantee that this contribution goes beyond the formal aspects of media functioning and pays attention to such issues as quality of news and information, people's media literacy, public participation and commitment for citizenship.

Notes

[1]   This group owned three general information dailies, but one of them (*24 Horas*) closed in June 2010.

[2]   One of the most known is *Mediascópio*, an observatory of media activity, belonging to the research centre of the Communication Sciences Department in the University of Minho – Braga (NOTE: The author of this report is a member of that centre).

[3]   The existence of a news ombudsman both in the public Radio and in the public Television is mandatory by law, since the last version of the Law on the Public Service Broadcasting (2006). Although TV and Radio belong to the same public company, there is an ombudsman for each medium.

[4]   This traditional right to journalists' "professional secrecy" was changed in the last revision of the Statute: the right not to disclose the identity of information sources is still granted in general terms, but an exception is previewed in the Penal Code. This means that, if and when a judge in a court of law decides that the identity of an information source is essential to pursuing justice, the journalist may be compelled to reveal it. But the journalists' Code of Ethics plainly states that those professionals must not disclose the identity of their sources. Because of this, one journalist has already been convicted in court because, in spite of an order given by the judge, he insisted on protecting his sources.

[5]   The number of journalists has decreased in the past three years, but it grew very quickly during the previous two decades: between 1987 and 2006, it increased from 1281 to 7402 professionals, most of them (ca. 60%) with some academic degree in journalism or communication sciences (Fernandes 2008). It should also be noted that only 19.8 % of them were women in 1987, but the figure was about 41% of the total in 2006 (Salim 2008). Presently, there are about 6,900 journalists in the country.

Data sources

ANACOM – Autoridade Nacional de Comunicações. <www.anacom.pt>

APCT – Associação Portuguesa para o Controlo de Tiragem e Circulação. <http://site.apct.pt/homepage_00.aspx>

ERC – Entidade Reguladora para a Comunicação Social. *Regulation Reports 2006-2007- 2008-2009.* <www.erc.pt>

EUROSTAT – *Europe in figures – Eurostat yearbooks 2006-2007 and 2010.* <http://epp.eurostat.ec.europa.eu/portal/page/portal/eurostat/home/>

INE – Instituto Nacional de Estatística. *Anuários Estatísticos de Portugal 2006 and 2009.*

INE – Instituto Nacional de Estatística. *Estatística das Comunicações 2006 and 2009.*

MARKTEST – *Anuários de Media & Publicidade 2006 and 2009.* <http://www.marktest.com/wap/g/?e=2>

MARKTEST – *Netscope (Ranking de tráfego de entidades Web)* <http://netscope.marktest.pt/>

OBERCOM – *Anuário da Comunicação 2005-2006 and 2009.* <http://www.obercom.pt/>

PORDATA – *Base de Dados Portugal Contemporâneo* <http://www.pordata.pt/azap_runtime/>

SEF – Serviço de Estrangeiros e Fronteiras [http://sefstat.sef.pt/distritos.aspx]

SJ – Sindicato dos Jornalistas <http://www.jornalistas.online.pt/>

WAN – World Association of Newspapers (2009), *World Press Trends.*

References

Bourdieu, P. (2005) 'The Political Field, the Social Field, and the Journalistic Field', in Benson, R. & Neveu, E. (ed.) (2005) *Bourdieu and the Journalistic Field,* Cambridge: Polity Press, pp. 29-47.

Cádima, F.R. (2009) 'Web TV local/regional em Portugal: Que alternativa à TV?', in AAVV (2009) *Anuário Internacional de Comunicação Lusófona 2008 – Comunicação e Cidadania.* LUSOCOM / SOPCOM / CECS: Braga.

Cardoso, G., Espanha, R. & Araújo, V (2009) *Da Comunicação de Massa à Comunicação em Rede.* Porto: Porto Editora.

Correia, F. & Baptista, C. (2007) *Jornalistas – Do ofício à profissão.* Lisboa: Caminho.

Fernandes, J.L. (2008) 'Motivações e modos de acesso na profissão de jornalista', *Trajectos,* nr. 12, Primavera 2008, pp. 97-115.

Férin, I. (2009) *Imigração, diversidade étnica, linguística, religiosa e cultural na Imprensa e na Televisão: 2008.* Lisboa: Entidade Reguladora para a Comunicação Social (ERC)

Fidalgo, J. (2008a) *O lugar da ética e da auto-regulação na identidade profissional dos jornalistas.* Lisboa: Fundação Calouste Gulbenkian / FCT.

Fidalgo, J. (2008b) 'Novos desafios a um velho ofício ou... um novo ofício? A redefinição da profissão de jornalista', in Pinto, M. & Marinho, S. (2008) *Os media em Portugal nos primeiros cinco anos do século XXI,* Porto: Campo das Letras, pp. 109-128.

Garcia, J.L. (org.) (2009) *Estudos sobre os Jornalistas Portugueses.* Lisboa: Imprensa de Ciências Sociais.

Graça, S.M. (2007) *Os jornalistas portugueses: dos problemas da inserção aos novos dilemas profissionais.* Coimbra: MinervaCoimbra.

Hallin, D. & Mancini, P. (2004) *Comparing Media Systems – Three Models of Media and Politics.* Cambridge: Cambridge University Press.

Kovach, B. & Rosenstiel, T. (2001) *The Elements of Journalism.* New York: Three Rivers Press.

Lopes, F. (2007) *A TV das Elites – Estudo dos programas de informação semanal dos canais generalistas (1993-2005).* Porto: Campo das Letras.

Ribeiro, V. (2009) *Fontes sofisticadas de informação.* Lisboa: Editora Media XXI.

Salim, I. (2008) 'A 'feminização do jornalismo em Portugal', *Trajectos,* nr. 12, Primavera 2008, pp. 117-124.

Santos, R. (2010) *Do jornalismo aos media – Estudos sobre a realidade portuguesa.* Lisboa: Universidade Católica Editora.

Schulz, W. & Held, T (2004) *Regulated Self-Regulation: An Analysis of Case Studies from Media and Telecommunications Law.* Luton: University of Luton Press.

Souza, P.D. (2008) 'Apropriação e representações das TIC e seu impacto em jornalistas de duas gerações', *Trajectos,* nr. 12, Primavera 2008, pp. 125-136.

Chapter 10

Sweden
A Mixed Media Model Under Market Pressures

Torbjörn von Krogh & Lars Nord

Sweden is the largest of the Nordic countries, in terms of both geographic size (449,964 km²) and population (9 million people). Swedish democracy is based on a multiparty parliamentarian system, where the political parties have traditionally been more important than the candidate in national elections. Traditionally, Swedish modern political history has been dominated by a single party. The Social Democrats have been in power for 65 of the past 78 years, and the party has been positively associated with the principles of the welfare state, economic growth and outstanding political leadership. However, the two most recent national elections in 2006 and 2010 have resulted in centre-right alliance governments, and the previous Social Democratic hegemony seems to be broken. Sweden joined the European Union in 1995, but is not a member of the euro currency zone.

The Swedish media system can generally be described as a mixture of classical liberal notions of the press as an independent and monitoring 'fourth estate', and social responsibility ideas about the necessary relationships between the political system and the media system in order to maintain diversity and public service in the broadcast media. Historically, the prospects for independent journalism could not possibly be better. Sweden was the first country in the world to include a Freedom of Information Act in its constitution, as early as 1766, and since then freedom of expression and freedom of information have been embedded in the Swedish consti-tution, which gives stronger protection than common law. However, in reality this liberal media approach has co-existed with numerous state regulations of the media sector and with an active media policy.

Traditionally, there have been very stable and fixed relations between the politi-cal system and the media system. The party press system, with different newspapers representing different political views and diverging societal interests, guaranteed a foreseeable – but nevertheless effectively working – external pluralism in the printed media during the 20th century (Nord 2001; Höyer 2005). The public service broadcasting system in radio and TV contributed to this picture, when introduced in 1924 and 1956, respectively, by offering internal pluralism in programmes based upon the concepts of objective and non-partisan reporting about political events (Hadenius 1998).

In all media today, Swedish journalists are highly professionalized, and the country has a developed and institutionalized system for self-regulation as well as state regulations regarding, for example, the public service media, impartial and neutral programming in the broadcast media, programming for children and press subsidies to second-ranking newspapers in a region (Petersson et al. 2005). Sweden has no law against limiting media ownership despite many political suggestions in this area. Thus far, the problems associated with implementing such a law effectively have stopped the process. Besides the legal system, with its strong constitutional protection for freedom of information and freedom of speech, Sweden is characterized by a system of institutionalized self-regulation on the printed market (cf. Hallin & Mancini 2004). The Swedish Press Council is part of this corporatist structure. The Swedish Press Council is not affiliated with the government; the council makes decisions concerning media ethics issues in public and also publishes regular reports with its considerations and explanations regarding its policy positions (von Krogh 2008).

The party press system in the printed media (including the press subsidy system) and the public service broadcast media were undoubtedly the core concepts of Swedish media policy during the period 1950-2000. However, they have gradually lost some of their importance as established media policy positions have been challenged by the new media technology development, the deregulation of media markets and the increasing fragmentation of media audiences (Ewertsson 2004; Nord 2008). Digitalization of the television market was completed in the whole country in 2007, while the parliament decided in 2006 not to continue to develop digital radio broadcasting on a large scale.

In recent decades, the Swedish media landscape has undergone considerable changes: more commercial radio stations and television channels and free tabloid metro newspapers have been introduced, and Internet use has expanded rapidly, offering the audience unlimited access to news and entertainment websites. Still, traditional newspapers and public service broadcast companies in Sweden have been fairly successful in distancing themselves from their former political affiliations and in facing new commercial competitors, using their institutional strength and developed company brands.

Sweden has a relatively long history of Internet penetration and computer use and ranks among the leading countries in the world in this respect (Norris 2000). Public use of the Internet has increased steadily, and in 2009 on overwhelming majority, 86 %, of the Swedish population reported that they had a personal computer with Internet access in their homes. Young people were over-represented among the users, as were men and more highly educated persons. However, these differences seem to have diminished over the past years due to the higher penetration of the Internet (Carlsson & Facht 2010).

News media sample

The data in the present study are based on media statistics and some assessments concerning the general media situation, while the interviews relate to six national and four regional media outlets. The interviews were conducted in May-June 2010 and included the following media professionals:

Table 1.   News Media Sample

	Media type	Ownership	Interviewee
Dagens Nyheter	Daily morning paper	Bonnier	Political Editor
Svenska Dagbladet	Daily morning paper	Schibsted	Managing Editor
Aftonbladet	Daily tabloid	Schibsted/LO	Online Editor
Expressen	Daily tabloid	Bonnier	Editor-in-chief
Sveriges Television	Public service TV	Public service	Deputy Director
Sveriges Radio	Public service radio	Public service	Deputy Director
Sundsvalls Tidning	Regional daily	Mittmedia	Editor-in-chief
SVT Mittnytt	Regional TV station	Public service	Managing Editor
SR Västernorrland	Regional radio station	Public service	Regional Director
TV4 Sundsvall	Regional TV station	Bonnier	News Editor
Journalists' Union			Vice chairman

The head of political coverage and analysis at *Dagens Nyheter*, Sweden's biggest morning paper (subscribed), circulation 315,000 copies (2009), published in Stockholm. Unique online visitors 1.3 million per week (summer 2010). The editorial pages take a liberal perspective.

The managing editor at *Svenska Dagbladet*, the second biggest morning paper in Stockholm (subscribed), circulation 200,000 copies. Online visitors 0.7 million. The editorial pages are conservative.

The head of online publication at *Aftonbladet*, the biggest afternoon paper (single copy sale), circulation 360,000 copies, and by far the biggest online news provider with 4.3 million online visitors. The online operation is one of the very few online general news operations that show a profit. The editorial pages of Aftonbladet take a social-democratic perspective.

The editor-in-chief of *Expressen*, the second biggest afternoon paper (single copy sale), circulation 290,000 copies, online visitors 1.9 million. The editorial pages are liberal.

The deputy head of *Swedish Television*, responsible for all news content. Swedish Television is a public service broadcaster, financed by licence fees, with about 30 per cent of the television audience and 1.3 million weekly online visitors.

The deputy head of *Swedish Radio*, responsible for all news content. Swedish Radio is a public broadcaster, financed by licence fees, with about 65 per cent of the radio audience and 0.7 million online visitors.

The editor-in-chief of *Sundsvalls Tidning*, the largest regional daily newspaper in the area of Västernorrland, circulation 31,000 copies and 80,000 weekly online visitors.

The regional director of *Sveriges Radio Västernorrland*, the regional public service radio station in the area of Västernorrland, with a daily reach in the region about 40 per cent.

The managing editor of *Sveriges Television Mittnytt*, regional public service news programme in the area of Västernorrland, and the news editor of the commercial regional broadcaster *TV4 Sundsvall*.

In addition to these media representatives, we have also interviewed the vice chairman of the Swedish Journalists Union, who possesses knowledge of the European situation in his capacity as chairman of the European Journalists Union and hence is able to place Swedish circumstances in a European context.

Indicators

Freedom / Information (F)

(F1)   Geographic distribution of news media availability   3 POINTS

News available all over the country, and strong local and regional markets.

Sweden is the third largest country in Europe and the population is concentrated to the southern part, while only one of nine million people live in the much more sparsely populated northern part. However, the supply of news media is satisfactory wherever people live. Newspapers are distributed all over the country, broadcast media reach all regions and broadband infrastructure is well developed.

Swedish daily newspapers are available for subscription all over the country, and evening tabloids are sold everywhere. Traditionally, local and regional newspapers have relatively strong market positions and cover all parts of Sweden. The number of newspaper titles has gradually decreased, but is still high compared to other countries. In 2008, 155 dailies existed in Sweden and 64 of them were published five days a week or more (TS-boken 2009). The newspaper market is rather stable in terms of the number of titles. On explanation for this is the state press subsidy system that has existed in Sweden since 1971. The system supports newspapers with a weak market position in order to keep them in the market. The biggest changes in availability can be noted in suburban metropolitan areas. New free newspapers in city areas like Metro, which is distributed in public areas and transportation systems, have been commercially successful. Most people, 64 % in the age range 15-85 years, claimed in 2008 that they lived in a household with a daily newspaper subscription (Carlsson & Facht 2010).

Broadcast media markets have historically been characterized by a de-facto monopoly of public service radio and public service television covering the whole nation. For the past 40 years, both public service radio and TV have offered regional news and programmes. An exclusive public service radio channel for 25 regional stations was established in 1977. Due to the introduction of new media technologies and an active deregulation of media policy (supported by a majority of the political parties) in the early 1990s, the number of available radio stations and television channels has increased dramatically. In 2008, there were 53 public service radio stations (4 FM, 7 digital, 27 regional and 15 on the Web), 89 local commercial radio stations and 150 community radio stations. The same year there were 7 public service TV channels and 51 Swedish private TV channels available to the audience (Carlsson & Facht 2010). Digitalization of the national television net was completed in fall 2007. Digital terrestrial television, satellite and cable are three almost equally important distribution systems in Sweden today. In 2008, 44 % of households used cable TV, 38 % DTT, 23 % satellite and 6 % IP-TV (Radio- och TV-verket 2009). There is no national commercial radio station in Sweden.

Internet infrastructure is well developed and broadband connections are now available for the majority of Swedish households. In 2008, around 3.5 million people or 82 % of all Internet customers were connected via broadband (Carlsson & Facht 2010). All national news media and all leading regional media offer online news services. Basic news is free, but additional content may sometimes require monthly subscriptions.

National news media, and some of the major regional news media companies, also offer mobile news for free. The mobile 3G net covers major parts of the nation. The next generation of 4G is implemented in some geographic areas, as in metropolitan regions, but the plan is to develop the net all over the nation in forthcoming years.

(F2)   Patterns of news media use (consumption of news)   3 POINTS

A newspaper reading nation still, and public service broadcast media still popular.

In previous media and communication studies, Swedish citizens claim that they receive most of their information about what is going on in society from the news media. Personal communication and personal experiences are regarded as less powerful information channels (Nord & Strömbäck 2009). Generally speaking, media reach a huge majority of the population on a daily basis.

Table 2.   Daily news media reach 2007-2009

	2007	2008	2009
Newspapers	77	76	75
Radio	26	26	27
Television	52	51	51
Internet	32	34	33

Source: Holmberg & Weibull 2010.

Sweden is, together with Norway, Finland and Japan, among the most newspaper-reading countries in the world. 75 % of the population (9-79 years) read the news in a newspaper everyday in 2009. The average newspaper reader spends about 30 minutes everyday with the paper, but there are great differences across age groups. Teenagers spend only 15 minutes on newspaper reading, while senior citizens spend around 45 minutes with their paper (Carlsson & Facht 2010). The most read sections in newspapers are local news, domestic news and foreign news. However, the same patterns with regard to age categories appear when consumption of newspaper content is compared (Mediebarometern 2009).

Radio news listening is not particularly high among the population, neither on regional nor on national levels. 27 % of the population (9-79 years) listen to radio news everyday. Public service regional listening figures have been about the same in recent decades, despite increased competition from new local commercial radio stations. In 2008, both public and private channels on the local/regional level reached about 30 % of the population in the area (Mediebarometern 2009).

Television news reaches 51 % of the population everyday. The habit of watching TV is highly concentrated to the evening peak hours between 19:00 and 22:00, and the average time spent with TV everyday is about 160 minutes (Flisen & Harrie 2010). The audience market share of public service TV is 33 %, a figure that is gradually declining because of the number of news channels, domestic and international, instantly introduced on the Swedish TV market. Daily news is only offered in the main public service channels and in the biggest private channel, TV4. More television viewers have also moved to the Internet, and all leading national TV channels offer web TV services. The most popular service, *SVT Play* (public service), has nearly two million viewers every month (SVT Annual reports).

Online news media use is growing rapidly. The outstanding online news service is provided by the tabloid *Aftonbladet*, whose website *aftonbladet.se* was successfully established in the early stages of the Internet era and has maintained its huge popularity in the audience.

Table 3.   Top ten online news media

	Type of media	Unique visitors
aftonbladet.se	National tabloid	4 039 029
expressen.se	National tabloid	1 758 951
svt.se	Public service TV	1 235 120
dn.se	National daily	1 015 845
Tv4.se	Private TV station	820 258
sr.se	Public service radio	672 223
svd.se	National daily	620 443
gp.se	National daily	373 936
sydsvenskan.se	National daily	285 637
hd.se	Regional daily	179 480

Source: KIA index 2010, week 40.

(F3)   Diversity of news sources   2 POINTS

*Awareness of importance of balanced reporting, but domination of elite sources
in the news.*

As in most other countries, powerful interests in society, representing the political and
economic elite groups, generally seem to be over-represented in the news. Systematic
content analyses of Swedish news media confirm this picture, regardless of whether
election campaigns, crises or news reporting during ordinary conditions are studied
(Sahlstrand 2000; Strömbäck 2008).

However, the misrepresentation of sources is not extreme, and there is a general
awareness among news media representatives about this problem. The issue of news
source diversity is also addressed in written media declarations. Public service media
operations are based on charters in which diversity in news reporting is central, and
most private news media organizations have policy documents with the same recommendations (Andersson Odén 2001).

Most interviews with representatives of leading national media outlets indicate a
high degree of awareness concerning the problematic traditional prominence of elite
sources. Countermeasures include broad analytical pieces that are not tied to just
a couple of sources, internal monitoring of sources appearing in the news (female,
male, age, spokesperson, decision-maker, ordinary person, etc.) and setting goals for
the appearance within different categories, enterprising and investigative projects,
using social media to identify and find new sources and thoroughly fact-checking
political statements in the election campaigns during 2010. The representatives of
the afternoon papers viewed themselves as more people oriented than elite oriented
and praised the new online opportunities for diversification.

Regional media representatives also recognized the problem of favouring elite sources in the news. Both private and public media companies referred to news policies supporting an increased presence of hitherto unrepresented source categories. At the same time, the difficulties associated with achieving increased diversity were generally explained by daily newsroom routines and practices.

(F4) Internal rules for practice of newsroom democracy   2 POINTS

Journalists do not elect editor-in-chief, but are considered influential in shaping news routines.

To put it simply, the debate on conditions for quality journalism in Sweden has never centred on the issue of newsroom democracy. One of the main explanations for this is the Swedish Constitution, which places all legal responsibility for newspaper content in the hands of the editor-in-chief (appointed as responsible by the owner, in accordance with the press laws). It is always the editor-in-chief who pays fines or goes to jail if editorial content is deemed illegal by a court of law; this is thought to make it more difficult for external forces to intimidate reporters. Hence no newsrooms in Sweden have internal rules for electing their editor-in-chief. Instead editors-in-chief are all appointed by the owners and the board of the newspaper. The same general rules in these processes are applied to broadcast media.

However, the minimal influence from journalists regarding the appointment of editor-in-chief does not mean that they lack influence on other editorial matters. Daily news selection and news value processes are transparent, and the framing of political issues openly discussed in the newsrooms.

National media interviews indicate a mixture of ways to enhance impartiality and quality in framing and reporting political issues. The public broadcasters, one of the morning dailies and one of the afternoon papers have written rules (in one case reporters have to sign a four-page quality contract); none has institutionalized sanctions, partly because of the Swedish press laws.

Regional media interviews confirmed a perceived great opportunity for single journalists to make their voices heard on news decisions, and this was particularly true for journalists specialized in specific fields. The influence of journalists was stressed even more in the interviews with representatives of public service media, and was described as "scary" by the interviewee at *Sveriges Radio Västernorrland*.

(F5) Company rules against *internal* influence on newsroom / editorial staff 2 POINTS

Media owners most often do not influence daily newsroom practices.

According to the Swedish Constitution, and its Freedom of the Press Act, the owner has no right to interfere with the editorial content; only the person who is filed as responsible according to the press law (editor-in-chief) has that right. If the owner wishes to decide over editorial content, she or he has to fire the responsible person and appoint a new editor-in-chief.

National interviews mainly show that influence on the news from the advertising/ commercial side of the enterprise is generally not at hand – not at all in the public broadcasting companies, and very little in most of the printed newspapers. In one of the morning papers, the editor-in-chief is also chief executive officer, and there is some debate as to whether that leads to editorial influence over the economy or vice versa. When it comes to the online operation, one afternoon paper describes a much harder commercial climate in uncharted territory with ownership pressure for profitability, which leads to an ongoing debate within the newsroom about the borders between news and ads.

Any influences from owners and management were also denied by regional public service media representatives. Private media newsrooms had the same experiences, and underlined the division between journalism and business, even if the major regional newspaper *Sundsvalls Tidning* admitted a "tougher climate" with regard to increased competition and a more market-oriented media environment.

(F6) Company rules against *external* influence on newsroom / editorial staff 3 POINTS

Outside influences on newsroom decisions are not problematic according to news editors.

National interviews reveal no manifest anxiety or unsettled conflicts in this area. The editor-in-chief holds a strong position according to press laws, and the bonds that once existed between political parties and their press are almost non-existent, except for the editorial pages. When it comes to radio and television, public broadcasters have built-in shields against political influence on the news. Public service charters are normally decided for six-year periods. As the election cycle is four years, new governments cannot change conditions for public service media when they take power.

The income streams vary across media. Public broadcasters rely almost only on licence fees, while advertising is not at all allowed in public service media. Private broadcast media are financed by advertising or subscriptions (pay TV). Morning papers' incomes come from advertising, 65-70 %, and the rest mainly from subscriptions, afternoon tabloid papers' print editions receive about 75 % of their revenues from copy sales and 25 % from advertising, while online news services' revenues mainly come from advertising and a small part from subscriptions.

Sponsorship in public television is strictly regulated and the current government has further sharpened the conditions and the number of yearly events possible to sponsor. In commercial TV, rising revenues might be hidden product placements by external production companies. The public service company *Swedish Television* has started in-house training to enhance the capacity of their personnel to identify and avoid product placements.

Regional media companies see no real problems with external pressure in terms of lobbying, news management efforts or linkages between newsroom work and outside business interests.

(F7) Procedures on news selection and news processing   3 POINTS

Written editorial policies exist, but are mainly guidelines in daily newsroom work.

Most Swedish newsrooms refer to some kind of news policy documents in their work. Still, these rules are not used for detailed regulation of daily newsroom work. Professional criteria of newsworthiness are probably much more important for these procedures than are commonly shared official principles. Recent national surveys among Swedish journalists confirm their stable perceptions of news values based on professional judgements of the social significance and deviation of an event. Editorial routines are also perceived as increasingly relevant for decisions on news processes (Ghersetti 2007).

National interviews show that four out of six investigated newsrooms have written policies and a structured set of daily and weekly news meetings to implement the policies. The two others also have a structured news process, even though their policies are not written down. Two newsrooms also employ so-called quality editors who have internal as well as external tasks (daily columns). Most newsrooms strive to combine weekly/monthly planning (allowing for enterprising and investigative reporting according to policies) with the important political events of the day, emerging themes in social media and suggestions from specialized reporters within the newsroom.

Among regional media, the newspaper *Sundsvalls Tidning* has a written multimedia policy discussing the principles for news processing on different platforms such as newspapers, radio stations, the Web and mobile platforms. However, these principles should be perceived as guidelines, and the daily newsrooms practices are more shaped by the daily flow of events, available editorial resources and the interests of single journalists. Public service regional media, with limited editorial staff and budget, admit that there is a risk that news processes are decided to too great a degree by who happens to be working on a particular day.

Equality / Interest mediation (E)

(E1)   Media ownership concentration national level   2 POINTS

Ownership is more concentrated, but the influence of the biggest owners remains about the same.

Sweden has no law against media ownership concentration. In the newspapers market there are four dominant players: Bonnier (*Dagens Nyheter, Expressen, Sydsvenskan*), Schibsted (*Aftonbladet, Svenska Dagbladet*), Stampen (*Göteborgs-Posten* and regional newspapers) and Stenbeck (*Metro*). Bonnier is the biggest owner group, and its business interests have expanded in other parts of the country outside Stockholm. However, there is intense market competition between newspapers from different owner groups, both between national morning dailies and between national tabloids. As shown in the table below, the two biggest owners – Bonnier and Schibsted – maintain about the same market share as before. Owner concentration has increased on other levels. Still, owner concentration is not high compared to other markets.

Table 4.   Owner concentration in the newspaper market (% of total circulation)

	1993	2000	2008
Biggest owner	26.7	27.3	26.4
2 biggest owners	43.9	41.8	42.5
4 biggest owners	56.9	54.2	66.6
8 biggest owners	73.2	71.0	87.0
16 biggest owners	89.2	89.7	97.6

Source: Sundin 2010.

The national radio market is completely dominated by public service radio, as there are no other national private radio stations. The national television market has three dominant players: *Sveriges Television, SVT,* (public service), *Bonniers* (TV4) and *Stenbeck* (TV3, TV8). They control a large part of the TV market, but their share of the market has slightly declined due to the increasing number of 'niche' channels specialized in sports, films, documentaries, etc.

Table 5. Owner concentration in the television market (% of total viewing time)

	1999	2004	2009
Biggest owner (PSB)	47.0	40.7	32.8
2 biggest owners	73.4	66.5	61.7
3 biggest owners	92.9	88.4	88.0
3 biggest private owners	46.1	47.7	55.2

Source: Sundin 2010.

(E2) Media ownership concentration regional (local) level 2 POINTS

Regional media ownership concentration is a trend affecting most parts of the country.

The ownership concentration on the regional level has not been discussed as much as the controversial media mergers involving national media players. However, the strong concentration of local and regional newspaper ownership is evident on regional media markets. The number of regional newspaper titles has not changed dramatically, but most regional newspaper markets are completely dominated by a single owner group. Today, there are many examples of diverging models of media mergers, ranging from complete take-overs to different forms of joint ventures. True competitive regional newspaper markets exist only in five areas (Dalarna, Värmland, Kalmar län, Karlskoga and Motala). The country is divided into 100 regional/local newspapers markets, and most of them are controlled by one dominant newspaper owner group.

Table 6. Newspaper companies' markets shares in newspaper regions

Market share (%)	Number of newspaper regions	Accumulated numbers
≥ 98	25	
90-97	16	41
80-89	13	54
70-79	8	62
60-69	5	67
50-59	3	70
40-49	2	72
30-39	3	75
20-29	8	83
10-19	17	100

Source: Sundin 2010.

Regional public service radio offers 25 regional stations. The fourth public service radio channel, P4, is dominated by regional news and programmes. The private radio market was deregulated in 1993, but the number of station owners has decreased significantly, and today only two owner groups control all local commercial radio stations: *MTG Radio* (Radio Rix) and *SBS Radio* (Mix Megapol). Regional TV has only two major players: *Sveriges Television* (public service) and *TV4* (Bonnier). Regional TV news is not offered in regional channels, but appears in regional news "windows" on the national channels.

(E3) Diversity of formats   3 POINTS

Anything for anyone, any time – almost.

There are no longer any newspaper publishing houses in Sweden, neither at the national nor at the regional level. Today, they all refer to themselves as *media* publishing houses offering a wide range of formats from printed papers, online services (including social media), mobile platforms and in many cases also broadcast media. Cross-media formats such as newspaper as PDF, web-TV and pod radio are offered by most multi-media companies.

News is available at any time on the Internet and on text-TV. Public service radio newscasts are updated every hour of the day. Journalistic work is increasingly influenced by the variety of publishing platforms, and journalists are expected to produce news material for different formats when reporting on current events.

The request for diverging media formats has also encouraged hitherto unknown collaborations between public and private media, as in the region of Jämtland where the two daily newspapers *Länstidningen Östersund* and *Östersunds-Posten* (both owned by Östersunds Tidningar) offer regional public service web-TV news on their websites.

(E4) Minority / Alternative media   1 POINT

Minority interests are not met by minority media.

Sweden is increasingly becoming a multi-cultural society and has received more immigrants per capita than most other European countries. 11 % of the population (and 17 % in the capital of Stockholm) are first-generation immigrants.

Still, media content largely does not reflect these minorities, and they are not particularly well represented in the news (Nygren 2005; Hultén 2006). Journalists and editors are mainly ethnic Swedes and news consumption is generally lower among immigrant groups.

Programmes in immigrant languages are offered by public service radio, and newspapers published in these languages may receive state subsidies for production and distribution. However, the supply of regular news is relatively limited in suburban areas where many immigrants live.

The alternative news media scene is not particularly impressive. Progressive weekly newspapers such as *Stockholms Fria Tidning*, *Flamman* and the syndicalist paper *Arbetaren* reach a very limited audience and play no crucial role in news and opinion processes.

(E5)   Affordable public and private news media   3 POINTS

More money is spent on the media.

Prices for newspapers, broadcast media and Internet are reasonable, as Sweden is a comparably rich country. The annual license fee for public TV was € 211.40 in 2008, slightly cheaper than in the other Nordic countries (Carlsson & Harrie 2010). The payment rate is high, with about 90 % of Swedish households paying the license fee. National surveys have confirmed that most Swedes think it is morally unacceptable to try to avoid paying the fee. There is no specific license fee for public service radio, as this service is included in the TV license fee.

Swedish households also spend much more money on private television, and pay-TV is the fastest expanding financing model on the television market in Sweden. Television viewers paid almost five times more for TV in 2006, compared to ten years before, despite the fact that the total viewing time has been fairly constant (approx. two hours/day) (Engblom & Wormbs 2007).

In 2008, the average price for an annual subscription to a daily regional newspaper was € 201.22 and € 311.11 for a metropolitan newspaper. Since 2000, the price of regional newspapers has increased by 12 % and the price for metropolitan papers has increased by 30 % (Carlsson & Facht 2010).

(E6)   Content monitoring instrument   1 POINT

Media monitoring is random.

Media scholars monitor political reporting in the national media prior to parliamentary elections (Asp 2006; Strömbäck 2009). Private opinion-polling companies monitor national media coverage of politicians and political issues on a macro level. Besides these, there is no effective and publicly available monitoring instrument.

(E7) Code of ethics at the national level (structure)   3 POINTS

The code is well known and an important tool within the self-regulatory system.

The first embryonic ethical recommendations were issued as early as in 1900, and have since been updated regularly. They are very well known in the newsrooms and are often referred to in the debate on media performance. They are issued by *Pressens samarbetsnämnd*, which is an umbrella organization for the main publishers' associations and the journalists' union. Pressens samarbetsnämnd also directs and finances the national press council, *Pressens opinionsnämnd.*

Sweden also has a number of specialized journalists' associations for different purposes (investigative journalism, environmental journalism, science reporting, etc.) that discuss ethical issues within these sectors. Interviews at the national and the regional levels verify the importance attached to the recommendations made in the national code of ethics.

(E8) Level of self-regulation (performance)   2 POINTS

A well-integrated system though sometimes under debate.

The first Press Council was established in 1916. It was restructured in 1969 when members of the public were included in the council, a national Press Ombudsman was added and economic sanctions were introduced against erring newspaper organizations. The Press Ombudsman facilitates complaints from the public and selects cases from the public to bring to the press council. Then the council decides whether or not the publication deserves the blame. Blamed newspapers with under 10,000 copies in circulation pay about € 1000 in a so-called administrative fees to the council, and newspapers with more than 10,000 copies pay about € 2500. The code of ethics includes referral to democratic values and rights of reply. The journalists' union has a committee that – in theory, but rarely in practice – can sanction members for unethical behaviour. As previously noted, in the Swedish model sanctions are mainly aimed at the editor-in-chief, not the individual reporter.

The Press Council and the national Press Ombudsman handle complaints regarding the newspaper organizations' print material and online publications. Broadcasters are also committed to the code of ethics, but have their own ethical guidelines that are supervised by a committee of researchers and experts appointed by the government.

The Publicists' Club, which is a member of the umbrella organization Pressens samarbetsnämnd, upholds a continuous function of self-criticism with regular panel-debates on critical media matters. Top editors at the morning paper *Svenska Dagbladet* and the tabloids *Aftonbladet* and *Expressen* regularly write columns and blog about the motives for the journalism in their papers and enter into dialogues with critics.

The system is frequently under debate, but has hitherto shown its strength. The editor-in-chief of the regional daily *Sundsvalls Tidning* publishes a weekly column where current publication issues are discussed.

(E9)   Participation   2 POINTS

Some media organizations have pushed for participation and the overall trend points in that direction.

Interviews with representatives of national media organizations paint a somewhat diversified picture of citizen participation in the news process. The public broadcasters have experimented with open newsrooms and present a great deal of background material / extra material about controversial publications (raw interview transcripts, etc.), but have not yet reached as far with public participation in the news process. They are at present struggling to find ways to achieve more participation without compromising quality aspects.

The online operations of the newspapers have been much more active during recent years in finding ways to implement user participation. A recent study (Karlsson 2010) shows that reader comments, links to external blogs and user contributions of texts, pictures and videos have multiplied from 2005 to 2010. National interviews contain some examples: *Aftonbladet* (tabloid) listed 34 separate mechanisms for user participation on its site. The newsroom rewards reporters who are active in comment sections and who engage in dialogues with the readers. *Svenska Dagbladet* (morning paper) has developed a prizewinning investigative project online built on a combination of traditional reporting and user suggestions/participation.

Regional media try to increase public participation by the same means. However, the regional public service TV station acknowledges participation as one of the major problems in regional online news, as the policy is to deny the public access to news commentaries.

Generally speaking, the main reasons given for user participation are democratic values, more perspectives, more value for readers in online forums discussing the relevance of news and possibilities to develop new forms and formats of journalism.

(E10)   Rules and practices on internal pluralism   2 POINTS

Many newsrooms are aware of the benefits of pluralism and strive to find solutions.

National and regional interviews show awareness of the values of pluralism. The homogeneity of the newsrooms regarding age and ethnicity is regarded as a problem in most companies, and various counterstrategies have been implemented. Some examples are internal monitoring, internal goals, targeted recruiting, special online projects, workgroups with representatives from newsroom management and journalists' union, daily and weekly newsroom debates, and encouraging online the participation of special groups / interests.

Control / Watchdog (C)

(C1) Supervising the watchdog 'control of the controllers' 2 POINTS

Public service radio has a tradition of media criticism that is now joined by initiatives on the Web.

Apart from the previously mentioned debates at the Publicists' Club, the national Press Ombudsman, the Press Council and the government appointed committee to handle complaints about radio and television content, there are a number of venues for media scrutiny and debate. Almost every major news event that is covered by Swedish media contains a meta debate on how the coverage is framed and conducted. This is done in the national newspapers, magazines and among broadcasters as well as on the Web by news organizations, in the comments sections, by bloggers (often visible on the traditional media site as links to the article in question) and on special sites for debate and/or media scrutiny (for instance www.second-opinion.se – a site where professional journalists, readers/users and organizations/authorities are paid/ invited to criticize media coverage of processes/events).

The leading regular venue for critical reporting on the media for the past 35 years has been the Swedish public radio corporation, *Sveriges Radio*, which now airs two weekly media programmes and a lot of daily debates as well. Magazines and websites financed by different stakeholders like publishers, advertisers, journalists' union and investigative journalists criticize and debate media matter. Private and state-financed institutes publish books on media performance based on investigative journalism and/ or academic research, and arrange public seminars/debates to discuss the findings.

(C2) Independence of the news media from power holders 3 POINTS

Institutional as well as professional barriers create a distance between media and power holders.

The Swedish constitution forbids journalists from revealing their sources (except, for instance, in cases of imminent threat to national security) and forbids authorities from searching for sources who have given secret material to the media for publication purposes. Journalists are also, as previously noted, not sentenced by law for offensive publications. Only the editor-in-chief is responsible by law. The exceptions deal not with content, but with conduct while gathering information. For instance, journalists can be prosecuted for posing as officials or for trespassing on private property.

The public broadcasters *Sveriges Radio, Utbildningsradion* and *Sveriges Television* have clauses in their charters to publish news items that are factual and impartial; power-holders in society (which includes the state itself) are to be scrutinized. The only imposed partialities concern defending democracy and human rights. The financing of public service media is decided in periods of six years at a time. There is a certain distance between the government/parliament and the public broadcasters. The government appoints a committee, which in turn appoints board members of the different broadcasters: radio, education and television.

On a national level, public radio and public television have editorial resources that are greater than the commercial corporations considered separately. Swedish Radio has, for instance, 18 foreign correspondents; no newspaper has even half that number. However, on a regional and local level, the commercial newspapers have bigger news operations than the regional radio and television operations do. The national and regional interviews do not reveal any particular worries on the part of the media representatives regarding their independence from influential interests in society.

(C3)   Transparency of data on media system   2 POINTS

Data are available, although they could be easier to find.

In 2006, the latest parliamentary general investigation of press conditions was published (SOU 2006:8), the eighth investigation since 1963. It is available at the government website as is an investigation from 2003 made by the Swedish Competition Authority. There have also been several general investigations on public service radio and television, and the latest one was published in autumn 2008 (SOU 2008:64).

Every year the academic research institution Nordicom at University of Gothenburg publishes a report on the media situation, including the ownership structure, that is easy to download from the Internet. This material does not seem to be well known or frequently in demand by the public, as it does not appear among the first 100 hits on a Google search (made by the authors, August 2010) for Swedish media ownership concentration.

The newspapers in our sample do not print information about their owners in every daily issue. Their websites, however, contain information on, for instance, owners, circulation, finances and editorial policies. The public service websites include information on management, financing and government relations.

(C4) Journalism professionalism   3 POINTS

A professional ideology and practice have a longstanding hold on Swedish journalists.

According to national surveys (Asp 2007), about 80 per cent of Swedish journalists strongly endorse the professional goals of independent scrutinizing of powerholders, gathering and distributing information to citizens that is needed for their informed decisions in the democracy and giving a voice to the voiceless. 99 per cent endorse the ideals to some degree. Though many (84 per cent) are not satisfied with their efforts and want journalism to be more non-conformist.

According to the national interviews, the news organizations include enterprising and investigative reporting in their content planning. The journalists' union stresses the increased workload of journalists when newsrooms are downsized and expresses concern about the professional identity of those who combine journalistic freelance work or short-term employments with other kinds of communication/information occupations.

In the regional interviews, all media representatives claim that investigative journalism is poorly developed in many respects. No regional media have journalists or routines designed for investigative journalism. When such journalism does occur, it is more likely to be the result of ad-hoc decisions than of long-term editorial planning.

As previously noted, there are quite a number of associations of journalists that promote and discuss ethical problems of journalism and that initiate public debates on these issues. Many newsrooms encourage further education and training in ethical reasoning.

(C5) Journalists' job security   2 POINTS

Threats are said to be more common, but the union as well as employers act accordingly.

Journalists have a 'clause de conscience' in their collective agreement with the employers' association. It is probably very seldom used, at least that is what surveys have shown. Swedish labour laws protect employees from being dismissed for their personal convictions. The Journalists' Union argues for less short-term employments in order to protect members' financial situation, but also in order to foster a more secure work atmosphere with healthy opposition and debate on journalistic issues. The union feels that the Labour Court increasingly favours loyalty over freedom of speech when solving labour contract disputes.

The union also notices that threats against journalists seem to have become more common – not just from extremist political groups, but also from relatives to persons in the news, entertainment companies and sports fans. The union finds that the employers do assume their responsibilities in this field and make the necessary precautions.

(C6) Practice of access to information   3 POINTS

Sweden has many preconditions for an open government, but shows signs of increased secrecy.

Sweden has a very old tradition of open government, and the default position for governmental documents since 1766 is that they are public. They are open to anyone, not just to journalists, although journalists are more experienced than the ordinary citizen in gathering and using public documents. During the past 50 years, secrecy clauses have become increasingly common in the legislation. The motives are often said to be the power of digital documentation, protection of personal integrity and protection of commercial and state interests.

Swedish citizens (and journalists) still have good opportunities to gain access to most kinds of governmental documents, but for instance the Journalists' Union argues that other countries have now implemented legislation that gives better access to electronic documents than in Sweden. Some cases have been reported when government officials have not documented their decisions in writing in order to avoid public scrutiny.

(C7) The watchdog and the media's mission statement   2 POINTS

Media have mission statements and perform watchdog duties, but the first element need not be the cause of the second.

Svenska Dagbladet's mission statement includes an obligation to engage in critical scrutiny of powerholders in society. Sveriges Radio states in their 196-pages handbook that their task is to review and investigate different forms of power. These examples show that the watchdog function of the media is present both in written documents and, as previously noted, in the overall rhetoric motivating news gathering. But few observers in Sweden ascribe any decisive force to the mission statements; they are most important during the process of formulation and not particularly important afterwords (Andersson Odén, 2001; von Krogh 2008). None of the regional media studied here has editorial policy documents that explicitly mention the watchdog role.

The editor of the Swedish magazine for investigative reporting, interviewed for this project, states that the practical actions in the newsrooms are far more important than – and often not linked to – goals set in mission statements. It is also evident that enterprising and investigative reporting are being performed at many levels in the Swedish media system (more on this in C9).

(C8)   Professional training   2 POINTS

Training is available, but the demand is higher than the supply.

The overall attitude on the part of employers as well as employees is very positive towards further professional training. There is a special government financed institute for further education of journalists in the south of Sweden, *Fojo*, most often offering week-long courses at no charge, and where journalists keep their salaries during the course period. In addition there are a number of funds to which journalists can apply for scholarships for further education.

The public broadcasters *Sveriges Radio* and *Sveriges Television* have ambitious programmes for structured in-house training. Some national newspapers underline the possibilities for on-the-spot training by skilled veterans as news events unfold. The Journalists' Union still thinks the efforts are too minuscule and lagging behind other sectors of knowledge-based production. Their goal is a week of further education each year for every journalist.

(C9)   Watchdog function and financial resources   2 POINTS

Resources for investigative reporting – commitment, energy and money – are rarely sufficient.

The national and regional interviews are unanimous on one point: there will never be enough resources for investigative journalism. But as some interviewed representatives point out, commitment and energy are at least as important to obtaining results. This view is supported by earlier Swedish research (von Krogh 1991; Nord 2007).

The public broadcasters devote parts of their budgets to special programmes built on long-term investigative journalism. *Sveriges Radio* also designates resources within the main newsroom for daily news for shorter projects (weeks, rather than months) and uses a network of reporters within its 25 local radio stations for joint investigative projects.

The tabloid *Expressen* has a special unit with three reporters for investigative projects. *Aftonbladet* claims that investigative reporting is important for the content mix in the paper, but it must be presented so that the relevance to readers is clear. To *Svenska Dagbladet* investigative and agenda-setting journalism is vital for the survival of the national daily press.

Dagens Nyheter, on the other hand, is more pessimistic about the level of its investigative reporting, and believes that is has shrunk more for Dagens Nyheter than for leading dailies in other European countries.

The editor of the Swedish magazine for investigative reporting, interviewed for this project, estimates a rather high level of investigative journalism in the public broadcasters and a somewhat lower level in the commercial national newspapers. Some local/regional news organizations are very successful with investigative projects, but overall dedication is not as high as it ought to be.

A comparison of European investigative journalism (van Eik, 2005) found that the quality of top Swedish projects is generally lower than in some other countries, but on the other hand, that investigative reporting is more widespread in regional media than in most other countries.

The union representative interviewed for this project points out that traditional media produce much more investigative journalism than do bloggers and social media, that public broadcasters do a considerable amount of good work, but that Swedish news media could and should do more.

The number of foreign correspondents has been reduced somewhat over time in commercial media, and some of them have been replaced by part-time stringers. The public broadcasters, especially *Sveriges Radio* with 18 correspondents, have been more successful in defending their own exclusive international reporting.

Conclusions

The study of media performance in Sweden indicates that the democratic criteria of the media are meet to a considerable extent. The media structure on both the national and regional levels includes a diversity of news media, easy accessible to everyone. Despite increased owner concentration in print media markets, the number of available dailies is still rather high, not least because of the remaining press subsidy system. The deregulation of broadcast media has resulted in increased competition, above all in the television market. However, public service media have been successful in maintaining dominating market positions.

Freedom of information is secured in the Swedish media system. News reporting is generally based on professional values and norms and is not directly influenced by powerful interests in society. Traditionally, openness and transparency are core values of the Swedish democracy. Newsworthiness is in most cases not decided by the consequences a news item may have for political power-holders or private business interests. There is a competition in news markets on both the national and regional levels.

Equality is generally achieved, but not to the same extent as freedom of information. There is a diversity of formats offered, and there is a common awareness of the benefits of audience participation in the media. However, some media companies feel a bit pressured between professional journalistic values and the need for equal representation in the news. Even if all media principles argue for fair and balanced reporting, some groups of Swedish citizens, representing minorities, are obviously not particularly well covered by the media.

Finally, the watchdog function of the media is probably the most problematic goal for the media to fulfil. The intention to promote more investigative journalism is expressed by all media, but does not meet the real capacity to produce such journalism. Thus, all media representatives express frustration when discussing the difference between investigative journalism principles and practices.

References

Andersson Odén, T. (2001) *Redaktionell policy. Om journalistikens mål och inriktning i svensk dagspress*. [Editorial Policy. On Journalistic Objectives and Orientations in Sweidsh Dailies] Göteborg: University of Gothenburg.

Asp, K. (2006) *Rättvisa nyhetsmedier*, [Fair News Media] Göteborg: JMG Rapport.

Asp, K. (ed.) (2007) *Den svenska journalistkåren*, [Swedish Journalists] Göteborg: JMG, University of Gothenburg.

Carlsson, U. & Facht, U. (2010) *Medie Sverige 2010. Statistik och analys*, [Media Sweden 2010. Statistics and Analysis] Göteborg: Nordicom.

van Eijk, D. (ed.) (2005) *Investigative Journalism in Europe*, Amsterdam: Vereniging van Onderzoeksjournalisten

Engblom, L.Å. & Wormbs, N. (2007) *Radio och TV efter monopolet* [Radio and Television After The Monopoly], Stockholm: Ekerlids.

Ewertsson, L. (2004) *Dansen kring guldkalven. En historia om uppbyggandet av TV4 1984-1991*. [The Construction of TV4 1984-1991], Stockholm: SNS.

Flisen, T. & Harrie, E. (2010) *Medietrender i Norden 2010*. [Media Trends in the Nordic Countries], Göteborg: Nordicom.

Ghersetti, M. (2007) Vad bestämmer nyhetsvärdet? [What Decides News Value?], In Asp, K. (ed.) (2007) *Den svenska journalistkåren*, [Swedish Journalists] Göteborg: JMG, University of Gothenburg, pp. 97-108.

Hadenius, S. (1998) *Kampen om monopolet – Sveriges radio och TV under 1900-talet*, [The Battle of the Monopoly – Swedish Radio in the 1900's] Stockholm: Prisma.

Hallin, D.C. & Mancini, P. (2004) *Comparing Media Systems. Three Models of Media and Politics*, Cambridge: Cambridge University Press.

Holmberg, S. & Weibull, L. (2010*) Nordiskt ljus. 37 kapitel om politik, medier och samhälle* [Nordic Light. 37 Chapters on politics, media and society], Gothenburg: SOM-institutet.

Høyer, S. (2005) The Rise and Fall of the Scandinavian Party Press. In *Diffusion of the news paradigm 1850-2000*, edited by S. Høyer & H. Pöttker, pp. 75-92. Göteborg: Nordicom.

Karlsson, M. (2010) *Nätnyheter*, [News on the Net] Stockholm: Institutet för mediestudier, Sim(o)

von Krogh, T. (1991) *Grävande journalistik och redaktionell miljö*, [Investigative Journalism and Editorial Environment] JMK:s skriftserie 1991:13, University of Stockholm

von Krogh, T. (ed.) (2008) *Media Accountability Today...and Tomorrow*, Göteborg: Nordicom

Nord, L.W. (2001) *Vår tids ledare – en studie av den svenska dagspressens politiska opinionsbildning*, [Contemporary Editorials – A Study of Political Opinion Formation in the Swedish Press], Stockholm: Carlsson.

Nord, L.W. (2007) Investigative journalism in Sweden. A not so noticeable noble art. *Journalism. Theory, practice & criticism* 5: 517–521.

Nord, L.W. (2008) *Medier utan politik – de svenska riksdagspartiernas syn på dagspress, radio och TV*, [Media without Politics – The Swedish Political Party Opinions on Press, Radio and TV], Stockholm: Santérus.

Norris, P. (2000) *A Virtuous Circle. Political Communications in Postindustrial Societies*, Cambridge: Cambridge University Press.

Nygren, G. (2005) *Skilda medievärldar – lokal offentlighet och lokala medier i Stockholm*, [Different Media Worlds – Local Public Sphere and Local Media in Stockholm], Stockholm/Stehag: Symposion.

Petersson , O. et al. (2005) *Mediernas integritet*, [The Integrity of Media], Stockholm: SNS.

Sahlstrand, A. (2000) *De osynliga – nyhetskällor i svensk storstadsmorgonpress,* [The Invisibles –News Sources in Swedish National Press], Stockholm: JMK.

SOU 2006:8. Mångfald och räckvidd. [Diversity and Reach] Slutbetänkande av Presskommittén 2004.

SOU 2008: 64. Kontiniuitet och förändring [Continuity and Change], Slutbetänkande av public service-utredningen.

Strömbäck, J. (2008) Swedish election news coverage: Towards increasing mediatization. In *Handbook of election news coverage around the world*, edited by J. Strömbäck and L. L. Kaid, pp. 160-174. New York: Routledge.

Sundin. S. (2010) En mediemarknad i förändring. Ägar- och mediekoncentration, [A Changing Media Market – Owner and Media Concentration], In Carlsson, U. & Facht, U. (2010). *Medie Sverige 2010. Statistik och analys,* [Media Sweden 2010. Statistics and Analysis] Göteborg: Nordicom, pp. 45-54.

SVT Annual Reports.

TS-boken (2009).

Chapter 11

SWITZERLAND
Swiss Quality Media:
A Reduced Protective Forest for Democracy

Werner A. Meier, Alexandra Gmür & Martina Leonarz

Switzerland is a small, landlocked country. It enjoys a remarkably long and continuous tradition of independence, stability and political neutrality. The country's political structure is based on strong federalism with a high degree of autonomy in each of the 26 cantons.

One key feature of Switzerland is its cultural diversity. There are as many as four different official languages – German (spoken by 64 %), French (19 %), Italian (8 %),and Rhaeto-Romanic (< 1 %) – which more or less define four different mentalities. Each language area has its own media (Meier 2010; Meier 2007).

The diversified Swiss society structure, with its high esteem for civic engagement, has been an important precondition for a differentiated press and media landscape. There are renowned high quality newspapers that are read by opinion leaders as well as boulevard media such as the *Blick*. In the past ten years, free-of-charge sheets targeting commuters in the large economic areas intensified the competition among newspapers. Especially *20 Minuten* (*20 minutes* in the French speaking part) has been most successful.

In radio and television, the public broadcaster SRG SSR is the most important player. Institutionalized by law and financed by license fees, this organization provides for the most successful programmes both in radio and television. SRG SSR is entrusted with a special mandate to provide all linguistic regions with programmes of equal quality on a public service basis. Its programming mandate reads as follows: serving the public, freedom and responsibility, integrity, committed to truthful and impartial reporting, transparency, fairness, consideration for the audience and accountability.

In the past years, the Swiss television landscape has experienced some fundamental changes. In 2006, the Swiss Parliament adopted a new Federal Radio and Television Act (RTVG) to ensure the dominant role of SRG SSR. In parallel, the Act supports local and regional commercial broadcasters by sharing the licence fee revenues.

An extensive cable network allows most Swiss homes to access programmes from neighbouring countries sharing one of Switzerland's national languages. Increasing access to electronic media, particularly via the Internet, has further expanded the availability of news and information sources.

The Federal Constitution guarantees the freedom of the media (Art.16). Furthermore, the Constitution prohibits censorship, and guarantees editorial secrecy. Freedom of the press (i.e., the ability to gather and publish information and opinions freely) is traditionally interpreted in Switzerland as protecting the right to establish newspapers or other media outlets. The independence of SRG SSR is specifically underlined in the RTVG. Swiss television and radio stations have the mandate to reflect and maintain the linguistic and cultural diversity of the country by providing specific programming. Media polity is governed by different national and international interest groups who influence the norms and values of the Swiss media landscape (Meier 2007: 187): the Swiss Parliament, the Federal Department for Transportation, Communication and Energy (UVEK), the Federal Office for Communication (BAKOM) and the Independent Authority of Program Complaints (UBI). Political parties and media organizations also have a say in governmental media policy strategies.

The sample

The following indicators are based on relevant statistical media data and current scientific findings on the media landscape in Switzerland. Furthermore, seven in-depth interviews were conducted with leading professional heads of large publishing houses and the public broadcast company (SRG SSR) as well as a representative of the biggest journalists' union. They give more insight and a clear picture of the media's performance for democracy as well as the everyday routines employed in practice. We decided to focus on the German-speaking part of Switzerland, where the media with the highest audience reach and the largest publishing houses are located. The following media professionals were interviewed (Table 1):

Table 1.   Overview interview partners

Person/function	Organization	Feature
Editor-in-chief	20Minuten	Daily free sheet
Editor-in-chief	NZZ-Online	Quality paper, online edition
Editor-in-chief	Tages-Anzeiger	Regional paper
Vice editor-in-chief	Blick	Tabloid
Director	Swiss Radio DRS	Public service broadcast
Head News Office	SF DRS (television)	Public service broadcast
President	Syndicom (formerly Comedia)	Journalists' Union

Indicators

Freedom / Information (F)

(F1) Geographic distribution of news media availability   3 POINTS

News media are available to the Swiss population with no major restrictions.

News media are widely available in Switzerland. The media landscape is characterized by high levels of public access and technical reach. There are no regional divides. Each linguistic area is provided with its own media: private, commercial and public service radio and television stations, daily and weekly newspapers as well as various periodicals.

The public broadcaster SRG SSR runs between three and six radio stations for each part of the country (German, French and Italian). For the Rhaeto-Romanic part, there is an almost full-service radio programme. In each linguistic region there is a television studio (Geneva, Zurich, Lugano), producing independent programmes, two for each region and one in the Rhaeto-Romanic language (only a few hours per week). In addition, the German part of Switzerland is provided with a 24-hour information channel, repeating the latest news programmes initially shown on one of the two regular channels. Furthermore, 87 private radio stations and 105 private TV stations broadcast in local and regional markets (BAKOM 2010).[1]

Table 2.   Number of broadcast media in Switzerland

Category	Number
SRG SSR (German, French, Italian)	26
TV	8
Radio	18
Private TV broadcasters: with license	15
Private TV broadcasters: programme services subject to the obligation to notify (without license)	90
Private Radio broadcasters: with license	49
Private Radio broadcasters: programme services subject to the obligation to notify (without license)	38

Sources: SRG SSR idée Suisse Geschäftsbericht 2009, p. 36-37; 50-51,
Federal Office of Communications / BAKOM 2010:
http://www.bakom.admin.ch/themen/radio_tv/marktuebersicht/index.html?lang=en

Almost every Swiss household has one or more radio receivers, and 92 per cent are equipped with one or more television receivers (BfS, 2008[2]). 80 per cent of all households have access to cable TV and receive over 50 channels; 15 per cent of all Swiss households have access to a satellite dish (Meier, 2010).

The existence of 203 different newspapers (including non-dailies) makes Switzerland one of the richest countries in terms of number of newspapers published in proportion to its population and geographical size (data for 2008, BfS; Meier 2010). Newspapers are widely available in all regions. All cantonal capitals and almost all major Swiss cities have at least one regional newspaper. Nonetheless, the number of existing newspapers has decreased rapidly in the past decades. In 1939 there were exactly twice as many titles on the market. Furthermore, big publishing houses are in possession of different newspapers in different regions. This fact diminishes the diversity of newspapers, as they often share most of the sections and only provide a minimum on exclusive local or regional content. The following table illustrates impressively that only a few publishing houses control the leading newspapers in the 26 cantons. The number of independent newspapers is around 30[3].

Table 3a.   Newspapers focusing language regions

Language region	Newspaper	Character of newspaper	Main editorial office	Owner
German	Blick	Tabloid	Zürich	Ringier
French	Le Matin	Tabloid	Lausanne	Tamedia
French	Le Temps	Elite	Geneva	Tamedia/Ringier
French	Le Courrier	Critical, non profit oriented, socially involved	Geneva	Nouvelle Association du Courrier

Table 3b.   Leading regional newspapers in the 26 cantons

Canton	Newspaper	Characteristics	Main editorial office	Owner
Aargau	Aargauer Zeitung	Main edition	Aarau/Baden	AZ Medien
Appenzell Ausserhoden	Appenzeller Zeitung	Strong content syndication* with St. Galler Tagblatt	St. Gallen	NZZ-Gruppe
Appenzell Innerhoden	Appenzeller Volksfreund		Appenzell	Druckerei Appenzeller Volksfreund
Basel-Land	Basellandschaftliche Zeitung	Strong content syndication with Aargauer Zeitung	Aarau/Baden	AZ Medien
Basel-Stadt	Basler Zeitung (BaZ)		Basel	Basler Zeitung Medien
Bern	Berner Zeitung		Bern	Tamedia
	Bund	Content syndication with Tages-Anzeiger**	Bern	Tamedia
	Bieler Tagblatt (German)	Content syndication with Berner Zeitung	Biel	Gassmann Medien AG
	Journal du Jura (French)		Biel	Gassmann Medien AG
Fribourg	Freiburger Nachrichten (German) La Liberté (French)	Strong content syndication with Berner Zeitung	Fribourg Fribourg	Paulus Druckerei (Imprimerie Saint Paul) Paulus Druckerei

SWISS QUALITY MEDIA: A REDUCED PROTECTIVE FOREST FOR DEMOCRACY

Canton	Newspaper	Characteristics	Main editorial office	Owner
Genf	Tribune de Genève		Geneva	Tamedia
Glarus	Südostschweiz Glarus	Strong content syndication with Südostschweiz	Chur	Südostschweiz Medien-gruppe
Graubünden	Südostschweiz	Main edition	Chur	Südostschweiz Medien-gruppe
	La Quotidiana (Rom.)		Chur	Südostschweiz Medien-gruppe
Jura	Le Quoditien Jurassien		Delémont	Editions D+P SA
Luzern	Neue Luzerner Zeitung	Main edition	Luzern	NZZ-Gruppe
Neuchâtel	L'Express	Main edition	Neuchâtel	Hersant
	L'Impartial	Strong content syndication with L'Express	Neuchâtel	Hersant
Nidwalden	Neue Nidwaldner Zeitung	Strong content syndication with Neue Luzerner Zeitung	Luzern	NZZ-Gruppe
Obwalden	Neue Obwaldner Zeitung	Strong content syndication with Neue Luzerner Zeitung	Luzern	NZZ-Gruppe
Schaffhausen	Schaffhauser Nachrichten	Content syndication with Der Landbote	Schaffhausen	Meier + Cie AG
Schwyz	Neue Schwyzer Zeitung	Strong content syndication with Neue Luzerner Zeitung"	Luzern	NZZ-Gruppe
Solothurn	Solothurner Zeitung	Strong content syndication with Aargauer Tagblatt	Aarau	AZ Medien
St.Gallen	St. Galler Tagblatt	Main edition	St. Gallen	NZZ-Gruppe
Tessin	Il Corriere del Ticino		Muzzano	Società editrice Corriere del Ticino
	La Regione		Bellinzona	Giacomo Salvioni Editore
	Il Giornale del Popolo		Lugano	Diocese di Lugano/ Società editrice Corriere del Ticino
Thurgau	Thurgauer Zeitung	Strong content syndication with St. Galler Tagblatt	St. Gallen	NZZ-Gruppe
Uri	Neue Urner Zeitung	Strong content syndication with Neue Luzerner Zeitung	Luzern	NZZ-Gruppe
Vaud	24 Heures		Lausanne	Tamedia
Wallis	Walliser Bote (German)		Visp	Mengis Druck + Verlag
	Le Nouvelliste (French)		Sion	Hersant
Zug	Neue Zuger Zeitung	Strong content syndication with Neue Luzerner Zeitung	Luzern	NZZ-Gruppe
Zürich	Neue Zücher Zeitung		Zürich	NZZ-Gruppe
	Tages-Anzeiger		Zürich	Tamedia
	Zürcher Landzeitungen	Alliance of single titles	Stäfa	Tamedia
	Der Landbote		Winterthur	Ziegler Druck AG

* Strong content syndication: newspaper is subsidiary and only produces regional section and takes over complete sections (e.g., culture, foreign politics, national politics, economy) from its "mother" newspaper/main edition.

** Content syndication: newspaper relies on content of another newspaper insofar as it prints a selection of articles from its "mother" newspaper/main edition. The newspaper DER BUND consists of 60 % of articles from TAGES-ANZEIGER. Others rely less on purchased content.

There is only one national news wire service (SDA) that produces output in German, French and Italian. After having bought the news agency office of Associate Press in January 2010, SDA has the monopoly.

(F2)   Patterns of news media use (consumption of news)   3 POINTS

The Swiss population is well supplied with news from different sources.

Swiss citizens are generally well informed on political issues due to regular public debates on referenda. The news media compete for an audience with an adult literacy of 99 % and a relatively high income. Radio and television, as well as newspapers, are the main sources of information for Swiss citizens. However, the Internet has also turned into an important source of information (Meier 2007: 185).

Broadcast media
In the German-speaking region, citizens (older than three years) spent 144, in the French-speaking 161 and in the Italian-speaking 188 minutes every day watching TV in 2009 (BfS).

Only very few Swiss people watch television programmes from other Swiss language areas. However, they intensively use the television channels originating in neighbouring countries speaking the same language. In 2009, national public TV channels had an average market share of about 30 per cent (German-speaking part: 33 %, French-speaking part; 29 %, Italian-speaking part: 30 %).

National public radio predominates in all language regions of Switzerland. In the German-speaking part, the national public radio scored an average market share of 62 per cent (French-part: 60 per cent, Italian-part 71 per cent) (SRG SSR Marktanteil 2009). Commercial radios in all regions are also important, while radio stations from abroad only play a minor role.

Newspapers
Dailies have been losing readers for the past years. Free sheets, very well received by young people (but not solely), could weaken this downtrend a bit. In a representative survey, 60 per cent of the interviewed people still said that they had read a newspaper the day before (Bonfadelli 2009).[4] However, in this survey newspapers scored lower than television. Swiss citizens spend 30 minutes on average per day reading print media.

The distribution of Swiss newspapers reflects the linguistic composition of the population. The German-language newspapers predominate. Among the Swiss newspapers, the free sheet *20 Minuten* (distributed to commuters from Monday to Friday) had the largest circulation with 1.31 million readers in 2010 (Table 4).

The paper is mainly read by younger people and surpasses the former market leader tabloid *Blick*.

Table 4.   The most read daily newspapers 2010 in Switzerland's linguistic regions

Language region	Newspapers	Reader	Reach %*	Circulation	Publishing house
German	20 Minuten	1,315,000	30.3	494,368	Tamedia
	Blick	628,000	14.5	214,880	Ringier
	Blick am Abend	495,000	11.4	329,418	Ringier
	Tages-Anzeiger	472,000	10.9	203,636	Tamedia
	NZZ	306,000	7.0	125,228	NZZ-Gruppe
	Aargauer Zeitung GES**	206,000	4.8	192,234	AZ Medien
	NLZ GES**	303,000	7.0	127,244	NZZ Gruppe
French	20 minutes	495,000	35.1	207,112	Tamedia
	Le Matin	251,000	17.8	57,894	Tamedia
	24 Heures	231,000	16.4	78,964	Tamedia
	Tribune de Genève	140,000	9.9	54,068	Tamedia
	Le Temps	132,000	9.4	44,450	Ringier
Italian	Corriere del Ticino	123,000	43.9	37,092	Società editrice Corriere del Ticino
	La Regione	103,000	36.8	32,479	Giacomo Salvioni Editore
	Giornale del Popolo	53,000	19.0	16,229	Diocese di Lugano/Società editrice Corriere del Ticino

* Reader per edition in per cent of the population of the linguistic region. Source: WEMF (MACH Basic 2010/II)

** Numbers of readers and circulation number reached with several subsidiaries.

Online media

The increasing access of Swiss homes to electronic media (in particular to the Internet) has expanded the availability of news and information sources. This has shaped the country's media landscape of the twenty-first century. The number of people using the Internet on a daily or almost daily basis (narrow user group) has grown from 32.6 per cent in 2000 to 57.3 per cent in 2003 to the current 74.5 per cent in 2010 (MA Net, Net Metrix 2/2010). 77 per cent of all private households have access to the Internet, most of them (90 per cent) even a high speed connection (BFS Aktuell 2011: 5). With 37 broadband subscribers per 100 inhabitants, Switzerland ranked three worldwide in broadband penetration in 2010 (OECD Breitband Statistik June 2010[5]).

In addition, most of the Swiss newspapers are available as online editions. Most of them provide their content for free. Thus, there is a tendency to let non-subscribers pay.

The Internet is used by different people in different ways: Highly educated people use the Internet in a rather instrumental way, while less educated people seem to use the Internet almost exclusively for entertainment purposes (Meier 2010: 5). There is still a digital divide mostly based on age, education and income. A gender gap is also detectable, but only in the age cohort over 30 years (BFS Aktuell 2011: 11).

Table 5.   Reach of the top 10 news websites in 2010 (basis: 4,964,000 users = 100 %)

Websites	Owner	Unique Users per Month	In %
Search.ch	Tamedia	1,799,000	36.2
Bluewin	Swisscom	1,742,000	35.1
20minuten.ch/20minutes	Tamedia	1,359,000	27.4
sf.tv	SRG SSR	1,324,000	26.7
Blick Online	Ringier	1,089,000	21.9
tagesanzeiger.ch	Tamedia	718,000	14.5
NZZ online	NZZ Gruppe	715,000	14.4
tsr.ch	SRG SSR	474,000	9.5
drs.ch	SRG SSR	356,000	7.2
Lematin.ch	Tamedia	330,000	6.7

Source: NET-Metrix-Profile 2010/II[6]

(F3)   Diversity of news sources   2 POINTS

The diversity of news sources has become smaller in the past years.

The reduction of staff leads to a reduction in diversity of news sources. There are only a few publishing houses left that can afford foreign correspondents and regional offices. In other words, newspapers and other media strongly depend on a few information sources such as the Swiss wire service. There is neither time nor personnel to countercheck the information they get. The public broadcaster SRG SSR and the quality newspaper Neue Zürcher Zeitung still count on their foreign correspondents. Swiss radio maintains regional offices.

Working pressure and working constraints have increased drastically under the current media crisis. This results in journalists succumbing more easily to PR material from stakeholders. Powerful actors from politics and industry bring their interests into the media without difficulties (see also Grossenbacher 2010: 133f.). Furthermore, journalists increasingly use the Internet for their stories and neglect investigation outside the newsroom. Diversity also suffers due to the collaboration among the different newspapers and news editors. Content syndications at different levels are common. Newspapers take over whole sections or single articles from other newspapers. Especially on the level of national news and very strongly on the level of international news, the performance of most newspapers has diminished. Readers get the same news about national or international politics in almost all newspapers. Since 2010, there has been only one national news wire service left. The Schweizerische Depeschenagentur (SDA – in French ATS, in Italian ATI) provides material in three languages. Most media are clients of the SDA. According to the interviewees, the SDA has been losing ground as a controlling authority. Instead, media products from the same media company are being taken as a reference and a source. The introduction of integrated newsrooms also results in information sources being used for several outputs.

(F4) Internal rules for practice of newsroom democracy   1 POINT

Leading Swiss news media do not work according to written newsroom rules.

Our interviewees alluded rather to restrictions than to democratic structures in the newsrooms. A newsroom council does not exist in any of the selected media outlets. For all cases, nomination of the editor-in-chief is exclusively in the hands of the management. In some instances, the acting editor-in-chief holds informal conversations, concerning his or her deputies with the heads of the editorial sections. However, this does not seem to influence the management's final decision. Some interviewees stated that there are no formal procedures (or company rules) to ensure journalists' participation in decision-making. But still, the moods from the journalists in the newsrooms are being taken into account when a new editor-in-chief or a new newsroom chief is being nominated. Past experience has shown that editors-in chief who take over the job against the will of the staff have a hard time succeeding. There is, so to speak, an informal equality but no "bottom-up" democracy.

(F5) Company rules against *internal* influence
on newsroom / editorial staff   2 POINTS

Leading Swiss media are keen on separating economic management from journalistic management. Still, a complete restriction of the internal influence on the newsrooms is not feasible.

Even if there are no formal rules to separate the newsroom and management, all interviewees ensured there was a separation and denied any interference from the owner as well as from the shareholders. The interviewees pointed to the fact that they experience different needs (from the publishing and journalistic side), which sometimes leads to friction – like in other companies. For the interviewees, the journalistic principle always comes first when media content is involved.

However, in some cases, the publishing house manager and the editor-in-chief meet at regular conferences. All editors told us that they have never experienced any interference by management in editorial decisions. If we take a closer look at the board of management, we can see that there is nearly no representation of journalists. This may also be a disadvantage, because the administrative board has little knowledge of journalism. A former editor-in-chief puts it this way: "The administrative board has no journalistic competence. They do not know what good journalism consists of" (Medienwoche.ch).

Editors-in-chiefs are more involved in economic and strategic management than they were in the past. The public broadcaster SRG SSR has a greater separation of management from the journalistic work than this is the case in the commercial media. The heads of the newsrooms are less involved in strategic decisions. They carry the journalistic responsibility.

Even if none of the selected media has internal rules to safeguard their independence, it can be concluded that journalists can normally decide independently on editorial matters. Altogether, the newsrooms of the Swiss media seem to be sufficiently autonomous.

(F6) Company rules against *external* influence on newsroom / editorial staff   1 POINT

There are hardly any company rules against external influence.

The external influence on media content is a well-known problem and part of the daily business. However, our current findings and statements from the interviews with editors-in-chief show that there is a certain danger in downplaying (or justifying) the influence of external stakeholders. In fact, the question seems to be delicate. The given answers pointed more to (non-)existing external influence but not to (non-)existing company rules.

Interviews with editors and journalists conducted in the course of another research project show that only a few media companies have some basic rule meant to prevent an external influence on media output. One regional newspaper does not allow their editorial staff to be active members of a political party (cf. Meier et al. 2011). Thus, rules are rare.

(F7) Procedures on news selection and news processing   2 POINTS

News selection is strongly audience research oriented. Furthermore, news selection is also based upon the characteristics of the media.

All big media have a daily editorial meeting in which topics are selected. The selection is made in accordance with the medium and its readership, viewers or listeners. Public radio and public TV have to fulfil their public service contract.

When it comes to political controversial topics and elections, all media try to report fairly, with no bias and considering both sides, pro and con – according to the interviewees. Current findings also show that Swiss media have a tendency to focus on the powerful. Established power holders get more room in the media. This is legitimated insofar as they have relevance in the society or in the specific discourse. Journalism for the weaker ("anwaltschaftlicher" Journalismus) is quite rare.

Furthermore journalistic criteria are important. Not every topic on the political agenda is suited to every medium. Especially media with a tendency towards "boulevard" journalism select according to the assumed wishes of their audience.

Equality / Interest mediation (E)

(E1) Media ownership concentration national level   2 POINTS

On the national level three big publishing houses dominate the print media sector. The public broadcaster SRG SSR dominates the electronic sector in all three language regions in Switzerland.

At the national level, Switzerland experiences all forms of press concentration: Ownership concentration (a declining number of publishing houses), journalistic concentration (a declining number of fully staffed papers) and a concentration of circulation can be observed. The trend seems to be heading towards a two-tier newspaper landscape. Only a few high-circulation papers will serve the economic centres and the suburbs, meanwhile many small newspapers will have to fill the gaps, taking advantage of narrow local advertising and readership markets. In addition, cross-media concentration is also a fact. Big publish houses have entered other media markets – more expansion is due to occur (cf. Meier 2010: 10; Meier 2007: 189). The dominant publishing houses hold different products; cross-media portfolios are common.

Because Switzerland has no single language and thus no national media, we define national concentration according to the three main linguistic areas: the German, French and Italian parts of the country. The concentration of newspapers seems to be much greater at the regional than at the national level. The large number of newspapers in Switzerland disguises the fact that most dailies are owned by the same publishing houses.

According to Künzler (2011: 84), the most profitable publishing houses that publish a daily are the following: Ringier, Tamedia, NZZ-Gruppe, Basler Zeitung Medien, AZ Medien and Südostschweiz Mediengruppe. Publishing houses from abroad play a minor role. In the French-speaking region, the publishing house Hersant has expanded, but the most invasive corporation is Tamedia from Zurich. With its takeover of Edipresse Tamedia also controls the French part of Switzerland.

In the Italian-speaking region, the daily newspaper Corriere del Ticino has a market-share of 43.9 % of the total newspaper circulation. Its competitors reach 36.8 % (La Regione) and 19 % (Giornale del Popolo) (Wemf MACH Basic 2010/II).

Regarding the broadcasting sector, the degree of media concentration can also be calculated according to the market data for the three linguistic regions (audience market share). Generally, Switzerland's audiovisual media market is dominated by programmes provided by the public service broadcaster SRG SSR. In fact, the combined market share of the public radio programmes in the German-speaking part of Switzerland is 61.7 per cent, in the French-speaking part 60.1 per cent and in the Italian-speaking part even 71 per cent (Source: SRG SSR 2009). Unlike the television sector, radio programmes from foreign broadcasters have only little relevance.

The SRG SSR television channels face competition from a large number of foreign broadcasters sharing one of Switzerland's national languages (Table 6). About one third of the total watching time is dedicated to Swiss public programmes, while two thirds are spent watching foreign channels. However, the advantage of SRG SSR is its Swiss perspective and the provision of domestic information. Moreover, there are no private commercial television stations on a national level. Private commercial television channels are just able to assert themselves on a regional level with a small audience and limited commercial success.

In the German part of Switzerland, the leading channel of the public service television SF TV reaches an audience market share of 33.3 per cent. Private commercial regional channels achieve only 6.4 per cent, while the foreign channels reach 59.6 per cent (Source: SRG SSR 2009).

In the French and Italian part of the country, the two leading SRG SSR TV channels have the highest reaches (TSR 29.2 per cent and RSI 30.3 per cent). However, their runners-up are foreign channels from France and Italy (Source SRG SSR 2009).

Taken together, citizens in the three linguistic areas that are defined as national level in Switzerland can choose from newspapers, public and private radio and television and a considerable number of freely accessible online media. We therefore consider national media concentration to be less relevant than regional media concentration.

Table 6.   TV concentration in the linguistic regions

Market Share TV (24h, Mo-So) 2009

German-speaking region (in %)			
Public (SRG SSR): 33.3 %	Swiss commercial station: 6.4 %	Foreign	59.6 %
...the biggest thereof: SF1 22.7 %		... the biggest thereof: RTL SAT 1	 6.7 % 5.5 %
Viewer per day: 2,866,000	1,518,000		

French-speaking region (in %)			
Public (SRG SSR) 29.2 %	Swiss commercial station: 0.8 %	Foreign	68.4 %
...the biggest thereof: TSR 1 22 %		TF 1 M6	13 % 9.3 %
Viewer per day: 913,000	215,000		

Italian-speaking region (in %)			
Public (SRG SSR) 30.3 %	Swiss commercial station: 1.7 %	Foreign	64.4 %
...the biggest thereof: RSI 1 23.6 %		Canale 5 Rai 1	11.9 % 11.2 %
Viewer per day: 180,000	63,000		

Table 7.   Radio concentration in the linguistic region

Market Share Radio (24h, Mo-So)

German-speaking region (%)			
Public (SRG SSR) 61.7 %	Swiss commercial station: 28.8 %	Foreign	5 %
...the biggest thereof: DRS1 36.4 %			
Listeners per day: 2,929,000	2,351,000		

French-speaking region (in %)			
Public (SRG SSR) 60.1 %	Swiss commercial station: 22.3 %	Foreign	10.2 %
...the biggest thereof: La Première 39.9 %			
Listeners per day: 861,000	681,000		

Italian-speaking region (in %)			
Public (SRG SSR) 71 %	Swiss commercial station: 8.1 %	Foreign	7.8 %
...the biggest thereof: Rete Uno 49.6			
Listeners per day: 195,000	80,000		

Source: SRG SSR 2009.

(E2)   Media ownership concentration regional (local) level   1 POINT

There is strong concentration of newspapers at the regional level. There is hardly any competition. Only in the Italian-speaking part and in the greater area of Zurich does more than one independent publishing house compete.

Switzerland has been known as a country rich with regional subscription newspapers. This situation has changed drastically. Classical journalistic high profile newspapers are losing ground to the commercially powerful free sheets. Entrepreneurial decisions have changed the ownership structures in the regional markets. There are only two regions (Zurich and Tessin) where two media houses of the same size exist.

The following overview shows the three dominant newspapers and their reach in selected parts of all three language regions.

Table 8.   Selected regions: the three biggest newspapers and their reach in the region

Economic region	Newspaper	Owner	reach	%
Economic region Basel Population: 448,000	20 Minuten (free)	Tamedia	179,000	39.8
	BaZ	Basler Zeitung Medien	173,000	38.7
	Blick am Abend (free)	Ringier	62,000	13.8
Total reach				92.3
Economic region „Berner Mittelland" Population: 431,000	Berner Zeitung Bund	Tamedia	219,000	50.8
	20 Minuten	Tamedia	160,000	37
Total reach				87.8
Economic region „Greater-Zurich" Population: 1,039,000	20 Minuten	Tamedia	350,000	33.7
	Tages-Anzeiger	Tamedia	310,000	29.8
	Blick am Abend	Ringier	202,000	19.4
Total reach				82.9
Economic region Tessin Population: 153,000*	Corriere del Ticino	Società editrice Corriere del Ticino Diocese di	73,000	47.8
	La Regione	Giacomo Salvioni Editore	62,000	40.6
	Giornale del Popolo	Lugano/Società editrice Corriere del Ticino	31,000	20
Total reach				108.4

Cont.

Table 8. *Cont.*

Economic region Geneva Population: 381,000	20 Minutes	Tamedia	150,000	39.5
	Tribune de Genève	Tamedia	138,000	36.3
	Le Matin	Tamedia	52,000	13.6
Total reach				89.4

Economic region Vaud Population: 458,000	24 Heures	Tamedia	198,000	43.3
	20 minutes	Tamedia	174,000	38.1
	Le Matin	Tamedia	82,000	18.0
Total reach				99.4

Economic region "Innerschweiz" Population: 499,000	Neue Luzerner Zeitung (GES)	NZZ Gruppe	298,000	59.7
	20 Minuten	Tamedia	147,000	29.5
	Blick	Ringier	79,000	15.9
Total reach				105.1

* This economic region matches the canton Tession, though not the whole language region. This explains that the reaches for the newspapers in this table are a bit higher than the reaches in Table 4 (F2).

Source: Wemf MACH Basic 2010/2

In nearly all Swiss regions the printed and audio-visual media are controlled by a single company.

Table 9. Some Swiss regions with dominant publishing houses (selection)

Region	Publisher	Dalies	Radio	TV
Aargau/Midland	AZ Medien	Aargauer Zeitung	Radio Argovia	Tele M1 Tele Tell
Grisons/ Southeastern Switzerland	Südostschweiz Medien	Die Südostschweiz	Radio Grischa Radio Engadina	Tele Südostschweiz
Berne (metropolitan area)	Tamedia	Berner Zeitung Der Bund Bernerbär	Capital FM	Tele Bärn
Greater Zurich	Tamedia Ringier NZZ Gruppe	Tages-Anzeiger Blick NZZ	Radio 24 Radio Energy	Tele Züri

Source: Own compilation.

(E3) Diversity of formats   2 POINTS

The Swiss news media landscape is still rich in news formats. In the newspapers, the traditional media sections have been eliminated more and more in the past years. This trend is alarming. The diversity suffers.

At first glance, Switzerland's media landscape is diverse with several public and private television channels and radio stations as well as many newspapers (daily, tabloid and weekly), presenting news in a large variety of formats. Swiss publishing houses provide all major categories of media publications, including full-featured daily newspapers, regional and local weekly editions as well as free-sheets.

Switzerland's public service broadcaster SRG SSR, with its radio and TV channels, delivers news throughout the day. In addition, SF info frequently repeats the German-language television news and information programmes. Besides regular news programmes (noon, prime time and midnight), the public broadcaster also allocates time and space for other news formats, like magazines, debates, interviews, etc.

Regarding radio, SRG SSR transmits along with regular news several times a day the programme *Echo der Zeit,* which includes background information and analyses on current topics. In addition, a high number of private, non-commercial radio stations broadcast mainly local and regional news programmes. The formation of private commercial national broadcast television channels is impeded by the relatively small and highly competitive market. During the 1990s, the political pressure to deregulate the broadcast media increased, opening some new business opportunities to private broadcasters. Today, there are only a few regional privately owned news channels (e.g. Tele Züri, Tele M1), mostly with only a limited number of news formats. Finally, many news-related online media have entered the Swiss news market. In addition, online editions of most Swiss newspapers are available and most of the public and private broadcasters disseminate their content online. Online news coverage, thus, happens in various formats: news articles can be read on websites, live radio streams can be listened, and television programmes can be watched online – or downloaded as podcasts.

At second glance – and in comparison with the situation about ten years ago – we can state that the diversity of news format and news content has decreased significantly. The traditional quality press has come under heavy pressure. Together with the public radio and – with some distance – public TV, the traditional newspapers provide the public with all relevant information required for a democracy. They still try to sustain their public service in politics, economy and culture. They have a hard time competing against the solely commercially aligned free sheets, tabloids, commercial radio, TV channels and online-media, which all focus on individual interest and on sports, human interest and showbiz. Furthermore, they very successfully reprocess issues from politics, economy and culture in a personal and emotional way (foeg 2010). The abolishment of the traditional news sectors leads to a "all-round journalism" that very often neglects quality criteria. The core sectors such as politics, economy, etc., lose importance in favour of human interest topics.

Altogether we can state that the diversity on the level of different products as well as on the level of different forms of news presentation is sufficient (see also Kradolfer 2010: 94). The latter shows a clear tendency towards tabloidization.

(E4) Minority / Alternative media   2 POINTS

(Swiss) linguistic minorities are well equipped with mass media in Switzerland. The public broadcaster SRG SSR guarantees that all official languages and cultures are covered with information. There are no special media for immigrants. Alternative media products exist.

One key feature of Switzerland is its ethnic and linguistic diversity. Multilingualism is dominant and determines the media landscape radically: Dailies, weeklies, magazines, radio and TV programmes exist for each lingual region – German, French, Italian and Rhaeto-Romanic. The national broadcasting cooperation SRG SSR is mandated by law to provide programmes reflecting and maintaining the linguistic and cultural diversity of the country. It produces radio and TV programmes in all four official languages. Six radio studios located in Zurich, Berne, Basel, Geneva, Lausanne and Lugano and four additional regional studios in Aarau, Chur, Lucerne and St. Gall produce 16 radio channels in addition to seven television channels. All media services are provided to the four linguistic groups on an equal basis, with the larger German sector subsidizing internally services for the smaller French, Italian and Rhaeto-Romanic communities. In contrast to the abundant news provision for its language communities, Switzerland has no policies to create special media channels for immigrant minorities. The SRG SSR undertakes some efforts in this regard. However, information news media attach only little relevance to this issue. A recent study shows that only 6.4 per cent of all media contributions (SRG SSR radio and TV programmes as well as private commercial radio programmes) are focused on immigrants minorities (cf. Bonfadelli 2008: 233).

There is no discernible religious orientation in the major newspapers and magazines. Special-interest publications represent the interests of various religious groups (e.g., Jüdische Rundschau).

Major international English-language newspapers and editions are available. The national public television broadcasts the leading news programmes with sign language on its repetition channel SFinfo. In addition, the SRG SSR sub-company Swiss TXT has provided subtitles for deaf people in German, French and Italian (teletext) since 1987.

Alternative, non-profit oriented media products do exist, such as weekly newspapers and non-profit radio stations (which receive some license fees from the state). Journalists who work for alternative media do so for little money or voluntarily. There is one feminist magazine for the French-speaking part, but no longer in the German-speaking part. Due to financial problems, the "Frauenzeitschrift FraZ" had to close down in September 2009. Alternative media fight even harder – unless they are subsidized – against the crisis.

(E5) Affordable public and private news media   3 POINTS

Switzerland is one of the richest countries worldwide and its mass media are relatively cheap.

In 2008, Swiss households spent 393 Swiss francs on average to cover their need for information and communication (Kradolfer 2010: 73). This makes 7.4 per cent of the overall consumption expenditure. Households with a low income spend proportionally more for communication and information in comparison with households with higher incomes.

An annual subscription to a daily newspaper is about 400 CHF (www.presseabo. ch). The Swiss billing company Billag collects license fees for public service radio and television, which amounts to 462 CHF per year per household (combined fee). The monthly subscription fee for cable television costs between 20 and 27 CHF, depending on the provider. Also depending on the provider as well as on the capacity, the monthly costs for access to broadband Internet are between 34 and 50 CHF. According to this, a full supply including radio, television, Internet, daily newspapers and cable-TV costs approximately 150 CHF per month.

Altogether 15.7 billion CHF were spent on communication and information in 2008, thereof 6.6 billion CHF (42 %) for mass communication (radio, TV, print media, books and audio-visual data media). One third goes to telephony and another 16 per cent to computer (hardware and software) and Internet access. In the past ten years, the cost for telephony, Internet and computing have clearly increased, while the costs for traditional mass media have increased indiscernibly. An even closer look reveals that the spending on newspapers and magazines decreased during that time span by about 10 per cent. At the same time, people spent more money on electronic media, especially TV-sets (Kradolfer 2010: 91). In other words – and relevant in the context of democracy – there is a shift from spending money on journalistic content to spending money on technologies and technical devices.

(E6) Content monitoring instrument   1 POINT

Efforts to monitor news media on a regular basis in Switzerland are institutionalized, but are still at an early, emerging stage.

The Public Councils of the SRG SSR (Publikumsräte) are a public issue monitoring instrument, which operate more or less on a regular basis. The Public Councils are independent advisory bodies, which critically monitor the programmes of the public service broadcaster SRG SSR. These Councils shall protect the values established as the foundations of political, legal and social structures of the democratic society. The programme monitoring is done by six work groups (each group consists of six to ten members), which report to the Councils on a regular basis.

The FOEG (Forschungsbereich Öffentlichkeit und Gesellschaft) is a Centre for Research on the Public Sphere and Society at the University of Zurich. It was founded with the aim to monitor communication events. In order to create an independent body that can monitor the media on a regular basis, the Swiss annual "Media quality" project was launched by the FOEG Schweizer Jahrbuch "Qualität der Medien". The large-scale research was first published in August 2010, accompanied by extensive media coverage. The state of the Swiss media and communication landscape will later on be evaluated continuously, with an annually published report.

(E7) Code of ethics at the national level (structure)   1 POINT

Although a code of ethics exists, it has limited effect in daily business.

Guidelines for editorial and journalistic practice are established by the major national and international professional associations to which the majority of newspapers and professional journalists belong. These include the liberal Swiss Union of Journalists (Schweizerische Journalistinnen und Journalisten Union), and the oldest professional association, the Swiss Federation of Journalists (Schweizer Verband der Journalistinnen und Journalisten), whose members subscribe to a specific "Declaration of Rights and Duties of Journalists". The Swiss Press Council (Schweizer Presserat) follows as well a policy of self-regulation based on standards of professional ethics that are laid down in the declaration mentioned above (www.presserat.ch/16310.htm) and its related guidelines (www.presserat.ch/16320.htm). The declaration emphasizes independence as a prerequisite for responsible journalistic action: "The right to information, to free speech and criticism is one of the basic human rights. The duties and rights of journalists derive from the public's right to know facts and opinions. The responsibility of journalists towards the public has priority over any other responsibility, particularly the responsibility to their employers and the state organs." Through its activities, the Press Council should contribute to public awareness of basic ethical problems within the media and stimulate editorial discussion of media ethics.

In addition, a variety of complaints procedures are available to deal with disputes: The Swiss Press Council (Schweizer Presserat) is the self-regulatory complaints authority that deals with media-related breaches of civil law.

The Swiss Press Council deals with complaints received regarding the print media. Furthermore, it can actively investigate issues related to the ethics of media and journalistic professionalism as well as matters of freedom of the press and opinion. However, the body does not operate on a permanent and continuous basis. All decisions of the Swiss Press Council are published on its website (www.presserat. ch). Important decisions are sent to the news agencies, major editorial offices as well as other parties involved. In this regard, the Press Council's conclusions are made known to a wide public.

(E8)   Level of self-regulation (performance)   2 POINTS

Editorial statutes and other internal newsroom rules exist, but are not used consistently in daily practice.

Looking at self-regulation at the level of the main news media to provide fair, balanced and impartial reporting and to fulfil the journalistic mission, we can see attempts on different levels. Firstly and for the sake of prevention, candidates are to be informed adequately about their rights and duties. The question of whether they will accept the ethical principles may determine whether someone gets the job. Secondly and after being hired, training programmes help ensure that journalists will comply with formalities. Training on a regular basis will guarantee that journalists are steadily confronted with their own work and their own performance. The public broadcaster SRG SSR is still very keen on continuing education, while other media have cut down on offering continued training. Thirdly, internal policy guidelines and codes of conduct are other instruments of self-regulation. Each of the main news media has an Editorial Statute, which contains a Mission Statement and elements of a Code of Conduct. However, apart from the public broadcaster, such statements seem not to matter a great deal. They are neither institutionalized nor an effective instrument of self-regulation. In our interviews, the editors-in-chief pointed to the fact that internal guidelines and codes of conduct are important, but often hard to implement in everyday practice. New employees need to read the papers, but often there is a friction between the principles and the journalistic work. Especially tabloids often work on the outer limits of "moral legality". The editors-in-chief count on the "common sense" of their journalists. Thus, editorial statutes and other internal newsroom rules exist, but are rarely used in daily practice.

Fourthly, many of our interviewees referred to the importance of the regular newsroom-meetings open for all journalists. However, besides this form of internal criticism, there are no formalized sanctions against journalists who violate ethical standards. We can say that most of the main Swiss news media do not have an effective system of self-regulation, which is implemented by formal rules. Self-criticism results rather from bilateral and informal forms of feedback. It depends strongly on the culture and tradition prevailing in each single newsroom.

Fifthly, there is an independent body (ombudsperson) for the employees as well as one for the audience. An ombudsperson, who oversees the operation of self-regulation and adjudicates between a media outlet/journalist and the subject of a report, does exist in most commercial news media. The public broadcaster is supervised by an ombudsperson – not least because of its specific legal requirement. If the resolution of the complaint is not satisfactory, an appeal can be lodged with the Independent Radio and Television Appeals Body (UBI). Further appeals to UBI decisions can be lodged with the Federal Supreme Court. Depending on the circumstances, individuals who feel personally affected and harmed by something that has appeared in the media have the right to complain, for example to the Swiss Press Council.

(E9) Participation   1 POINT

Leading Swiss news media hesitate to engage people to participate in the news process.

There are not many possibilities for people to participate in the news process. The newspaper section "Letters to the Editors" is the most frequently used feedback tool. This traditional way of giving a feedback still has weight and is subject to newsroom selection. Nowadays most letters to the editors are actually "emails to the editor". Journalists complain about the bulk of emails, which are very often written in a sloppy non-reflexive way. With it, letters to the editor have experienced degradation.

Most interviewees see the importance of getting the civil society (or at least their audience) involved, but interference is avoided if possible. Public involvement has no high priority. Even though they take feedback seriously, any real participation is not taking place. The audience has no possibility to set the agenda.

A current study illustrates that the Internet, and especially the possibilities offered by Web 2.0, intensifies the interactivities with the audience and changes participation. The Internet has become the most important interaction channel. However, citizens' comments are often filtered. Journalists collect comments on popular topics to re-use them in new articles. The audience – in rare cases – may thus influence the news selection (cf. Keel et al. 2010: 25). On a more regular basis, free sheets and tabloids use photographs sent in to their websites. Altogether, journalists and editors-in-chief are ambivalent towards the new possibilities offered by the Internet. A serious dialogue with the audience fails, due to the lack of time and the low quality of the feedback. More interaction mainly means more work (cf. Keel et al. 2010: 31)

(E10)   Rules and practices on internal pluralism   2 POINTS

Media organizations strive for pluralism. Their mission statements guarantee that different views and perspectives are being reported. The given circumstances restrain pluralism.

Pluralism is one of the main goals of all media products. These statements from the editors-in-chief can be affirmed by a current study on diversity in Swiss regional newspapers. There is no explicit exclusion of any groups, perspectives, opinions (cf. Meier et al. 2011). Media organizations strive for pluralism not only for democratic reasons, but also because they target a wide readership/audience. Yet free sheets and tabloids do not feel obliged to cover everything, especially because not every topic suits their format. The public broadcaster SRG SSR is bound to pluralism by law.

Even though mission statements constitute pluralism in the different media organizations, pluralism has suffered in recent years for different reasons. Lack of time to investigate, lack of diverse sources and other precarious job conditions due to the economic (and the media) crisis harm pluralism (cf. Meier et al. 2011). Furthermore, pluralism also suffers because there are not enough experts anymore. Journalists in Switzerland are well trained in the field of their profession but they have little expert knowledge on specific matters. Even their knowledge of national politics and administration is limited. They depend on external expertise.

Control / Watchdog (C)

(C1)   Supervising the watchdog 'control of the controllers'   2 POINTS

The Federal Office of Communication (BAKOM) is the external supervising body. Other watchdogs exist like blogs and Internet sites that observe and criticize the performance of the media.

There are a few institutions in Switzerland controlling the performance and role of the news media: The SRG SSR broadcasting corporation operates under the legal obligation (RTVG) to outsource viewer and listener research to the independent research foundation, Mediapulse. It is responsible for conducting research on usage that is ultimately unbiased and neutral. This also involves measuring television viewing figures, independent of the broadcasting technology used. The Federal Transportation, Communication and Energy Department (UVEK) and the Federal Office for Communication (BAKOM) are also in charge of supervising the performance of Swiss radio and television broadcasting. The Federal Office for Communication commissions content analyses on a regular basis (ca. 500,000 CHF per year) as well as other research according to problems at issue (another 500,000 CHF a year). The BAKOM itself does not conduct any research itself, as it must not control the media.

The following Internet sites supervise the performance of the media: Medienkritik-schweiz.ch, medienspiegel.ch, blattkritik.ch.

(C2) Independence of the news media from power holders   2 POINTS

For the leading media, pressures from external stakeholders are part of the daily business. Indirect influence exists.

The external influence on media content is a well-known problem and part of the daily business. Our current findings and statements from the interviews with editors-in-chief show that there is a certain danger in downplaying (or justifying) the influence of external stakeholders. According to their statements, they feel pressure from politicians as well as from industry. At the same time, they vow to withstand it successfully and underline their independence.

Altogether, it is correct to say that the media in Switzerland are independent from the direct influence of power holders. There are, indeed, indirect influences – on both sides. The media are willing to and in fact do look over stakeholders' shoulders. And, vice versa, the media are under the influence of various stakeholders.

A critical look at the interaction between the media and power holders reveals dependencies, at least at some points. Furthermore, the big question of what status the media enjoy within Swiss society and Swiss democracy remains open: namely whether the media themselves constitute a power holder.

The media – or more precisely the attitudes of journalists – are ambiguous. On the one hand, they complain about the pushy attempts of politicians to get attention from the media. On the other hand, they depend on "good stories" from politicians and thus are ready to jump on campaigns that promise controversies and may please the crowd. Furthermore, journalists often have a close relationship to certain politicians, which makes it difficult to maintain a distance.

When it comes to the advertising industry, the dependency is obvious – and one-sided. Especially commercial media (free sheets, online media) depend on advertising.

It is not very surprising that editors-in-chief of such commercial media judge the influence of the advertising industry to be non-problematic. After all, they depend heavily on them.

Commercial media have tried to avoid the pressure from the advertising industry with the introduction of pages or programmes where advertising merges with journalism (e.g., advertorials).

In contrast to the commercial media, the public broadcasting media are almost free of advertisement. Public radio has no advertising at all, public television is financed 23 per cent by advertising revenues. In 2009 advertising revenues were 232.8 Million CHF (Source: Geschäftsbericht SRG SSR 2009).

(C3) Transparency of data on media system   1 POINT

Detailed information about ownership structure and decision-making processes of private media organizations are not open.

Although media – or more precisely – journalists ask the important stakeholder for transparency, they themselves are very reluctant to lay bare internal information. In the recent course of takeovers of newspapers and changes of ownership in Switzerland, there are some examples of non-transparent activities, such as the buyout of a regional newspaper by a single person who refuses to give any information about his source of capital (cf. Strahm 2011).

The public broadcaster SRG SSR is obliged to present their data. The annual report gives insight into the structure and the finances.

(C4) Journalism professionalism   2 POINTS

Journalism professionalism is being challenged. Journalists have good skills but too little expertise and not enough knowledge about politics. New media products undermine journalism professionalism additionally.

Most journalists have special training – either achieved at a school of journalism (university, university of applied science) or attained on the job. Still, complaints about a lack of professionalism cannot be ignored. Even journalists themselves complain about their colleagues. (Elder) journalists notice that (younger) journalists have little expertise (cf. Meier et al. 2011). They are uncritical; they have no opinion of their own (cf. Medienkritik-schweiz.ch). Even more, they lack inspiration, they avoid investigation and they focus on emotions rather than on facts (which needed to be gathered). A former editor-in-chief put it this way: "The work ethic and the will to do journalism has vanished. The problem is that most of them believe that emotions are enough. However, investigation is needed" (Medienwoche.ch).

Tabloids, free sheets and online media not only legitimize but also glorify this style of journalism and reinforce the tendency towards deprofessionalism (FOEG 2010).

Yet, journalists are not the only ones to blame. Under the constraints caused by the media crisis, the quality of journalism also suffers. Professionalism can be better safeguarded if resources are abundant.

(C5) Journalists' job security   2 POINTS

In the course of the media crisis, job security cannot be guaranteed. Insecurity is bigger with commercial media.

Journalists' job security has diminished in the past few years. Especially in the course of the media crisis 2008 and afterwards, many journalists have become victims of reorganization. Journalists working for commercial media – especially newspapers – have been greatly affected. In 2010, the number of unemployed journalists was the highest in 40 years. In May 2010, 1465 journalists were jobless (comedia 2010). The following examples show the situation even more clearly: In May 2010, the regional newspaper *Tages-Anzeiger* dismissed 80 journalists; the tabloid *Blick* introduced its integrated newsroom and 45 journalists lost their jobs (comedia 2010). The situation has become especially critical for freelancers. They have fewer mandates for less money.

According to the interviewees, the situation at the public broadcaster SRG SSR regarding job security is still satisfactory. Still, the times when one got a secure job until retirement are over. There is, however, a Collective Labour Agreement (GAV) that protects all employees fairly well.

(C6) Practice of access to information   3 POINTS

In general Swiss journalists have free access to most public information.

The interviews with the editors-in-chief give no indication that they were hampered in getting information from different stakeholders. This finding corresponds with other statements from journalists who work at regional newspapers (cf. Meier et al. 2011). There is a consensus that especially the administration and authorities provide information well. According to the law, the State must provide information (Art. 180 Abs. 2 BV) (Mader 2010: 29). Refusal to do so is rare.

(C7)   The watchdog and the media's mission statement   2 POINTS

Mission statements partly contain reference to the democratic watchdog role, but they are of little importance in daily life.

When asked about journalists' role in a democracy, the self-image of a watchdog was not common to all the interviewees. While the role as a critically analytical intermediary between the public and the political elite is one that is taken seriously, some editors see their main task as being the providers of information. The need for independent information seems to be a principle common to all selected news media. There is no distinctive culture of investigative journalism in Switzerland. Some interviewees stated that the watchdog function is not as essential as it was some time ago. No one wants to be the "monopolistic watchdog" – not even the public broadcaster SRG SSR. On the other hand, there is a wish to work more with investigation and to spend more time finding stories and scandals. That would be "the icing on the cake"; however most media do not have sufficient funds.

(C8)   Professional training   2 POINTS

Journalistic training was downsized over the past years and lacks coherence. No particular emphasis is placed on democratic virtues.

There is a general lack of professional training opportunities for Swiss journalists. Journalism schools, press associations and other professional organizations that provide training in investigative skills are rare. There is in general insufficient training offered in the skills that are needed to execute strong watchdog journalism.

The public broadcaster SRG SSR runs an in-house training centre. SRG SSR puts effort into their professional training programme and calls up their employees to benefit from internal and external programmes during their whole career. Big publishing companies also offer internal courses for their employees. They put particular value on special courses in the field of new technology to keep current on the online sector. Thus, they have been cut down lately for reasons of lack of resources or no need. Even the large media conglomerate Ringier AG, which has been offering courses in its own School of Journalism (Journalistenschule) since 1974, has put training on hold. In German-speaking Switzerland, there is only one journalist's training centre MAZ (Schweizer Journalistenschule), which has offered journalism training courses since 1984.

(C9) Watchdog function and financial resources   1 POINT

Before the current recession, leading Swiss news media have been financially viable. Since then, there has been less staff for investigative reporting.

The recent and ongoing financial crisis prompted many Swiss news media to eliminate or cut back their investments. In particular, the number and availability of reporters who have the time, institutional backing, and resources to perform effective watchdog journalism are being reduced. Due to limited resources, some of the selected media depend a great deal on news agencies. Once again, the public broadcasters seem to have fewer problems in this regard. Due to financial aid (e.g., licence fees), they have enough personnel and time resources to engage in thorough research. In some departments, journalists are on the payroll for the purpose of doing investigative journalism.

However, among the editors, watchdog journalism is not universally seen as an absolute role that the media ought to play. Investigative reporting seems rather to be an exception. The accurate coverage of daily news and information is considered more important.

Concluding remarks

The traditional quality papers, public radio and TV are the means of providing the Swiss public with information relevant for democracy. However, the traditional quality press has come under heavy pressure and has been pushed into a defensive role. Still, traditional quality papers are trying to sustain their mandate to inform appropriately about politics, economy and culture. On the contrary, highly commercialized free sheets, tabloids, commercial radio and TV stations as well as online media are on the move. They concentrate on individual interests and cover first and foremost human interest, sports and showbiz. Furthermore, they have a strong tendency to personalize, emotionalize and to give every story a private spin.

Switzerland was once a country known for its great variety of newspapers. In the past decade, subscription papers with high quality journalistic content have been losing readers, reach and advertising revenues to the free sheets. The introduction of free sheets and news sites has pushed the commercial and journalistic concentration forward. Fewer titles and fewer publishing houses share geographically growing markets. Furthermore, there are some other developments in the media sector as well as in politics that hamper a lively democracy rather than boosting it:

On the national level, the media show an increasing orientation towards their own country or region. Switzerland has opened up and has become more global and multicultural – sometimes against its own will. Still, the leading newspapers give the impression that Switzerland is the hub of the universe. National stories and, to an even greater extent, regional stories have gained in importance at the expense of international coverage. Especially commercial news media reduce their perspectives. They – if at all – cover neighbouring countries that share the same language or focus on wars, crises and catastrophes.

On the regional level of the languages, free sheets for commuters produced on the cheap and flashy online news sites delegitimize the important role of the media in democracies. They marginalize other high quality journalistic products. The increasing commercialization of the media enhances the tabloidization of politics. Political actors cannot resist the temptation of the tabloids and free sheets, which are fighting every day for the readership. Thus politics and media mutually fuel the mutual loss of legitimacy instead of combating it.

On the regional level, monopolies of dailies have emerged. There are only two regions left (Zurich, Tessin) where journalistic competition between equally strong dailies is a fact.

Altogether, politically independent newspapers (Forumszeitungen) are less capable or less willing to offer politically relevant platforms to the communities that are small scale and often very diverse. They withdraw from local areas and focus more on regional centres.

On the individual level, we can show that young generations prefer media with a strong tendency towards tabloidization and with little information that is relevant for democracy. Furthermore, looking at the expenses for information and communication, we can also state that Swiss households are increasingly spending more money on hardware, while the expenses for journalistic information have decreased.

Altogether, all the stated developments are pieces of a puzzle that reveals a smouldering crisis of democracy. British political scientist Colin Crouch (2009) has started a discussion using the buzzword "postdemocracy". The media are embedded in economy and politics. They seem to be more part of the problem and less part of overcoming postdemocracy.

Notes

[1] http://www.bakom.admin.ch/themen/radio_tv/marktuebersicht/index.html?lang=en
[2] http://www.bfs.admin.ch/bfs/portal/de/index/themen/16/04/key/approche_globale.indicator.30103.301. html?open=308#308 (2.2.2011)
[3] The number of independent newspapers varies in the literature – depending on the definition (see Künzler 2011, Kradolfer et al. 2010).
[4] Univox-Studie: see also www.gfs-zh.ch/?pid=7
[5] http://www.oecd.org/document/23/0,3746,en_2649_34225_33987543_1_1_1_1,00.html (2.2.2011)
[6] http://www.net-metrix.ch/sites/default/files/files/Report_NMP_2010-2_d.pdf

References

BFS aktuell (2011) *Internet in den Schweizer Haushalten.* Information, Kommunikation, Konsum, Reisen und Freizeit: Das Internet ist allgegenwärtig. BFS Sektion Struktur und Konjunktur. Neuchâtel.

Bundesamt für Kommunikation (BAKOM) www.bakom.admin.ch/themen/radio_tv/marktuebersicht/

Bundesamt für Statistik (BfS). www.bfs.admin.ch/bfs/portal/de/index/themen/16/04/key/approache_globale. indicator.30103.301.html

Bonfadelli, Heinz (2008) *Migration, Medien und Integration.* Forschungsbericht zuhanden des Bundesamtes für Kommunikation BAKOM. IPMZ-Universität Zürich, April 2008.

Bonfadelli, Heinz (2009) Bereits fast 40 % nutzen täglich das Internet. Univox-Studie. http://www.gfs-zh. ch/?pid=7

Comedia (2010) Was von den Medien übrig bleibt. www.comedia.ch/de/aktuelle/news/

Crouch, Colin (2009) *Post-democracy.* Polity. Cambridge.

FOEG – Forschungsbereich Öffentlichkeit und Gesellschaft (2010*) Medienkonzentration und Meinungsvielfalt. Informations- und Meinungsvielfalt in der Presse unter Bedingungen dominanter und crossmedial tätiger Medienunternehmen.* Bericht zuhanden des Bakom. Zürich.

FOEG – Forschungsbereich Öffentlichkeit und Gesellschaft/Universität Zürich im Auftrag der Stiftung Öffentlichkeit und Gesellschaft Zürich (Hg.) (2010) *Jahrbuch 2010*: Qualität der Medien. Schweiz – Suisse – Svizzera. Basel.

Grossenbacher, René (2010) Staatskommunikation und Medien – die ungleichen siamesischen Zwillinge. In: Ehrenzeller, Bernhard/Saxer, Urs (Hrsg.) *St Galler Tagung zur Öffentlichkeitskommunikation des Staates. Recht und Praxis.* pp. 131-144.

Keel, Guido et al. (2010) *Auswirkungen des Internets auf die journalistische Praxis und berufskulturellen Normen.* Schlussbericht für das BAKOM. Winterthur.

Kradolfer, Edi/Custer, Ueli/Künzler, Matthias (2010) *Die wirtschaftliche Entwicklung der Medien in der Schweiz 2000-2010. Strukturen und Perspektiven.* Projektbericht zuhanden des BAKOM. Biel.

Künzler, Matthias (2011) *Mediensystem Schweiz.* Konstanz.

MA Net, *Net Metrix* 2/2010

Mader, Luzius (2010) Rechtliche Schranken staatlicher Öffentlichkeitsarbeit – was darf der Staat, und was darf er nicht. In: Ehrenzeller, Bernhard/Saxer, Urs (Hrsg.) *St Galler Tagung zur Öffentlichkeitskommunikation des Staates. Recht und Praxis.* pp. 27-46.

Meier, Werner A. (2007) The Swiss Media Landscape. In G. Terzis (ed.) *European Media Governance: National and Regional Dimensions.* Chicago: Intellect Bristol, p. 181-190.

Meier, Werner A. (2010) Media Landscape: Switzerland. In: *European Journalism Centre.* www.ejc.net/ media_landscape/article/switzerland/

Meier, Werner A. et al. (2011) *Pluralismus und Vielfalt in Regionalzeitungen. Auswirkungen von Medienkonzentration und Medienkrise auf die Lokalberichterstattung in ausgewählten Regionen in der Schweiz.* Schlussbericht zuhanden von Bakom. Zürich.

NET-Metrix-Profile 2010/II. www.net-metrix.ch/sites/default/files/files/Report_NMP_2010-2_d.pdf

OECD (2010). Breitbandstatistik Juni 2010. www.oecd.org/document/23/0,3746,en_2649_34225_33987543_1_1_1_1,00.html

SRG SSR idée suisse (2009) Geschäftsbericht 2009.

SRG SSR Marktanteil www.srgssr.ch/de/radio/schweizer-radio-und-fernsehen/

SRG SSR idée suisse (2008) Schwerpunktthema Integration. In SRG SSR idée suisse Update 2/2008, p.1-8.

Strahm, Rudolf (2011) Demokratie ist nicht käuflich. In: *Tages-Anzeiger* 8.2.2011. p. 9.

Verband Schweizer Medien. www.presseabo.ch

WEMF MACH Basic 2010/II

Online references

www.bakom.ch

www.bfs.admin.ch

www.medienkritik-schweiz.ch

www.medienwoche.ch

www.presserat.ch

www.srgssr.ch

Chapter 12

UK

UK News Media and Democracy
Professional Autonomy and its Limits

Peter Humphreys

In Hallin and Mancini's (2004) famous typology the UK corresponds to the 'North Atlantic/Liberal' model, characterized by medium newspaper circulation, a neutral commercial press, internally pluralistic journalism, strong professionalization, non-institutionalized self-regulation, and market domination. However, it is certainly not a straightforward fit. The UK's distinctive institutions of public service broadcasting and externally pluralistic national press contrast with the US media system. Other prominent distinctive features of the UK system have been:

- high professional standards in the 'quality press' but a strong 'downmarket' popular press;

- a lack of deference to the political class;

- weakness of privacy laws;

- strong libel laws, with a 'chilling effect' on press freedom;

- a tradition of weak freedom of information (Humphreys 1996; Humphreys 2009: 198).

UK newspapers have been free, by international standards, from state intervention. Public service broadcasting has been free from politicization. However, market pressures have been a major constraint on news media output. The following analysis is based on desk research of primary and secondary sources. It proved impossible for various reasons to conduct interviews, though one respondent (a former BBC executive) did reply to a survey questionnaire sent to media professionals. The main focus is on the main television corporations and companies (BBC, ITV, Channel 4 and BSkyB) and national newspapers (both 'quality' and 'popular').

Indicators

Freedom / Information (F)

(F1) Geographic distribution of news media availability   3 POINTS

A wide variety of news media is available to UK citizens.

UK news media are widely available. According to industry regulator Ofcom (2009), at the end of March 2009 consumer satisfaction with communications services stood at 89 %. Nine in ten homes had digital television and two-thirds broadband. Multiplatform news delivery was high and there existed no regulatory restrictions on access to online-news. Three digital TV platforms offered a free-to-view service which provided news and current affairs programmes. The BBC's *Freeview* was available via terrestrial TV, while satellite offered two non-subscription options: *Freesat* from ITV/BBC and *Freesat* from Sky. Viewers could choose from different UK television news services with their own distinctive brands (BBC, ITV, Channel 4, C5 and Sky). The three major television news providers (BBC, ITN and Sky News) each provided a 24-hour service as well as peak-time news reports. Strict news and current affairs programming quotas applied across all the UK's designated public service broadcasters – namely, BBC, ITV, C4, C5 and S4C – ensuring that high quality international, national and regional news content was widely available. Ofcom (2009: 111) reported that all the public service broadcasters had mostly exceeded their quotas for news and current affairs programmes over 2004-2008. *Sky News,* a non- public service provider, operated a 24-hour news service that regularly won awards for the quality of its reporting (Royal Television Society awards, BAFTAs, etc.). In 2010, the Audit Bureau of Circulations (ABC) counted no fewer than 28 national newspapers in the UK (seven of these were Scottish and Welsh). The Newspaper Society counted 1,212 regional/local newspapers in January 2010.

(F2) Patterns of news media use (consumption of news)   3 POINTS

Television is the primary source of news, followed by newspapers. The Internet is important, especially for the young for whom it is the prime source. Traditional media are adapting and the BBC website is a particularly important source.

According to a survey conducted by NEMS Market Research for Keynote (2010) 54.3 % of adults cited TV as their main source of news information, 16.5 % cited newspapers, 14.5 % cited the Internet, and 12 % cited radio.[1] Respondents in their late 20s and early 30s used the Internet the most for news gathering and showed lower penetration rates than other age groups for radio and newspapers. The survey found age to be a big factor in newspaper readership, with the young becoming less interested in newspapers and showing a higher propensity to access the Internet for news and entertainment. The survey noted an accelerating decline in newspaper circulation. A worrying trend was that the market for 'quality' newspapers was dropping much faster than the market for 'popular' papers (Keynote 2010). A House of Lords Select Committee on Communication report (2008a: 24-25) identified the reasons for the decline in news viewing and reading as: lifestyle changes, proliferation of television channels, growth of the Internet, and increasing technological opportunities for personal scheduling or non-linear viewing. In order to retain audiences and readerships, newspapers and television news providers are developing a multiplatform presence. The BBC website, the centre-piece of which is news, is the third most used website in the country and the *Guardian* newspaper's website has been recognized as the 'Best Newspaper' online by the international Webby Awards.

(F3)   Diversity of news sources   2 POINTS

Research indicates reliance on official and PR sources of information and strong commercial pressures militating against investigative journalism. Yet there remains a reasonably healthy degree of independent and critical journalism.

How diverse are the *sources* of news? There is growing literature on the 'public relationsalization' of journalism (see e.g. Aeron Davis 2002). In his provocatively titled critique *Flat Earth News*, Nick Davies (2009), an award winning journalist with years of experience of working on UK newspapers and television, reported disturbing findings of research commissioned from the journalism department of Cardiff University. The Cardiff researchers, Lewis et al. (2006: 15-16), found that 30 per cent of stories in the newspapers surveyed – *The Guardian, Independent, Times, Telegraph* and *Daily Mail* – were all from wire services or other media and a further 19 were mainly from wires or other media. However, only 1 % of stories were directly attributable to PA or other wire services. The research also looked at broadcast news items – namely BBC and ITV evening news, and BBC Radio's *World at One* and *Today* programmes – and found their dependence on wires and other media was less. Nonetheless '27 % of [broadcast] news contained material that appeared wholly or mainly derived from wires or other media'. The Cardiff research also found that 'nearly one in five newspaper stories and 17 % of broadcast stories were verifiably derived *mainly* or *wholly* from PR material or activity' (Lewis et al. 2006: 17). Davies (2009) explained this as part of a decline in journalistic standards linked to commercial pressures. Indeed, the Cardiff research (Lewis et al. 2006) provides strong evidence of a link with employment conditions and in particular the drive for journalistic productivity (see C5 below). The House of Lords Select Committee on Communications (2008a: 19-20) has also expressed concern about a general trend among newspapers to cut the numbers of special correspondents and to rely on agency feed and PR (House of Lords 2008a: 19-20).

Despite commercial pressures that militate against quality news and investigative journalism, widely perceived by journalists and academics alike to be in decline, examples abound. Just a few recent cases from the national quality press serve to underline this point. In 2009 *The Guardian*'s Ian Cobain won the Paul Foot award for an investigation into British involvement in the torture of terror suspects detained overseas. Another *Guardian* journalist, Paul Lewis, won the Bevins Prize[2] for his reports about the death of Ian Tomlinson during the G20 riots in London, revealing that he died after being struck from behind by a police officer. Perhaps the biggest recent story was *The Telegraph*'s investigation into how politicians – from cabinet members to backbenchers of all parties – had exploited the system of parliamentary allowances to subsidize their lifestyles and multiple homes.[3] In all these cases, the press impressively performed its democratic watchdog function as a result of the work of journalists searching for evidence and not reliant on agency feed or PR.

(F4)   Internal rules for practice of newsroom democracy   1 POINT

There is little evidence of formal newsroom democracy and research suggests a pattern of strong managerial dominance, particularly in the newspaper sector. However, there are exceptions to this rule.

In the newspaper sector there is no requirement or expectation of impartiality and internal democracy within newsrooms. As elsewhere among liberal capitalist democracies, proprietors and their chief editors determine the philosophical, political, social and cultural perspective of the publications. In his seminal work on Britain's national press, Tunstall (1996)[4] hardly paints a picture of vibrant democracy within newspapers, finding instead that newspaper editors have always wielded 'commanding powers'. Journalists have had little professional defence against editorial power except perhaps during the high tide of trade unionism in the period 1960-80. In the case of the popular tabloid newspapers, the editor would be ubiquitous in the daily operation of the paper. In the case of the quality press, some editors were less hands-on; nonetheless, chief editors typically chose the 'editorial high command'.

An indicator of the degree to which a more limited democracy might flourish within the company is whether or not the paper's journalists have any say in the choice of editors. Thus, the *Guardian*'s editor, Alan Rusbridger had to stand for 'election' for the first stage of the process of his selection. According to his evidence to a parliamentary committee's report on *The Ownership of the News*:

'We did hustings, we set out a manifesto and there was an indicative vote conducted by the Electoral Reform Society, which went to the Scott Trust {the owner of the paper]. I then went through the same process with the Scott Trust along with the other candidates. They saw the vote from the journalists but said they would not consider themselves bound by that and I was appointed by the Scott Trust (House of Lords 2008b: 39).

However, *The Guardian* was exceptional. Normally, chief editors have been chosen in the traditional way by the newspapers' owners. In the case of the *Times* and *Sunday Times* in 1981 the government insisted that there should be safeguards against proprietorial dominance as a condition for their takeover by Rupert Murdoch's *News International*. This included provision for a board of independent directors to approve the appointment of Editors. Nonetheless Robert Thomson, Editor of *The Times*, informed the parliamentary committee inquiry that, when appointed, he had been on 'a short list of one' that the newspaper's proprietor Rupert Murdoch had put to its independent directors (House of Lords 2008b: 48). Not even in the case of the BBC is there any *formal* democracy within the newsroom. However, it is normal practice for there to be editorial meetings and processes that generally encourage participation. There exist clear guidelines on impartiality and there prevails a view that the impartiality of public service broadcasting:

'is best defended through a combination of editorial cultures [in different production teams], public accountability, rules and regulation, and complaints handling, rather than "newsroom democracy"…In addition there is an open culture that means that management attempts to impose a single line – for the wrong reasons – would tend to backfire in adverse public comment' (survey questionnaire response from former BBC executive, July 2010).

(F5) and (F6) Company rules against *internal* and *external* influence on newsroom / editorial staff   2 POINTS EACH

There is little evidence of any direct external influence on the UK media, though general commercial pressures adversely influence the quality of news. The main area of potential direct influence is proprietorial guidance/pressure relayed via the internal management structure, but the actual extent is disputed. The public service broadcasters – and certain newspapers – are free from such pressures.

In *Flat Earth News*, Nick Davies (2009: 14-16) suggests that, contrary to much theorizing about the media, influence by proprietors and commercial interests such as advertisers is limited. He says that '[i]n thirty years in Fleet Street, [he] never came across a case of advertisers influencing an editorial line, directly or indirectly. Nor [could he] find any other journalist who has ever known it to happen'.

Nor do owners interfere with the editorial process of their publications 'in quite the way that outsiders imagine….the new corporate owners interfere far less than their propagandist predecessors', namely the famous press barons of an earlier era. For Davies, it is rather the 'forces of commercialism which now provide the greatest object to truth-telling journalism'. In *Flat Earth News*, he provides a detailed analysis of how the changed conditions of journalistic production, under the pressures of commercialism, have diminished the integrity of news. However, writing in the *Guardian*, Roy Greenslade (2009), another experienced UK journalist (since 2003 professor of journalism at London's City University), suggests that proprietorial intervention, though usually subtle, remains the rule. Greenslade notes 'honourable exceptions' such as the *Independent* newspaper during Tony O'Reilly's eleven year ownership (until 2009)[5], the *Guardian* newspaper, owned by the Scott Trust, and also the *Daily Mail*, whose owner, Lord Rothermere, Greenslade also deems to be a 'hands-off' proprietor. However, he concludes that generally 'the publisher holds the whip hand'. Greenslade suggests that self-censorship and managerial control abounds.

The House of Lords Select Committee on Communications report (volume 1, 2000a: 33) noted that '[i]n all that evidence only one person was willing to admit openly to acting as a "traditional proprietor": Rupert Murdoch' (whose News International owned two of the UK's leading quality papers *The Times* and the *Sunday Times*, as well as its leading popular tabloids the *Sun* and the Sunday *News of the World*). The committee's minutes of a meeting in the US with Rupert Murdoch himself revealed:

> 'Mr Murdoch did not disguise the fact that he is hands on both economically and editorially. He says that "the law" prevents him from instructing the editors of The Times and The Sunday Times….. [but] ….For The Sun and News of the World he explained that he is a "traditional proprietor". He exercises editorial control on major issues—like which Party to back in a general election or policy on Europe. (House of Lords 2008a: 119-120).

When the committee asked former *Sunday Times* and (briefly) *Times* editor, Andrew Neil, whether Rupert Murdoch had honoured the legal requirement to desist from 'instructing' the editors of the *Times* and the *Sunday Times*, this having been a condition for their take-over in 1981, Andrew Neil's response gets to the heart of the matter:

> 'He does not instruct the quality newspaper editors of *The Times* and *The Sunday Times*, but that does not mean to say that he does not have influence and he does not let you know what he thinks…. I was never left in any doubt what he wanted' (House of Lords 2008b: 338).

A couple of editors of leading quality national papers were very forthright about their independence. Simon Kellner, of the *Independent* and *Independent on Sunday*, stated:

> 'With the *Independent* the clue is in the title. What you see in the paper is entirely as a result of our journalism. We do not have proprietorial interference and we do not have allegiance to any political party….The paper is the product of journalism, untainted by any sort of commercial influence or political influence' (House of Lords 2008b: 117-118).

Alan Rusbridger, of *The Guardian*, could point to the undeniable fact that his independence was 'guarded by the [Scott] Trust' – there being no proprietor other than the trust created in 1936 precisely to safeguard the newspaper's values of independent and liberal journalism (House of Lords 2008b: 39).

With regard to broadcast news, the committee concluded that the 'presence of content regulation and impartiality rules limits the kind of influence an owner can have' (House of Lords 2008a: 39). Aside from the impartiality requirement, for the commercial public service broadcasters issues of quantity, scheduling and (in ITV's case) resources devoted to news are regulated by Ofcom, whilst in the BBC's case, news output is monitored by the BBC Trust. As for the third force in UK broadcast news, Sky News, in his interview with the parliamentary committee Murdoch appeared to complain that rather than just the UK's strict impartiality rules, it was more the journalistic standard set by the BBC in the UK's broadcasting culture, that prevented him from transforming Sky News into something more like his US news channel Fox News operation, claiming that one of he reasons that Sky News 'is not a proper alternative to the BBC is that no broadcaster or journalist in the UK knows any different'. He stated that the only reason that Sky News was not more like Fox news was that 'nobody at Sky listens to me' (House of Lords 2008a: 119). This is an argument that has frequently been made about the standard-setting role of the BBC with regard to other UK broadcasters. Andrew Marr, a leading UK political journalist with years of experience working for the BBC, observed: 'In America, Fox News openly avows Rupert Murdoch's politics: but its British cousin Sky News, constrained and influenced by British television culture, does not' (Marr 2005: 306).

(F7)   Procedures on news selection and news processing   2 POINTS

The UK's commercial press functions according to some unwritten and unstated rules of production which can impact negatively on the quality of news. However, there is a marked difference between the popular press, on the one hand, and the quality press and the more regulated television news providers, on the other.

Based on extensive insider experience of the UK news media, Davies (2009: 113-154) has described a set of 'unwritten and unstated rules of production' which determine the quality and content of much news output. The first rule is to 'run cheap stories'. The pressure to keep costs down has served as a disincentive to conduct investigations and an incentive to produce what he terms 'churnalism'[6], second-hand news provided by press agencies and PR services. Another unstated rule encourages journalists to favour safe factual statements, especially those attributable to official sources which carry authority, provide quick copy, and protect journalists against being sued for defamation.[7] Another rule is to extend 'the rule of safe facts to an encouragement of deference to any organisation or individual with the power to hurt news organisations'. Accordingly, media content is determined by 'electric fences' such as the UK's restrictive Official Secrets Act and the 'chilling effect' of UK libel law, widely regarded to have constrained free press reporting.[8] Another rule, that news stories should increase readerships or audiences, has certainly always defined the UK's popular newspapers, but many media commentators and scholars have become concerned that it has spread to the quality media (see e.g. Franklin 1997).

The publicly funded BBC is insulated from direct commercial pressures and the commercial public service broadcasters[9] are strictly regulated. The House of Lords select committee on communications found that each of the latter framed their editorial requirements differently. In line with its statutory remit to cater to minorities, Channel 4 consciously looked for depth, range and perspectives 'not pursued elsewhere' and had a multiculturalist approach.

> '[E]ach news programme had a detailed editorial specification to achieve those aims ....., although the day-today realisation of those aims was up to [Channel 4's news provider] ITN. There was daily contact about the content of particular bulletins and a weekly meeting to discuss forward strategy. It is therefore clear that, while ITN is free to implement Channel 4's news brief according to its own standards of journalistic professionalism and integrity, the overall news agenda and news framework is laid down by Channel 4. The channel, in turn, derives its approach to news from its statutory obligations laid down by the Communications Act 2003' (House of Lords 2008a: 38-9).

For the more commercial ITV, with a lighter public service remit, it was important to be 'accessible without being frivolous', though editorial control remained with the editorial management with ITN and was 'sacrosanct'. For Channel 5, with the lightest public service remit, there was no ambition to do long-form investigative reports, and the channel did not see investigative journalism as its hallmark. The report concluded:

> In all three cases, it is clear that the news requirements are designed to fit in with the culture, branding and general approach of the respective channels (House of Lords 2008a: 39).

Equality / Interest mediation (E)

(E1) Media ownership concentration national level 2 POINTS

There is a quite diverse and highly competitive national news media market, with a range of competing news media. However, ownership is highly concentrated in both the newspaper and the television sector.

At first sight, the UK has a highly competitive broadcasting market. The extensive penetration of multi-channel television means that a large number of news providers are available, including foreign services like CNN, Fox News, Euronews, France 24 and Russia Today. However, news viewing is concentrated. The House of Lords Select Committee on communications (2008a: 23) noted that:

> 'While the choice of news programmes has increased, BBC1 and ITV1 still attract the largest audience shares for news programmes. An analysis of TV news viewing in October 2006 showed that BBC1 had a 50.6 % share, ITV1 had a 26.8 % share, Channel 4 had a 4.5 % share, Five a 2.8 % share and BBC2 a 4.6 % share. BBC News 24 had a 5.2 % chare and Sky News a 4.9 % share.'

Only three UK companies actually produce TV news: the BBC, ITN (which provides ITV and Channel 4) and Sky (which provides its own channel and Five). Regional television news is produced by the BBC and by the Channel 3 licence holders. ITV plc currently owns 11 of the 15 Channel 3 regional licences that compose the ITV network. ITN is 40 % owned by ITV plc, 20 % by Thomson Reuters, 20 % by United Business Media, and 20 % by the major UK press company Daily Mail and General Trust.[10] National radio news is produced by three companies. The BBC produces bulletins for its own channels, and Independent Radio News and Sky News Radio supply the commercial radio sector. ITN has a 20 % share of Independent Radio News. Sky News and Sky News Radio are part of the Murdoch-controlled BSkyB operation.

London plays host to the largest and most competitive national press in Europe. London-based UK national newspapers, rather than local papers, are the main source of national and international news (though the Scottish newspapers also serve this function). The UK national press market is generally characterized as being composed of three categories of newspapers. 'Quality papers', with an 'upmarket' educated middle class readership (just under a quarter of total readership), are the *Guardian*, the *Independent*, the *Daily Telegraph*, and the *Times*, together with their Sunday editions (the *Observer*, in the *Guardian*'s case) and also the *Financial Times*. A much larger readership is shared between the 'midmarket' *Daily Mail* and *Daily Express* and their Sunday editions, catering to a mainly white collar middle class readership (just over a quarter of total readership). The 'downmarket' or 'popular' papers – notably the *Sun*, the *News of the World*, the *People*, the *Mirror* and the *Star* and their Sunday editions – appeal to the remaining largely lower middle and working class readership (they account for about half of the total readership). Although highly competitive, with a range of titles that allows for considerable diversity of style and a partisan range of political and social orientations (the external pluralism noted by Hallin and Mancini as being exceptional for the North Atlantic/Liberal model), ownership of the UK national press is highly concentrated (by the CR3 measure, C = 73).[11]

Table 1. National Newspaper Ownership in 2010

Group	Market Share	Titles	Executive Control
News International	35.1 %	Sun, Times, Sunday Times, News of the World	Murdoch family
Daily Mail & General Trust	22.2 %	Daily Mail, Mail on Sunday	Viscount Rothermere
Trinity Mirror	15.7 %	Daily Mirror, Sunday Mirror, People	Victor Blank
Northern & Shell	12.9 %	Daily Express, Daily Star, Sunday Express, Star on Sunday	Richard Desmond
Telegraph Group	6.7 %	Daily Telegraph, Sunday Telegraph	Barclay brothers
Guardian Media Group	3.5 %	Guardian, Observer	Scott Trust
Pearson	2.1 %	Financial Times	Pearson board
Independent Print Ltd.	1.8 %	Independent, Independent on Sunday	Alexander Lebedev

Note: As the book went to press in July 2011, News of the World was closed down by News Corporation in the wake of a scandal over illegal phone-hacking.

Source: Data from Keynote 2010.

The principal instance of diagonal ownership concentration in the UK is that of News International, the UK subsidiary of the global media corporation News Corporation (in which Rupert Murdoch's family is the controlling shareholder). As seen, News International owns a number of UK national newspapers, with a combined readership market share of 35 % in 2010. *New Corporation* also controls (through a 37 % share) the UK's most important pay-TV platform, *BSkyB*. BSkyB also had a 17.9 % share in ITV plc, though it has been compelled on competition grounds to reduce this to 7.5 %.

(E2) Media ownership concentration regional (local) level　　1 POINT

Local media markets are much less competitive than at the national level; local newspaper monopolies are the rule (not counting free papers). Ownership of the UK regional/local press is concentrated.

The UK regional press is far less competitive than the national market; indeed, local newspaper monopolies are the norm (if free papers are discounted). According to Keynote (2010) the top ten regional newspaper publishers in January 2010 were:

Table 2. Top 10 regional newspaper publishers in 2010

Rank	Publisher Group	No. of titles	Weekly circulation
1	Trinity Media	134	9,581,662
2	Johnstone Press	284	7,949,205
3	Newsquest Media Group	191	7,148,470
4	Northcliffe Media (part of the Daily Express group)	129	6,609,588
5	Associated Newspapers (part of the Daily Mail group)	1	3,672,810
6	Archant	62	1,971,219
7	Guardian Media Group	40	1,968,117
8	DC Thomson & Company	6	1,729,691
9	The Midlands News Association	17	1,723,353
10	Tindle Newspaper	68	1,252,984

Source: Data from Keynote 2010.[12]

The continuing long-term trend was for the sector to become even more concentrated. In February 2009, Guardian Media Group sold its regional newspapers – except for two in Surrey – to Trinity Mirror PLC.

(E3) Diversity of formats   3 POINTS

There is a healthy diversity of news media formats.

There is a healthy diversity of news formats in the UK media. The quality, mid-market and popular press present the news in a range of vernacular, thereby engaging a broad public, though mostly the already politically interested, in political and social issues (see Norris 2003). That diverse news formats are at least accessible cannot be in question. Most UK households have access to a choice of rolling 24 news channels, foreign news channels (most UK homes are now multi-channel homes) and online-outlets. All leading UK broadcasters and newspapers provide online news. There is a diverse range of news and current affairs content.

(E4) Minority / Alternative media   3 POINTS

There is a wide range of alternative and minority media, though their needs are not so well catered for in mainstream media.

Media 08, the Guardian's media directory (2008)[13], listed no fewer than 77 UK minority press outlets, catering to the UK's rich multicultural diversity. This included numerous titles for the numerous British ethnic minorities and religious minorities. Through non-terrestrial channels these communities were also able to access a range of programming that featured culture, heritage, news and language associated with their ethnic background (Ofcom 2007). The MediaWise website links to a sizeable number of alternative media websites.[14] However, there is argument about how well minority needs are catered for by the mainstream media, and indeed about the need for special programming for them. In 2010, the BBC announced the closure of its Asian programmes unit, saying 'departments catering specifically for particular minority groups are no longer required' because the representation of different communities had become an integral part of its commissioning process. The BBC, however, still produces the BBC Asian Network and the black music radio station 1Xtra.[15] Lastly, in this context, it is noteworthy that national minority languages within the UK have been catered for, notably by S4C, the Welsh TV channel established in 1982 and by government subsidies for Gaelic programming in Scotland and Northern Ireland; the 2003 Communications Act provided for the establishment of a Gaelic Media Service, which launched in 2008 under the operating name MG ALBA, funded by the Scottish government.

(E5) Affordable public and private news media   3 POINTS

The UK news media are reasonably affordable.

UK media are generally affordable. UK popular tabloid newspapers are cheap. The UK national quality papers all cost a £1:00, the Sunday papers around £2:00, still less than a cup of coffee. So far only the *Times* and *Sunday Times* website have introduced 'paywalls' for their web content, charging £1:00 per day or £2:00 for a week's access to its content online. The household television licence fee stands at £145.50 per annum for a colour TV (paid per household rather than TV set). This is about 40p per day (per household). Moreover, this grants access to multi-channel television, including the contract-free, subscription-free *Freeview/Freesat* services. Pay-TV is, of course, more expensive and the cost depends on the package (films and sport put the price up). The two main pay-TV operators are BSkyB (satellite) and Virgin Media (cable). Ofcom (2000: 17) reports that 'UK households' average spend on communications (including telephone, broadcasting, Internet) was £93.69 a month, down £4.39 on 2007. Spend on communications services accounted for 4.63 % of total monthly household outgoings, down from 4.8 % a year earlier.

(E6) Content monitoring instrument   2 POINTS

There is no public body dedicated to news monitoring, but the operation of the UK news media is subject to the scrutiny of parliamentary committees.

The media's regulatory bodies aside, there is no dedicated public news monitoring instrument. However, a number of media monitoring organizations subject the news media to critical scrutiny (see CI below). Moreover, two parliamentary institutions hold the media and media policy accountable, the House of Commons Culture, Media and Sports Committee and the House of Lords Select Committee on Communications, both of which have a cross-party membership. Recently, the House of Commons Culture, Media and Report Committee (2010) produced a report on press standards, privacy and libel, which is quite critical and suggests some important reform measures. The House of Lords Select Committee on Communications (2008a and 2008b) conducted a probing inquiry into the quality of UK news media and produced a comprehensive and revealing snapshot of the current state of the UK news media's industry structure. The report includes perspectives from all sides in the debate about the quality of news output. This can be taken as evidence of a system that is democratically accountable and transparent (both reports are posted on the web).

(E7) Code of ethics at the national level (structure)   2 POINTS

The public service broadcasters have comprehensive ethical guidelines and there exists a code of ethics for the commercial press sector, which however is not backed up by strong enforcement powers.

There is no shortage of detailed guidelines about journalistic standards and ethics. The BBC has a comprehensive set of Editorial Guidelines (230 pages long!), outlining the standards the BBC expects of all BBC content on TV, radio and online.[16] The Guidelines contain sections on the BBC's editorial values, accuracy, impartiality and diversity of opinion, fairness, privacy, harm and offence, and a host of other matters, including the reporting of war and terror.[17] Ofcom, the regulator of all UK licensed private television providers, also implements a Broadcasting Code (109 pages long), serving the same purposes.[18] UK newspapers are signed up to the editorial code of the Press Complaints Commission (PCC), an industry funded body whose board is composed of 10 lay members and seven editors. The PCC operates a Code of Practice for journalists and deals with complaints from members of the public. Complaints are adjudicated by reference to its Code of Practice. The Code is written and revised by the Editors' Code Committee, composed of editors of national, regional and local newspapers and the Chairman and Director of the PCC. The Code consists of 16 clauses, which include provisions on accuracy, opportunity to reply, privacy, the use of clandestine devices and subterfuge, discrimination, financial journalism, and the protection of confidential sources. However, the Code is not binding in law and judges are not obliged to take account of PCC adjudications. Nor does the PCC have the power to issue fines or punish other than public 'naming and shaming'. The National Union of Journalists also has an Ethics Council and Code, which sets out the principles of responsible independent journalism, and all journalists have to agree to uphold its terms when they join the union. Unlike the PCC Code, the NUJ code includes a "conscience clause" which states that journalist have a right to refuse work that would break the letter or spirit of the code. It states: "The NUJ will fully support any journalist disciplined for asserting her/his right to act according to the code."

(E8)   Level of self-regulation (performance) 2 POINTS

The effectiveness of self-regulation of the press has long been a matter of public controversy, notably with regard to the popular press's excesses regarding accuracy of reporting and invasion of privacy. Self-regulation is widely seen as having functioned much better in the case of the quality press and the BBC (the commercial broadcasters are subject to external regulation).

Accounts vary as to the effectiveness of UK press self-regulation. There has always been criticism. Periodically there have been official inquiries and critical reports. In 2007 a parliamentary report concluded that self-regulation continued to be the best way to maintain press standards while ensuring freedom of the press. Statutory regulation, it argued, 'is a hallmark of authoritarianism and risks undermining democracy' (House of Commons 2007). Supporters of the PCC claim that it sets a standard and acts as a deterrent. The most recent House of Commons Media, Culture and Sport committee report (2010: 118) observed that 'voices from inside the industry, including editors, journalists and media lawyers, generally supported the PCC and saw little or no need for change'. However, the same report noted that 'in the evidence presented to our inquiry, the general effectiveness of the PCC has been repeatedly called into question'. Concern had been voiced by media lawyers, independent organizations like The Media Standards Trust, the Campaign for Broadcasting Freedom, the National Union of Journalists, some journalists and editors, and media commentators. The report recommended that the PCC's powers be enhanced, that PCC membership be rebalanced to give the lay members a two thirds majority, and that practising journalists be invited to serve on the PCC's Committees'.

Some newspapers do go further than the PCC guidelines. For example, the *Guardian* and its Sunday stable-mate *The Observer* have their own editorial codes and readers' editors – journalists who listen to the complaints and concerns of the audience and act on their behalf, correcting errors and writing columns on the papers' journalism. *The Guardian*'s reader's editor reportedly handled 14,435 communications and published 664 corrections in the paper in the seven months ending May 2010. Stephen Pritchard, reader's editor of the Observer, handled more than 10,000 complaints in 2009, and was also President of the Organisation of News Ombudsmen (ONO) (*The Guardian* 2010). At the time of writing, the ONO's website did not list any other UK members other than the reader's editors of the *Guardian* and the *Observer*.[19] Other newspapers do respond to complaints, though. *The Times*, too, has rigorous procedures for responding to reader's queries and complaints (House of Commons 2008b: 54).

As noted, the broadcasting codes are more comprehensive. They also have the backing of law. Thus, Harcup (2007: 117) observes: 'the contrast with the cosier world of print self-regulation can be seen as soon as you go onto the Ofcom website and browse the adjudications on complaints about broadcasters' (p. 117). The BBC, too, has an impressive Complaints Homepage on its website where it posts regular reports on the main themes in all complaints received monthly, those complaints referred to the Editorial Complaints Unit, and any appeals to the BBC Trust.[20]

(E9) Participation   2 POINTS

Traditionally UK news media have operated in a top-down manner, but recent years have seen a considerable expansion of participatory developments and the Internet has had a major impact in this respect.

As in other areas of journalistic standards, the BBC has pioneered interesting formats for providing audience participation in high quality news and current affairs debate in both radio and television. Its weekly flagship television programme *Question Time* is a good example. The 'public' contribute by putting questions to a range of panellists who represent broadly right, left and centre political positions. In McNair's (1995: 75-6) view:

> 'Here, one might argue, the liberal democratic role of broadcasting is found in its purest form, *mediating* between the public and the politicians, providing the former with access to raw political discourse, and providing the politicians with a channel of direct access to the people.'

The BBC has also been front-runner in adopting new technologies. The programme's webpage invites the public to 'join the Question Time audience' and provides an application form.[21] The general public can also participate in the debate during the programme by sending text messages, emails and most recently messages on Twitter. The programme is also publicly available on the BBC's online download service.

Generally, the BBC website has set a high standard for employing the new media in the cause of interaction with the public and encouraging participation. The BBC's website devotes considerable space to user-generated content, online postings, various BBC outreach initiatives, and editors' blogs. In the words of one informed expert: at the BBC 'public engagement and openness are taken more seriously than ever' (survey questionnaire response from former BBC executive, July 2010). All leading UK news media providers now have sophisticated websites and make provision for online blogs in the cause of interaction with their audiences and readerships. The *Guardian* has repeatedly been deemed best online newspaper at the internationally Webby awards.[22]

(E10)   Rules and practices on internal pluralism   2 POINTS

UK newspapers are not bound by internal pluralism rules. Though they do practice a degree of internal pluralism, most have a distinct political, social and cultural orientation. The public service broadcasters are bound by regulation to provide internal pluralism, and all UK news broadcasters are bound by an impartiality rule.

One of the unwritten newsroom rules identified by Davies as determining the content of the news (see F7 above) is: 'always give both sides of the story'. The UK news media – certainly television and quality press – are generally serious about practising a degree of internal pluralism and giving space to a reasonably diverse range of different viewpoints. Rather than an absence of an internal pluralism of at least mainstream debate in the UK news media, criticism has always focused on the marginalization of minority and 'alternative' perspectives (Harcup 2007). Recently, there has been criticism of the transformation of newspapers into 'viewspapers', a trend towards blurring of the line between news and views (House of Lords 2008a: 18). Further, there is a concern about a trend towards a 'softer news agenda' (for a consummate critical academic study on this theme, see Franklin 1997).

Control / Watchdog (C)

(C1)   Supervising the watchdog 'control of the controllers'   2 POINTS

The UK media are subject to considerable scrutiny by official regulators and civil society media monitoring organizations, but there is little involvement on the part of the general public.

The UK news media are subject to a quite impressive number of mechanisms that control their performance and there is considerable lively discussion of the media's watchdog function, though this is more a matter for the concerned elites than the general public. Aside from 'official regulators', notably the BBC Trust, Ofcom, and the Press Complaints Commission, the first two of which can be considered to be very creditable regulators, there exist a number of 'non-official' media monitoring organizations. The Voice of the Listener and Viewer (VLV) is an independent, not-for-profit society focused on ensuring independence, quality and diversity in broadcasting.[23] Aligned with media unions, the Campaign for Press and Broadcasting Freedom (CPBF) has monitored the media industry and campaigned for diverse, democratic and accountable media since it was founded in 1979.[24] Yet another monitoring and campaigning organization is MediaWise (formerly PressWise), an independent charity, established in 1993 and supported by concerned journalists, media lawyers and politicians in the UK, which professes to 'operate on the principle that press freedom is a responsibility exercised by journalists on behalf of the public, and that the public have a right to know when the media publish inaccurate information'.[25] Significantly, the Media Standards Trust, an independent charity that exists specifically to promote high standards in news, has recently established a website called 'churnalism.com'[26] designed to identify news based on press releases and thereby help the public distinguish between journalism and 'churnalism' (see F3).[27]

(C2) Independence of the news media from power holders   3 POINTS

The UK news media enjoy a high degree of independence from political power holders.

The BBC is bound by its Royal Charter (DCMS 2006) to be 'independent in all matters concerning the content of its output, the times and manner in which this is supplied, and in the management of its affairs.' It is widely recognized that the BBC has enjoyed, by international standards, an outstanding degree of independence from government. Scholars have pointed to how the BBC's governors, now the BBC Trust, have characteristically served as a buffer between the Corporation and governments. Though appointed by government, they have tended to act as 'trustees of the public interest' in a politically independent manner. Of course, there have been times when the limits to the BBC's governor's independence have been exposed. As one former BBC insider has summarized: 'The BBC is very independent. However, as with any publicly funded body accountability and the requirement for impartiality can act as a limitation on absolute independence' (survey questionnaire response from former BBC executive, July 2010).

The BBC has set the standard for other news media. Channel 4 News is widely regarded as excellent, for instance considered by a recent study to have outperformed the BBC in independent reporting of the 2003 Iraq War (Robinson et al. 2010). As mentioned, there can be little doubt that the standard established by the BBC part-explains the high quality and independence of the non-public-service *Sky News*, which has also collected its share of Television awards. Of course *Sky News*' independence *vis-á-vis* political power holders is also underpinned by its commercial freedom. The same applies to the UK press, which receives no subsidies (apart from exemption from value-added-tax), so governments have never had this particular potential lever for political pressure. Finally with regard to independence, UK journalists are not only lacking in deference to politicians, they have in the view of one controversial account actually pursued their cynicism and 'attack journalism' so far that they have undermined respect for politicians and damaged British politics (Lloyd 2004).

(C3)   Transparency of data on media system   2 POINTS

There is a fairly high degree of transparency of data on the UK media.

On this measure, the UK scores quite well. The BBC is committed to transparency and accountability and its website bears testimony to this. Ofcom, too, has an excellent website and produces a wealth of data on UK communications sector, including biennially a very comprehensive Communications Market Report (with less detailed annual interim reports). Data on newspaper circulations is published by the Audit Bureau of Circulations (ABC), data on television audiences by the Broadcasters' Audience Research Board (Barb), and data on radio audiences by Radio Joint Audience Research (Rajar), all of which have websites which make core data available on a cost-fee basis. However, there could be more transparency with regard to measuring and informing the public about media ownership and control and the commercial interests of news media.

(C4)   Journalist professionalism   2 POINTS

There is a highly professional journalistic culture in the broadcasting sector, with the BBC setting a high standard. In the press sector the picture is mixed.

UK public service broadcasting has always displayed strong characteristics of professionalism, defined in terms of collective identity and organization, journalistic autonomy, distinct professional norms, and professional training. The BBC fostered a strong ethos of journalistic autonomy and established a high public service quality standard which was emulated by ITV during the duopoly era, and later by the other commercial public service broadcasters Channels 4 and 5, and – as noted – also the non-public service Sky News. When discussing journalistic professionalism, the example set by the BBC in promoting quality journalism that serves the public interest cannot be over-emphasized. The managing editor of the award-winning *Guardian* quality newspaper has pointed to the standard setting role of the BBC: 'We have to be aggressive and cover more things in creative ways because we aren't just competing with other newspapers, we are competing with the BBC that is serious about journalism' (Chris Elliott, cited in McChesney & Nichols 2010: 162). The UK broadcasting industry at large displays strong signs of professional identity, organization and norms, promoted by institutions like the Royal Television Society,[28] the British Academy of Film and Television Arts (BAFTA)[29] and the annual MediaGuardian Edinburgh International Television Festival. The sector also is also strongly unionized in the shape of the Broadcasting, Entertainment, Cinematograph and Theatre Union (BECTU), which represents those working in broadcasting, film, theatre, entertainment, leisure, interactive media and allied areas.[30]

In the press sector, professionalism has weaker roots. For a long time, there was an element of truth in the old adage that newspaper journalism was a 'trade' not a profession. The route into Fleet Street was through 'learning on the job' in a provincial newspaper and/or having privileged contacts. However, a profound change has occurred. Nowadays, overwhelmingly entrants to newspaper journalism are openly competitively recruited and university educated, often with postgraduate qualifications in journalism. Training is ubiquitous and multimedia skills are *de rigeur* (see C8 below). However, this stride towards professionalization has been countered by a marked increase in workload pressures (C5), a decline in job security, and a relative decline in the unions' ability to stand up to management. Since the 1980s, in broadcasting too (even the BBC), there has occurred a rise in the numbers of workers on freelance and short-term contracts. This 'casualization' trend, it is reasonably argued, has diminished journalistic autonomy and militated against professionalism.

(C5) Journalist's job security

1 POINT

The overall stability of employment levels disguises the fact that journalists operating in a climate of employment insecurity and casualization (short term contracts, freelancing, etc.) have faced markedly increased productivity pressures, which is bound to impact on quality.

As Lewis et al. (2006) have observed, data about employment within the UK media are 'notoriously difficult to gather'. Nonetheless, drawing on annual accounts filed at Companies House for national newspaper groups between 1985-2004, the Cardiff University researchers have drawn a detailed picture of employment, workload and commercial pressures in the UK national press. The sector saw a decline in total numbers of employees from over 4000 in 1985 to less than a quarter of that in 1990, since when the figure has remained more or less stable. This reflected largely the impact of new production techniques and the laying off of large numbers of print-workers. However, the figures for editorial employees remained stable through the period: the national press had 786 editorial employees in 1985, and 741 in 2004. The Cardiff team also discovered that national newspapers had generally retained fairly healthy levels of turnover and profits during the twenty-year period, though the aggregate figures hid a variety of performances both between years and across newspaper groups. In general, the popular 'tabloid' groups 'demonstrated the most consistent and highest levels of profitability', the most lucrative titles being the News International (Murdoch controlled) titles *The Sun* and the *News of the World*.

The Cardiff researchers show how this 'fairly rosy picture' disguised a significant increase in journalistic productivity, measured in terms of pagination over the period 1985-2006. By the end of this period, national newspapers had, on average, two and half times as many pages as twenty years earlier. Whilst

'the *proportion* of total newspaper content taken up by advertising ha[d] actually fallen slightly.....*the average number of editorial/news pages across national newspapers had almost tripled*, rising from a 14.6 page average in 1985 to 41 pages by 2006' (p. 11).

Their quantitative research was backed up by qualitative research (interviews with journalists), from which they concluded that journalists were required to 'do more with less time, a trend that inevitably increases their dependence on "ready made" news [see F3 above] and limits the opportunities for independent journalism' (p. 3).

The employment situation has certainly worsened since 2006 because of the impact of an advertising recession, competition from the Internet, declining circulations, and most lately, the financial crisis – the impact of the resultant productivity pressures can only be assumed to be becoming even more negative. The degree of legal protection for journalists' job security is no greater than it is for any other employee, whose rights are protected by the UK's general labour law. There is no UK *clause de conscience* law for journalists. Moreover, a National Union of Journalists report (NUJ 2007) complained that the UK 'media industry ha[d] gone through a long period of increasing casualisation leading to greater insecurity of employment'.

(C6) Practice of access to information   2 POINTS

Until recently the UK would have scored low on this criterion (1) but the enactment of Freedom of Information legislation in 2000 has significantly improved access to information.

Until recently the UK would have scored rather lower than a number of other western European democracies with regard to this criterion of democracy (Humphreys

1996: 53-57). However, in 2000 a Freedom of Information Act was enacted which finally came into force in 2005. Its considerable effectiveness has been summarized by a 2008 report of the Campaign for Freedom of Information. The report itemized 1000 stories, published in national and regional papers in England, Scotland, Wales and Northern Ireland during 2006 and 2007, based on Freedom of Information disclosures made upon the request (mainly) of journalists. They included significant disclosures about the Iraq conflict and innumerable reports about high expenses claims and dubious public spending (Campaign for Freedom of Information 2008). It is also noteworthy that the UK hosts a number of active campaigning organizations committed to freedom of information and expression, such as the Campaign for Freedom of Information,[31] the *Index on Censorship*,[32] and Article 19.[33]

(C7) The watchdog and the media's mission statement   2 POINTS

The public service broadcasters score highly on this criterion, and so do the Guardian Media Group and the Guardian quality newspaper. However, in the newspaper sector at large mission statements (beyond the pithy) are not evident.

The media's watchdog role is only implicit in mission statements or what might be taken as such. Thus, the BBC specifies its mission as being 'to enrich people's lives with programmes and services that inform, educate and entertain'.[34] The 2007 Royal Charter states that the Corporation exists to serve the public interest and to promote its public purposes, which are: sustaining citizenship and civil society; promoting education and learning; stimulating creativity and cultural excellence; representing the UK, its nations, regions and communities; bringing the UK to the world and the world to the UK; and helping to deliver to the public the benefit of emerging communications technologies and services and, in addition, taking a leading role in the switchover to digital television.[35] Ultimately, it is a task of the BBC Trust to ensure fulfilment of these purposes.

The remits of the commercial public service broadcasters are statutory and detailed in broadcasting laws as well as posted on their websites. Thus, Channel Four's special public service remit is laid out in the statement of programme policy, attached to its licence. It specifies that C4 should 'foster the new and experimental in television… [and] encourage pluralism, provide a favoured place for the untried and encourage innovation in style content perspective and talent on and off screen'. Among C4's promises is the aim to 'reflect the diversity of Britain; culturally and geographically… [and]…reflect the energy of our multicultural society, by representing the voices of a new generation of programme makers from the ethnic minorities'.[36]

The Guardian Media Group (GMG) also has a clear mission statement, which reflects the public service values of the *Manchester Guardian*, a newspaper 'created to support social reform in the early 19th century'. These values, 'honesty, cleanness (now interpreted as integrity), courage, fairness, [and] a sense of duty to the reader and the community' are promoted by the GMG's owner, the Scott Trust, in the 'business conduct and the editorial content of [its] newspapers, websites and other media'.[37] Innovatively, the *Guardian* newspaper has gone a step further by launching a 'sustainability vision' with a commitment to 'to play our part as a leading media organisation in creating a fair society that lives within the means of our planet'[38].

All these mission statements reflect the particular journalistic orientation and principles that, by and large, the respective media organizations have respected. However, such public expressions of a detailed journalistic remit appear to be a comparative rarity for the commercial news media. Website home-pages and annual reports provide some guidance, featuring ethical commitments concerning corporate governance and social responsibility (e.g. working with the community, commitment to good working practices, etc.).[39] However, such statements about the precise journalistic mission as can be found tend to be pithy. Thus, the Daily Mail and General Trust website announces that it is about '[e]mpowering people through information'[40]. The *Independent* newspaper proclaims that it is 'free from party-political ties' and 'free from proprietorial influence' directly beneath its title banner on its front page, which is certainly as bold a statement of its independent ethos as could be imagined. Beyond question, UK newspapers have distinct, established brands, which can embody a certain sense of mission. *The Times*, for instance, has traditionally seen itself – and been widely seen – as a 'newspaper of record', with the mission to be 'objective above all' (*The Times* editor Robert Thomson cited in House of Commons Select Committee on Communication 2008b: 49).

(C8)   Professional training   3 POINTS

Professional training has always been good in the broadcasting sector, not least because of the BBC. The situation in the press sector has undergone a marked professionalization. Most UK journalists nowadays have degrees and on the job training opportunities appear to be prevalent.

Precise data about journalism training are not easy to assemble. One detailed report was published by the Journalism Training Forum (2002) based on research by the publishing sector's National Training Organisation (NTO) and its broadcasting sector counterpart Skillset. The report was based on an extensive survey of UK journalists, responding to a comprehensive range of questions about their individual experiences of working in the UK press and broadcasting industries.[41] The report included illuminating sections on journalists' backgrounds, qualification levels, working conditions, contractual status, and the like. It also contained a section on their skills, needs and learning opportunities. This section found that the majority of the practising journalists (76 %) had undertaken some learning activities in the previous year; in the majority of cases this training related to the development of professional skills; and in two thirds of the cases the training was paid for by an employer. Over half believed that news skills were needed, these being largely core journalistic skills, new media competences and some legal training. 58 % stated that their employers had been very or fairly helpful, whilst 34 % disagreed (Journalism Training Forum 2002: 49).

The report indicated the highly educated quality of UK journalists, in contrast to an earlier era of 'learning on the job'. A remarkable 98 % of the respondents had a degree or postgraduate qualification; nearly half of them had a postgraduate qualification, usually in journalism from universities with reputed journalism courses such as Cardiff and City University London. According to a sample analysis carried out for the Guardian (Wilby 2008)

'nearly half of the postgraduate students in City University's journalism school, still one of the main gateways to Fleet Street [the collective term for the UK's national newspapers] and the BBC, come from just four [elite] universities: Oxford, Bristol, Leeds and Cambridge'.

In some regards this is a sign of professionalization. However, as Wilby (2008) remarks it is also indicative of a 'narrow social and ethnic base' (this is, of course, not a new phenomenon.). There is a growing awareness of this bias, and there have been attempts to remedy the situation. Wilby (2008) notes that the National Council for the Training of Journalists (NCTJ), has had a journalism diversity fund since 2005.[42]

As regards the broadcasting sector, it should be noted that the BBC has always played a special role as a training organization. Within the BBC there is a 'very strong sense of journalistic professionalism' and since the Hutton report 'there has been an increased focus on training in the BBC. The BBC College of Journalism website[43] is an example' (survey questionnaire response from former BBC executive, July 2010).

(C9) Watchdog function and financial resources 2 POINTS

Financial constraints in a highly competitive commercialized sector have constrained the UK media's ability optimally to perform its democratic watchdog function, yet investigative journalism has benefited from leaked information and the recent enactment of freedom of information legislation.

As already described, there is growing concern that economic pressures, such as the drive for productivity, and the laying off of editorial staff, are having an adverse affect on news journalism. Studies have indicated a marked increase in workload pressures (C5) and a decline in job security – even at the BBC. Since the 1980s, there has occurred a rise in the numbers of workers on freelance and short-term contracts. This 'casualization' trend, it is reasonably argued, has diminished journalistic autonomy and militated against professionalism. The voices of concern range from critical journalists like Nick Davies, author of *Flat Earth News* (2009), to academics like Bob Franklin, author of *Newszak and News Media* (1997), to the House of Lords Select Committee on Communications (2008a and 2000b). The employment situation has certainly worsened since 2006 because of the impact of an advertising recession, competition from the Internet, rapidly declining newspaper circulations, and most lately, the financial crisis – the impact of these pressures can only be assumed to be becoming even more negative. As noted, even the BBC has cut staff and increased its reliance on contract staff, though '[f]rom the perspective of any UK commercially funded organisation the BBC is still extremely well resourced…BBC journalists are in practice more secure than most commercial colleagues in the UK. There are short term contracts, but generally the contracts and terms and conditions are better than elsewhere' (survey questionnaire response from former BBC executive, July 2010).

Nonetheless, it would be false to conclude that the UK news media no longer fulfil their watchdog function. The above account shows that there still exists a reasonably diverse range of high quality news organizations in the UK, staffed by journalists who do not display deference to the political class. In the UK political scandals have always made for good press; admittedly much reporting has been trivial tabloid style material, but there have been a number of recent examples of public interest exposure of serious malpractice as well, which has resulted from leaked information (by 'whistleblowers') and also a much improved freedom of information climate. The report by the Campaign for Freedom of Information (2008) cited in C6 (above) lists an extensive catalogue of how freedom of information legislation has supported the news media's continued fulfilment of their watchdog function in the UK.

Conclusion

To conclude, the professional quality of broadcast news and current affairs has undoubtedly made an important contribution to the cause of healthy democracy in the UK. It has been argued herein that the standard setting role of the BBC has been particularly significant. The institutional cultures of other news media, newspapers as well as broadcast media, have been strongly influenced by standards established by the BBC. Broadcasting policy and regulation have also played an important role; for instance, the special 'alternative' remit of Channel 4 has fostered a culture of independent reporting. Along with the BBC example, the regulatory impartiality requirement helps explain why Sky News has not become Fox News. Despite concentration, the highly competitive nature of the UK national press market, combined with a healthy degree of professional autonomy and a partisan culture, makes for a relatively plural pattern of news and current affairs reporting, clearly evident surrounding the 2003 Iraq war when a range of pro- and anti-war – therefore, pro- and anti-government policy – stances were reflected (Robinson et al. 2010). The key weakness of the UK news media would appear to be the negative effects on the quality of day-to-day news that arise from commercial pressures (Franklin 1997; Lewis et al. 2006; Davies 2009). The economic challenges facing traditional media, in particular the quality press and the local press (whose markets are conspicuously uncompetitive), but also public service broadcasting in an increasingly marketized environment, are a major cause for concern. Here the 'North Atlantic/Liberal' bias against intervention in markets, which – alongside the BBC – has undoubtedly helped underpin the political independence of the UK news media, is a double-edged sword.

Notes

[1] NEMS Market Research surveyed 1,000 adults across the UK regarding their buying habits and attitudes of adults towards newspapers, magazines and books in the 12 months preceding February 2010.

[2] The Bevins Prize is awarded for investigative journalism by a trust established to honour Anthony Bevins, the leading political journalist who worked for a wide range of newspapers during his career. See: http://www.bevinsprize.org/index.html

[3] See: http://www.telegraph.co.uk/news/newstopics/mps-expenses/

[4] For which he interviewed 217 newspaper journalists and executives during the 1990s, as well as drawing on earlier interview-based studies.

[5] The *Independent* announces itself directly under its title banner as being 'free from party-political ties/ free from proprietorial influence'.

[6] A leading UK media scholar, Bob Franklin, has coined the terms 'Newszak' (Franklin 1997) and 'McJournalism' (Franklin 2005), to describe much of this kind of news content.

[7] It should be noted that this bias towards official news is by no means a UK phenomenon. There is a large academic literature on the dependence of news media on official sources.

[8] London has become a major venue for 'libel tourism' because UK libel law favours the plaintiff and does not grant legal aid. If the plaintiff is rich and powerful it can serve as a powerful deterrent for cost conscious media organizations.

[9] As ITV, Channel 4 and Channel 5 are referred to in official media policy discourse.

[10] See: http://corporate.itn.co.uk/about-itn/board-of-directors.aspx – Accessed July 2010.

[11] According to the commonly used CR3 indicator, C3 is the sum of three largest market shares where 0-35: low concentration, 36-55: moderate concentration and 56+: high concentration.

[12] Keynote's sources were The Newspaper Society, based on figures supplied by the Audit Bureau of Circulations, Verified Free Distribution and independent audits.

[13] Unfortunately, this appears to be the last in a series of this very useful publication.

[14] See: http://www.mediawise.org.uk/display_page.php?id=320 – Accessed July 2010.

[15] Haroon Siddique 'Minority report: The media has never been more alive to minority issues. But does that mean there is no longer a need to cater specifically for niche groups?' *The Guardian*, see: http://www.guardian.co.uk/media-diversity/minority-report. Accessed 14.01.2011.

[16] http://www.bbc.co.uk/guidelines/editorialguidelines/ – accessed July 2010.

[17] The BBC also has a set of guidelines specifically regarding financial journalism. See http://www.bbc.co.uk/guidelines/editorialguidelines/assets/advice/financial_journalism.pdf

[18] http://stakeholders.ofcom.org.uk/binaries/broadcast/code09/bcode.pdf – accessed July 2010.

[19] http://www.newsombudsmen.org/regmem.htm#gb – Accessed July 2010.

[20] http://www.bbc.co.uk/complaints/homepage/

21 http://news.bbc.co.uk/1/hi/programmes/question_time/1858613.stm –
22 See: http://www.guardian.co.uk/media/2009/may/05/guardian-wins-three-webby-awards – Accessed February 2011.
23 See: http://www.vlv.org.uk/ .
24 See: http://www.cpbf.org
25 See: http://www.mediawise.org.uk/display_page.php?id=83 – Accessed July 2010.
26 See: http://churnalism.com/
27 See: http://mediastandardstrust.org/
28 See: http://www.rts.org.uk/
29 See: http://www.bafta.org/
30 See: http://www.bectu.org.uk/about
31 See: http://www.cfoi.org.uk/
32 See: http://www.indexoncensorship.org/
33 See: http://www.article19.org/ – Accessed July 2010.
34 See: http://www.bbc.co.uk/aboutthebbc/purpose/
35 The Charter can be found at: http://www.bbc.co.uk/bbctrust/assets/files/pdf/about/how_we_govern/charter.pdf
36 See: http://www.channel4.com/about_c4/promises_2001/promises_intro2.html
37 See: http://www.gmgplc.co.uk/Responsibility/tabid/132/Default.aspx
38 See: http://www.gmgannualreview2010.co.uk/files/sustainability/GMG_Sustainability.pdf
39 News Corporation, for instance, has a detailed set of guidelines regarding corporate governance. The DMGT has a statement on corporate responsibility.
40 See: http://www.dmgt.co.uk/about-dmgt – accessed July 2010
41 Some 10,737 questionnaires were mailed out. In total, 1,238 completed and usable questionnaires were returned (Journalism Training Forum 2002: 12)
42 The NCTJ is a body established in 1951 to oversee the training of journalists for the UK's newspaper industry and which offers accreditation recognized throughout the industry.
43 http://www.bbc.co.uk/journalism/ – This training website is open to the UK (i.e. the licence fee paying) public.

References

Campaign for Freedom of Information (2008) *1000 FOI Stories from 2006 and 2007*. See: http://www.cfoi.org.uk/pdf/FOIStories2006-07.pdf – Accessed July 2010.

Davis, Aeron (2002) *Public Relations Democracy: Public Relations and the Mass Media in Britain*. Manchester: Manchester University Press.

Davies, Nick (2009) *Flat Earth News*. London:Vintage Books.

Department for Culture, Media and Sport (2006) *Broadcasting: Copy of Royal Charter for the Continuance of the British Broadcasting Corporation*. London: HMSO 2006. Available at: http://www.bbc.co.uk/bbctrust/assets/files/pdf/about/how_we_govern/charter.pdf

Franklin, Bob (1997) *Newszak and News Media*. London: Edward Arnold.

Franklin, Bob (2005) 'McJournalism: the local press and the McDonaldization thesis', in Stuart Allan (ed.) *Journalism: Critical Issues*, Maidenhead: Open University Press, pp. 137-150.

Greenslade, Roy (2009) 'Controlling interest', The *Guardian*, 27 July 2009.

The Guardian (2010) 'Working to strengthen the trust with our readers', The Guardian, Tuesday 6 July 2010. http://www.guardian.co.uk/sustainability/readers-editor-trust-audience-complaints/print – accessed 14 July 2010.

Hallin, Daniel C. and Mancini, Paolo (2004) *Comparing Media Systems: Three Models of Media and Politics*. Cambridge: Cambridge University Press.

Harcup, Tony (2007) *The Ethical Journalist*. London: Sage.

House of Commons Culture, Media and Sport Committee, *Seventh Report of Session 2006–07, Self-regulation of the press*, HC 375.

House of Commons Culture, Media and Sport Committee (2010) *Press Standards, Privacy and Libel*. London: The Stationary Office, 24 February 2010. Available online at: http://www.publications.parliament.uk/pa/cm200910/cmselect/cmcumeds/532/532.pdf

House of Lords Select Committee on Communications (2008a) *The Ownership of the News – Volume I: Report*. London: The Stationary Office. Available at: http://www.publications.parliament.uk/pa/ld200708/ldselect/ldcomuni/122/122i.pdf

House of Lords Select Committee on Communications (2008b) *The Ownership of the News – Volume II: Evidence*. London: The Stationary Office. Available at: http://www.publications.parliament.uk/pa/ld200708/ldselect/ldcomuni/122/122ii.pdf

Humphreys, Peter (1996) *Mass Media and Media Policy in Western Europe*. Manchester: Manchester University Press.

Humphreys, Peter (2009) 'Media freedom and pluralism in the United Kingdom', in Andrea Czepek, Melanie Hellwig and Eva Nowak (eds) *Press Freedom and Pluralism in Europe: Concepts and Conditions*. Bristol UK/Chicago USA: intellect, pp. 197-211.

Jones, Nicholas(1995) *Soundbites and Spin Doctors: How Politicians Manipulate the Media – and Vice Versa*. London: Indigo (Cassell).

Journalists Training Forum (2002) *Journalists at Work*. London: Publishing NTO & Skillset. Available at: http://www.skillset.org/uploads/pdf/asset_2081.pdf?1 – Accessed July 2010.

Keynote, *The Publishing Industry 2010*.

Lewis, Justin, Williams, Andrew, Franklin, Bob, Thomas, James and Mosdell, Nick (2006) *The Quality and Independence of British Journalism: Tracking the Changes over 20 Years*. Cardiff School of Journalism, published by MediaWise. Available at: http://www.cardiff.ac.uk/jomec/research/researchgroups/journalismstudies/fundedprojects/qualitypress.html

Lloyd, John (2004) *What the Media Do to Our Politics*. London; Constable & Robinson.

Marr, Andrew (2005) *My Trade: A Short History of British Journalism*. London: Pan.

McChesney, Robert W. & Nichols, John (2010) *The Death and Life of American Journalism: The Media Revolution that Will Begin the World Again*. Philadelphia: First Nation Books.

McNair, Brian (1995) *An Introduction to Political Communication*. London & New York: Routledge.

National Union of Journalists (2007) *Submission to the Commission on Vulnerable Employment*. November 2007. A submission to the Trade Union Council commission on vulnerable employment. See: http://www.nuj.org.uk/innerPagenuj.html?docid=594 – Accessed 16 July 2010..

Norris, Pippa (2003) *A Virtuous Circle: Reinventing Political Activism*. Cambridge: Cambridge University Press.

Ofcom (2007) *Communications Market Special Repor: Ethnic minority groups and communications services*. Available at: http://stakeholders.ofcom.org.uk/binaries/research/cmr/ethnic_grps.pdf

Ofcom (2009a) *Communications Market Report*. Ofcom 2009. Available at: http://stakeholders.ofcom.org.uk/binaries/research/cmr/cmr09.pdf

Ofcom (2009b) *UK adults' media literacy: 2009 interim report*. Ofcom 2009. Available at: http://stakeholders.ofcom.org.uk/binaries/research/media-literacy/adult_ml.pdf

Robinson, Piers, et al. (2010) *Pockets of Resistance: British News Media, War and Theory in the 2003 Invasion of Iraq*. Manchester: Manchester University Press.

Tunstall, Jeremy (1996) *Newspaper Power: The New National Press in Britain*. Oxford: Clarendon Press.

Wilby, Peter (2008) 'A job for the wealthy and connected', The Guardian, Monday 7 April, 2008. Available at: http://www.guardian.co.uk/media/2008/apr/07/pressandpublishing4/ Accessed July 2010.

Chapter 13

Democratic Functions under Pressure: Conclusions

Lars Nord, Hannu Nieminen & Josef Trappel

This comparative study of leading news media performances in ten countries largely confirms previously expressed concerns about the complex and interdependent role of the news media in democratic societies. The main and perhaps somewhat surprising observation is that, contrary to the most pessimistic predictions (Christians et al. 2009), the news media still have a great deal of capacity to fulfill their basic democratic functions. This picture is, however, mixed.

There exists, undoubtedly, in all countries examined a constitutionally guaranteed freedom of the press. In practice, most governments also tend to accept the role of free and independent media. Media communication remains central to public information and public debate, and the leading news media still reach the majority of the population. The idea of professional journalism seems to be deeply rooted and is linked to a commonly shared awareness of the basic democratic roles of journalists.

Generally speaking, the three root concepts of democracy analyzed here – *freedom*, *equality* and *control* – are largely fulfilled by news media in the ten countries. In the 30 cases studied here, the countries scored more than 50 percent of the total possible points in 29 cases (Lithuania scored 48 per cent in the *control dimension*).

At the same time, we should be reminded that the data for this study were gathered between 2008 and 2010 – a period of global economic and financial crisis. It was also a time of major reorientation for most if not all media companies in the countries studied here. The full consequences from their new orientations will be felt only after some years. However, some reflections can be seen already today.

Commercial pressures

A major trend that the news media have faced in most countries can be summarized in the word *pressure*. Discussions about new pressures on the democratic performance of the news media appear in almost every country chapter. The nature and origins of this pressure may be described in different ways and in different contexts, but it is generally perceived as a threat to the news media's democratic functions. When analyzing the possible reasons for media shortcomings in reaching democratic goals, these pressures stand out as the most important factors in most cases.

Economic pressure – or the commercial logic – seems to be one of the main problems for contemporary news media. Due to the globalization of media and more liberal communication policies, media markets are increasingly commercialized. New commercially oriented media players are successfully challenging the hitherto dominating national news media, such as traditional newspapers and public service radio and television. The pressure from commercial competitors affects traditional news media in different ways. The high costs required to produce quality journalism are not easy to meet in the more market-driven media landscape, where constant battles for audiences and advertisers tend to favor less informational media content. The trend is from *fact-based news journalism* toward *attention-seeking journalism*. There are also signs that power relations within media companies are shifting, and business and market divisions are becoming more influential in strategic decision-making processes within media organizations.

Economic considerations also change media structures on national and regional levels. Media ownership concentration is a distinctive feature in most countries studied. Media mergers, and different models of collaboration between media companies, decrease diversity in news and concentrate media power in fewer hands. This was experienced as especially problematic on regional and local levels. Structural changes in media markets are mainly driven by economic decisions and top management strategies, and decision-makers are largely indifferent to the consequences such changes may have for the basic democratic functions of the news media. Thus, the overall result of media diversity decline must be perceived as a democratic problem.

The market paradigm, or the commercial logic, does not only affect company strategies and long-term priorities, but also daily editorial decisions. Journalists pressed by a heavy workload and increased demands for profitable journalism are probably not in the best position to defend quality journalism when faced with internal and external pressures. This is particularly true of the countries analyzed in which there are no written editorial policies or rules for newsroom practices and news selection, and where self-regulation systems do not work particularly well. In such cases, many news decisions lack transparency.

Seeking a new business logic

The general commercialization of the media sector observed in the country chapters is also important for media consumers' willingness to pay for news. Most news on the Internet is free, although most online news services consist only of headlines and newsflashes. The same concerns the news offered by urban metropolitan tabloids as well as the limited amount of news in commercial broadcast media. Paid-for daily newspapers report declining circulation and subscription figures, even in the formerly strong newspaper-reading countries of Northern Europe. As evidence has shown, news journalism is not especially attractive to advertisers, and this means that the emphasis in the commercial media is shifting from news to less costly and more attractive contents, both in print and in the online environment.

The same pressures concern the public service broadcast media. They are faced with shrinking audience market shares and, in some countries, legitimacy problems and political opposition to the license fee system. In many countries, especially in the UK, the Northern European, and the German-speaking countries, strong public service broadcasting has been seen as enhancing the overall quality of journalism in the commercial media sector, too. Now the public service companies must compete not only for their place in the new multichannel environment, but they also have to fight the ideological opposition trying to reduce their role to providing services for niche audiences only, instead of the entire nation.

For the media companies, economic pressures are increasingly mixed with the challenge presented by the Internet. As people spend more money on broadband and mobile subscriptions as well as on narrow niche media and pay-TV, traditional news media are desperately seeking new sustainable business models. Some major news media companies have been successful players on new digital media platforms, but mainly because of revenues from other media activities.

Audience fragmentation and participation

Media are still affordable for the majority of households in most countries studied. As a result of digitalization and media convergence, there is a multiplicity of new channels. At the same time, media consumption has continuously increased. This has led to media use becoming more fragmented: consumption is shared between several channels and different media. As a consequence of the financial crisis, there is a risk that this will lead to the segregation of audiences and to increasing information and knowledge gaps: that news media consumption will become polarized between citizens who are able to pay for high-quality journalism, and citizens without any other choice than to stick to less costly, or free, tabloid news on different platforms.

Finally, it is worth noting that not all pressures on journalism are based on commercialization trends. As many country chapters confirm, media technology development now allows for increased audience participation in the media. User-generated content is appearing on many platforms: in commentary spaces on online news websites, in blogs and micro blogs, in other social media and in contributions with photos, films or texts to daily journalism. This audience participation, facilitated by new technology, may be perceived as an improvement in the forum function of media, where potentially more voices are heard and more views on more topics are expressed. However, journalists sometimes seem to be rather skeptical about this development, arguing that content is of low quality and has very limited impact on the public discourse. Thus, some media companies still have a restrictive policy in this area (see Chapter 1).

To conclude, this overview has basically underlined some general observations of the news media situation in the ten countries studied. The focus has been on shared practices and on some transnational trends with an impact on the democratic performances of news media. Still, there are of course considerable differences between the countries when the basic concepts of freedom, equality and control are more carefully analyzed.

Freedom, equality – and some control

Comparing the three dimensions, the empirical findings indicate that the news media are generally most successful in meeting the demands for free information, closely followed by the equality criteria. The control functions of news media seem to be the most difficult to fulfill. Disseminating information and providing equal access to news media are obviously, and not so surprisingly, slightly easier goals to achieve than are acting as a watchdog and scrutinizing powerful political and economic interests in society.

Comparing the different indicators on *freedom* used for the analysis, the best scores are noted for basic criteria of media availability and media use patterns. In almost every country examined here, there are no huge geographic gaps with regard to the number of media channels available for the population living in different areas. The analysis of media consumption also confirms that people actually use a wide range of news media. Thus, national media structures generally facilitate a free flow of information. The lowest scores in this part of the study are noted for the indicator on internal rules for practice of newsroom democracy. In most countries analyzed, journalists are not at all involved in processes for election of editors-in-chief or other persons in leading positions.

The *equality* indicators roughly display the same wide range of scores. Media are perceived as affordable for the average household everywhere, and there is equal access to news media, regardless of socio-demographic differences. The main problems with regard to equality are associated with the media ownership concentration that is taking place both on national and regional levels in many countries. The reduced number of media owners, and the lack of competition, tend to create strong monopoly markets, where the successful entrance of newcomers becomes much more costly and unlikely. Worrying is the score for content monitoring. In many countries, a systematic instrument for assessing media performance is either weak or missing, making serious evidence-based analysis of media contents occasional and case-dependent.

Finally, *control* indicator scores are generally lower than for the two previous criteria. Interestingly, the best scores are not noted for journalism practices, but for journalists' awareness of professional values, and for mechanisms of 'controlling the controllers' or supervising the watchdogs. The lowest scores are noted for the estimated editorial independence from power holders outside the media and for the practice 'access of information' for reporters. Thus, the scores may be summarized as follows: journalists are generally aware of what they should do, and their work is satisfactorily checked. However, they are not that often able to do what they think they should do.

Overview of the indicators

The following overview shows the main arguments for each indicator and all countries participating in the MDM. In the right column there are the points assigned by each country team to each indicator. What is, however, more important than these indicative points is the justification presented for each indicator.

Dimension Freedom / Information:

(F1) Geographic distribution of news media availability		
AU	Due to Australia's geography and population distribution, regional areas are less well served than the metropolitan centers, where all media are available.	2
AT	A wide variety of news media is available to Austrian citizens. The distribution of news media, however, varies by media type.	3
FI	The mainstream news media are accessible throughout the country and there are no major regional divides.	3
DE	All relevant news media are available to all citizens, there are no regional divides or regional shortages.	3
LT	Although the mainstream news media is heavily used in the country, the population in Lithuania is segmented (dispersed into different audience groups) according to its socio-economic status and socio-cultural needs (the type of media and how it is used)	3
NL	A wide variety of news and information media is available to all Dutch citizens, although regional news coverage varies from province to province.	3
PT	Relevant news media are generally available to all citizens	3
SE	News available all over the country, and strong local and regional markets.	3
CH	News media are available to the Swiss population with no major restrictions.	3
UK	A wide variety of news media is available to UK citizens.	3

(F2) Patterns of news media use (consumption of news)		
AU	The Australian citizen is well supplied with news from different sources.	3
AT	Newspapers and public service television are the main sources of information concerning political issues. Among the younger population the importance of the Internet is increasing. The reach however is limited.	2
FI	The mainstream news media reach a very high proportion of the population in Finland.	2
DE	In Germany, news media use is – with certain reservations regarding the media use of young people – at a quite high standard.	2
LT	Although the mainstream news media are heavily used in the country, the population in Lithuania is segmented (dispersed into different audience groups) according to its socio-economic status and socio-cultural needs (the type of media and how it is used)	2

NL	Seven out of ten Dutchmen read a newspaper every day. Of all television channels, it is the first public channel that has the largest market share with one out of four Dutchmen tuning in every-day. The reach of most online media is on the rise.	3
PT	Consumption of news is less important than entertainment or fiction, especially given the overwhelming presence of television	2
SE	A newspaper reading nation still, and public service broadcast media still popular.	3
CH	The Swiss population is well supplied with news from different sources.	3
UK	Television is the primary source of news, followed by newspapers. The Internet is important, especially for the young for whom it is the prime source. Traditional media are adapting and the BBC website is a particularly important source.	3

(F3) Diversity of news sources		
AU	For Australians, as part of the English-speaking community, the Internet offers a wide array of news sources. Also the world-wide media network of News Corporation feeds the Australian market, whereas the public broadcaster has cut its commitment to foreign correspondents.	2
AT	All editors-in-chief emphasized the predominant role of journalistic research and pointed out that external content could at best serve as a starting point for further investigation.	2
FI	The diversity of sources is seen to have increased with the Internet, but the influence of PR material and recycling of other media's material are identified as threats in some sectors.	2
DE	Most of the German news media rely on different sources, though there is a tendency towards one dominant news agency	2
LT	News media use diverse sources; however, none of the mainstream news media have a bureau in a foreign country: for international news reporting, news media rely on Internet-based sources or international news agency material. Citizen journalism is popular in news portals.	2
NL	For quite a long time the Dutch press agency ANP used to enjoy a dominant position in providing news and scoops. Recent developments on the Internet have put an end to that hegemony. Other sources mentioned are the national and regional newspapers and the regional broadcasters, which often function as pointers to given issues.	3
PT	There is little diversity of news sources, with a high dependency on the single national agency	1
SE	Awareness of importance of balanced reporting, but domination of elite sources in news.	2
CH	The diversity of news sources has become smaller in the past years.	2
UK	Research indicates reliance on official and PR sources of information and strong commercial pressures militating against investigative journalism. Yet there remains a reasonably healthy degree of independent and critical journalism.	2

(F4) Internal rules for practice of newsroom democracy		
AU	There are no written rules for newsroom democracy in the Australian media.	1
AT	Newsroom democracy is established by editorial statutes, which are common in most Austrian newsrooms. But journalists have limited influence on the decision about the editor-in-chief.	1
FI	Individual journalists seem to enjoy a high level of autonomy in daily journalistic decisions, but formal procedures to ensure internal democracy are few.	2
DE	In Germany, journalists are not in full democratic control of the newsroom. There are some significant barriers to an effective and democratic organization of newsrooms, especially with regard to the engagement of new staff.	1
LT	In most media organizations there are no formalized procedures for how to involve journalists in decisions on personnel or editor in chief choices	1
NL	Nearly all news media have internal rules or by-laws outlining a procedure for appointing an editor-in-chief. The management will not easily disregard the viewpoint of the editorial board.	2
PT	Several laws and mechanisms for journalists' democratic participation exist, but they are not always followed in practice	2

SE	Journalists do not elect editor-in-chief, but are considered influential regarding news routines.	2
CH	Leading Swiss news media do not work according to written newsroom rules.	1
UK	There is little evidence of formal newsroom democracy and research suggests a pattern of strong managerial dominance, particularly in the newspaper sector. However, there are exceptions to this rule.	1

(F5) Company rules against internal influence on newsroom/editorial staff	
AU	Media proprietors have long been dominant figures, also in newsroom decisions.	1
AT	The separation of newsrooms from management is formally practiced by all media organizations in this media sample and can be interpreted as common for the Austrian media system.	2
FI	The autonomy and independence of the newsroom is generally regarded as a central value in the Finnish journalistic culture.	2
DE	The autonomy of newsrooms is generally well-established and implemented in most of the main news media, even though sometimes formal rules are still lacking.	2
LT	In most cases, the news media do not have written editorial policies (only few media have these documents available online); some of the news media that do not have written policies acknowledge that having such document is an important strategic policy decision and are planning to develop such documents in the near future.	1
NL	Editorial by-laws endorse the chief editor's final responsibility and protect the strict separation between editorial staff, on the one hand, and management and shareholders, on the other. However, present-day practice shows that the editor-in-chief's role is shifting away from editorial responsibilities to general management. The litmus test on whether editorial by-laws really function well is not taken until things begin to go badly for the news medium concerned.	2
PT	The degree of independence of the newsroom against ownership is high in the leading media but weak in others.	2
SE	Media owners most often do not influence daily newsroom practices.	2
CH	Leading Swiss media are keen on separating the economic management from the journalistic management. Still, a complete restriction of the internal influence on the newsrooms is not feasible.	2
UK	There is little evidence of any direct external influence on the UK media, though general commercial pressures adversely influence the quality of news.	2

(F6) Company rules against external influence on newsroom/editorial staff	
AU	The strong position of Australian media proprietors protects the newsroom from external influence.	3
AT	All editors-in-chief strictly denied direct influence of external parties on newsroom work and content, although such attempts were occasionally reported.	2
FI	Direct influence by external parties on newsroom decisions is not seen as a major problem.	2
DE	There are no reported cases of external influence, but in the case of the commercial media, there are neither explicit rules nor structural boundaries against it.	2
LT	It is difficult to draw a consistent conclusion here: some of the news media have clear and transparent rules (reporting policies), but this is not applied as a regular and established practice in all media organizations. One of the failures to meet this criterion is the public service broadcaster, which not only lacks a transparent and planned funding procedures, but its funding is negotiated with the government on an annual basis.	1
NL	Rules or by-laws provide for the formal separation between editorial and commercial considerations. The majority of the journalists interviewed are in principle opposed to any outside influence. Some news media tend to accept more non-spot advertising and advertorials or commercial specials for the job, real estate and travel markets. Such practice will make it more difficult to insist on respecting the editorial rules.	2

PT	Although news media generally receive revenues from a multitude of advertisers, they are increasingly permeable to advertising formats that allow some confusion between the editorial and the commercial areas.	1
SE	Outside influences on newsroom decisions are not problematic according to news editors.	3
CH	There are hardly any company rules against external influence.	1
UK	The main area of potential direct influence is proprietorial guidance/pressure relayed via the internal management structure, but the actual extent is disputed. The public service broadcasters – and certain newspapers – are free from such pressures.	2

(F7) Procedures on news selection and news processing		
AU	Although no formal rules on how to select and process news exist, informal rules are followed in the news selection and processing.	1
AT	Institutionalized ways of criticizing journalistic working habits only exist in a few newsrooms and are not regularly practiced.	1
FI	Stylebooks that include guidelines on the processing of news items are becoming more common, but their significance is still limited.	2
DE	Rules on how to select and present the news are based on journalists' professional education and regular debates within the newsrooms and therefore widely practised. Stylebooks and other written documents do exist in some media.	2
LT	Some news media have written documents (stylebooks) for news presentation; these instructions, however, are very general.	2
NL	In the absence of formal rules underlying the selection of news or documents outlining a definition of what news is and what it is not, the meetings and discussions held by the editorial staff can be considered informal procedures for making the selection.	2
PT	Rules and standards for news processing exist, but they are not always present in the day-to-day routines.	2
SE	Written editorial policies exist, but are mainly guidelines in daily newsroom work.	3
CH	News selection is strongly audience research oriented. Furthermore, news selection is also based upon the characteristics of the media.	2
UK	The UK's commercial press functions according to some unwritten and unstated rules of production which can impact negatively on the quality of news. However, there is a marked difference between the popular press, on the one hand, and the quality press and the more regulated television news providers, on the other.	2

Dimension Equality / Interest mediation

(E1) Media ownership concentration national level		
AU	Australia has a high media ownership concentration on a national level, which is only slowly broken up by increased availability of media on the Internet.	1
AT	Ownership concentration on a national level is very high as the market is divided among few big media companies.	1
FI	The national media market is relatively concentrated with a handful of companies dividing the market in each sector.	2
DE	At the national level, there are two or more competitors for all news media, but an increased level of concentration in the TV and print sector can be observed.	2
LT	Concentration is high in all sectors of media with a national coverage (especially in television).	1
NL	The overall market of national, regional, free and specialist newspapers is dominated by three large groups, as is the overall television market. Although less concentrated, the overall radio market too is dominated by just a handful of players. No figures on market shares are available for the Internet.	2

PT	There are three or more competitors for every area, but the level of ownership concentration is rather high.	2
SE	Ownership is more concentrated, but the influence of the biggest owners remains about the same.	2
CH	On the national level, three big publishing houses dominate the print media sector. The public broadcaster SRG SSR dominates the electronic sector in all three language regions in Switzerland.	2
UK	There is a quite diverse and highly competitive national news media market, with a range of competing news media. However, ownership is highly concentrated in both the newspaper and the television sector.	2

(E2) Media ownership concentration regional (local) level		
AU	Australia's demographic distribution and resulting economy of scale have led to a high media ownership concentration on a regional level.	0
AT	On a regional level ownership concentration is very high. In most Austrian regions one newspaper is dominant; the ORF dominates the local radio market.	1
FI	Apart from newspapers, the leading news media in Finland are nationally oriented. There are no significant regional or local television channels.	1
DE	There is some limited competition between regional broadcasters in most of the German states, but monopolization in the field of local press is increasing at the same time.	2
LT	In general, regional concentration is fairly low in Lithuania; in most cases more than two competing news media outlets are available in each sector.	2
NL	Three major players dominate the regional newspaper market. By contrast, concentration in the regional radio and television market is considerably lower.	1
PT	Ownership concentration at the regional level is very low.	3
SE	Regional media ownership concentration is a trend affecting most parts of the country.	2
CH	There is strong concentration of newspapers at the regional level. There is hardly any competition. Only in the Italian-speaking part and in the greater area of Zurich more than one independent publishing house compete.	1
UK	Local media markets are much less competitive than at the national level; local newspaper monopolies are the rule (not counting free papers). Ownership of the UK regional/local press is concentrated.	1

(E3) Diversity of formats		
AU	Australia has sufficient news presentation formats of news and current affairs.	2
AT	Austrian daily newspapers provide a wide variety of news coverage in different categories usually including local, national and international news as well as politics, economy, culture and sport sections.	3
FI	Formats of news presentation have proliferated especially online, and nearly all major news formats are widely available in Finland.	3
DE	There is a huge variety of news formats in every media sector in Germany.	3
LT	Different types of content are offered, but entertainment dominates in mainstream media.	1
NL	Although the chief business of print media remains the production of a paper version, the Internet is increasingly used to offer complementary functions and services. All news bulletins of the public and private broadcasters are available online, offering the latest news.	2
PT	There is an increasing homogenization of formats, meaning less diversity.	1
SE	Anything for anyone, any time – almost.	3
CH	Swiss news media landscape is still rich in news formats. In the newspapers the traditional media sections have been abolished more and more in the past years. This trend is alarming. The diversity suffers.	2
UK	There is a healthy diversity of news media formats.	3

(E4) Minority/ alternative media

AU	Australia offers an abundance of broadcast and print media in languages other than English.	3
AT	The availability and institutionalization of minority media depends on whether or not the minority is legally recognized. Overall, a wide range of minority media is available; however their reach is limited.	2
FI	The supply of media in Swedish and Sámi languages is extensive in relation to the size of the population in Finland, but other minority and alternative media are limited.	2
DE	Minorities' informational needs are respected and served by the German news media.	3
LT	Media for national minorities exists only as a niche media.	2
NL	The public broadcaster aims at inclusive broadcasting through which the largest possible number of groups in society, among them (ethnic) minorities, can make their voice heard. In spite of quite a number of subsidized actions undertaken to support newspapers for minorities, their future is far from rosy.	3
PT	Relatively little attention is given to minorities in the mainstream media, and they have few media of their own.	1
SE	Minority interests are not met by minority media.	1
CH	(Swiss) linguistic minorities are well equipped with mass media in Switzerland. The public broadcaster SRG SSR guarantees that all official languages and cultures are covered with information. There are no special media for immigrants. Alternative media products exist.	2
UK	There is a wide range of alternative and minority media, though their needs are not so well catered for in mainstream media.	3

(E5) Affordable public and private news media

AU	Media are readily affordable in Australia.	3
AT	All news media are relatively cheap compared to the average income of an Austrian household.	3
FI	The prices of media services in relation to household income are affordable.	3
DE	A full media supply is affordable for large sectors of the German society.	3
LT	All media is inexpensive and available at a low cost.	3
NL	Pricing is highly flexible: news consumers can choose the subscription that best fits their budget.	3
PT	Prices are decreasing and much free content is offered, but the cost of news media is still relatively high for an average household.	2
SE	More money is spent on the media.	3
CH	Switzerland is one of the richest countries worldwide and its mass media are relatively cheap.	3
UK	The UK news media are reasonably affordable.	3

(E6) Content monitoring instrument

AU	Australia has a number of monitoring instruments, but largely of a self-regulatory nature.	2
AT	Institutionalized and independent media monitoring instruments are rare in Austria.	1
FI	There are some attempts to develop more systematic instruments for media content monitoring, but they have yet to become fully institutionalized or widely publicized.	1
DE	Content monitoring is delivered on a regular and to some extent on a free basis.	3
LT	There is an organized and regular media monitoring performed by diverse organizations such as NGOs, media regulatory bodies, and higher education institutions; large-scale and regular media monitoring practice, however, are lacking.	2
NL	The Dutch Media Authority publishes the Media Monitor, an annual report analyzing the ownership relations and markets pertaining to newspapers, television, radio and opinion magazines. In addition, the News Monitor is published periodically.	3

PT	There are different monitoring instruments and they are publicly available.	3
SE	Media monitoring is random.	1
CH	Efforts to monitor news media on a regular basis in Switzerland are institutionalized, but are still at an early, emerging stage.	1
UK	There is no public body dedicated to news monitoring, but the operation of the UK news media is subject to the scrutiny of parliamentary committees.	2

(E7) Code of ethics at the national level (structure)		
AU	The journalists' code of ethics is well-known in the print industry but is becoming less suited to new online environments.	2
AT	A code of ethics exists, but the Austrian Press Council has been re-established in 2010 only.	1
FI	All leading news media have committed to the common code of ethics.	3
DE	A national code of ethics exists, is implemented and widely used.	3
LT	Lithuania has an institutionalized system of media self-regulation with two institutions established according to media law; in 2009, the Lithuanian Journalists Union has established their own self-regulation institution.	2
NL	Most media stick to the Guidelines of the Press Council and the Code of the Association of Editors-in-chief and/or observe a behavioral code of their own. Ethical decisions are usually made ad hoc in discussions among journalists and editorial staff. The advent of Internet journalism is seen as one of the most important causes of the weakening of journalistic standards and values.	2
PT	There is a national Code of Ethics but is not always widely implemented.	2
SE	The code is well known and an important tool within the self-regulatory system.	3
CH	Although a code of ethics exists, it has limited effect in daily business.	1
UK	The public service broadcasters have comprehensive ethical guidelines and there exists a code of ethics for the commercial press sector, which however is not backed up by strong enforcement powers.	2

(E8) Level of self-regulation (performance)		
AU	While the self-regulatory system is far from perfect, a fair attempt is made to implement it.	2
AT	Self-regulation occurs rather informally; institutionalized or codified rules and procedures are rare.	1
FI	Self-regulation is based on the ethical guidelines whose application varies from media to media.	2
DE	There are parts of a self-regulating system, but these parts are not implemented by formal rules, even though more media seem to establish codes of conduct.	2
LT	Sophisticated means of media self-regulation do exist in some newsrooms; there are also examples of organized self-criticism in some media.	2
NL	The Press Council, examining complaints about media coverage, is an organization for self-regulation. The News Monitor, funded by grants from the Press Promotion Fund, provides empirical material for the evaluation of news coverage.	3
PT	Some self-regulation mechanisms exist on the level of the main news media.	2
SE	A well integrated system though sometimes under debate.	2
CH	Editorial statutes and other internal newsroom rules exist, but are not used consequently in daily practice.	2
UK	The effectiveness of self-regulation of the press has long been a matter of public controversy, notably with regard to the popular press's excesses regarding accuracy of reporting and invasion of privacy. Self-regulation is widely seen as having functioned much better in the case of the quality press and the BBC (the commercial broadcasters are subject to external regulation).	2

(E9) Participation		
AU	Although there is an increasing interaction between journalists and the public, there is no actual participation in the news process.	2
AT	Audience participation is limited to "classical" means of participation, e.g. letters to the editor. Austrian newsrooms are not open to citizens.	1
FI	Audience participation in the news process is increasing, but there was some scepticism about the productiveness of all new forms of participation.	2
DE	Audience participation is widely established with classical instruments, but there is a growing amount of new means of audience involvement.	2
LT	Media in Lithuania offer a variety of ways for their audiences to take part in the public sphere.	2
NL	Every newspaper has an online version with a facility to post a response. Various social media have intensified the trend of reacting to and participating in news distribution.	3
PT	People are not particularly encouraged to participate in the news process, in spite of some improvements in the online context.	2
SE	Some media organizations have pushed for participation and the overall trend points in that direction.	3
CH	Leading Swiss news media hesitate to engage people to participate in the news process.	1
UK	Traditionally UK news media have operated in a top-down manner, but recent years have seen a considerable expansion of participatory developments and the Internet has had a major impact in this respect.	2

(E10) Rules and practices on internal pluralism		
AU	There is evidence of internal diversity but little of internal pluralism.	1
AT	As Austrian newsrooms usually do not have codified guidelines, contradictions and discussions are also subject to informal agreements.	1
FI	Internal pluralism is encouraged and valued, but aside from general professional guidelines and values, there are few formal rules.	2
DE	Internal pluralism is widely respected and established, though codified guidelines often do not exist.	2
LT	No written rules exist and most of the newsrooms have their own non-interference norms and practices; research studies, however, show that mainstream media are susceptible to external pressures, and with the media crisis this has worsened.	1
NL	Most news media enjoy a culture of openness: their editors-in-chief are accessible and willing to listen to young journalists with a fresh view of things who make their views known, solicited or not.	2
PT	Internal pluralism is fairly promoted in the main news media.	3
SE	Many newsrooms are aware of the benefits of pluralism and strive to find solutions.	2
CH	Media organizations strive for pluralism. Their mission statements guarantee that different views and perspective are being reported. The given circumstances restrain pluralism.	2
UK	UK newspapers are not bound by internal pluralism rules. Though they do practice a degree of internal pluralism, most have a distinct political, social and cultural orientation. The public service broadcasters are bound by regulation to provide internal pluralism, and all UK news broadcasters are bound by an impartiality rule.	2

Dimension Control / Watchdog

(C1) Supervising the watchdog, 'control of the controllers'		
AU	Australia has a number of independent observers of the news media.	3
AT	Even though weblogs are becoming more popular in Austria there are only a few media-blogs so far. Media criticism and public debates are centered on the press, but absent in radio and television.	2

FI	Organized media criticism in general is seen as lacking in Finland.	1
DE	There is a quite high degree of media monitoring by media journalism, professional journalistic journals and to a growing extend by blogs, although there is no permanent public debate about the role of media as watchdogs.	2
LT	Public criticism and regular public debates on media performance are found in the media; this, however, happens on irregular basis only.	2
NL	One leading example is the 'Foundation Media Debate Bureau'; the website denieuwereporter. nl is another. Both invite media professionals as well as citizens to think about quality, reliability and diversity in the media.	2
PT	There are institutionalized mechanisms to control media performance as watchdogs, but these issues are not very present in the public debates.	2
SE	Public service radio has a tradition of media criticism that is now joined by initiatives on the web.	2
CH	The Federal Office of Communication (OFCOM) is the external supervising body. Other watchdogs exist like blogs and Internet sites that observe and criticize the performance of the media.	2
UK	The UK media are subject to considerable scrutiny by official regulators and civil society media monitoring organizations, but there is little involvement on the part of the general public.	2

(C2) Independence of the news media from power holders		
AU	Legal instruments to guarantee greater independence from power holders have only just become law. However, defamation law is used as another pathway by the rich and famous to silence critics.	2
AT	Overall, a special status is granted to journalists by several laws emphasizing the value of independence for journalistic work. However "promise and practice" often diverge.	1
FI	Independence of the Finnish news media from power holders is generally strong.	2
DE	Independence from power holders is guaranteed by law and widely respected, though there are some minor cases of potential owner influence.	2
LT	Mainstream media do not have established rules and procedures to cope with pressures from power holders.	0
NL	The Dutch news media enjoy relative independence from power holders. There are examples of diagonal concentration involving a publisher and a broadcaster in the same group as well as an investment company as the largest shareholder.	1
PT	Some independence is guaranteed by different laws, but the actual practice shows increasing difficulties.	2
SE	Institutional as well as professional barriers create a distance between media and power holders.	3
CH	For the leading media pressures from external stakeholders are part of the daily business. Indirect influence exists.	2
UK	The UK news media enjoy a high degree of independence from political power holders.	3

(C3) Transparency of data on media system		
AU	Data on media are rarely a topic of debate.	1
AT	Transparency is given with regard to media legislation and the ORF. Ownership structures of private media companies, however, lack transparency.	1
FI	Relevant information about the media system is generally available, but not necessarily easily accessible.	2
DE	Transparency of the complete media system is given and available for the public.	3
LT	Media ownership data are available to the citizens.	2
NL	On its website mediamonitor.nl the Media Authority describes the most recent situation as to media ownership relations.	3
PT	Information on news media exists and is easily accessible	3

359

SE	Data are available, although they could be easier to find.	2
CH	Detailed information about the ownership structure and decision-making processes of private media organizations are not open.	1
UK	There is a fairly high degree of transparency of data on the UK media.	2

(C4) Journalism professionalism		
AU	Most journalists receive professional training.	2
AT	The position of journalists concerning professional ethics and standards is quite ambivalent. On the one hand such principles are high valued and a crucial status is attributed to them; on the other hand journalists show little enthusiasm regarding institutionalized forms of self-criticism and reflection.	2
FI	The news media are characterized by a strong professional ethos and a high level of unionization.	3
DE	There are signs of high professionalism, such as strong unions and frequent ethical debates, but the increasing workload of German journalists is a menace to the quality of news.	2
LT	Professionalism values vary across different media and this is associated with transformations taking place in media field, such as economic (media crisis and budget cuts) and technological (media convergence and new requests to journalists).	1
NL	The Dutch newsrooms engage in various forms of self-reflection on and appraisal of the work they do and the way in which they do it. However, most self-reflection occurs on an ad hoc basis and usually after the fact.	3
PT	The professional ethos is not too high in global terms, considering the heterogeneity of the professional group.	2
SE	A professional ideology and practice have a longstanding hold on Swedish journalists.	3
CH	Journalism professionalism is being challenged. Journalists have good skills but too little expertise and not enough knowledge about politics. New media products undermine journalism professionalism additionally.	2
UK	There is a highly professional journalistic culture in the broadcasting sector, with the BBC setting a high standard. In the press sector the picture is mixed.	2

(C5) Journalists' job security		
AU	It is difficult to provide job security for journalists in this time of change.	1
AT	Journalists are formally well protected by several laws. Nevertheless, in the daily journalistic routine pressures occur.	2
FI	There are few specific legal provisions that apply only to journalists, but general legal provisions and labor contracts give journalists strong occupational protection.	2
DE	Journalist only have rudimentary legal protection.	1
LT	In most media organizations journalists are working on job contracts.	2
NL	In general, the Association of Journalists controls the basic working conditions for professional journalists in the Netherlands.	2
PT	There is a relatively high level of job security in the legal framework	2
SE	Threats are said to be more common, but union as well as employers act accordingly.	2
CH	In the course of the media crisis job security cannot be guaranteed. Insecurity is greater in the commercial media.	2
UK	The overall stability of employment levels disguises the fact that journalists operating in a climate of employment insecurity and casualization (short term contracts, freelancing, etc) have faced markedly increased productivity pressures, which is bound to impact on quality.	1

(C6) Practice of access to information		
AU	The law provides access to public information, but practical problems persist.	1
AT	Formally the access to information for journalists in Austria is unlimited even though some restrictions are present.	2
FI	The existing law provides extensive access to public information, but problems remain in practice.	2
DE	Formally the access to information to governmental documents is unlimited, though it does not work in a completely satisfactorily manner in daily practice.	·2
LT	Additional requests are formulated for journalists.	1
NL	One important source is government information, for which Dutch legislation on the public nature of government records is the primary tool, as it gives citizens (and journalists) the right to access government data. The way in which the law functions and the lengthy procedures involved have recently come under attack.	1
PT	No legal barriers exist to access public information, but access is often difficult in practice.	2
SE	Sweden has many preconditions for an open government, but show signs of increased secrecy.	3
CH	In general Swiss journalists have free access to most public information.	3
UK	Until recently the UK would have scored low on this criterion but the enactment of Freedom of Information legislation in 2000 has significantly improved access to information.	2

(C7) The watchdog and the media's mission statement		
AU	Australia's media sees itself as a watchdog.	3
AT	A significant value is attributed to the watchdog function of media in Austria.	2
FI	The importance of the watchdog role is widely recognized by Finnish media organizations.	2
DE	There is no widespread use of mission statements thar explicitly foster investigative journalism. However, most interviewees emphasized the importance of investigative journalism.	1
LT	Watchdog mission is understood (and sometimes also implemented) as an important, but not a primary function of contemporary news media	2
NL	The media themselves decide on the basis of their distinctive characteristics to what extent they play their role as watchdog seriously.	3
PT	News media only indirectly refer to the watchdog function in their mission statements	1
SE	Media have mission statements and perform watchdog duties, but the first element need not be the cause of the second.	2
CH	Mission statements partly contain reference to democratic watchdog role but they are of little importance in daily life.	2
UK	The public service broadcasters score highly on this criterion, and so do the Guardian Media Group and the Guardian quality newspaper. However, in the newspaper sector at large mission statements (beyond the pithy) are not evident.	2

(C8) Professional training		
AU	Some mid-career training is on offer.	1
AT	Supply for further education is abundant in Austrian newsrooms; nevertheless workshops on democratic values and ethical standards are rare.	2
FI	The importance of continuous professional training is broadly acknowledged, but not all journalists take full advantage of the opportunities available.	2
DE	In Germany, there is no serious lack of opportunities for journalism training.	2
LT	There exists a well-established practice of continuous training of media professionals	2

NL	Practically all news media offer their employees a chance of following courses or completing their education. Due to economies and falling revenues from the advertising market, possibilities are limited.	1
PT	Very little importance is given to journalists training, except for technical skills attached to the new 'convergence' efforts	1
SE	Training is available, but the demand is higher than the supply.	2
CH	Journalistic training was downsized over the past years and lacks coherence. No particular emphasis is put on democratic virtues.	2
UK	Professional training has always been good in the broadcasting sector, not least because of the BBC. The situation in the press sector has undergone a marked professionalization. Most UK journalists nowadays have degrees and on the job training opportunities appear to be prevalent.	3

(C9) Watchdog function and financial resources		
AU	Commitment to investigative journalism is the Australian media's way to brand themselves.	3
AT	Austrian newsrooms usually try to provide resources for in-depth research as much as possible. The decision of which issue is most promising is up to the editor-in-chief.	2
FI	The leading news media give priority to their own material and also seek to undertake investigative journalism.	2
DE	The main German news media are in a quite good financial situation for in-depth investigations.	2
LT	No pre-planned budgets are allocated to perform investigative journalism and fulfill watchdog function.	1
NL	The worldwide financial crisis did not affect the time or the budget made available for investigative journalism. Even before the crisis economies had been imposed, mainly as a result of shrinking revenues from advertising and recent take-overs of broadcasters and publishers.	1
PT	Investing in investigative journalism is more an exception than a rule in the main news media.	1
SE	Resources for investigative reporting – commitment, energy and money – are rarely sufficient.	2
CH	Before the current recession, leading Swiss news media have been financially viable. Since, there is less staff for investigative reporting.	1
UK	Financial constraints in a highly competitive commercialized sector have constrained the UK media's ability optimally to perform its democratic watchdog function, yet investigative journalism has benefited from leaked information and the recent enactment of freedom of information legislation.	2

Table 1 shows the final scoring of the MDM for each country, all dimensions and all indicators. It is important to emphasize that this table – and all gradings and points – are reflections of qualitative arguments based on empirical findings. Therefore, the points in Table 1 are by no means objective measures of any kind. They are presented as illustration of the complex instrument. Each indicator can and should be regarded together with the qualitative explanation given by the country teams.

This said, the final scoring table shows substantial differences between countries. Sweden achieves high scores in all dimensions. Taking the three dimensions on a par, Sweden reaches 78 percent. Second and third and fourth are the Netherlands, the United Kingdom and Germany, all close runners-up, with Finland following on their heels. Northern European countries, all with a strong press tradition, score very highest. At the bottom end of the overall scoring we find Lithuania and Austria. For different reasons: While Austria scores lowest of all countries in the freedom/ information dimension due to a highly concentrated news media landscape and with low scores also in the equality/interest mediation dimension (little participation, little internal pluralism), Lithuania suffers from the lowest scores in the freedom/ information and in the control/watchdog dimension. In this respect, Lithuania still has some room for improvement in order to catch-up with the standard of the other countries. Switzerland scores similar to Portugal and Australia, which might come as a surprise. But again, high levels of regional concentration and low scores in the equality/interest mediation dimension characterize this small country with a strong press tradition.

The United Kingdom is in no dimension either particularly high or low scoring. Despite media concentration especially at the regional and local level, little sensitivity to internal democracy and low levels of journalistic security combined with economic problems in financing investigative journalism, several strong features lead to this country scoring in the upper mid-range of the field, notably the variety and independence of news media and the standard set by the BBC.

Reference

Christians, C.G., T.L. Glasser, D. McQuail, K. Nordenstreng and R.A. White (2009) *Normative Theories of the Media. Journalism in Democratic Societies.* Urbana, Chicago: University of Illinois Press.

Table 1

Indicators	Australia	Austria	Finland	Germany	Lithuania	Netherlands	Portugal	Sweden	Switzerland	UK
(F1) Geographic distribution of news media availability	2	3	3	3	3	3	3	3	3	3
(F2) Patterns of news media use (consumption of news)	3	2	2	2	2	3	2	3	3	3
(F3) Diversity of news sources	2	2	2	2	2	3	1	2	2	2
(F4) Internal rules for practice of newsroom democracy	1	1	2	1	1	2	2	2	1	1
(F5) Company rules against *internal* influence on newsroom / editorial staff	1	2	2	2	1	2	2	2	2	2
(F6) Company rules against *external* influence on newsroom / editorial staff	3	2	2	2	1	2	1	3	1	2
(F7) Procedures on news selection and news processing	1	1	2	2	2	2	2	3	2	2
(F) Freedom / Information (max. 21 points)	**13**	**13**	**15**	**14**	**12**	**17**	**13**	**18**	**14**	**15**
	62%	**62%**	**71%**	**67%**	**57%**	**81%**	**62%**	**86%**	**67%**	**71%**
(E1) Media ownership concentration national level	1	1	2	2	1	2	2	2	2	2
(E2) Media ownership concentration regional (local) level	0	1	1	2	2	1	3	2	1	1
(E3) Diversity of formats	2	3	3	3	1	2	1	3	2	3
(E4) Minority / Alternative media	3	2	2	3	2	3	1	1	2	3
(E5) Affordable public and private news media	3	3	3	3	3	3	2	3	3	3
(E6) Content monitoring instrument	2	1	1	3	2	3	3	1	1	2
(E7) Code of ethics at the national level (structure)	2	1	3	3	2	2	2	3	1	2
(E8) Level of self-regulation (performance)	2	1	2	2	2	3	2	2	2	2
(E9) Participation	1	1	2	2	3	3	1	2	1	2
(E10) Rules and practices on internal pluralism	1	1	2	2	1	2	3	2	2	2
(E) Equality / Interest mediation (max. 30 points)	**17**	**15**	**21**	**25**	**19**	**24**	**20**	**21**	**17**	**22**
	57%	**50%**	**70%**	**83%**	**63%**	**80%**	**67%**	**70%**	**57%**	**73%**
(C1) Supervising the watchdog 'control of the controllers'	3	2	1	2	2	2	2	2	2	2
(C2) Independence of the news media from power holders	2	1	2	2	0	1	2	3	2	3
(C3) Transparency of data on media system	1	1	2	3	2	3	3	2	1	2
(C4) Journalism professionalism	2	2	3	2	2	3	2	3	2	2
(C5) Journalists' job security	1	2	2	1	2	2	2	2	2	1
(C6) Practice of access to information	1	2	2	2	1	1	2	3	3	2
(C7) The watchdog and the media's mission statement	3	2	2	1	2	3	1	2	2	2
(C8) Professional training	1	2	2	2	2	1	1	2	2	3
(C9) Watchdog function and financial resources	3	2	2	2	1	2	2	2	1	2
(C) Control / Watchdog (max. 27 points)	**17**	**16**	**18**	**17**	**13**	**17**	**16**	**21**	**17**	**19**
	63%	**59%**	**67%**	**63%**	**48%**	**63%**	**59%**	**78%**	**63%**	**70%**
Total (max. 78 points)	**47**	**44**	**54**	**56**	**44**	**58**	**49**	**60**	**48**	**56**
	60%	**56%**	**69%**	**72%**	**56%**	**74%**	**63%**	**77%**	**62%**	**72%**
Mean percentage three dimensions	**61%**	**57%**	**69%**	**71%**	**56%**	**75%**	**63%**	**78%**	**62%**	**72%**

The Authors

Auksė Balčytienė, Department of Public Communications, Faculty of Political Science and Diplomacy, Vytautas Magnus University, Lithuania

André Donk, Department of Communication, University of Muenster, Germany

Leen d'Haenens, Centre for Media Culture and Communication Technology, Katholieke Universiteit Leuven (KU Leuven), Belgium, and Department of Communication, Radboud Universiteit, Nijmegen, Netherlands

Joaquim Fidalgo, Department of Communication Sciences / Communication and Society Research Centre, University of Minho, Portugal. Contact: jfidalgo@ics.uminho.pt

Alexandra Gmür, SwissGIS – Swiss Centre for Studies on the Global Information Society, University of Zurich, Switzerland

Manuela Grünangerl, Department of Communication Research, University of Salzburg, Austria. Contact: manuela.gruenangerl@sbg.ac.at

Peter Humphreys, School of Social Sciences, University of Manchester, UK

Beate Josephi, School of Communications and Arts, Edith Cowan University, Perth, Australia

Kari Karppinen, Media and Communication Studies, Department of Social Research, University of Helsinki, Finland

Quint Kik, The Social and Economic Council of the Netherlands, The Hague, Netherlands

Martina Leonarz, SwissGIS – Swiss Centre for Studies on the Global Information Society, University of Zurich, Switzerland. Contact: leonarz@bluewin.ch

Anna-Laura Markkanen, Media and Communication Studies, Department of Social Research, University of Helsinki, Finland

Frank Marcinkowski, Department of Communication, University of Muenster, Germany

Werner A. Meier, SwissGIS – Swiss Centre for Studies on the Global Information Society, University of Zurich, Switzerland. Contact: wameier@ipmz.uzh.ch

Hannu Nieminen, Media and Communication Studies, Department of Social Research, University of Helsinki, Finland

Lars Nord, Department of Information Technology and Media, Mid Sweden University, Sundsvall, Sweden. Contact: lars.nord@miun.se

Josef Trappel, Department of Communication Research, University of Salzburg, Austria. Contact: josef.trappel@sbg.ac.at

Torbjörn von Krogh, Department of Information Technology and Media, Mid Sweden University, Sundsvall, Sweden. Contact: fam.vonkrogh@swipnet.se